Alexander of Aphrodisias
On Aristotle's Prior Analytics 1.1-7

Alexander of Aphrodisias

On Aristotle's Prior Analytics 1.1-7

Translated by
Jonathan Barnes, Susanne Bobzien,
Kevin Flannery, S.J., and
Katerina Ierodiakonou

Cornell University Press

Ithaca, New York

First published 1991 Cornell University Press.

Library of Congress Cataloging-in-Publication Data
Alexander, of Aphrodisias.
   On Aristotle's Prior analytics 1.1-7 / Alexander of Aphrodisias :
translated by Jonathan Barnes ... [et al.].
      p.   cm. — (Ancient commentators on Aristotle)
   Translated from the Greek.
   Includes bibliographical references and indexes.
   ISBN 0–8014–2689–8
   1. Aristotle. Prior analytics.   2. Logic—Early works to 1800.
I. Barnes, Jonathan.   II. Title.   III. Series.
B535.A6304513   1991
160—dc20   91–55257

The present translations have been made possible by
generous and imaginative funding from the following
sources: the National Endowment for the Humanities,
Division of Research Programs, an independent federal
agency of the USA; the Leverhulme Trust; the British
Academy; the Jowett Copyright Trustees; the Royal
Society (UK); Centro Internazionale A. Beltrame di Storia
dello Spazio e del Tempo (Padua); Mario Mignucci;
Liverpool University. The general editor is very grateful to
Ian Crystal and Paul Opperman for their help in
preparing the volume for press.

Printed in Great Britain

Contents

Preface

This book is the work of a collaborative partnership. Each partner is equally responsible for everything in it. The work was done in a series of weekly meetings held in Balliol during 1988 and 1989. We were from time to time joined by Antonina Alberti, Barbara Cassin, Jim Hankinson, Anna Maria Ioppolo, James Irvine, Mario Mignucci and Voula Tsouna, to each of whom we owe valuable suggestions. And we are indebted to Ian Mueller for a sheaf of written comments.

Oxford   JB
August 1990   SB
                                                           KF
                                                           KI

Introduction

Alexander of Aphrodisias

Alexander addressed his essay *On Fate* to the Emperors Septimius Severus and Caracalla. The address dates the work between the years 198 and 209 AD.[1] Alexander explains that in the essay he will present and discuss Aristotle's views on fate and human freedom; for

> I am the champion of his philosophy, having been nominated a teacher of it on your recommendation. (*Fat.* 164,14-15)

The Emperors had thus helped Alexander to a Chair in Aristotelian Philosophy. It is a plausible guess – but no more – that this was one of the four philosophy chairs which had been established at Athens some twenty-five years earlier by Marcus Aurelius.[2] (If the guess is lucky, then Alexander will have taught at Athens.[3])

Alexander, we may reasonably infer, was an eminent Aristotelian who flourished at the beginning of the third century AD. This conclusion is consistent with the other evidence, scanty and indirect, which we have about his life and activity – for apart from the passage in *On Fate* we hear nothing detailed and datable about his career.[4] We do not even know for sure where he came from: he was

---

[1] See *Fat.* 164,1-3. Caracalla was made Augustus on 28 January 198; in 209 Geta became Augustus to make an Imperial trio. It is reasonable – but not perhaps absolutely mandatory – to date *On Fate* to the period between the elevation of Caracalla and the elevation of Geta. See further Thillet, pp. LXXV-LXXIX.

[2] The year was 176: see e.g. Cassius Dio, LXXII xxxi 3; cf. e.g. Oliver, pp. 80-5; Lynch, pp. 169-77; Glucker, pp. 146-50.

[3] Arabic sources actually state that Alexander taught at Athens; but they derive from a passage in Galen (*Anat. Admin.* II 218K) which refers to Alexander of Damascus – and there is no reason to identify the Damascene with the Aphrodisian (see e.g. Thillet, p. XLI). At *in Metaph.* 415,29-31, Alexander refers, in an illustrative example, to 'this statue – say, of Aristotle – which stands in Athens'; but this hardly implies that Alexander was lecturing in Athens at the time. Note that there is nothing to be said for the old view that Alexander was the official Peripatetic scholarch at Athens: see Lynch, p. 214. On Alexander's 'school' see Sharples (1990).

[4] For discussion and bibliography see Thillet, pp. VI-LXXIII; Sharples (1987), pp. 1177-8.

1

Alexander 'of Aphrodisias', but more than one town went by that name and it is at best a reasonable conjecture that he was born in the rich and flourishing Aphrodisias in Caria.[5] As for his personal features and foibles, we learn nothing – unless we may believe that he was 'lean and pale'.[6]

His teachers included Sosigenes and Herminus – whom he criticises at some length in his commentary on the *Prior Analytics*.[7] We know little about these scholars. Their pupil emerged as a learned philosopher; but we cannot tell to what extent and in what ways the pupil's ideas were shaped and formed by his teachers.

His writings contain critical and polemical passages, many of them directed against the Stoics.[8] It is easy to suppose that he was a controversialist, engaged in living dispute with his contemporaries. There is indeed evidence that he broke a lance or two with Galen, his senior by some years and a leading intellectual figure of the day.[9] Yet it may be suspected that some, at least, of Alexander's attacks were bookish – delivered in the calm of the study or the lecture-room against dead or hypothetical opponents.[10]

Bookish he certainly was. A dozen major works survive, in addition to several collections of shorter pieces. And much more has been lost than survives. Although Alexander did not rival the productive energy of Galen, his collected works would have occupied an impressive amount of shelf space.[11] Moreover, they had some influence:[12] on his contemporaries (such as Galen), on the later Greek philosophers (on Plotinus[13] and on the Neoplatonic commentators), and also on Arabic philosophy.[14]

---

[5] On Aphrodisias see e.g. Reynolds. The name 'Alexander' is found on Aphrodisian inscriptions (e.g. *Monumenta Asiae Minoris Antiqua* VIII 414, 574); but it is an extremely common name.

[6] See [Alexander], *in Metaph.* 531,25-6 (cf. 532,7-19) – but this part of *in Metaph.* is not from Alexander's own feather.

[7] See Moraux (1973/84), II, pp. 335-60 (Sosigenes) and pp. 361-98 (Herminus). On the controversial figure of Aristotle of Mytilene see Moraux (1973/84), II, pp. 399-425; Accattino; Goulet, pp. 411-12; and esp. Thillet, pp. XI-XIX.

[8] See Todd (1976); Sharples (1987), p. 1178.

[9] For the evidence see esp. Thillet, pp. XXXII-XLIX; cf. von Müller, pp. 424-5; Pines; Zimmermann, p. lxxxi n. 2; Nutton (1984), pp. 318-24; Nutton (1987), pp. 45-51; Sharples (1987), p. 1179.

[10] The evidence for living and contemporary debate in Alexander's school is sifted by Sharples (1990), pp. 90-2, 104-10.

[11] For a general characterization and a full catalogue see Sharples (1987), pp. 1179-99; cf. Thillet, pp. LII-LXXIII; Goulet, pp. 128-39.

[12] See, in general, Cranz, pp. 79-82; Sharples (1987), pp. 1220-4.

[13] See Porphyry, *Vit. Plot.* 14; and the Index Fontium to the Henry-Schwyzer edition of Plotinus. Note that Eusebius cites Alexander (*Fat.*) at *PE* VI ix.

[14] See esp. Maróth. Many of Alexander's writings were translated into Arabic, and some have survived only in their Arabic versions: see Badawi (1987), pp. 109-14; Strohmaier; Sharples (1987), pp. 1187-8, 1192-4. For Alexander's influence on mediaeval thought see Ebbesen (1981b), (1982), (1990).

In philosophy, he was thoroughly Aristotelian.[15] Indeed, his philosophical activity can be roughly characterised as an attempt to organise and present a comprehensive, consistent and contemporary Aristotelianism. This being so, it is unsurprising to discover that much of his writing took the form of commentaries on Aristotle's works; and although there is a substantial body of material, always in Aristotelian vein, which is less closely tied to the words and works of the Master, the Aristotelian commentaries constitute the core of his philosophical achievement.

He wrote commentaries on all the constituent works of Aristotle's *Organon* or logical *corpus*: the commentaries on the *Categories*, *On Interpretation*, *Prior Analytics* 2, *Posterior Analytics*,[16] and the *Sophistical Refutations*[17] are lost. But in addition to the work on *Prior Analytics* 1, we possess a substantial commentary on the *Topics*.[18] There were also independent books on logical matters: an essay on the conversion of propositions,[19] and an essay on utterances, both preserved in Arabic versions;[20] several brief discussions on questions to do with the concept of possibility, found among the so-called *Quaestiones* and closely related to Alexander's interest in determinism;[21] a lost essay on hypothetical syllogistic;[22] a one-volume work on syllogisms with modally mixed premises, and some *Scholia Logica* or *Logical Notes*, both referred to in the commentary on the *Prior Analytics* and both lost.[23]

The chronology of Alexander's writings cannot be established.[24] The only absolute date is given by the opening of *On Fate* – and even that is not precise. For the internal or relative chronology, we must rely on occasional cross-references. Thus we know that the essay on conversions, and perhaps the commentary on the *Topics*, were

---

[15] For a sketch see Donini, pp. 220-48; Sharples (1987), pp. 1199-220; the account in Zeller, III i, pp. 817-31, is still worth reading.

[16] For fragments, *testimonia* and discussion see Moraux (1979).

[17] The commentary preserved under his name and published in *CAG* II 3 is a much later work: see Ebbesen (1981a), I, pp. 242-4; Sharples (1987), p. 1184.

[18] Edited by Wallies in *CAG* II 2.

[19] Arabic text in Badawi (1971); referred to below by 'Alexander, *Conv.*'.

[20] See Sharples (1987), p. 1193. An Arabic source refers to a second, shorter, commentary on *An. Pr.*: see Badawi (1987), p. 113.

[21] See Sharples (1982), (1983).

[22] Known to Avicenna: see Maróth, pp. 7, 139.

[23] For the *peri mixeôn* see *in An. Pr.* 125,30; 127,16; 207,35; 213,26; 238,37; 249,38 (cf. Philoponus, *in An. Pr.* 126,20-3); for the *Scholia* see 250,2 (cf. Sharples (1987), p. 1196). Zeller, III i, p. 820 n. 2, asserts that the reference to the *Scholia Logica* at *in An. Pr.* 250,2 is a later gloss; but he offers no reason for this opinion. Perhaps there was also an essay on affirmations: see our note to *in An. Pr.* 36,6 below. Note also the indeterminate cross-references at *in An. Pr.* 188,16; 191,17; 284,17; 390,9; and the proleptic references at *in An. Pr.* 70,20; 110,20; 193,21; 328,6.

[24] See Sharples (1987), p. 1181.

written after the commentary on the *Prior Analytics*;[25] and we know
that the commentary on the *Prior Analytics* had itself been preceded
by two shorter writings on logical matters. Such results are meagre
and unsatisfying. But in any case, chronological questions are
probably of little significance.[26] For the commentaries presumably
represent the substance of Alexander's lectures on Aristotle;[27] the
lectures were presumably delivered year in year out; and the passing
years presumably brought revisions of various sorts. In such circumstances it makes little sense to speak of a relative chronology: in a
way, we might rather suppose that Alexander wrote his commentaries concurrently, and perhaps over a decade or more.

Commentaries

Numerous ancient commentaries on Aristotle have survived. And
many more have perished. Alexander's commentaries are, by
general consent, among the best: modern scholars praise him – and
so did some of the ancients.[28] But he was not the first in the field: on
the contrary, he was writing in a tradition already some centuries
old.

Aristotle's immediate successors, Theophrastus and Eudemus,
wrote on the same subjects as their master had done; and, to some
extent at least, they conceived of their task as correcting, expanding
and completing Aristotle's work.[29] Their works can no doubt be

---

[25] See *Conv.* p. 60; *in Top.* 7,11. (But note that cross-references in the
commentaries are primarily concerned with the order in which the readers or the
audience will read or hear the works – they do not necessarily provide evidence for
the order of *composition*.)

[26] The same may be said for the chronology of some of Aristotle's writings: see e.g.
Barnes (1981).

[27] But note the doubts expressed by Sharples (1990), p. 97.

[28] See e.g. Simplicius, *in Phys.* 80,15-16; 795,33-5; *in DA* 52,27-8. It is regularly
asserted that Alexander was later known simply and honorifically as 'The
Commentator'. The passages adduced to support this claim include: Simplicius, *in
Phys.* 707,33; 1170,13; 1176,32; Philoponus, *in An. Pr.* 126,21; Olympiodorus, *in
Meteor.* 263,21. In all these texts Alexander is indeed referred to by phrases such as
'the commentator' or 'Aristotle's commentator'; but these phrases are not honorific
titles – they are ordinary referring expressions. (If, at the end of a book review, you
read 'The author deserves our thanks', you will rightly take this for praise – but you
will not think that the author has been honoured as The Author *par excellence*.)
Alexander is also said to have been called 'the second Aristotle'; but the two relevant
texts ('Elias' [i.e. David], *in Cat.* 128,13; Syrianus, *in Metaph.* 100,6) are peculiarly
difficult (and 'Elias' is certainly corrupt): for opposing views see Moraux (1973/84), II,
p. 401; Thillet, pp. XX-XXXI. Note, too, that Alexander was often criticised (e.g.
Plutarch of Athens, *apud* Philoponus, *in DA.* 21,20-3; Philoponus, *in An. Post.*
111,31-112,6) and sometimes accused of bias (e.g. 'Elias', *in Cat.* 123,4-8).

[29] See Boethius' comment on Theophrastus at *in Int.* ed. sec. 12,3-16; cf. Barnes
(1985a) for an attempt to reconstruct one such Theophrastean supplement.

called interpretations or exegeses of Aristotle, in a loose sense;[30] but there is no reason to believe that they wrote commentaries on his writings;[31] and it seems unlikely that any Aristotelian work received a commentary before the renascence of Aristotelian studies in the late first century BC.[32] By then the tradition of literary commentaries, which had been consolidated in Alexandria in the third century BC,[33] was well established, and the *hupomnêma* or commentary was a recognised genre.[34] There were already commentaries on scientific texts – namely, on the medical writings in the Hippocratic corpus.[35] Perhaps, too, there were commentaries on philosophical texts, and in particular on Platonic texts. According to Proclus, Crantor was 'the first interpreter of Plato';[36] and whether or not Proclus means that Crantor wrote *commentaries* on Plato,[37] it is likely that such commentaries were written during Crantor's life-time – for two papyri dating from the third century BC preserve small fragments of what seems to have been a commentary on the *Phaedo*.[38] The earliest philosophical commentary of which we can form any general impression is the anonymous commentary on the *Theaetetus*, partly preserved on papyrus.[39] The papyrus itself is dated to the first century AD, but the text it contains may go back to

[30] Compare the way in which later Epicureans interpreted the works of their master: see esp. Sedley; Puglia.

[31] *Pace* Geffcken, pp. 406-7: Geffcken's study is a useful survey of the antecedents of philosophical commentaries; but he fails to distinguish essays in interpretation from commentaries proper.

[32] On this renascence see most recently Moraux (1973/84), I, pp. 1-94; Gottschalk (1987), pp. 1083-97.

[33] See e.g. Pfeiffer, pp. 210-33; Fraser, pp. 447-79; Turner, pp. 112-24; and esp. del Fabbro, who gives lucid accounts of the forms and varieties of early commentaries (pp. 70-2; 93-5), of commentatorial style (pp. 97-100), and of the sorts of topics which a commentary standardly covered (pp. 106-23).

[34] For the history of the term see e.g. Bömer.

[35] See Fraser, pp. 363-7. Our MSS of Galen ascribe a commentary on Hippocrates' *Aphorisms* to Herophilus (*in Hipp. Aph.* XVIIIA 186-7K); but the text should be emended to ascribe the commentary to Herophilus' pupil, Bacchius: see now von Staden, pp. 75-6.

[36] See *in Tim.* I 75,30-76,10 (cf. II 276,31-277,14).

[37] See most recently Dörrie, pp. 328-38. The use of the word *exêgêsis* does not in itself imply a commentary: thus we should not suppose that the *pleistoi ... hosoi exêgêntai* the book of Heraclitus, and who included the shadowy Antisthenes (not, *pace* Geffcken, p. 399, the celebrated Antisthenes but the *Hêrakleiteios* mentioned at Diogenes Laertius, VI 19) and Heraclides of Pontus (Diogenes Laertius, IX 15), wrote commentaries (even though Heraclides' work was entitled *Hêrakleitou exêgêseis*: Diogenes Laertius, V 88).

[38] Namely PMon 91 [Carlini (1986), pp. 10-14] and PHeid 28 [Carlini (1978), pp. 201-9]; see also Carlini (1975).

[39] See Diels-Schubart; Praechter (1909b) (a new text is being prepared for the *Corpus dei Papiri Filosofici*). Note that the anonymus had also written commentaries on the *Timaeus* (XXXV 10-12), on the *Phaedo* (XLVIII 7-11), and on the *Symposium* (LXX 10-12).

the first century BC.[40] There are scattered references to other commentatorial activity on Platonic texts.[41]

The earliest surviving commentary on Aristotle is Aspasius' commentary on the *Nicomachean Ethics*.[42] Aspasius was a generation senior to Alexander. Earlier Peripatetics had written earlier commentaries: Andronicus, Boethus and Ariston in the first century BC; Sotion, Apollonius, Achaicus and Alexander of Aegae in the first century AD.[43] Of these scholars, Boethus and Ariston are known to have written about syllogistic;[44] and Boethus had indeed proposed substantial modifications to Aristotle's theories.[45] But it is not explicitly said that they wrote commentaries on the *Prior Analytics*. Sotion wrote a commentary on the *Topics*; and a papyrus preserves part of a commentary on the *Topics* dating from the first century AD.[46] Contemporary with Aspasius were Adrastus, who was perhaps Alexander's compatriot,[47] and Alexander's teachers, of whom Herminus almost certainly had written a commentary on the *Prior Analytics*.[48] In addition, thinkers outside the Peripatetic school had addressed themselves to Aristotelian logic; and the two earliest logical handbooks to have survived – Galen's *Introduction to*

[40] So Tarrant; but see Glucker (1989).

[41] See e.g. Diogenes Laertius, III 65-6; POxy 1609 (a reference to a commentary on the *Timaeus*); Suetonius, *apud* Eustathius, *in Od.* I 107; Porphyry, *Vit. Plot.* 14; Proclus, *in Rep.* II 96. On Albinus' commentaries see Diels-Schubart, pp. XXVIII-XXX; on Adrastus' commentary on the *Timaeus* see Moraux (1973/84), II, pp. 296-313; on Posidonius' alleged commentary on the *Timaeus* see Kidd, pp. 338-40 (on PGen 203 see Burkert (1987)). In general see Gudeman, cols. 687-91; Untersteiner, pp. 205-22; Dillon, pp. 54-7; Westerink (1976), I, pp. 7-19.

[42] Edited by Heylbut in *CAG* XIX 1 (see Mercken; cf. Goulet, pp. 635-6).

[43] See esp. Moraux (1973/84), I, pp. 97-142 (Andronicus), 143-80 (Boethus), 181-96 (Ariston); II, pp. 211-14 (Sotion), 216-17 (Apollonius), 217-21 (Achaicus), 222-5 (Alexander of Aegae); also Moraux (1986b); Gottschalk (1987), pp. 1097-121 (who also refers to Platonists, such as Eudorus, and to Stoics, such as Athenodorus, who discussed – but did not compose commentaries upon – Aristotle's logical ideas).

[44] For Ariston see esp. Mariotti, pp. 59-74.

[45] Notably in his thesis that *all* categorical syllogisms are 'perfect': Themistius, *Max.* 190-1; Ammonius, *in An. Pr.* 31,11-32,7; scholiast to Aristotle, 156b43-157b9 (see our note to 23,14 below). Note too Boethus' claim that hypothetical syllogistic is prior to categorical: Galen, *Inst. Log.* vii 2.

[46] PFayum 3: see Moraux (1973/84), I, pp. 215-16.

[47] For his presence in the surviving commentary on Books II-V of *EN* (edited by Heylbut in *CAG* XX) see Moraux (1973/84), II, pp. 323-30; Gottschalk (1987), p. 1155; Mercken; Goulet, pp. 56-7. Note too the fragmentary commentary on *GC* preserved in 'Ocellus Lucanus', 20-35: the date of this work is uncertain, but it may be as early as the first century BC (see Moraux (1973/84), II, p. 606; (1986b), pp. 133-4).

[48] For commentaries on *An. Pr.* see also Ebbesen (1981b); Lee, pp. 9-12, 36, 128. (POxy 3320 may possibly come from an early commentary on *An. Pr.*) For early commentaries on *Cat.* see Galen, *Lib. Prop.* XIX 42K; Simplicius, *in Cat.* 1,3-2,29; 159,23-33 (cf. Moraux (1973/84), II, pp. 519-27; Gottschalk (1987), pp. 1101-12); for commentaries on *de Int.* see Zimmermann, pp. lxxx-xcii.

Dialectic[49] and the *On Interpretation* ascribed to Apuleius[50] – both contain accounts of Peripatetic syllogistic.[51]

Alexander thus had at his disposal a wealth of scholarly work on Aristotelian logic in general and on the *Prior Analytics* in particular; and at least some of this work had been expressed in the form of commentaries. Alexander rarely names his predecessors.[52] But it is clear from his own commentary that he was thoroughly familiar with their work. It is clear, too, that the tradition had produced interpretations of considerable detail and ingenuity. And it is clear that the tradition was not uniform or univocal: Alexander reports deviant interpretations; and he also reports the views of logicians who wished to modify or even reject some parts of Aristotle's logical system.

Alexander's commentary was influential in its turn. Two later commentaries on the *Prior Analytics* survive: one, truncated, by Ammonius,[53] and the other by Ammonius' pupil, John Philoponus.[54] Ammonius and Philoponus were intimate with Alexander's work, and each draws upon it. Indeed, there are substantial passages in Philoponus' commentary which paraphrase, with or without acknowledgment, the corresponding passages in Alexander's work. The two later commentators were Platonists, and they did not share Alexander's general philosophical stance. But their differences from Alexander in matters of logic were relatively trifling; and their commentaries provide us with interesting, and sometimes illuminating, parallels to Alexander's discussion.[55]

Alexander, *On the Prior Analytics*

The later commentators were conservative creatures. They worked to a standard form; and they borrowed shamelessly – or perhaps

[49] Note also Galen's commentaries on *An. Pr.*, *An. Post.* and *Cat.*: *Lib. Prop.* XIX 47K (see Moraux (1973/84), II, pp. 688-91).

[50] For the latest surveys of the long-standing controversy over the authorship of this work see Hijmans, pp. 408-11; J.-M. Flamand, in Goulet, pp. 298-317.

[51] Note also the brief description in Albinus, *Didasc.* 158-64H.

[52] In the first part of *in An. Pr.* Herminus is the only commentator named (72,27; 89,34; 91,21); but note the several anonymous references to exegetes and critics of Aristotle: 20,31; 23,3; 65,18; 68,21; 75,11; 81,17; 95,29; 100,17. Sometimes other evidence allows us to name these people (see e.g. our note to 95,29; and compare *in An. Pr.* 125,3-6 with [Ammonius], *in An. Pr.* 39,31).

[53] Edited by Wallies in *CAG* IV 6.

[54] Edited by Wallies in *CAG* XIII 2: the commentary was taken from Ammonius' seminars on *An. Pr.* There is also an Armenian version of David's commentary on *An. Pr.*, and a fragment of the commentary by Elias (see Westerink (1961)). We perhaps have references to lost commentaries by Porphyry (see Ammonius, *in An. Pr.* 31,15), Iamblichus (Philoponus, *in An. Pr.* 26,5), Themistius ([Ammonius], *in An. Pr.* 39,2), Syrianus ([Ammonius], *in An. Pr.* 39,2), Eutocius (Elias, *in An. Pr.* 134 Westerink), Proclus ([Ammonius], *in An. Pr.* 43,30-1), Marinus (Leo Magentinus: Ebbesen (1981b), p. 10). For Byzantine commentaries see Benakis.

[55] On the substantial issues see Lee, *passim*. We draw attention to the more interesting parallels in our notes to the translation.

reverentially – from their predecessors.[56] Moreover, they had
reflected upon the obligations and duties of a commentator, and they
had established certain canons of procedure.[57] Earlier scholars had
also thought about the matter. Thus Galen:

> Before the detailed interpretation, you should learn in general what
> the function of any interpretation is, namely to render clear whatever
> is unclear in the work. To prove that what is written is true, or to
> refute it as false, or to defend it against sophistical criticisms – these
> are not part of interpretation, but they have become standard tasks
> for pretty well everyone who writes a commentary. Now there is
> absolutely no reason why an interpreter should not touch lightly on
> these matters; but a thorough examination of the author's doctrines
> falls outside the boundary of interpretation. (*in Hipp. Fract.* XVIIIB
> 318-19K)

No doubt such elementary ideas had presented themselves to
Alexander; and if the later canons had not been fixed by his time,
most of their prescriptions are in fact observed by him – he will, for
example, discuss such preliminary issues as the purpose of the work
before him, its utility, the significance of its title. In any case, the
requirements for a commentary – and especially for a commentary
on a logical text – are relatively obvious and uncontroversial; and
Alexander's works no doubt followed, more or less closely, an
established pattern.

The commentary on the *Prior Analytics* begins with a Preface, on
the nature of the subject-matter and on the name and scope of
Aristotle's treatise. Then follows the commentary proper, divided
into sections by 'lemmata' or citations from Aristotle's text.[58] The
intensity of comment is uneven: some Aristotelian passages receive
minute scrutiny, others are ignored. And the unevennesses do not
invariably correspond to the differing degrees of difficulty which a
modern reader will find in the text: what an ancient commentator
considered interesting is not always the same as what a modern
reader finds perplexing. The nature of the comments is diverse:

[56] For the later commentatorial tradition see e.g. Praechter (1909a), pp. 526-33;
Richard; Sorabji (1990a); Westerink (1990).
[57] The canons were codified by Proclus (see 'Elias', *in Cat.* 107,24-5; cf. esp.
Westerink (1990)); but they can be traced back to the third century (see I. Hadot) and
perhaps even earlier (see e.g. Moraux (1986b), pp. 134-5). For their description of the
role of the commentator see e.g. Simplicius, *in Cat.* 7,23-32; 'Elias', *in Cat.*
122,25-123,11.
[58] On lemmata in ancient commentaries see Turner, pp. 114-15; del Fabbro, p. 78.
Ross, p. 91, says that 'it is agreed among scholars that the lemmata were written not
by the commentators but by copyists'. If Ross means that the commentators supplied
no lemmata at all, he is wrong. If he means that the lemmata in our MSS never
represent the lemmata written by the commentators themselves, he is at best half
right (cf. Lamberz, pp. 7-15): see below, p. 17.

there are textual notes;[59] there are explications of points of language; there is much explanatory paraphrase of Aristotle's argument; there are short disquisitions interpolated into the commentary, where Aristotle has hinted at an issue without discussing it or where other philosophers have ventured dubious opinions.

Usually Alexander makes his own judgment plain. Occasionally he sets out the different possibilities without indicating a preference. From time to time he refers explicitly to the views of other scholars – other Peripatetics or members of other schools – but almost invariably in order to criticize and refute their views. On the other hand, he rarely offers a substantive criticism of Aristotle himself:[60] he often finds Aristotle obscure and in need of explanation (why else would he be writing a commentary?[61]); but, like any good commentator, he implicitly adopts a 'Principle of Charity' and strives to find an interpretation of the text which will place it on the side of the truth.[62]

For whom was Alexander's commentary written? What is its style and tone? What is its value, as a commentary and as a contribution to logical studies?

The commentary is not a literary production, written for a large public. Rather, as we have said, it may be supposed to represent the lectures which Alexander gave to his students, perhaps in his capacity as Professor of Aristotelian Philosophy. Lectures are usually given more than once, and the incorporation of later revisions will often leave the text disjointed and uneven. In Alexander's commentary there are some odd transitions and some strange *non sequiturs*.[63] They are no doubt to be explained by the nature of the work. An early comment was later judged to be inadequate in some fashion; further notes were written and added to the text; but the new coat showed its seams, and the original

[59] See Moraux (1986b), pp. 134-7; note Galen's remarks on this subject at *in Hipp. Off.* XVIIIB 630-2K.

[60] The only serious exception to this in the part we have translated is at 116,29-35; but note that Alexander's criticism here must be read in the light of his claim that Aristotle, in the passage in question, intends to train or exercise his readers (*gumnasion*: 113,10). In later parts of the commentary there are more substantial criticisms, notably in connexion with 'mixed' modal syllogisms; see e.g. *in An. Pr.* 213,11-27; 214,12-18; 236,8-11; 238,22-38; 240,32-241,9; 249,25-32; 270,6-8.

[61] Note that the question 'Why is Aristotle obscure?' was one of the preliminary topics prescribed by the Procline canon (above, n. 57).

[62] No doubt some commentators strove too hard: the Procline canon gravely insists that 'the interpreter must not force and strain and announce that everything said by the old author whom he is interpreting is true. He must always repeat: "The man is my friend, but so too is truth; and while both are friends, truth is the more so"' ('Elias', *in Cat.* 122,32-123,1): cf. Tarán. Alexander sometimes forced and strained: note his remark at *DA* 2,4-9.

[63] See e.g. 116,36 note; 118,10 note.

material was neither cut out nor refashioned to make the text cohere.

The lecture audience was expected to have a text of Aristotle's *Prior Analytics* to hand, and to be prepared to give it a close reading, with meticulous attention both to dubious exegetical points and to substantive matters of logical theory. Students would already have studied the *Categories* and *On Interpretation*. It is presupposed that they have a general competence in Peripatetic philosophy and in its terminology. (Thus Alexander can use, without explanation, such technical or semi-technical terms as *hulê* and *tropos*.[64]) It is also presupposed that they have an elementary logical training.[65]

As for the style, you may call it, unkindly, professorial.[66] Alexander makes no attempt to write 'good Greek', nor does he enliven his argument with stylistic tricks and tropes. (Contrast the writings of his contemporary Galen: Galen's works, even the most technical, are composed in a rich and flowing style, and they are full of rhetorical embellishments and polemical *tours de force*. Contrast, too, the later Greek commentators who are usually fluent and sometimes elegant.) Alexander's vocabulary is limited. He avoids variation. He is frequently repetitive. There are no light touches – and no jokes.

His syntax sometimes slips. More notably, his sentence construction is at the same time lax and tortuous. Sentences meander across the page, flowing languidly toward a finite verb and sometimes seeping away before they find one. 'Anacolouthon' is the polite – or the technical – term for such things; but Alexander's anacoloutha are not conscious rhetorical tricks, designed to heighten the emotional tone.

Alexander's subject is logic, and it might be said in his defence that logic does not lend itself to simple syntax or to flowery prose. Logicians must be spare, and they must be explicit: we should expect long sentences and we should not expect pleasing embellishments. But Alexander's style is no model for the logician: it achieves explicitness only at the cost of a tedious opacity. The long sentences are difficult to construe. The language hangs like a dense fog over the logical terrain.[67] Compare Alexander with another of his contemporaries, Sextus Empiricus. Sextus' plain prose possesses a limpidity and a precision even when he is discussing matters of considerable logical complexity.

If the style of Alexander's commentary does not commend itself to the candid reader, what of the substance? As a commentary on

[64] See 6,17; 26,15.

[65] Alexander will sometimes refer to a separate monograph for a fuller discussion of technical issues: see esp. *in An. Pr.* 238,22-38; 249,15-250,2.

[66] On commentatorial style see esp. del Fabbro, pp. 97-100, who justly describes it as 'dry and devoid of any stylistic embellishment' (p. 97). Del Fabbro thinks that the style reflects the serious and sober aim of the commentator (p. 100); Turner (p. 113) supposes rather that it reflects the oral origin of the commentaries.

[67] A prize example at 72,26-74,7 – which is, syntactically, a single sentence.

Aristotle, the work is not without merit. Aristotle's *Prior Analytics* is densely written, particularly in its early formal chapters. The text is sometimes allusive, often obscure. Alexander has an eye for the difficulties, and he will often make them plain. His paraphrastic comments are especially useful in this respect; for their aim is simply to state expansively what Aristotle had stated in rude and crabbed form. Sometimes Alexander's interpretations are questionable; and on occasion they seem contrived and implausible. But all in all readers of Aristotle will gain from consulting Alexander – and they will gain more from him than they will gain from many a later commentary.

In addition, Alexander will often elaborate on issues towards which Aristotle merely gestures. These little essays, which sometimes draw on later Peripatetic theories and sometimes involve polemic against the enemies of Aristotelianism, enrich the content of the commentary. They afford historical information which we cannot get, or cannot get so well, from other sources.[68] They also collectively delineate Aristotelian syllogistic at the midpoint of its historical development.[69] The conception of logic which manifests itself in Alexander's pages is in some respects different from Aristotle's – and different from our own. Consider, for example, Alexander's interest in the 'generation' of the syllogistic figures;[70] or his concern with the proper 'ranking' of the figures, and of the syllogisms within the figures.[71] Such issues will strike modern logicians as utterly alien to logic: for Alexander, they have the same interest and the same standing as such 'genuinely' logical topics as the reduction or analysis of syllogisms. No doubt Alexander was wrong, his conception of logic muddled and inadequate. But it was a conception of considerable historical influence and importance; and that in itself gives the commentary a peculiar interest.

Alexander was not an original logician. There is no evidence that he made any substantial logical discoveries or inventions of his own. There may have been a few terminological innovations;[72] some of the arguments which he deploys against various of Aristotle's critics he may have excogitated himself; and he may have contributed

---

[68] See e.g. the material on 'unmethodically concluding' arguments at 21,10-22,30; or the account of Herminus' views on major and minor terms at 72,17-75,34.

[69] On this aspect of the commentary see esp. Lee. Lee's monograph contains the best and most substantial modern treatment of Alexander's logic, but it does not purport to be comprehensive. Of older treatments, Prantl (see pp. 620-6) offers nothing of value, and Volait is mostly jejune.

[70] See 47,27 note.

[71] See 47,22 note; 51,8 note.

[72] Thus the words *suzugia* and *sumplokê*, in their logical senses, meet us for the first time in Alexander's commentary. But Alexander gives no hint that he is neologizing, and we may well suppose that he is using an established vocabulary.

something to the method of 'reducing' all syllogisms to the two first syllogisms of the first figure.[73] However that may be, it is plain that he is essentially a presenter, not a producer, of logical ideas. (Here, again, he contrasts with Galen, who made – and was acutely conscious of having made – no small contribution to logical theory.[74]) That in itself is no disgrace. But it must be confessed that Alexander's presentation of logical ideas is less than perfect. Not only, as we have said, is his style at odds with the needs of his subject: there is also evidence that he sometimes failed to understand what he presented. One example of his failure is worth elaborating; for it runs through the whole commentary and it may puzzle an unwary reader.[75]

In his syllogistic, Aristotle was concerned to show not only that certain pairs of propositions yield a syllogistic conclusion but also that certain other pairs do not. He proves that pairs of propositions are 'non-syllogistic' by providing counterexamples. Thus he shows that no syllogistic conclusion follows from a pair of propositions of the form

A holds of no B, B holds of no C

in the following way.[76]

First, it will be proved that you cannot infer a conclusion of the form

A does not hold of some C.

Take the terms: science, line, medicine. No line is a science; no medicine is a line; but every medicine is a science. (The example, which is Aristotle's own, may sound strange: read 'medicine' as 'branch of medicine'.) Hence three propositions of the forms

A holds of no B, B holds of no C, A holds of every C

may all be true together. Hence a pair of propositions of the form

A holds of no B, B holds of no C

do not yield a conclusion of the form

A does not hold of some C.

---

[73] See 115,18-116,36: the state of the text suggests (but does not prove) that this passage was a later addition to Alexander's original text, and it *may* be the case that it represents a later discovery by Alexander himself. But equally, of course, Alexander may have *read* about the method later in a work by some other logician. There is in general much in Alexander which we find in no earlier source – but we possess virtually no relevant earlier sources. The text of the commentary rarely gives us any reason to *suspect* originality; and since Alexander never *claims* originality, it seems probable that he rarely *is* original.

[74] See e.g. Barnes (1985b).

[75] See Łukasiewicz, pp. 67-8; Patzig, pp. 169-72; Barnes (1990a), III 7. The misunderstanding is not proprietary to Alexander: it can be paralleled in most of the ancient commentators (see e.g. Apuleius, *Int.* 186,5; 194,23; Philoponus, *in An. Pr.* 34,7-10; 74,30-75,15 – and very often) – and in some of the moderns; it *seems* to appear from time to time in Aristotle himself (e.g. *An. Pr.* 38a29-31, b18-20; 39b3-6).

[76] See *An. Pr.* 26a9-12 (Alexander's comments are at *in An. Pr.* 57,7-18).

Another triad of terms shows in the same way that a pair of propositions of the form in question will not yield a conclusion of the form

A holds of some C.

Now, since the pair does not yield

A does not hold of some C,

it does not yield

A holds of no C;

and since it does not yield

A holds of some C,

it does not yield

A holds of every C.

(For 'A holds of every C' entails 'A holds of some C'. Hence if the pair yielded the former, it would also yield the latter. Similarly for 'A holds of no C' and 'A does not hold of some C'.)

Hence no syllogistic proposition predicating A of C can be deduced from the pair in question. Hence the pair is 'non-syllogistic'.

Alexander frequently discusses this method of proving that a pair of propositions is non-syllogistic. He always misunderstands it.[77] He takes it that – in the first example we cited from Aristotle –

Every medicine is a science

follows from the pair of propositions

No line is a science, No medicine is a line.

Thus he takes it that

A does not hold of some C

does not *always* follow from

A holds of no B, B holds of no C

because

A holds of every C

sometimes follows. This is Alexander's own view of the logical structure of Aristotle's method; and he supposes that he is simply following Aristotle's view.

It is clear that something has gone seriously wrong. Alexander is in effect confusing the relation of *being compatible with* with the relation of *following from*. The method of counterexample in fact employs the relation of *being compatible with*: that is the relation which the method requires, and it is the relation which Aristotle's examples actually exhibit. Alexander speaks instead of the relation of *following from*: the method does not and cannot employ this relation; and Aristotle's examples evidently do not exhibit it.

It is hard to have much faith in a logician who can make such an elementary error; and it must be allowed that Alexander was not a

[77] He may seem to get it right at *in An. Pr.* 101,14-16 and 328,10-30; but in these passages it seems reasonable to think that he has succeeded by mistake.

first-rate logician. Nonetheless, the second-rate are often worth reading. Even Alexander's blunders have their interest: logic is not an easy subject; it is salutary to see how readily bad mistakes are made; and one way of avoiding error yourself is to observe the errors of others.[78] Moreover, the errors in Alexander's commentary are balanced by a decent weight of truth. And in any event, the commentary has (as we have indicated) an unparalleled value as an historical document; for we possess no other contemporary logical text of comparable length and detail.

The translation

Book 1 of the *Prior Analytics* divides into three main sections: first, in 1.1-7, Aristotle introduces his syllogistic theory and expounds the non-modal syllogisms; then, in 1.8-22, he discusses modal syllogisms; and thirdly, in 1.23-46, he offers a loosely organized series of metalogical observations. The first part can sensibly be read on its own; for, apart from the discussion of modal conversions in 1.3, it is entirely self-contained. Alexander's commentary also, and unsurprisingly, divides into three parts. This translation is of the first part – that is to say, the commentary on 1.1-7. This accounts for about one third of the total bulk of Alexander's work.

We have endeavoured to do Alexander into plain and intelligible English. Our readers, we suppose, will be primarily interested in the history of logic and in Aristotelian syllogistic; and the translation is designed for such readers. It will be of little interest to anyone whose main concern is with Alexander's prose style – not that such people are common.

Our English is sometimes clumsy or ambiguous or obscure. In principle these failings are deliberate: they reflect failings in Alexander's Greek, failings which an English reader should be aware of. We have not, however, attempted to match Alexander's stylistic inelegancies with analogous inelegancies of our own: mere bad writing – as opposed to bad thinking – has been effaced. (But we have no doubt introduced some bad writing of our own.) In particular, we have consciously striven to break down Alexander's long and contorted periods into ordinary English sentences. This betrays Alexander's style, but it does service to his argument. And Alexander's style merits no loyalty.

We have added a few things of our own. Occasionally we have interpolated numerals to indicate the division of an argument into its parts. These numerals have no counterpart in the Greek, and we have added them only where the train of thought seemed

---

[78] See *in An. Pr.* 8,19-29.

disagreeably obscure without them. The Chapter and Section headings are also our addition. They too have no counterpart in the Greek, which is broken only by the Aristotelian lemmata.[79] But they should not be misleading; and they may serve any reader who wishes to scan through the pages looking for matters of particular interest – and also any hardened spirit who may determine to read the book from cover to cover.

As far as vocabulary is concerned, we have not affected a rigorous purism. Different Greek words are often given the same English translation if they are synonyms or used synonymously. Conversely, a single Greek word will get different English renderings if it is ambiguous – or even if normal English idiom requires or suggests a variation. (It should be unnecessary to state these elementary principles of translation; but in recent years a foolish purism, based on a false conception of fidelity, has become fashionable.) Where logical terminology is involved, we have, however, been a little more scrupulous. Here we have allowed ourselves a few barbarisms; for here it is – or it may be – important to know that Alexander used the same word in this sentence as in that. The next section of the Introduction says something about Alexander's logical terminology and our attempts to translate it. The Greek-English Index and the English-Greek Glossary offer a more extensive view of our linguistic decisions.

It will surprise some readers that we have altogether avoided logical symbolism. There is a temptation to employ modern logical notation (or at least the standard symbols deployed in modern treatments of Aristotle's syllogistic) in the translation, or at any rate in the notes. For symbolism is both concise and precise. But Alexander himself was no symbolic logician. Like Aristotle, he uses a technical and semi-technical vocabulary. But he writes in Greek, and the 'mathematical' aspect of modern logic is entirely foreign to him (as indeed it is to Aristotle himself).[80] Hence (and also for other reasons) we have dispensed altogether with symbols. We write 'A holds of every B' rather than 'AaB'. We write 'If P, then Q' rather than 'P→Q'.

The annotations are mere notes: they do not, and are not intended to, amount to a commentary (or metacommentary). They are of five kinds. (1) They provide precise references and cross-references to ancient texts which Alexander cites or alludes to. Where Alexander simply remarks 'X says' (or 'I have said'), we pedantically supply the appropriate numbers. Sometimes Alexander's allusions are covert

---

[79] On our treatment of the lemmata see below, p. 17.

[80] Alexander follows Aristotle in using letters (A, B, C; M, N, O; P, R, S) to express syllogistic forms; but these letters are not variables in the modern sense (see note to 53,30).

(for he knew Aristotle and Plato backwards and his language often echoes them): we have sometimes made such allusions explicit – but we cannot pretend to have hunted all of them down. (2) The notes also record parallel passages in other ancient texts: in Alexander's other works; in the later commentaries of Ammonius and Philoponus; and occasionally in other authors. These records, again, make no claim to completeness; rather, they suggest starting-points to anyone who wishes to look further into the ancient history of the issues which Alexander discusses. (3) There are references to the modern literature. This literature is not in fact vast; for Alexander's logic has not been a favourite topic among modern scholars. Even so, there is more than we have looked at, and our notes are selective. (4) From time to time, Alexander's arguments appear to us to be obscure and difficult to follow. In such cases we have provided a paraphrase: some of the paraphrases are no more than tentative attempts to articulate one possible interpretation of a puzzling text; and although we have (of course) picked the interpretation which we think is least bad, we do not suppose that our interpretation is the only interpretation worth considering. (5) Finally, there are some textual notes – but they require a fresh paragraph.

The only critical edition of Alexander's commentary on the *Prior Analytics* is the text published by Maximilian Wallies in volume II 1 of the Berlin series of *Commentaria in Aristotelem Graeca*. Wallies relied mainly on three manuscripts (BLM) and on the early Aldine edition, which he took to represent an inferior manuscript tradition. There are several manuscripts which Wallies did not consult; and some of those which he did consult he consulted briskly: a full critical edition of the commentary would have demanded far more time than the Berlin Academy allowed its editors.[81] And a properly scholarly edition is yet to be done. (We have looked idly at a few pages in a late Florentine manuscript;[82] this has, unsurprisingly, brought only one small improvement to Wallies' text – and Wallies' error was perhaps due to a minor lapse at the proof-reading stage.[83])

We have ventured to depart from Wallies' text at some eighty places. The departures are signalled in notes of the fifth sort.

---

[81] For an enthusiastic account of the origins and the progress of *CAG* see Usener, pp. 199-202. Wallies signed the Preface to *in An. Pr.* on 1 September 1883: the Berlin Academy had given its formal approval to the *CAG* project on 9 May 1878.

[82] Laurent LXXII 11, which Wallies calls C.

[83] At 17,4 Wallies prints *ê en têi entolêi ê en têi klêsei*; and his critical apparatus records no variants. Laurent LXXII 11 has *ê en têi erôtêsei* after *entolêi*. It is likely that this is the correct text (for it is hard to imagine a scribe's being moved to interpolate the words). But we should not infer that the Laurentian MS uniquely preserves Alexander's text. In fact, the same text is printed in the Aldine edition; and we suspect that the words in question are to be found in all the MSS – they have been lost from Wallies' text by some nineteenth-century oversight.

(These textual notes are collected in Appendix 3.)

As a matter of fact, Alexander's text seems to be in pretty good order; and we do not suppose that a new critical edition would often differ substantially from Wallies. But there is one point where some uncertainty might be felt. It concerns the lemmata or snippets of Aristotelian text which punctuate the commentary. There are two problems here. First, the lemmata run to different lengths in different manuscripts: it seems likely that different copyists (or their paymasters) chose to copy more or less of the Aristotelian text; and it is not clear that we know how extensive the lemmata were in Alexander's own copy of his commentary. Secondly, the proper wording of the lemmata is sometimes a matter of doubt. Alexander's text of the *Prior Analytics* often differs (usually in trifling particulars) from more recent texts;[84] and copyists would sometimes take their lemmata from a manuscript of Aristotle rather than from the manuscript of Alexander which they were reproducing. (This is proved by the fact that the text of a lemma will sometimes disagree with the text cited in the course of the commentary.[85]) Thus we cannot always be sure that the text which we read in the lemmata was the text which Alexander himself had before him.

In the translation we have adopted the following policy: in every case, we have translated all of the lemma which Wallies prints; but we have often continued the citations beyond the text in Wallies, and we have occasionally interpolated new lemmata on our own initiative. All such additions are clearly marked, being enclosed by angle brackets. They are made, solely for the convenience of the modern reader, when Alexander's subsequent comments bear specifically on a part of the text which does not appear in the lemma which Wallies prints.

Logical terminology[86]

Alexander had at his service a rich and developed logical

---

[84] See notes to Appendix 1.

[85] There is a trivial example of this in the part of *in An. Pr.* which we have translated: at *An. Pr.* 26a15 our texts of Aristotle read *ontos te*, and so does the lemma at *in An. Pr.* 58,24 (except that the Aldine edition prints *tou* for *te*); when Alexander cites the same line of Aristotle in the body of the commentary, he writes *ontos ge* (58,9: the manuscripts have *ge*, the Aldine has nothing – and Wallies prints *te*). For a more interesting case compare *in An. Pr.* 282,14-15 (the lemma, agreeing with our text of Aristotle) with 283,3 (and 284,20.29), which cites a variant text. Note that the lemmata in the Aldine edition have often (but not invariably) been written to fit the current text of Aristotle (e.g. 9,4; 13,27; 23,20 – further references in the notes to Appendix 1).

[86] The Greek-English Index contains references to discussions in this section.

vocabulary.[87] Many of his Greek terms are difficult to translate; and
any translation is certain to break some of the semantic connexions
which link the different Greek terms. In this section we survey
Alexander's logical vocabulary, stating and sometimes explaining
our choice of translation. We do not discuss every word which might
be deemed logical in a broad sense of the term; and we are primarily
interested in Alexander's *syllogistic* vocabulary.[88] The section is
written as a continuous narrative: we begin with a few terms of very
general application; then we turn to arguments and syllogisms;
thirdly, we deal with words connected with propositions and their
interrelations; and finally we discuss the terminology for the parts
and internal structure of propositions.[89]

Alexander insists that the logician should attend not to words but
to what words mean;[90] nonetheless, the objects of his study are, of
course, essentially expressed in words: *phônê*, which we normally
translate 'word' and *lexis*, which is normally 'expression', pick out
parts of language – words, phrases or sentences. These linguistic
items have a semantic force – they *mean* something.

Alexander's semantic repertoire includes the following words:
sêmainein (with *sêmantikos* and the associated *sêmeion*); *dêloun*
(with *dêlôtikos*); *mênuein* (and *mênutikos*); *endeiknunai*. It is
initially tempting to suppose that these different words must have
different senses, and so to establish different English versions for
them. But there is no evidence of any subtle semantic distinctions
among the words, whether in Alexander or in any other Greek
author. (Greek philosophers were scarcely interested in theories of
meaning; Greek grammarians did not develop any semantic
theory.[91]) Accordingly, we have been content to use 'mean' as a
standard translation for the first three of these four verbs. For the
fourth, *endeiknunai*, we do reserve a special translation, 'indicate';
but we do so only because the word is used elsewhere in a technical
sense, and an English reader might be interested to see how
Alexander uses it in a non-technical way. (In addition, the four verbs
may have a slightly different meaning in certain contexts. Thus
dêloun means 'make *dêlos* or clear';[92] and 'make clear' may

[87] Little work has been done on Alexander's style and language; but see Todd (1974).
[88] For a brief account of syllogistic see Appendix 2.
[89] But a desire to group together words from the same stem has occasionally interfered with this general scheme.   [90] See 84,15-19 and note.
[91] The grammarian Apollonius Dyscolus has an extensive semantic vocabulary (see e.g. the opening section of *Conj.*); but he makes no systematic distinctions among the words he uses, all of which can usually be translated by the one word 'mean'.
[92] 'Clear' is always *dêlos*: 'obvious' renders *enargês*, 'plain' gives *saphês*, and 'evident' translates *phaneros*. The Greek words are in fact synonyms. But it is useful to signal occurrences of *phaneros*, since the word has a vital role in the account of

sometimes carry the sense not of 'mean', i.e. 'make clear in language', but rather of 'betoken' or 'show'. Similarly, *mênuein* may be 'mark'; and *sêmainein* is sometimes 'signify'.)

Two different *lexeis* may be said *isodunamein* or *ison dunasthai* – they may be equal in power or capacity to one another. We have used the English 'equivalent' for this. (The etymology of 'equivalent' is exactly that of *isodunamos*.) A modern philosopher will ask whether *isodunamein* amounts to synonymy (sameness of meaning), or whether some weaker equivalence is intended.[93] The question cannot be answered: the important distinction between synonymy and logical equivalence seems not to have been observed by any ancient logician.

Lexis comes from *legein*, which is one of several verbs we translate by 'say'. (Sometimes 'mean' is better, and we have used it.) *Legein* also breeds *logos*, a word often cited as a paradigm of the untranslatable. It is true that no one English word will pick out the range of meaning of *logos*. But that does not make *logos* a puzzling, let alone a metaphysically exciting, term. The central idea is perfectly simple: a *logos* is what you say. There is no noun in English which means precisely 'what is said'. We have followed custom and taken 'account' as our normal rendering. But there are contexts in which this translation would be pointlessly misleading: first, the *logos* in question is sometimes an *argument*; and secondly, it is sometimes a mere *utterance*. In these cases the word *logos* does not *mean* 'argument' or 'utterance'. But clarity and the exigencies of English demand that we *translate logos* by 'argument' or by 'utterance'. Sometimes a translator should be content to preserve reference and let sense go.

Logoi which are *arguments* are the subject of Aristotle's work. The kind of argument with which he is concerned in the *Prior Analytics* is taken by Alexander to be a species of *pistis*.[94] A *pistis* is a way of warranting or justifying something; and we use 'justification' for *pistis*, with 'justify' and 'justified' for the cognate verbs (*pisteuein*, *pistousthai*) and adjective (*pistos*). (The adjective *pistos* sometimes rather has the force of 'justifiable', 'warrantable'. More generally, to call something *pistos* is sometimes to say that you are *entitled* to believe it. But in the commentary 'justified' will normally do, and we have stuck by it.)

Arguments yield conclusions. Alexander most often says that an argument *sunagei* its conclusion. We translate *sunagein* by

'perfect' syllogisms.

[93] Note that there are also *very* weak uses of the word: e.g. Philoponus, *in An. Pr.* 63,12; 98,6 (cf. Ammonius, *in Int.* 114,22-3; 122,20-26; 246,9; 257,30-258,4; and note Apuleius, *Int.* 181,6).

[94] See 43,11 note.

'deduce'. ('Infer' would do as well, but we keep this for another verb, *epipherein*, where it is used as a synonym for *sunagein*.) A *sunagôgê* is a deducing or, more naturally, a deduction; and we use 'deduction'.

An argument will also *perainein*, or more often *sumperainein*, something. We use 'conclude' for both verbs. And the noun, *sumperasma*, is 'conclusion'. The conclusion *hepetai* or *akolouthei* the premisses: we use 'follow (from)' for both verbs – which both carry the spatial and temporal sense of 'follow' (i.e. 'come after') in non-logical contexts. *Akolouthia* is the cognate noun: there is no good English noun from 'follow', so we use 'implication' for *akolouthia* and lose the transparency of its connexion with *akolouthein*.

The arguments in which Alexander is interested can be systematized or subsumed under general rules: there is a *methodos* – a method – in their case; and they contrast in some passages with arguments said *amethodôs perainein*, to conclude unmethodically.

An argument, or an arguer, may establish and prove, or refute and disprove. 'Disprove' gives *diaballein* and 'refute' *elenkhein*.[95] (An *elenkhos* is a refutation.) 'Establish' is *kataskeuazein*. 'Prove' is normally *deiknunai* – and the associated noun, *deixis*, comes out as 'proof'. In ordinary Greek, *deiknunai* means, quite generally, 'show'; and in some Alexandrian contexts it is clear that 'show', rather than the more specific 'prove', is required. You might use 'show' throughout for *deiknunai*; but then, since 'show' has no appropriate noun, the connexion between *deixis* and *deiknunai*, self-evident in Greek, will be lost in the English version. Hence we use both 'prove' and 'show' for *deiknunai*, as the context suggests. (In using 'prove' we are again attending to the reference rather than to the sense of the Greek verb.) The adjective *deiktikos* is sometimes 'probative'; but it is more often paraphrased by way of 'prove'.[96]

Apodeiknunai always has the specific sense of 'prove' rather than the generic sense of 'show'. Since we have arrogated 'prove' for *deiknunai*, we take 'demonstrate' for *apodeiknunai*. The translation is well established in the tradition. 'Demonstration' and 'demonstrative' are used for the cognates *apodeixis* and *apodeiktikos*. An argument may be demonstrative, in which case it is an argument which functions as a proof and it stands in contrast to dialectical or sophistical (*dialektikos*, *sophistikos*) arguments.[97] Again, Alexander frequently speaks of demonstrating an argument, i.e. of proving it to

[95] But where Greek idiom uses *elenkhein* English will sometimes demand 'prove' rather than 'refute': *elenkhein to asullogiston* is 'to prove to be non-syllogistic'.
[96] There is an odd Aristotelian use of the adjective which Alexander explains at 112,13-16 (cf. *in An. Pr.* 256,11-14).
[97] See 7,8 note.

be valid. By contrast, certain arguments, which are taken as basic, are called *anapodeiktoi*. We translate this by 'indemonstrable'. The word was used by the Stoics of the basic arguments in their logical system, and it is generally supposed that the Peripatetics came to adopt the Stoic terminology. We are told that the Stoics used the word *anapodeiktos* in the sense of 'not *needing* demonstration';[98] and it is likely that it should be construed in the same way in Alexander. But 'indemonstrable' is established as the orthodox translation in Stoic texts; and in any case there is no convenient alternative.

The special sort of *pisteis* to which the *Prior Analytics* is devoted are called *sullogismoi*. Some translators of Aristotle render the word as 'deduction' – in the sense in which deductions contrast with inductions. There is much to be said for the rendering. (Aristotle, and Alexander after him, contrasts *sullogismoi* with *epagôgai* or inductions.[99]) But there is also one fatal objection: Alexander, following Aristotle, recognizes the existence of deductive arguments which are not *sullogismoi*. This point is not a casual aside: it is central to Alexander's understanding of *sullogismoi*.[100] Hence we prefer to align ourselves with an older practice, and to transliterate rather than translate: *sullogismoi* are syllogisms.

The noun carries a verb, *sullogizesthai*. The word 'syllogize' is ugly, but it exists. Similarly, *sullogistikos* is 'syllogistic'. But note that 'syllogistic' in Alexander has two different uses. First, and generally, it means 'concerned with syllogisms', so that syllogistic is the science of syllogisms – just as arithmetic is the science of *arithmoi* or numbers. (*Sullogistikê* in effect means 'logic', and is more or less synonymous with *logikê* and *dialektikê*. But note that in some authors and contexts these three terms are sharply distinct.) Secondly, Alexander will regularly describe a pair of premisses as syllogistic: in this sense, to say of something that it is syllogistic is to say that it can syllogize something, i.e. to say that it will yield a conclusion by a syllogism.[101] 'Non-syllogistic' or *asullogistos* is the opposite of 'syllogistic' in this second use. A synonym of *asullogistos* is *adokimos*, 'unreliable'.

Some syllogisms are *teleioi* or 'perfect' (in the sense of 'complete', 'lacking nothing'): the term is technical – roughly speaking, it picks out a class of syllogisms which are basic inasmuch as their validity is evident. Other syllogisms are *ateleis* or imperfect. These can,

---

[98] See e.g. Sextus, *PH* II 156; *M* VIII 223; Galen, *Inst. Log.* viii 1; cf. Frede (1974a), pp. 127-9.

[99] And also with 'paradigms', *paradeigmata*: see 43,11 note.

[100] See Barnes (1990a).

[101] Note too the technical term *huposullogistikos*, which we give as 'subsyllogistical'.

however, be perfected – the verb is *teleioun* or *epitelein*. To perfect a syllogism is in effect to prove it valid: Alexander also uses *apodeiknunai* in these contexts, as we have already noted; and like Aristotle he will speak of analysing or reducing an imperfect syllogism into or to a perfect syllogism.

'Analyse' translates – or rather transliterates – *analuein*. There is a cognate noun, *analusis*; and an adjective, *analutikos*, from which Aristotle's work took its title. Alexander has a short essay on the notion of *analusis*.[102]

'Reduce' represents both *anagein* and *apagein*; and 'reduction' is *anagôgê* or *apagôgê* (the latter noun being by far the more common, and always occurring in the phrase 'reduction to the impossible'). In some texts there may be a difference between *anagein* and *apagein*; but we discern none in Alexander and hence do not scruple to use a single English word.

There are various ways in which syllogisms may be perfected, analysed, or reduced; each of them involves certain operations – to which we shall return – on the syllogism or on its component parts.

For a syllogism is a compound item – it is composed of a *conclusion* and a pair of *premisses*. Each of these three components is a proposition. Where the word 'proposition' occurs in our translation it represents *protasis*. (And *proteinein*, the cognate verb, comes out as 'propound'.) A proposition is not a linguistic item nor yet a psychological event – it is neither a sentence nor an uttering of a sentence. Rather, it is what you propound when you utter a sentence of a certain sort. Alexander notes[103] that the word *protasis* also has a more specific sense: it is used for a premiss of an argument – i.e. it refers specifically to what you propound when you put forward propositions from which a conclusion is to be deduced. For this sense of *protasis* we reserve the word 'premiss'. It is not always clear when *protasis* means 'premiss' rather than 'proposition'; and sometimes our translation depends on the toss of a coin. But since both 'proposition' and 'premiss' are exclusively used for *protasis*, the reader will always know when the Greek text presents the word *protasis*.[104]

Propositions, or *protaseis* in the general sense, are true (or false), *alêthês* (or *pseudês*). Equivalently, they 'hold' (*huparkhein*) or fail to

---

[102] See 7,11-33 and notes.   [103] See 44,19-21.

[104] One particular point deserves notice. Alexander frequently speaks of pairs of *protaseis* from which no syllogistic conclusion can be deduced. It is natural to suppose that in such passages *protasis* means 'proposition' rather than 'premiss'; for it is odd to speak of *premisses* which generate no conclusion. Nonetheless, it emerges that in Alexander's view these *protaseis* are indeed premisses – premisses which yield now one conclusion and now another (see above, pp. 12-13). Hence we have supposed that 'premiss' is the correct translation in all these texts.

hold. The verb *huparkhein* is also used with two argument-places, when the arguments are terms rather than propositions. For A *huparkhei tôi* B we say 'A holds of B'.[105] (A *huparkhei tôi* B, or A holds of B, just in case A is truly predicated of B. Animal holds of man: man is an animal.)[106] Again, propositions (whether true or false) are either simple or complex. Alexander occasionally mentions complex propositions, for which his general name is 'hypothetical (*hupothetikos*) proposition'.[107] Thus he sometimes refers to conditionals (*sunêmmena*), which the Peripatetics called 'continuous' (*sunekhê*), and to disjunctions (*diezeugmena*), which the Peripatetics called 'disjoint' (*diairetika*). But Aristotelian syllogisms contain only simple propositions, and we may forget about complex propositions. From now on, when we refer to propositions we shall have non-complex propositions in mind.

Alongside *protasis*, in the general sense, we find *apophansis*. We use 'assertion' for *apophansis*, 'assert' for *apophainein*, 'assertoric' for *apophantikos*. Alexander makes a technical distinction between a *protasis* and an *apophansis*, which our English terms do not well reflect. But the distinction is explained in the text;[108] and in any case, *apophansis* is rare in the commentary, while *apophainein* is normally used as a mere synonym for *legein*, 'say'.[109]

Protaseis in the special sense, or premisses, come in pairs. A pair of propositions is called a *suzugia* or a *sumplokê*: etymologically, the words mean 'co-yoking' and 'co-weaving'. We use 'combination' for the first expression and 'conjunction' for the second.

The word *protasis* is only one of several devices by dint of which Alexander refers to the premisses of an argument. Two verbs are widely used – and each has several compound forms.

First, an arguer will *lambanein* a proposition. The verb is the normal Greek word for 'take'; and in many contexts (especially when it is terms which you must *lambanein*) this is how we translate it. But in the case of 'taking' a proposition, we need a word to express *to lambanomenon* or *to lêphthen*, 'what is taken'; and there is no suitable noun from 'take'. The right noun for the passive participle seems to be 'assumption'. (We have also used 'assumption' for the

[105] *huparkhein* in this usage is normally translated as 'belong to'; but 'belong to' has no advantage over 'hold of', and it disguises the connexion with the one-place use of *huparkhein*.
[106] *huparxis* is 'existence', and is thus distinguished from *hupostasis* or 'subsistence': in Alexander there seems to be no difference in sense between the two words; but the distinction is important in some Stoic contexts. On *huparkhousa* see below, p. 30.
[107] See esp. *in An. Pr.* 256,12-14 (cf. 258,24; 261,25-6; *in Top.* 2,6; Ammonius, *in Int.* 3,7-15); see e.g. Volait, pp. 24-7.
[108] See 10,17 and note.
[109] 'Statement' at 1,19 represents *axiôma*; elsewhere in Alexander this ambiguous word is 'axiom'.

noun *lêmma* and – once – for the abstract noun *lêpsis*, which is usually paraphrased.) Hence it seems sensible to use 'assume' for the verb when its object is a proposition or premiss.

Lambanein a proposition is sometimes contrasted with *erôtan*, to request, a proposition. Dialectical arguers must 'request', i.e. they may argue from P only if an interlocutor 'grants' (*didonai*) a request (*erôtêsis*) or gives an affirmative answer to the question 'P?'. Demonstrative reasoners on the other hand are not thus dependent on an interlocutor – they should simply 'take', without asking, what appears to be true. But this contrast between *lambanein* and *erôtan* is not always present in Alexander: in particular, when he uses the word 'assumption' he does not usually have demonstrative syllogisms specifically in mind.

Of several compounds of *lambanein*, the most important are *proslambanein*, *metalambanein* and *paralambanein*. *Proslambanein* is used as a term of art. (We also find *proslêpsis* and *aproslêptos*.) It applies specifically to the assumption of the *second* premiss of a syllogism: you assume one premiss; and then you assume in addition, or 'co-assume', a second. We translate 'co-assume'; and *proslêpsis* is 'co-assumption'.

Metalambanein is once used in a technical sense as a synonym for *proslambanein*: we there use 're-assume'.[110] Normally the word (which has a cognate noun *metalêpsis*) means 'take ... instead of ...': we sometimes use 'transform' and sometimes paraphrase.

(*Paralambanein* does not seem to be technical. Alexander uses it of introducing material – a term or a proposition – into a given context. And so 'introduce' is apposite enough.)

The second verb is *tithenai*. Its general meaning is 'put' or 'place'. It, its cognates, and its compounds are widely used by Alexander in technical and semi-technical senses. You may *tithenai* a proposition, and in particular you may *tithenai* a proposition as a premiss for an argument. Here we use 'posit': the verb is unattractive (and its normal English overtones are inapposite); but nothing preferable presents itself. We use 'posit', the noun, for *to tethen* or *to tithemenon* (passive participles). The abstract noun *thesis*, cognate with *tithenai*, is normally used in connexion with terms rather than with propositions. Here too we sometimes use 'posit' – but we also use 'position' and paraphrase.[111]

In normal Greek, *keisthai* ('lie') is often used as a perfect passive of *tithenai*. For it we use 'be supposed', thus preserving a link with 'posit'. The participle, *to keimenon*, is frequently applied to what has been posited or what is supposed – i.e. to a putative premiss; hence

[110] See 19,5 and note.

[111] On the *thesis* of terms, and the related notion of *taxis* ('order' or 'ranking'), see 47,22 note.

'supposition'. (The verb also has other, less technical, uses.)

There are five important compounds of *tithenai*, four of which it seems best to discuss here, although they are not directly connected to the concept of a proposition or a premiss.[112]

Alexander commonly uses *paratithenai* and *parathesis* in connexion with the production of specific concrete terms, especially of terms designed to provide counterexamples to a putative syllogism.[113] We use 'set down' for this verb.

Protithenai and *prothesis* connote a putting forward; what you *protithês* is what you aim at or purpose. For example, Alexander will explain the *prothesis* of the *Prior Analytics*, i.e. what Aristotle intends or purposes to do in the work. We normally use 'purpose' or 'propose'; but the words are not technical, and we have chosen different renderings as idiom suggests. There is, however, one semi-technical use of the verb – or rather of the associated passive verb and participle, *prokeisthai* and *prokeimenon*. In the context of a syllogism, *to prokeimenon* is, as it were, what the syllogism or the syllogizer is aiming at: it is the putative conclusion of the syllogism. If you say to yourself 'I want to find an argument to show X', then X is *to prokeimenon*. We have found no simple word for *to prokeimenon* in this usage: we generally make do with the clumsy paraphrase 'the point at issue'.

Hupotithenai and *hupokeisthai* have three distinct uses. First, *to hupokeimenon* is regularly the subject-term of a proposition – it is, as it were, what 'lies under' or 'is placed under' the predicate. For this use we keep the traditional word 'subject'; and for the verb: 'be subject for'. Secondly, the verbs, and also the associated noun *hupothesis*, are often used in the context of a particular type of argument, namely a *reductio*. In a *reductio* you make a *hupothesis* and then show that something absurd or impossible follows. As a result of this you reject the *hupothesis* and thereby establish its negation.[114] Here we transliterate, with the tradition, to 'hypothesis' and 'hypothesize'. Thirdly – and relatively rarely – Alexander will use *hupokeisthai* of the premisses of an argument. Here it is a synonym of *keisthai*, and we translate 'suppose', thereby obliterating the distinction between the compound and the simple verb.

Finally there is *ektithenai*, *ekthesis* and *ekkeisthai*. The words are not uncommon in a non-technical sense, where they denote the setting out of a term or a proposition or a problem. And we use 'set out'. But there is also an important technical usage (but not, strictly speaking, a technical *sense*): one of the methods of analysing or

[112] For the fifth, *antitithenai*, see below, p. 26.
[113] See below, p. 30.
[114] See 24,18 note.

reducing a syllogism employs what Aristotle calls *ekthesis*.[115] We retain 'set out' for the verbs in this usage. The translation is adequate. But there is no corresponding noun; hence for *ekthesis* in this usage we have adopted the traditional Latinism 'exposition'.

Propositions stand in a variety of relations to one another. If two propositions are both true, they are said to be true together with one another (*sunalêtheuein*)[116] or to hold at the same time as one another (*sunuparkhein*). Again, there is *akolouthia*, the relation of following or implication, which we have already mentioned.[117] One proposition may yield another by *akolouthia*, and it may also *anairein* it. X *anairei* Y when the truth of X determines the falsity of Y. The verb literally means 'destroy'; but 'destroy' is too dramatic a metaphor in English, and we prefer 'cancel'. (But when the verb has a *personal* subject we use 'reject'; for then 'destruction' is simply denial.) Similarly for the cognates *anairesis, anairetikos*; and for the compound *sunanairein*. If X destroys Y and Y destroys X, then X and Y 'fight', *makhontai*: they conflict, we shall say (and there is a conflict, *makhê*, between them). More soberly – and more frequently – they are said to be opposed, *antikeisthai*.

We normally translate *antitithenai, antikeisthai, antithesis* and *antikeimenon* by 'oppose', 'be opposed', 'opposition' and 'opposite': X and Y are opposed when they conflict, i.e. when they cannot both hold at the same time. There are different varieties of opposition. In particular, there is a distinction between *enantia* ('contraries') on the one hand and items which are opposed *antiphatikôs* ('contradictorily') on the other. X and Y are opposed *antiphatikôs* just in case X and Y cannot both hold at the same time and also cannot both fail to hold at the same time. (For example, and most obviously, a proposition and its explicit negation are contradictorily opposed.) If X and Y are opposed *antiphatikôs*, then they are or form an *antiphasis*.[118] We usually translate this word by 'contradictory pair'; but sometimes the abstract term 'contradiction' is more appropriate.

In Stoic logic *antikeisthai* has the specific sense of 'be contradictorily opposed',[119] and sometimes Alexander uses *ta antikeimena*, without any qualification, to refer to a *contradictory* pair of opposites. Does he use *antikeisthai* in the Stoic sense in these passages? Sometimes it is certain that he does, and there we translate the word by 'contradictories'. But in many passages it is

[115] See 32,33 and note.
[116] But *sunalêtheuein* is also used non-symmetrically: see 29,18 note.
[117] *antistrophê* or conversion will be discused later, p. 31.
[118] See the discussion of *antiphasis* at Ammonius, *in Int.* 81,13-84,25 (cf. 77,13-15), which depends on Aristotle, *Int.* 17a33.
[119] Note also Aristotle, *An. Pr.* 59b8-10.

plain that Alexander uses *ta antikeimena* to *refer to* contradictories but unclear whether he uses it in the *sense* of 'contradictories'; and in these passages we have preferred 'opposites'. (It is always clear from the context whether the opposites in question are in fact contradictories.)

Enantia or contraries cannot be true together but can be false together; paradigm contraries in the context of Aristotelian syllogistic are propositions of the form 'Every A is B' and 'No A is B'. The pair 'Some A is B' and 'Some A is not B' are not contraries: they may both be true but they cannot both be false. The relation in which they stand is known as 'subcontrariety' – and *hupenantios* is rendered by 'subcontrary'.[120] Further, 'Some A is B' is 'subaltern' (*hupallêlos*) to 'Every A is B', and 'Some A is not B' to 'No A is B'. These various relations are the constituents of the so-called 'square of opposition'.[121]

In addition to standing in these relations, the members of a pair of propositions may also be 'similar in form' or 'dissimilar in form', *homoioskhêmôn* or *anomoioskhêmôn*. These are terms of art and their explanation demands a detour. Every proposition is either affirmative or negative. 'Affirmative' gives *kataphatikos*: 'affirm' is *kataphaskein*, 'affirmation' *kataphasis*. 'An affirmative' is *kataphatikon*. (Aristotle – and hence Alexander – sometimes uses *katêgorikos* as equivalent to *kataphatikos*. We render this word by 'predicative', for reasons to be given later.[122]) 'Negative', 'negation' and 'a negative' are *apophatikos*, *apophasis*, *apophatikon*. But for the verbs *apophaskein* and *apophanai* 'negate' will not work, and we use 'deny'. (Aristotle and Alexander sometimes use *sterêtikos* as a synonym for *apophatikos*. We translate 'privative' – the root verb *sterein* means 'deprive'; but the intended *sense* of 'privative' is no different from that of 'negative'.) The status of a proposition as affirmative or negative is called by Alexander its quality, *poiotês*. Propositions differ in quality, *kata to poion*, when one is affirmative and the other negative. If the propositions in a pair differ in quality, they are *anomoioskhêmones* or dissimilar in form; if they are of the same quality, they are *homoioskhêmones* or similar in form.[123]

A proposition has a quantity as well as a quality: propositions may differ or agree *kata to poson*, in quantity. For in every

---

[120] Alexander appears to mean that 'Some A is B' is subcontrary to 'Some A is not B', so that 'subcontrary' means something like 'quasi-contrary'. (The prefix *hupo-* often has this semantic force.) Note, however, that Ammonius (*in Int.* 92,21-24) supposes that 'Some A is B' is subcontrary to 'Every A is B', and that 'Some A is not B' is subcontrary to 'No A is B': the particular propositions are 'subcontraries' inasmuch as they fall under the universals, which are contraries.

[121] See e.g. Ammonius, *in Int.* 91,4-93,18; Boethius, *Syll. Cat.* 800AC.

[122] See below, pp. 30-1.

[123] The terms do not seem especially apposite, but they are Aristotle's own.

proposition, the predicate is predicated (or denied) of *all* or of *some* of its subject; and differences in 'all' and 'some' are differences *kata to poson*. A proposition which has the 'all' quantity is called *katholou*, the word being used as an undeclinable adjective. In Greek 'A holds of the whole of B' is 'A holds *kath' holou tou* B'; the preposition *kata (kath')* and the quantitative adjective *holos* then coalesce, giving *katholou*. We translate by 'universal'.

For 'some'-propositions Aristotle and Alexander use *epi merous*, *kata meros* or *en merei*. For all three expressions, which do not differ in sense, we use the adjective 'particular'. Corresponding to *en merei* for 'some'-propositions, there is a use of *en holôi* – 'in a whole' – for 'all'-propositions. Now you might expect 'A is *en holôi tôi* B' to mean 'A is in the whole of B', i.e. A is found everywhere in B, or A holds of every B. But in fact the Greek means exactly the opposite: A is *en holôi tôi* B if B is true of every A. B is, as it were, a whole for A. To make this reasonably clear, we have followed the customary – and awkward – translation, writing 'A is in B *as in a whole*'.[124]

(*Meros* occurs in other contexts, and is always translated 'part'. In normal Greek, the diminutive *morion* is synonymous with *meros*. And we have usually translated it too by 'part'. But *morion* sometimes means 'subpart' – one of the few places being the opening pages of Alexander's commentary.[125])

Propositions are complex items: they *sunkeitai* ('are compounded': *suntithenai* is 'to compound', *sunthesis* is given by the noun 'compounding'); they have a *sustasis* or 'construction' (the verb is *sunistanai*, 'to construct'); in them, one element is linked (*sunaptein*) or connected (*suntattein*) to another. (*Suntattein* gives the noun *suntaxis*, from which derives the English 'syntax'; but in Alexander 'syntax' is not strictly a *linguistic* notion: it is parts of propositions, not parts of sentences, which are connected.)

The chief components of a proposition are terms or *horoi*. But a proposition may also contain a *diorismos*, or a sign to mark its quantity,[126] and a *tropos*, or a sign to mark its modality. A proposition with no specific indication of quantity, such as 'Pleasure is good', is called *adioristos*. The best English for this is 'indeterminate'. Hence we use 'determination' for *diorismos* (and 'determine' for *diorizein*). Strictly speaking, there are only *two* determinations of propositions, a universal and a particular; but the

---

[124] For a clear account of the locution see Boethius, *Syll. Cat.* 810B. In Greek, as in English, it is natural to take part and whole as mutually exclusive things; hence if A is *en holôi tôi* B, it might seem to follow that A is *not en merei tôi* B. But in Aristotle's logic, 'Every A is B' entails 'Some A is B'; hence in this context wholes and parts are not mutually exclusive. (In the modern jargon, 'part' here does not mean '*proper* part').

[125] See Barnes (1988), pp. 240-2.   [126] Later authors prefer *prosdiorismos*.

commentators all speak of *four* – 'Every', 'Some', 'No' and 'Some ...
not'. Hence the determination in effect gives the quality as well as
the quantity of the proposition. Thus in the determinate proposition,
'Every pleasure is good', 'Every' is or marks the *diorismos*. (We say
'is or marks'; for it is unclear in Alexander whether a *diorismos* is a
sign of quantification, i.e. a quantifying particle, and hence part of a
sentence; or whether it is, so to speak, the quantity signified by the
sign.)

Note that the word *adioristos* is also used in a different context,
involving the truth-conditions of particular propositions. We use
'indeterminate' here too – Alexander himself explains what he
means by this sort of indeterminacy.[127]

Tropos has a wide non-technical use: 'way', 'method', 'mode' are
variously appropriate, and we have used them as the context
suggests. In addition, there is a technical use of the word: here we
always use 'mode' (some might prefer 'mood'). If you say *'ex anankês,
A is B'* then *'ex anankês'* is or marks a mode.[128] ('is or marks': the
same uncertainty arises.) We always translate *ananke* as 'necessity'
and *ex anankês* as 'by necessity'. *Anankaios* is usually 'necessary'.
Dei also marks necessity: we render it by the word 'must'. And for
the occasional *opheilein* we use 'should'. (In our part of the
commentary modal issues occupy a minor place; but elsewhere they
are of central importance, and we have therefore been uncharacter-
istically pedantic in translating modal words.)

A second *tropos* is that of possibility. Here there are familiar
difficulties for the translator. For Aristotle distinguishes different
sorts of possibility, and he also has two different words (or families
of words) to designate possibility, namely *dunasthai* and *endekhesthai*.[129] *Dunasthai* and *dunatos* are always translated as 'be
possible' and 'possible' where Alexander is explicitly discussing
modal propositions. (And *adunatos* is 'impossible'.) Elsewhere we
often use 'can', rather than the cumbersome 'be possible', for
dunasthai. *Endekhesthai*, in normal Greek, is virtually a synonym
for *dunasthai*; and in contexts which are certainly non-technical we
use 'be possible' or 'can' for it too. But where Alexander is discussing
modal propositions, it is important to mark the difference between
endekhesthai and *dunasthai*. Accordingly, we have used 'be
contingent' for *endekhesthai*. This works well in some places. (For
example, 'A is B *endekhomenôs*' comes out as 'A is contingently B',

---

[127] See 66,1-10 and notes; cf. e.g. Ammonius, *in Int.* 94,7-24; 118,7-8; Philoponus, *in
An. Pr.* 82,1-84,11; 98,4-12. For a further type of indeterminacy see Ammonius, *in Int.*
90,19-20.
[128] Hence the modern phrase 'modal logic' – but *tropos* embraces far more than the
modalities treated in standard modal logic (see Barnes (1991)).
[129] There are also other words – *enkhôrei, exesti, esti*, and so on.

i.e. 'A is B, but not by necessity' – and that is exactly the intended sense.) But whereas in English 'It is contingent that A is B' suggests that A is indeed B, it is not clear that the Greek carries the same suggestion – '*endekhetai* that A is B' may be true when A is *not* B. To this extent our translation is unhappy. But we see no alternative which is not at least equally bad.

Alexander holds that the 'plain' proposition 'A is B' also has a modality:[130] he has no special term for it, but (following Aristotle) he refers to such propositions by the participle *huparkhôn*, 'holding'.[131] We might say that 'A is B' is taken to say that A is *actually* B, as opposed to being necessarily or possibly B. And so we have used 'actual' for *huparkhôn* in this usage. (The translation disguises connexions which are patent in the Greek; and the expression 'an actual proposition' is vaguely comic. But, again, alternatives seem worse.)

Terms constitute the *hulê* or 'matter' of a proposition (and hence, indirectly, of a syllogism). And they contrast with its *eidos* or 'form', which – in effect – is determined by its logical structure, or its quality, quantity and mode. Aristotle and Alexander regularly use 'dummy letters' – ABC, MNO, PRS – in formulating syllogisms.[132] Thus they will represent the *form* of a proposition by such a formula as 'A holds of every B'. When he wants to give a genuine proposition, with genuine terms, Alexander will talk of setting down[133] *hulê*. (Here we translate *hulê* as 'material instance'.) When Aristotle gives a material instance or concrete term, he uses either a common noun ('man', 'swan') or a mass term ('snow') or an adjective in the neuter singular ('wild', 'rational'). We translate these straightforwardly into English. The result is usually barbarous; for in ordinary English such a formula as 'No wild is man' is ill-formed. Yet it is clear what those formulae are intended to express; and the Greek formulae which they represent are also barbarous.

In a simple proposition, one term is predicated of (*katêgoreisthai*) another; and it is called 'the predicate' (*to katêgoroumenon*) of the proposition. The other term is the subject (*hupokeimenon*, as we have already remarked). The verb *katêgorein* has compounds, *antikatêgorein*, 'counterpredicate', and *proskatêgorein*, 'co-predicate'. There is also an adjective *katêgorikos*: as we have said, it is used specifically to designate affirmative propositions; but it is also used generically to designate simple propositions,[134] and hence

[130] The point later aroused controversy: see Barnes (1991).
[131] The participle is usually in the feminine, *huparkhousa*, agreeing with an unexpressed *protasis*.
[132] See 53,30 note.
[133] *paratithenai*: above, p. 25.
[134] As opposed to complex or *hupothetikoi* propositions: above, p. 23.

to pick out those syllogisms whose component propositions are all simple.[135] We use the adjective 'predicative', to preserve the transparent connexion with *katêgorein*. (Latin authors regularly use *praedicativus*.) It is true that 'predicative' does not transparently designate these items – but then the same holds for *katêgorikos*.[136]

To express the predicative tie, Aristotle also uses *legesthai*, 'be said of', and *huparkhein*, 'hold of' (and especially in schematic formulae, he often omits a verb altogether). 'B is A', 'A holds of B', 'A is said of B', 'A is predicated of B' – all these are equivalent.[137] Note in particular that 'A is said (or: predicated) of B' does not mean 'Someone says: "A is B" '.

Subjects and predicates are alike terms: they belong to the same logical category. (In this they are fundamentally different from the subjects and predicates of modern 'Fregean' logic.[138]) Hence they may exchange places in a proposition. Alexander's technical term for this exchange is *antistrophê*, with the verb *antistrephein*. *Antistrophê* may denote either an *operation* on a proposition, viz. 'conversion', or else the *result* obtained by performing the operation, i.e. a converse. Thus if you operate on 'No B is A' to reach 'No A is B', you perform a *conversion* (*antistrophê*) and you get a *converse* (*antistrophê*). It is not always clear whether *antistrophê* means 'conversion' or 'converse'. We have chosen what in each context seems the more plausible option – in point of fact little turns on the issue.

The verb *antistrephein* sometimes takes a personal subject: the logician converts a proposition. More often the subject is a proposition. Then there are two grammatical constructions: *antistrephein* + dative, *antistrephein* + *pros* + accusative. There is a difference in usage here.[139] *Antistrephein pros* marks a symmetrical relation: if X *antistrephei pros* Y, then Y *antistrephei pros* X. We talk here of 'converting *with*'. *Antistrephein* + dative, on the other hand, is non-symmetrical: if X *antistrephei tôi* Y, then Y may or may not *antistrephei tôi* X. Moreover if X *antistrephei tôi* Y, then X may be derived from Y by a process of 'propositional conversion'. Hence we use 'convert *from*' for *antistrephein* + dative. (Propositional *antistrophê*, as Alexander explains, is simply an interchange of terms which preserves truth.[140])

[135] For ancient explanations of the Aristotelian use of the term see Dexippus, *in Cat.* 12,29; Ammonius, *in Int.* 70,7; 87,13.

[136] *katêgorikos* is usually transliterated to 'categorical'; hence Aristotle's logic is known as 'categorical syllogistic'.

[137] Note that, according to Apuleius (*Int.* 192,30-193,5) the Peripatetics prefer the expression 'A holds of B', whereas he normally uses 'B is A' (cf. below, 54,25-29; Albinus, *Didasc.* 158-9H).

[138] On this see esp. Barnes (1983).

[139] The difference emerges most clearly at *in An. Pr.* 392,19-26.

[140] See 29,1-29 and notes.

Two terms may stand in various relations to one another. If every B is A, then A 'includes' or 'encompasses' B, *periekhei* or *perilambanei*. (There is a noun *perilêpsis*.) A is 'over', *huper*, B, and B is 'under', *hupo*, A. A may, in addition, hold of things which are not B. Then A is of wider extension, *epi pleon*, than B, and it (or some part of it) 'falls outside' B (*piptein ektos*). Again, if no A is B, then A and B are 'disjoined' (*apezeugmenon*).

A *suzugia* or combination of premisses contains three terms in all: its two constituent propositions 'share', *koinônein*, a term. (*Koinônia*, and the adjective *koinos*, are also used in this connexion.) The shared term or the term taken twice – once in each proposition – is the middle term, *meson*; and the other two unshared terms are 'extremes', *akra*. Any further term which may be invoked to show that the combination is syllogistic is said to be taken 'from outside', *exôthen*. (And Alexander also speaks of operations, such as *antistrophê*, being introduced 'from outside', a locution which is not illuminating.)

The extremes are distinguished in two ways: first, one of them may be called 'first' (*prôtos*) and the other 'last' (*eskhatos*). Secondly, and more importantly, one may be called *meizôn* and the other *elattôn*. The standard translations are 'major' and 'minor'; and we have retained these English words, not without misgiving. Literally the words mean 'greater' and 'less'. They are comparative adjectives. A is greater than B if and only if B is less than A; and A is greater than B if A is more extensive (or holds *epi pleon*) than B. In English, 'major' and 'minor' do not carry such evident implications of relative extension; nor, of course, are they genuine comparatives. This means that our translation suppresses an important idea present in the Greek. In addition, in some passages Alexander speaks expressly of A being *meizôn than* B. In these passages we hedge by using phrases such as 'A is major in extension with respect to B'. (The notion of relative extension is important in certain contexts. Thus it is connected with definitions (*horismoi*), which standardly analyse the *definiendum* into genus (*genos*) and *differentia* (*diaphora*) – and which may do so by the method of 'division' (*diairesis*).[141])

Finally, the terms in a combination have an order and a position (*taxis, thesis*)[142] The order and position of the middle term determines the type or 'figure' (*skhêma*) of a combination.[143]

---

[141] Hence *diairein* is normally 'divide'. The compound verb *antidiairein* is used when you pick out items at the same level in a division: we use 'co-ordinate' here, losing the connexion with *diairein*.

[142] On these notions see 47,22 note.

[143] For the figures see Appendix 2.

Most readers will find some of our translations misguided. There is nothing much to be done or said about this. All translators are in a pickle, and logical texts are no easier to deal with than texts in ethics or metaphysics.

Alexander of Aphrodisias

On Aristotle Prior Analytics 1.1-7

Translation

Contents

4. The First Figure

5. The Second Figure

6. The Third Figure

7. Further Reflections

1

Preface

1.1 The status of logic

1.1.1 Instrument or part of philosophy?[1]

Logic[2] or syllogistic is the study now before us. Under it fall   1,3
demonstrative, dialectical and examinatory methods, and also
sophistical procedure.[3] It is the product of philosophy: some other   5
sciences and arts do indeed use it, but they take it from philosophy,
to which belong its discovery, its construction, and its most
important uses.

Since logic is the product of philosophy, some people think that it
is also a part of philosophy.[4] Others, however, say that it is not a
part but an instrument of philosophy.[5]

[1] For other accounts of this dispute see esp. Ammonius, *in An. Pr.* 8,15-11,21;
Philoponus, *in An. Pr.* 6,19-9,20 (other texts in Hülser, pp. 22-39 – to which add Elias,
in An. Pr. 134,4-138,13). We suppose that the dispute which Alexander rehearses
reflects a genuine historical debate; but the date of the debate is uncertain. (See,
perhaps, Seneca, *Ep.* 88,21-8 [= Posidonius, F 90 EK], which shows that Posidonius
engaged in an analogous debate about the parts and instruments of philosophy and
which at least indicates that the debate described by Alexander would not have been
unthinkable in the first century BC.) For some account of the nature and importance
of the dispute see e.g. Mueller (1969), p. 184; Moraux (1986a), pp. 268-9; Gottschalk
(1987), p. 1099; Lloyd (1990), pp. 17-21; and esp. Lee, pp. 44-54.
[2] 1.3-2.2 = *FDS* 27.
[3] For Alexander's explanations of 'demonstrative', 'dialectical', 'examinatory' and
'sophistical' methods see *in Top.* 2,20-3, 2,23-5, 22,10-14, and 2,25-6. For the species
of syllogisms see below, 7,9 note.
[4] This view is generally associated with the Stoics; but it was a commonplace of
Hellenistic and post-Hellenistic thought to maintain that philosophy had three parts,
logic and physics and ethics. (See e.g. Seneca, *Ep.* 89,9: '*Most, and the most
important, authors* say that there are three parts of philosophy – ethical, physical,
logical'; Apuleius, *Int.* 176,1-3: 'The study of wisdom, which we call philosophy, seems
to most people to have three parts ....' cf. P. Hadot.) The Peripatetics, who divided
philosophy into two parts (theoretical, which is roughly equivalent to physics, and
practical, which is roughly equivalent to ethics), were heterodox; and Alexander's
opponents need not have been exclusively Stoics.
[5] The 'others' include Aristotle, according to Alexander: *in Top.* 74,29-75,3 (cf.
94,7-10; and also below, 3,5, which implies that 'the ancients' had called logic an
instrument). No Aristotelian text expressly says that logic is an instrument of

41

10   Now[6] those who say that it is a part were led to their view by the
following consideration. Just as philosophy concerns itself with the
other items which are universally agreed to be parts of philosophy,
making it its business to discover and order and construct them, so
too it concerns itself with the study before us. But although this
study is the product of philosophy, it is not a subpart of either of the
other parts of philosophy – neither of the theoretical nor of the
15   practical part. For its subject matter is different from theirs, and the
purposes of the three are distinct. The theoretical and the practical
parts differ from each other in certain ways, and in virtue of these
differences they are co-ordinate with one another: logic differs from
each of them in the same ways, and therefore it may reasonably be
taken as co-ordinate with them. It differs from them both in
subject-matter (for its subject-matter consists of statements and
20   propositions[7]) and also in its end and purpose (for its purpose is to
prove that, when propositions are compounded with one another in
2,1   certain ways, something may be deduced by necessity from what is
posited or conceded – and this is not the end of either of the other
parts).

      Those who claim that logic is not a part but an instrument of
philosophy reply as follows. For something to be a part of an art or
5   science it is not enough that the art or science is concerned with it[8]
in the same way as it is concerned with each of the other parts which
it studies. For something is judged to be a part not merely because it
is an object of attention and study, but when, in addition, its end and
construction do not make reference to anything other than those
10   very things which the science in question studies, i.e. when it is not
investigated and constructed for the sake of these other items. For if
something makes reference to the needs of other items which fall
under the same science or art, then it cannot properly be taken as
co-ordinate with them, since it is for their sake that it exists and
comes into being; nor can it be a part in the way in which they are,
since it exists for their sake. For if something makes reference to
15   certain items, and if its end is given attention insofar as it
contributes to the discovery and construction of other items, then it
is the instrument of those items. With distinct arts, the product of
one is the instrument of another if its end makes reference to the
needs of what is made by the art whose instrument it is: similarly, if
the things made by a single science or art have such a ranking in

---

philosophy; but *Top.* 163b9-11, which uses the word *organon* in a pertinent context,
may have been in Alexander's mind (cf. *in Top.* 584,9-12).

    [6] 1,9-2,2 = *SVF* II 49a.

    [7] cf. Ammonius, *in An. Pr.* 9,26-7. Note that here Alexander uses *axiôma*
('statement') in the Stoic sense: see e.g. Frede (1974a), p. 32 n. 1.

    [8] Omitting *to morion*.

relation to each other, then one will be an instrument and the other   20
– the higher one – will be both the product and a part of the science.
A hammer and anvil are not precluded from being an instrument of
the smith's art by the fact that they are its product.[9]

Moreover, those who call logic a part of philosophy must admit
that a part of philosophy is an instrument of those other sciences
and arts which use syllogisms and demonstrations to establish and
construct the objects of their own concerns. For they use them, but   25
not as parts of themselves (since it is impossible for the same thing
to be a part of different sciences, nor does any of these sciences study
the construction and discovery of syllogisms); hence they will be
using them as instruments. But if so, and if one art or science
dominates another whenever it uses in its own production the
product and end of the other art, whose own product makes   30
reference to its needs (as bridle-making in relation to the art of
riding and ship-building in relation to the pilot's art),[10] then
according to these people there will be other sciences and arts more
perfect than philosophy, namely those which have a part of
philosophy as their instrument.

1.1.2 Useless parts of logic?[11]

They might say that not all the study of logic makes reference to the   35
discovery and construction of what philosophy investigates or of
what some other science or art theorises about or investigates, but
that there are things logic theorises about and investigates which   3,1
have no utility at all.

In that case, first, they will concede that the earlier thinkers[12]
who developed the study of logic to the extent of its utility were right
to call it an instrument and not a part.

Secondly, according to them, what is useful in logic is an   5
instrument and it is what is not useful which will be a part.[13] But if
what is useful is better and worth more attention and study, then
for them the better subpart of logic will be an instrument of
philosophy and the other sciences and arts, and what is worth less

---

[9] For the analogy see Ammonius, *in An. Pr.* 9,37-10,1; Philoponus, *in An. Pr.* 7,31.

[10] See Aristotle, *EN* 1094a6-16.

[11] For the utility of logic see further 8,19-22; 18,14-19,3; 20,12-13; 28,17-30; 30,29-30; 39,19-40,5; 44,4; *in An. Pr.* 164,23-165,6; cf. Aristotle, *Top.* 101a25-b4 (with Alexander, *in Top.* 9,20-10,16). See Barnes (1990b).

[12] The earlier thinkers, *hoi arkhaioi* or *hoi palaioi*, contrast with the more recent thinkers, *hoi neôteroi*. The designations have different referents in different contexts; but by and large it is true to say that, in *in An. Pr.*, Alexander is thinking of Aristotle and his immediate followers when he refers to the ancients and of the Stoics when he refers to the more recent thinkers (cf. 17,12; 19,5; 22,18; etc). See further Kieffer, pp. 130-3; Barnes (1990a), IV.3.

[13] Omitting *on*.

10 attention will be a part. Yet in all cases, an instrument has a lower status than any product which is a part.

Again, if logic is given attention in order to exercise the mind for making discoveries among items which the parts of philosophy investigate,[14] then in this way too it will have the status of an instrument. If, on the other hand, logic is studied in order to gain knowledge of the truths it contains in itself,[15] then it will become a subpart of theoretical philosophy; for it is this which has knowledge as its end. But if you theorise about useless items in accordance with
15 logical method, what good does *that* contain which might make it worth attention as a part of philosophy? What is worth attention should either make reference to something else which is desirable in itself, or else contain in itself something worthy of attention. For it is not all and any knowledge which is worthy of philosophy (some things it is better to be ignorant of), but only knowledge of what is divine and
20 valuable – that is, of the things created by the divine art of nature.[16] It is clear from its very name that theorising is concerned with the sight and knowledge of what is divine; for it means seeing what is divine.[17] That is why we say that theoretical philosophy is knowledge of what is divine and of what comes about or is constituted by nature;[18] for knowledge of such things is in itself worth attention. But where the
25 things theorised about neither make reference to anything else nor contain in themselves anything excellent[19] and valuable, then knowledge of them, being utterly superfluous, is not appropriate to philosophy – it is a waste of labour. For it is above all appropriate to philosophers that, as they should never act at random, so too they should never theorise in this way: their theorising, like their actions, should be delimited.
30 Geometry is not, as they think, similar to the useless part of logic – their comparison is mistaken. First, as they themselves say, geometry is not a part of what is called philosophy in the strict sense.[20]

---

[14] For this use of logic see Aristotle, *Top.* 101a28; Alexander, *in Top.* 27,7-31 (cf. below, 8,24-7).

[15] Reading *autêi* for *autois*.

[16] For creative nature, *hê dêmiourgêsasa phusis*, see esp. Aristotle, *PA* 654a6-23; cf. Alexander, *in Metaph.* 103,5-104,18.

[17] i.e. *theôrein* is fancifully derived from *theia* and *horan*. Note that 'theory', 'theorise' and their cognates are not ideal translations. (The standard 'contemplate', 'contemplation' and so on are no better.) To 'theorise' about an area is simply to study the area with a view to grasping the truth about it (and not with any further practical end in mind).

[18] cf. Aristotle, *Metaph.* 983a5-10; Alexander, *in Metaph.* 18,5-13. Compare the standard Stoic definition of philosophy as 'knowledge of things divine and human' (e.g. Seneca, *Ep.* 89,5; Sextus, *M* IX 13).

[19] Retaining *peritton* (Wallies prints *terpnon* with the Aldine). But note that *perittos* occurs in the following line with the sense of 'superfluous'.

[20] cf. e.g. Posidonius, F 90 EK (Seneca, *Ep.* 88,21-8).

Then, astronomy, being in a way a subpart of geometry,[21] theorises   4,1
about divine and natural substances, knowledge of which is in itself
noble and valuable.

In addition, very many aspects of geometry are useful for philosophy, and because of them it is reasonable to give it attention.[22] For
the fact that geometry deals not only with perceptible things but with
things which escape perception and are intelligible is very useful for   5
philosophical theory since the incorporeal and intelligible substances
about which philosophers theorise are primary and more valuable
than the perceptible substances. Further, geometry accustoms us
from our youth to deal with lines and planes and solids, none of which
are perceptible, and instructs us about each of these things by
themselves. Now if you are to engage in philosophical theorising, it is
absolutely necessary to be able to distinguish from one another in
account things which are different from one another in substance but   10
cannot be apart from one another in subsistence and existence. For
this is how philosophy grasps the principles of natural compounds,
i.e. matter and form: these are inseparable from one another in
subsistence and neither of them can be apart from the other. Again, it   15
is by separating in account what is confused[23] that philosophy makes
distinctions among intelligible objects and finds the number of the
genera under which all beings fall; for the other nine genera depend
on substance, which underlies them, and cannot subsist apart from
it.[24] And for this[25] geometry has proved necessary and useful by
accustoming us to talk separately about lines, as if they constituted a
certain nature by themselves, and separately about planes and   20
solids, even though none of these things can subsist outside physical
bodies.

Further, by using syllogisms and demonstrations in proofs about
its objects, geometry accustoms us to take the same attitude in
philosophy too, so that we do not follow and believe silly stories[26]
about its objects, but demand demonstrations and regard as justified   25
only what is either known through itself or posited by way of a
demonstration.

[21] That astronomy is a mathematical science is a commonplace: see esp. Plato, *Rep.*
528D-530C; cf. e.g. Aristotle, *Phys.* 194a7-9; *Metaph.* 989b31-3 (Alexander, *in*
Metaph. 72,9-12); Geminus, quoted by Proclus, *in Eucl.* 38,4-10; Ptolemy, *Synt.*
6,21-7,4. But we have found no other text affirming that astronomy is a subpart of
geometry.
[22] An idea developed by the Platonists: see e.g. Albinus, *Didasc.* 161H;
Iamblichus, *Comm. Math. Sc.* 55,21-2; Proclus, *in Eucl.* 21,15-22,16; cf. O'Meara. The
classic text is Plato, *Rep.* 526C-527C.
[23] cf. Aristotle, *Phys.* 184a21-3.
[24] Alexander refers to the ten Aristotelian genera or 'categories' of being, the first of
which is substance.
[25] Reading *pros touto* for *pros toutôi*.
[26] For *muthôdeis phluariai* see e.g. Ammonius, *in Int.* 181,5-7; 249,1-25.

Again, geometry uses proportions and symmetries for its own
proofs: many of the things which concern philosophy are also proved
by these means, none of which can be taken from the useless part of
dialectic and made to contribute to philosophy.

For these reasons this part of dialectic is completely useless and
superfluous and will rightly be banished from philosophical
theorising.

1.1.3 The value of logic[27]

30   But if analytics is an instrument and not a part of philosophy, it is
not therefore any less worthy of our attention. For the attention due
to an instrument is judged by the worth of what is made or proved
by it. But the objects of philosophy are proved by demonstration,
and they are of the greatest worth. For everything in philosophy is
5,1   worth full attention, and the theory and knowledge of the truth
above all else. For the truth is both most appropriate to men and
also their highest good.

That it is most appropriate is clear from the following fact. Just as
something is appropriate and natural to each of the animals
(running to one, flying to another, hunting to one, guarding to
5   another, bearing burdens to another, and so on), so knowledge and
theory are appropriate and natural to men. 'For all men by nature
seek after knowledge'[28] – and there is evidence for this in the facts
that they prefer those modes of perception which provide them with
more knowledge,[29] and that they are immediately from their youth
fond of listening to stories. For small children listen attentively to
10   stories[30] although they gain nothing from them apart from the
knowledge of them; and the more gifted children are distinguished
by the attention with which they listen to the stories – which
suggests that knowledge is natural for men.

Further, men are distinguished from other animals above all and
most evidently by knowledge of the truth.[31] You can find some
15   traces of the virtues and of virtuous actions in non-rational animals
too (for some of them seem to share in courage, some in temperance,

[27] According to Todd (1976), p. 17 n. 83, this passage (with which cf. e.g.
Philoponus, *in An. Pr.* 4,26-9) is 'an apologia for the study of logic', written at a time
when logical studies were often disparaged. But note that the question of the 'utility'
of logic was also seriously discussed among logicians (see above, 2,33 note). (Later,
the value or utility of a subject was one of the standard topics in the Procline canon of
commentatorial procedure: see Introduction, p. 8.)

[28] Aristotle, *Metaph.* 980a21.
[29] cf. Aristotle, *Metaph.* 980a21-6; Alexander, *in Metaph.* 1,10-2,3.
[30] A commonplace exploited by philosophers to various ends; see e.g. Olympiodorus,
in Gorg. 46,3; Elias, *Proleg.* 27,15-22.
[31] cf. Aristotle, *Metaph.* 980a27-981a12; Alexander, *in Metaph.* 2,24-5,13.

and some in justice, and further some of them have actually been thought in addition to be sagacious and others to be generous, as we can learn from the *History of Animals*,[32] which Aristotle wrote in several books); but for truth and theoretical understanding they have no sense at all. 20

Secondly, theorising is the highest of human goods. 'For truth it is which brings all goods to gods and to men.'[33] If we may express an opinion about what is above us, we must deem that apart from this there exists no other activity for the gods.[34] It cannot be allowed that they are active in accordance with any of the other virtues, since the virtues concern the emotions (insofar as they measure and 25 shape them), whereas the divine is free from emotion. Further, moral virtues involve choice. For they have been proved[35] to be dispositions connected with choice. And choice is deliberative desire,[36] and deliberation is about objects of deliberation, and we deliberate about what is up to us but of unclear outcome. (No one deliberates about scientific matters.[37]) So if for the gods none of the 30 things they bring about is of unclear outcome, then for them there will be no objects of deliberation. If so, no deliberation either; if no deliberation, no choice; and if no choice, no moral virtue. 6,1

Now, for the gods, theorising about truth is continuous and uninterrupted. But for men it is not possible to be continuously active in this way[38] – for many of the conditions of life which were allotted to them lead them away from things of higher value. Yet if a man emerges,[39] as far as he can, from the emotions and conditions of 5 human life, he may see the things of highest value and be active in a theorising which is divine and worthy of its name. Now when he is active with this faculty of his soul and exercises activities like those of the gods, then he will become like the gods. Thus if becoming like god is the greatest good for men,[40] and if this is attained by the

[32] See e.g. Aristotle, *HA* 488b12-26 (cf. *EN* 1144b8-9); for sagacity (*phronêsis*) in animals, see e.g. *HA* 611a15-19; 614b18-21; 618a25-30 (cf. *Metaph.* 980b22-5).

[33] Plato, *Laws* 730C. For Alexander's knowledge of Plato see Sharples (1990), pp. 90-2.

[34] The following argument is a paraphrase of Aristotle, *EN* 1178b7-23 (see also *Metaph.* 1072b13-30; cf. e.g. Cicero, *Nat. Deorum* III xv 38; Alexander, *in Metaph.* 2,3-21; 17,5-18,14; *Quaest.* 141,2-4: Dooley, pp. 13-14; 38-9).

[35] See Aristotle, *EN* 1106b36.

[36] *EN* 1113a10-11.

[37] *EN* 1112a34-b11.

[38] See Aristotle, *EN* 1177b26-31 (but note 1177a21-2); cf. *Metaph.* 1072b14-16.

[39] *Anakuptein*: for the metaphor see Plato, *Phaedrus* 249C, to which Alexander probably alludes.

[40] For *homoiôsis theôi* as the greatest good for man see esp. Plato, *Rep.* 613A; *Theaetetus* 176B; and for Aristotelian parallels see e.g. *EN* 1177b30-1178a4; 1178b25-8. The idea is a commonplace in later Platonism (e.g. anon., *in Theaet.* 7 14; Albinus, *Didasc.* 153, 179-80H; Plutarch, *Ser. Num.* 550D; Apuleius, *Dog. Plat.* 126,3-6); but it is also found elsewhere (e.g. Seneca, *Ep.* 92,27; Epictetus, *Diss.* II xiv

10 theory and knowledge of what is true, and if the knowledge of what
is true comes by way of demonstration, then demonstration will
rightly be held most valuable and worthy of most study – and so too,
therefore, will syllogistic, since a demonstration is a sort of
syllogism.[41]

1.2 The *Prior Analytics*

1.2.1 Contents and title[42]

That is why Aristotle first studies syllogisms in this work, the title of
15 which is *Prior Analytics*, before he discusses demonstration. He tells
us what a syllogism is, what syllogisms are compounded from, how
many syllogistic figures there are, and what are the differences
among them. (The figures are like a sort of common matrix: by
fitting matter into them, it is possible to mould the same form in
different sorts of matter.[43] For just as things fitted into one and the
20 same matrix differ not in form and figure but in matter, so it is with
the syllogistic figures.) He[44] says further how many combinations
there are in each figure, which of them are syllogistic and which are
non-syllogistic, what are the differences among the syllogisms in
each figure, which of the syllogisms are perfect and directly known
25 and in no need of demonstration, and which are imperfect and not
indemonstrable,[45] and how it can be that imperfect syllogisms are
said to be syllogisms at all. In this work he also discusses the
discovery of premisses, saying how we may discover premisses and
so obtain appropriate syllogisms in each figure. He also discusses
the analysis of syllogisms – and in general whatever is proper to the
study of syllogistic.
30   Having discussed these issues in the two books of the *Prior
Analytics*, he will next proceed to the discussion of demonstration –

11-13; and cf. Alexander, *DA* 90,10-91,6). See e.g. Praechter (1909a), pp. 541-3;
Merki; Jaeger.
   [41] Aristotle, *An. Pr.* 25b30; below, 6,32-7,11; 42,17-31.
   [42] See also Alexander, *in An. Pr.* 340,11-12; Ammonius, *in An. Pr.* 5,5-7,25;
Philoponus, *in An. Pr.* 5,15-6,6. For analogous discussions in other commentaries see
e.g. Simplicius, *in Cat.* 10,8-19 (quoting Alexander's lost commentary); cf. Praechter
(1909a), pp. 530-1; Todd (1976), p. 9 n. 39. Note that Aristotle himself refers to the
Analytics by the phrase *ta analutika*. But he does not use the distinguishing
qualifications 'Prior' and 'Posterior', which are first found in the catalogue of
Aristotle's writings preserved by Diogenes Laertius, V 23.
   [43] On matter and form in logic see e.g. below, 52,19-25; cf. Patzig, p. 171; and esp.
Barnes (1990a), III (to the references there add Alexander, *Conv.* 56).
   [44] 6,21-6 = *FDS* 1099.
   [45] The later tradition regularly connects 'perfection' with indemonstrability (on
which see Introduction, p. 21): see below 24,4-5; 55,3; 69,28; 113,7; Galen, *Inst. Log.*
viii 1-4; Apuleius, *Int.* 188,4-11; Sextus, *PH* II 198; Boethius, *Syll. Cat.* 823A; cf.
Frede (1974a), p. 128; Flannery.

which he does not propose to deal with here – in the books entitled
Posterior Analytics. (These are also two in number.)

Now the reason why he entitles the work on syllogisms *Prior
Analytics* and the work on demonstration *Posterior Analytics* is that
the syllogism is by nature prior to demonstration. We have learnt in
the *Categories* that one thing is prior by nature to another if it 7,1
follows when the other is posited but does not convert with it as to
implication of existence.[46] Genera are things of this sort: every
genus is prior by nature to each of the species which fall under it; for
if a species is posited, the genus must necessarily follow, whereas
the species does not follow the genus.[47] Similarly with species in
relation to the things of which they are species: species are prior. 5
And thus too is the syllogism related to demonstration. For if
there is a demonstration, there must be a syllogism, since a
demonstration is a sort of syllogism; but if there is a syllogism, there
need not be a demonstration,[48] because there are also dialectical
and sophistical syllogisms.[49] Thus since the syllogism is prior and
demonstration posterior, it is reasonable that Aristotle entitled 10
those books in which he discusses what is prior *Prior Analytics* and
those in which he discusses what is posterior *Posterior Analytics*.

They are called *Analytics* because the reduction of any compound
to the things from which it is compounded is called analysis.[50]
Analysing is the converse of compounding;[51] for compounding is a
route from the principles to what depends on them, whereas
analysing is a return route from the end up to the principles.[52] 15
Geometers are said to analyse when they begin from the conclusion
and proceed in order through the assumptions made for the proof of

[46] See Aristotle, *Cat.* 14a29-35: Alexander alludes to the second of five types of
priority there distinguished. (Aristotle does not explicitly call this *natural* priority;
but note 15a7-11.) The tortuous phraseology, which Alexander takes from Aristotle,
hides a simple thought: x is prior by nature to y provided that (i) if y exists, then x
exists, and (ii) it is not the case that if x exists then y exists.

[47] See e.g. Aristotle, *Cat.* 15a4-7; cf. e.g. Alexander, *in Top.* 367,16-20.

[48] Aristotle, *An. Pr.* 25b29: below, 42,17-27.

[49] On the different kinds of syllogism see below 8,19-29; 18,22-31; 28,24-30 (cf.
12,7-14,6); cf. e.g. Alexander, *in An. Pr.* 331,12-24; *in Top.* 2,15-3,24; 10,26-8; *in
Metaph.* 260,1-20. It is a commonplace to distinguish three kinds of syllogism (cf. e.g.
Albinus, *Didasc.* 158H); but note that at *Conv.* 57-9 Alexander adds a fourth kind, the
'examinatory' syllogism (see above 1,4; cf. e.g. Ammonius, *in An. Pr.* 2,18-29). At *in
An. Pr.* 2,29-3,30, Ammonius offers a schematic derivation of the division of
syllogisms into their kinds (cf. Philoponus, *in An. Pr.* 2,22-4,14).

[50] For analysis in Alexander see also *in An. Pr.* 275,32-7; *Quaest.* 4,4-7. On the
varieties of analysis see e.g. Albinus, *Didasc.* 156-7H; Ammonius, *in An. Pr.*
5,10-7,25; Philoponus, *in An. Pr.* 307,6-8; scholium on Aristotle, 140a35-41; see e.g.
Lloyd (1990), pp. 8-11; and esp. Ierodiakonou.

[51] 'Compounding' gives *sunthesis*, which is standardly translated as 'synthesis'.

[52] See e.g. Aristotle, *EN* 1095a30-b4; Plato, *Rep.* 511BC (and for the 'return route'
see 521C, 532B); cf. e.g. Ammonius, *in Porph. Isag.* 37,7-13; Proclus, *in Eucl.*
43,18-21; Eustratius, *in An. Post.* 3,4-7.

the conclusion until they bring the problem back to its principles.[53]
Again, if you reduce compound bodies to simple bodies, you use
analysis; and if you reduce each of the simple bodies to the things on
20   which their being depends – that is to say, to matter and form – you
are analysing.[54] Again,[55] if you divide speech into the parts of speech,
or the parts of speech into their syllables, or the syllables into letters,
you are analysing.[56] If you reduce compound syllogisms to simple
ones you are said to analyse in a special sense of the word, and so too if
you reduce simple syllogisms to the premisses on which their being
25   depends.[57] Again, reducing imperfect syllogisms to perfect ones is
called analysing.[58] Again, the reduction of a given syllogism to its
appropriate figure is said to be analysis – and it is in this sense of
analysis in particular that the books are entitled *Analytics*. For at the
end of the first book Aristotle outlines a method for us by means of
which we shall be able to do this[59] – and he also explains how we shall
30   be able to effect the reduction of simple syllogisms to the appropriate
premisses on which their being depends.[60] We shall also find him
saying[61] how compound syllogisms come from simple ones and how
we may reduce the former to the latter.[62]

8,1   The books in which he studies the analysis of syllogisms he entitles
Prior Analytics; those in which he studies the analysis of demonstrations he also calls *Analytics* – but *Posterior Analytics*.

1.2.2 Procedure

When you are giving instruction it is always[63] very useful to state

---

[53] The main texts on geometrical analysis are Pappus, 634-6, and a scholium to
Euclid XIII 1-5 (printed in Heiberg's Euclid, IV 363-6); see also e.g. Albinus, *Didasc.*
157H; Philoponus, *in An. Post.* 162,16-28. Geometrical analysis is said to have been
encouraged by Plato: Diogenes Laertius, III 24; Proclus, *in Eucl.* 211,18-212,4. See
e.g. Hintikka and Remes; Ierodiakonou, pp. 173-90.

[54] See e.g. Aristotle, *Cael.* 300a7-11; *GC* 329a20-4.

[55] 7,22-7 = *FDS* 1106.

[56] See e.g. Apollonius Dyscolus, *Synt.* 265,9-10; 326,11-327,12.

[57] cf. e.g. Ammonius, *in An. Pr.* 6,2-4; *in Porph. Isag.* 36,7-9; Philoponus, *in An.
Post.* 334,25-335,3; see Ierodiakonou, pp. 166-73.

[58] e.g. by Galen (*Inst. Log.* ix 1, 2; x 2). Aristotle does not use 'analyse' in precisely
this sense in *An. Pr.*; but he does use it in a closely related way, of reducing a
syllogism in one figure to a syllogism in another (e.g. 51a2, 3, 18, 22).

[59] i.e. at *An. Pr.* 46b40-47b14 (for *analusis* see 47a4): see Alexander, *in An. Pr.*
340,5-21 (with a reference to Theophrastus' work *On the Analysis of Syllogisms*: F 31
Graeser).

[60] i.e. at *An. Pr.* 47b15-50a4 (for *analusis* see 49a19); see Alexander, *in An. Pr.*
372,26-373,9. (At 7,30-31 we follow the punctuation proposed by Wallies on p. 711 of
his edition of *in Top.*)

[61] Reading *pou auton* (Aldine) for *tina autôn*.

[62] See *An. Pr.* 50a5-15 (but Aristotle does not use the word 'compound' of
syllogisms); Alexander, *in An. Pr.* 381,28-386,2; cf. Ierodiakonou, pp. 21-3.

[63] Reading *aei* (cj. Wallies) for *dein*.

the aim and purpose of what you are going to say;[64] for those who
know what each thing you say refers to learn more easily than those
who do not know. (The difference between such learners is like that   5
between people walking along the same road, when some know the
destination to be reached and others are ignorant of it: those who
know walk with more ease and accomplish their purpose without
exhaustion, whereas those who are ignorant tend to tire. In all cases
ignorance is like a sort of inexperience.[65]) Since this practice is   10
useful, Aristotle usually follows it in his other studies – and he does
so here too. At the very beginning he states what his purpose is; and
having done so quickly and briefly, he next tackles the items which
lead up to this purpose.[66] For just as 'that for the sake of which' is a
starting-point for things which come about, so too is it for things
which are said; for that for the sake of which certain things are said,   15
i.e. their aim, is the explanation for the things said for its sake. And
if this is a starting-point, we should use it as a starting-point and
start from it. Moreover, if the aim is recognized, it will help those
who speak to judge what to say and those who learn to judge what
they hear.

At the same time, by saying that the purpose of his study of
syllogisms is to speak about demonstrations, he tells us that the   20
account of demonstration must be considered the primary product of
syllogistic method as a whole. For the study of the other forms of
syllogism is a matter for philosophers only to the extent that dealing
with them is useful for demonstration and for the discovery of what
is true: if you have exercised in dialectical syllogisms and can   25
recognize what is plausible and what lies close to what is true, then
you can more easily discover what is true, not being deceived by the
similarity of the plausible to the true but being aware of their
difference;[67] and if you know how sophistical arguments come about
you will be able to guard against falsehood – and avoiding this helps
very greatly in the discovery of what is true.[68]

Aristotle does the same in the *Ethics* as he does here. There he   30
first says that 'our method aims at these things, being in a sense
political',[69] and he states that his purpose has to do with

---

[64] Alexander's general comment, and also the specific analogy with walking, allude
to Aristotle's celebrated remarks on Plato's lecture *On the Good* (see Aristoxenus, II
30; cf. Aristotle, *Metaph.* 995a33-b2).

[65] 'Inexperience' gives *apeiria*. The word may also mean 'infinity'; and Alexander
may be punning. At *Probl.* 955b9-21, [Aristotle] asks why a road seems longer if we do
not know how long it is; and he replies that it is in a sense infinitely long (*apeiros*).

[66] See *An. Pr.* 24a10-15; cf. below 10,9-23.

[67] See Aristotle, *Top.* 101a27; Alexander, *in Top.* 27,24-31.

[68] See Alexander, *Conv.* 59. Note the practice of the Stoic Zeno (Plutarch, *Stoic.
Rep.* 1034E); and cf. Ebbesen (1981a), I, pp. 88-9.

[69] See *EN* 1094b10-1.

constitutions or political power. But only after ten books does he give an account of these things,[70] thereby suggesting that it is 9,1 necessary first of all to speak of human character and to say which characters are required in those who are to make up a State, since they are the primary parts of a State.[71]

[70] i.e. at *EN* 1179a33-1181b23? Or does Alexander rather mean that the whole of *EN* is, so to speak, a preface to *Pol.*?
[71] See e.g. Aristotle, *Pol.* 1290b38-1291a8 (cf. Plato, *Rep.* 552A).

2

Introductory Explanations

2.1 The goal of the *Analytics*[1]

First, to say about what and of what the inquiry is: it is about demonstration and demonstrative science. [1.1, 24a10-11]

He states briefly what is the purpose and the aim of the science of analytics as a whole.   9,5

Having proposed[2] to say 'about what' ('about' demanding the accusative case) and 'of what' (which is in the genitive case), he gives his answer in the accusative case, saying only 'about demonstration and science', and leaving it to us to reformulate his remarks for the genitive case too. But in some copies[3] 'demonstrative science' is   10
written not with a nu but with a sigma;[4] and with this reading he will have replied to both the questions he propounded – to 'about what' with 'about demonstration', and to 'of what' with 'of demonstrative science'. If 'demonstrative science' is written with a   15
sigma, it is possible that his words 'about what' and 'of what' do not both refer to the subject matter of the work. Rather, one of them ('about what') refers to the subject matter (for that which something is about[5] is the subject matter), and 'of what' refers to the disposition which theorises about the subject matter. Thus the work is *about* demonstration as its subject matter, and *of* demonstrative science, which theorises about demonstration.[6] In this way, he will have

---

[1] The issue was disputed: some commentators said that the goal was demonstration, others that it was the syllogism in general: see Ammonius, *in An. Pr.* 4,36-7; Philoponus, *in An. Pr.* 10,3-25; scholium to Aristotle, 139a36-140a10.

[2] Reading *protheis* for *prostheis*.

[3] For other references in Alexander to variant readings see e.g. *in An. Pr.* 144,4-6; 151,14-16; 210,30-2. For textual criticism in Alexander see Moraux (1986b), pp. 136-7.

[4] i.e. in the genitive rather than in the accusative. All our MSS of *An. Pr.* have the genitive, and this is the only reading mentioned by Ammonius (*in An. Pr.* 12,6-10) and Philoponus (*in An. Pr.* 9,28-10,25).

[5] Reading *peri* (Aldine) for *pan*.

[6] Alexander means that the inquiry is 'of' demonstrative science in the sense that you exercise your demonstrative skills in pursuing it (so too Philoponus, *in An. Pr.* 9,28-32). But the genitive is certainly objective rather than subjective, and 'of

20 given an appropriate reply to each of the questions he proposed.

A demonstration is a demonstrative syllogism; and demonstrative science is the disposition by means of which it is possible to syllogize demonstratively – for to speak about demonstrations[7] is the mark of demonstrative science and of someone who possesses it.

2.2 Propositions[8]

2.2.1 The general account

> Then to determine what a proposition is, <and what a term, and what a syllogism, and what sort of syllogisms are perfect and what sort imperfect; and after that, what it is for this to be or not be in that as in a whole, and what we mean by being predicated of every or of none.> [1.1, 24a11-15]

25 Since an account of the syllogism is indispensable for an account of demonstration (as we have already said[9]), and syllogisms are compounded of propositions and propositions of terms, Aristotle reasonably speaks about the items on which the being of a syllogism depends before speaking about syllogisms themselves. (In the same way it is not possible to know about words unless you know about
30 syllables and letters.) Next he proposes to speak about syllogisms, indicating to us that it is because of syllogisms that he has given an account of these items – just as he has given an account of
10,1 syllogisms because of the account of demonstration. Proceeding further, he will make known which syllogisms are perfect and which imperfect. And he will explain that 'to be in as in a whole' and 'in no' (for this is what is meant by 'or not be') mean the same as 'of every'
5 and 'of no'. And 'of every' and 'of no' mean universal affirmation and universal negation, as he will go on to explain. But since, in his presentation of syllogisms and in general of combinations in the figures, he will make use of 'one thing is in another as in a whole' and 'in no', for this reason he mentions these items first.[10]

10 Now a proposition is an utterance affirming or negating something of something. It is either universal or particular or indeterminate. <By universal, I mean holding of all or of none,

---

demonstrative science' simply means 'about demonstrative science' (cf. *An. Post.* 99b15-17: see e.g. Ross, p. 288; Mignucci (1969), p. 181). But note the subtle interpretation in Brunschwig (1981).

[7] As a matter of fact, demonstrative sciences do not speak *about* (*peri*) demonstrations. Hence we toyed with emending *peri* to *dia* (or *meta*): demonstrative sciences speak *through* or *with* demonstrations.

[8] On Alexander's account of propositions see Lee, pp. 55-8.

[9] Above, 6,32-7,11.

[10] See below, 24,23-25,11 and note to 25,11.

by particular holding of some or not of some or not of all, by
indeterminate holding or not holding, without being universal
or particular ...> [1.1, 24a16-20]

One account of propositions will be the account Aristotle gave of
assertions in *On Interpretation*, namely: an utterance 'in which
there is truth or falsity'.[11] But, in fact, he gives a definition specific
to propositions; for even if propositions and assertions are the same
in what underlies them, they differ in account:[12] insofar as they are
either true or false, they are assertions;[13] insofar as they are
expressed affirmatively or negatively, they are propositions. Or: for
something to be an assertoric utterance is simply a matter of its
being true or false; for something to be a proposition is a matter of
how it contains truth and falsity. This is why propositions which do
not contain truth and falsity in the same way are the same
utterance but not the same proposition. The proposition which says
that justice is good is similar to the proposition which says that
injustice is bad – they are both true and both affirmations; but they
are not the same proposition, since their subjects and predicates
differ. Again, the affirmation and the negation, which are true,[14] are
similar in this respect and are the same utterance; but they are not
the same proposition, since the quality of the assertion is different
in them: they are not the same proposition but they are the same
assertion.

He seems to define propositions in terms of what falls under
them.[15] The reason is this. In *On Interpretation* he said that 'the
primary single assertoric utterance is affirmation; and next is
negation'.[16] Now where things are ranked – where one of the
subordinate items is primary and one posterior, so that the primary
shows up in the posterior – there the predicate which they share is
not predicated of them as a genus.[17] For in genera the proximate
species are co-ordinate with one another, and it is not the case that
one of them is primary and another posterior. Now since proposi-

---

[11] See *Int.* 17a2-3.
[12] For the difference between *protasis* and *apophansis* see e.g. Ammonius, *in An. Pr.* 13,17-14,4; 15,30-16,9; Philoponus, *in An. Pr.* 11,25-36; cf. Maier II 2, pp. 359-66; Lee, p. 32.
[13] cf. e.g. Ammonius, *in Int.* 2,21-5; Boethius, *Int. Syll. Cat.* 767C.
[14] The phrase is obscure, but Alexander must have in mind some particular pair of affirmation and negation; and it is most likely that he expects us to supply the affirmation of 10,22 ('Justice is good') with an appropriate negation (e.g. 'Justice is not bad'): cf. Alexander, *in Top.* 12,10-24. For a different interpretation of the argument see Volait, pp. 1-3.
[15] i.e. in terms of affirmation and negation, which might be taken to be the species of proposition.
[16] See Aristotle, *Int.* 17a8-9.
[17] For the thought see e.g. Alexander, *DA* 16,18-17,8; *in Metaph.* 208,28-209,34; and note Aristotle, *DA* 414b20-32; *Metaph.* 999a6-13; *EE* 1218a1-8.

15

20

25

30

11,1

tions are not of a genus or nature distinct from the things of which
they are predicated and on which their being depends (as is the case
5   with genera),[18] for this reason he makes clear what they are by way
of affirmation and negation, of which they are predicated.

What he said in *On Interpretation* – namely, 'Thus a simple
assertion is a significant sound concerning something's holding or
not holding'[19] – is equivalent to the present account. Equivalent too
is what he says in the *Posterior Analytics*: 'The one part of a
contradictory pair,[20] one thing of one thing.'[21] (In this definition he
10   no longer added an indication of quality or of times, because these
are comprised in the notion of a contradictory pair – contradictory
pairs actually involve these features.[22]) Similar, too, is: 'An
utterance assertoric of something about something'[23] – except that
this is more general, since in it the notions of affirmation and
negation have not yet been introduced.

15   (Theophrastus, in his *On Affirmation*, seems to think of
'proposition' as having several senses. At any rate, he does not
define propositions but rather affirmation and negation.[24])

These definitions apply not to all propositions but to simple and
so-called predicative propositions. Saying something of something,
and being universal or particular or indeterminate, are features
peculiar to predicative propositions; for in hypothetical propositions
20   truth and falsity depend not on something's being said of something
but rather on implication or conflict.[25] Moreover, the definition he

[18] Alexander's view (which may be Theophrastean in origin: below, n. 24) that *protasis* is not the genus of affirmation and negation was criticised by Ammonius (*in Int.*
15,16-30; 66,14-28; 67,30-68,9; 80,15-35), Philoponus (*in An. Pr.* 12,23-20,3), and Boethius (*in Int.* ed. sec. 16,6-18,26; 119,10-125,27, which cites Porphyry as rejecting
Alexander's view). Philoponus and Boethius report Alexander's arguments at some
length, presumably drawing on his lost commentary on *Int.* (Note that in Alexander's
view *protasis* does function as a genus for problems, axioms, and so on: below, 44,16-23.)
[19] See *Int.* 17a23-4 (Alexander has *oun* where our MSS of Aristotle have *d'hê men*).
[20] Reading *antiphaseôs* for *apophanseôs*: the emendation is demanded by 11,10-11.
[21] See *An. Post.* 72a8-9.
[22] The definition of 'contradictory pair' includes an explicit reference to affirmation
and negation (*An. Post.* 72a13-14); hence there is no need to make an express
reference to 'quality' in the *An. Post.* definition of propositions. What about 'times'?
Aristotle's account of 'simple assertion' contains the clause (which Alexander does not
cite) 'in one of the divisions of time' (*Int.* 17a24): hence his definition of 'contradictory
pair' implicitly refers to times; and hence – perhaps – no explicit reference to time is
needed in the *An. Post.* definition.
[23] This account is not found in Aristotle.
[24] See Theophrastus, F 2 Graeser. See Bochenski (1947), pp. 40-1, who argues that
Theophrastus was the author of Alexander's view (above, n. 18) that *protasis* is not
the genus of affirmation and negation.
[25] The distinction between predicative (or 'categorical') and 'hypothetical'
propositions was a commonplace by Alexander's time: see e.g. Albinus, *Didasc.* 158H;
Galen, *Inst. Log.* iii 1; Apuleius, *Int.* 177,3-10. Roughly speaking, a hypothetical
proposition is either a conditional ('implication') or a disjunction ('conflict'): see
Introduction, p. 23; cf. e.g. Sullivan, pp. 24-30.

gives does not apply to dialectical propositions (for they involve requests) but only to syllogistic propositions.[26]

He used 'something of something'[27] of negations too, since in negations too there is a subject term and a predicate term. For here 'of something' means not that something is affirmed but that 25 something is predicated – and it may be predicated either affirmatively or negatively. In *On Interpretation*, however, when defining affirmation and negation, he used 'of something' for affirmations – for negations he used not 'of something' but rather 'from something', saying that a negation asserts 'something from something'.[28]

There are two things by which predicative propositions are 30 determined, namely quality and quantity, and he introduces both of them into his account of propositions: quality, in saying that a proposition is an utterance which is affirmative or negative (this is the primary and common quality of propositions); quantity, in saying 'It is either universal or particular or indeterminate'. Here he 12,1 sets out the meanings of these words – in *On Interpretation* he discussed them at greater length.[29] Note that he does not present universals in the same way here and in the *Posterior Analytics*.[30]

2.2.2 Demonstrative and dialectical propositions[31]

A demonstrative proposition differs from a dialectical proposition in that a demonstrative proposition is the 5 assuming of one part of a contradictory pair <(for if you are demonstrating you do not request but assume), while a dialectical proposition is a request for one of a contradictory pair. There will be no difference with regard to there being a syllogism in each case. For whether you are demonstrating or requesting, you syllogize by assuming that something holds of something or that something does not hold. Hence a syllogistic proposition *simpliciter* affirms or negates something of something in the way already mentioned. It is demonstrative if it is true and is assumed by way of the initial hypotheses. It is dialectical if it is a request for one of a contradictory pair (if you

[26] For dialectical propositions see the next section, and esp. 13,30-14,5: it is plain that *here* Alexander uses 'dialectical proposition' in the *first* of the two senses which (following Aristotle) he later distinguishes.

[27] Retaining *ti* (del. Wallies) before *kata*.

[28] See *Int.* 17a25-6 (with Ammonius, *in Int.* 80,31-5); cf. Ammonius, *in An. Pr.* 17,10-32.

[29] Alexander is presumably referring to *Int.* 17a38-b16.

[30] See *An. Post.* 73b26-7: 'I call universal whatever holds of every case and in its own right and *qua* itself.' See also below, 25,11-13.

[31] See above, 7,9 note.

are inquiring) or an assumption of what is apparent and
reputable (if you are syllogizing) – as has been said in the
Topics.> [1.1, 24a22-b3]

Having given his general account of propositions, he adds the
differences by which demonstrative and dialectical propositions are
distinguished from each other, thereby showing that the general
10   account of propositions which he has given applies to them and that
it is not in this respect that they differ. The account he has given
applies to all syllogistic propositions. But it does not apply to
requests: requests are not propositions *simpliciter* but dialectical
propositions, the phrase being taken as a whole. Now when he
defined propositions in the *Topics*,[32] he gave an account to the effect
that dialectical propositions are reputable requests.[33] So lest anyone
15   should think that this is the account of propositions in general, he
marks the distinction here and makes clear the differences among
propositions, showing that the account of propositions in the general
sense – i.e. of propositions assumed for syllogizing in general – is the
account given here and not the account stated in the *Topics*; for the
latter is an account of dialectical propositions, which are not as yet
syllogistic.
20   The differences among propositions correspond to the differences
among syllogisms, there being a general account of propositions as
there is of syllogisms. In the *Posterior Analytics*[34] he describes at
greater length how demonstrative propositions differ from other
propositions: they differ both with regard to their matter (for they
are true and prior and known and necessary), and also in the way in
25   which they are used and assumed (for someone who is
demonstrating does not make requests).[35] Here he indicates their
difference from dialectical propositions first by the manner in which
they are assumed: demonstrative propositions do not involve
requests, i.e. are not assumed by way of a request. Someone who
requests one of a contradictory pair does so inasmuch as he is
prepared to object to anything supposed by his respondent and to
30   reject it by way of the syllogism which he will construct from what
the respondent grants. Such is the dialectician, who syllogizes from
reputable propositions; for it is possible to obtain reputable
propositions even for opposites.[36] But if you are demonstrating you
will not demonstrate from *anything* which is granted; for it is not

[32] Aristotle, *Top.* 104a8-9; cf. Alexander, *in Top.* 69,13-70,11; Ammonius, *in An. Pr.*
19,3-21,30; Philoponus, *in An. Pr.* 22,23-23,17.
[33] For *endoxa* or 'reputable' items see Aristotle, *Top.* 100a29-30 (cf. e.g. *Metaph.*
995b23-4); and see Barnes (1980b).
[34] Aristotle, *An. Post.* 71b20-72a24.
[35] On these two modes of difference see Ebbesen (1981b), p. 5.
[36] i.e. there are cases in which both 'P' and 'not-P' are reputable.

possible for opposites to be true. So if you demonstrate you do not
request but make your own assumptions: you assume what follows   13,1
from the principles and hypotheses. We see this to be the case in
geometry; for if you want to prove that the three angles of a triangle
are equal to two right angles you do not prove it by way of propositions
granted after a request. (Aristotle says here that a dialectical
proposition is 'a request for one of a contradictory pair' in the sense of   5
a proposition assumed by way of a request for one of a contradictory
pair – this is clear from the next phrase 'There will be no difference
…'. For someone who makes a request syllogizes on the basis not of
the request but of what is assumed by way of the request.) The
principles of demonstrations are hypotheses; for there is no demonstration of such propositions, i.e. of principles, but they are posited as
obvious and directly known or else as following from propositions of   10
this type; and something which is assumed without demonstration
they call a hypothesis (and also, more generally, a posit[37]) and say
that it is hypothesized.[38] It is on items of this sort that demonstrations are based.

Having said how they differ in use, he next adds their difference in
respect of matter, having first shown that the account of propositions
which he gave is general and applies both to demonstrative and to
dialectical propositions when they are assumed for the generation of   15
a syllogism. (He says: 'There will be no difference with regard to there
being a syllogism in each case. For whether you are demonstrating or
requesting, you syllogize by assuming that something holds of
something or does not hold' – and this is the account he gave of
propositions.) For although the manner in which they are assumed is
different, still the assumptions share the general account of proposi-   20
tions. Now it is dialectical propositions as assumed, not as requested,
to which the general account of propositions applies; and what holds
generally of propositions, whether assumed demonstratively or
dialectically, is the fact that they affirm or negate something of
something. It is propositions in this sense which we use for syllogisms
in the general and unqualified sense; for it is the fact that they are
affirmative or negative which is useful for syllogisms.   25

When he says 'something holds of something' and 'something[39]
does not hold', his expression makes clear to us that 'of something'
applies to negations too. And when he adds to the next sentence 'in
the way already mentioned', he seems to mean that 'of something' is
common to both sorts of proposition.[40] Or else 'in the way already   30

[37] cf. Ammonius, *in Int.* 9,7-10.
[38] On this broad sense of 'hypothesis', which became common in later Greek, see
Barnes (1990c), ch. 4.
[39] Reading *kai ti* with the MSS: Wallies prefers *ê* (Aldine, Aristotle).
[40] See above, 11,22-6.

mentioned' means 'universal or particular or indeterminate'.[41]

14,1   He also makes a division among dialectical propositions: he distinguishes between the dialectical proposition of someone inquiring and requesting ('a request for one of a contradictory pair'), which consists in demanding an answer from someone else and which is not yet an assertoric utterance nor an affirmation or a negation, and the dialectical proposition of someone syllogizing, which is part of the syllogism being constructed and which depends upon its matter; for a
5   request for one of a contradictory pair is not part of a syllogism.

In the *Topics*[42] he has said what he means by 'apparent and reputable.'

<In what follows we shall say with precision> what a proposition is and how syllogistic and demonstrative and dialectical propositions differ. [1.1, 24b12-14]

He has said that propositions are utterances affirming or negating
10   something of something, and this is his account of syllogistic propositions. Demonstrative propositions are, as he puts it here, 'true and ... assumed by way of the initial hypotheses',[43] whereas in the *Posterior Analytics* he says that they are true and immediate and primary and better known than and explanatory of the
15   conclusion.[44] A dialectical proposition is 'a request for one of a contradictory pair (if you are inquiring) or an assumption of what is apparent and reputable (if you are syllogizing)'.[45] There are also sophistical propositions – which he does not mention at this point – which are assumptions of what is apparently reputable.[46] For propositions in which the plausibility is superficial and rather easy to detect[47] are sophistical propositions.

He discusses them 'with precision' – demonstrative propositions
20   in the *Posterior Analytics*, dialectical propositions in the *Topics*, and sophistical propositions in the *Sophistical Refutations*. These books all follow the general study of syllogisms. By saying 'In what follows we shall say' he makes it clear that the present books are prior in order to those studies.

---

[41] i.e. it refers back to *An. Pr.* 24a17.

[42] *Top.* 100b21-3: 'Reputable opinions are those held by everyone or by most people or by the wise (and either by all the wise or by most of them or by the best known and most reputable)'.

[43] *An. Pr.* 24a30-b1.

[44] *An. Post.* 71b21-2.

[45] *An. Pr.* 24b10-12.

[46] Omitting *kai* before *endoxou* with LM: see Aristotle, *Top.* 100b23-5.

[47] i.e. it is relatively easy to discern that the propositions are *merely* plausible.

2.3 Terms

2.3.1 Subjects and predicates

I call a term that into which a proposition resolves <– i.e. the predicate and that of which it is predicated ...> [1.1, 24b16-17]

By saying 'I call a term' Aristotle seems to indicate that the word   25
'term' was not in common use or well known in its application to a
part of a proposition.[48]
He deals first with propositions because he is going to give his
account of terms by way of propositions. The terms in a simple
proposition are noun and verb.[49] The parts of propositions are called
terms because propositions are determined by[50] and compounded   15,1
from them. The term of which something is predicated is the subject
term; and about it the utterance is made. The term which is
attached to the subject and said about it is the predicate.[51] For every
predicative proposition is composed of a subject term and a
predicate term.

2.3.2 The copula

<... (when you add or remove 'is' or 'is not').> [1.1, 24b17-18][52]

He adds 'when you add or remove[53] "is" or "is not"' lest out of   5
ignorance people should divide up propositions in which 'is' is
co-predicated as a third item,[54] and should think that 'is' or 'is not' is
a third term. For in propositions of this kind 'is' is not a term.
Rather, when it is added, it signifies a compounding of the predicate
and the subject and betokens an affirmation; and when it is said in   10
the negative form, it removes and separates the terms from one
another and betokens a negation. Every proposition is divided into

[48] cf. Ammonius, *in An. Pr.* 14,13-22; scholium to Aristotle, 146a9-18.
[49] cf. Apuleius, *Int.* 178,1-18; Galen, *Inst. Log.* ii 2-3; Ammonius, *in An. Pr.* 14,22-5; 22,18-24 (the ultimate source is Plato: see *Theaetetus* 206D; *Sophist* 262D; *Cratylus* 431B; but note, in Aristotle, *Int.* 16a1-2; 17a9-10). This grammatical analysis of propositions is at odds with the standard logical analysis into subject term and predicate term: the predicate term is not a verb – it has the same logical syntax as the subject term, with which it is interchangeable (see Barnes (1983)).
[50] They are called terms, *horoi*, because they are determined, *horizontai*.
[51] cf. e.g. Ammonius, *in Int.* 7,32-8,4; *in An. Pr.* 22,12-30.
[52] The interpretation of this clause was (and is) controversial: see esp. Ammonius, *in An. Pr.* 22,34-24,24; Philoponus, *in An. Pr.* 25,30-30,20. (Ammonius and Philoponus discuss and reject Alexander's interpretation, preferring the more elaborate suggestion put forward by Iamblichus.) See also Ross, pp. 290-1, who cuts the knot by excising *ê diairoumenou*.
[53] For this use of *diairein* see e.g. Ammonius, *in Int.* 27,1-3.
[54] See Aristotle, *An. Pr.* 25b22; *Int.* 19b19; cf. esp. Ammonius, *in Int.* 165,4-30 (cf. 8,5-8); *in An. Pr.* 23,25-24,5.

two terms. That 'is' is neither a term nor part of a term[55] seems to be clear from the fact that opposite affirmations and negations are compounded from the same terms.

15   But 'is' does seem to be a term when it stands by itself, i.e. when it is predicated of the subject, as in 'Socrates is'.[56] For here the 'is' seems to be the predicate term. But in fact, if you consider the case precisely, 'is' is not even here a term in its own right. For the proposition which says 'Socrates is' is equivalent to 'Socrates is being', in which not 'is' but 'being', which goes with 'is',[57] forms the
20 predicate term. Since 'is' seems to be equivalent to 'being' (for it is an inflected form of it), for the sake of brevity and in order not to appear to say the same thing twice it alone is connected to the subject. And when it is connected in this way it becomes a term and a part of the proposition.

    After 'when you add[58] or remove', he adds ' "is" or "is not" '. The addition of 'is not' seems to make the expression somewhat
25 incongruous; for 'when you add or remove "is" ' seems to be in itself sufficient, since the addition of 'is' makes an affirmation and its removal a negation. But in fact he adds 'is not' in order to make clear how a negation comes about when 'is' is removed. For you remove 'is'
30 both if you delete it completely and also if you connect it with the negative particle, to make 'is not'. If you subtract 'is' completely from the proposition and remove it in *this* sense, then what remains is not an affirmation nor indeed a proposition at all. For if you subtract 'is' from the proposition 'Socrates is white' and leave 'Socrates white',
16,1 you have not made a negation nor even kept what remains as a proposition. For propositions are complete utterances which lack nothing.[59] Hence in order to show the way in which you should remove 'is' in order to get a negation, he added 'is not', so as to mean 'when you add "is" in affirmations, and remove the same thing in
5 negations by making it "is not" '. For 'is' is not completely removed and subtracted.

    Or else he adds 'when you add or remove "is" or "is not" ' in order to indicate that these items, i.e. 'is' and 'is not', are neither parts of the proposition nor terms, but that both 'is' and 'is not' are external to the terms, either being added externally to the predicate terms

---

[55] But see e.g. Alexander, *in An. Pr.* 406,32-5 (below, 44,28 note).

[56] The observation was made by Eudemus (scholium to Aristotle, 146a19-27 = F 27 Wehrli); see e.g. Ammonius, *in Int.* 14,18-26; 57,29-32 (cf. Boethius, *Int. Syll. Cat.* 769A): Ammonius repeats Alexander's analysis, which derives ultimately from Aristotle (see *Int.* 21b9-10; *Metaph.* 1017a27-30).

[57] Reading *to on <to> meta tou estin.*

[58] Reading *prostithemenou* for *suntithemenou.*

[59] See e.g. Ammonius, *in Int.* 44,11-19; 62,10-12; Apuleius, *Int.* 176,13-14. Compare to the Stoic definition of an *axiôma* as a *lekton autoteles*: Sextus, *PH* II 104; *M* VIII 70-1; Diogenes Laertius, VII 65; Varro, cited by Aulus Gellius, XVI viii 1-8.

when propositions are divided into terms or else being separated 10
from them. For the addition or subtraction of these items
contributes nothing to the division of propositions into terms: the
terms in 'Socrates is white' seem to be 'Socrates' and 'white'. His
expression would be more congruous if it were put[60] in this way:
'when you add "is" or "is not" or remove them'.

Or is it absurd to claim that the 'is' in these propositions is not 15
predicated in any sense? (Eudemus, in the first book of his *On
Expression*, shows this at some length.[61])

2.4 Syllogisms[62]

2.4.1 The premisses

A syllogism is an utterance in which, certain things being
posited, something different from the suppositions comes 20
about by necessity inasmuch as they are the case. <By
'inasmuch as they are the case' I mean that it comes about
because of them; and to come about because of them is to need
no external term for the generation of the necessity.> [1.1,
24b18-22]

Having discussed propositions and the parts of propositions (which
he called terms), he duly presents his account of what a syllogism
is.[63] Now that a syllogism is a sort of utterance – that it falls within
the genus of utterances – is clear.

He first takes its genus[64] – the genus is what betokens the
common nature of the *definienda*, by which they are distinguished 25
from what differs from them in genus. This is the point of positing
the genus for the *definienda*; for the *definiendum* must be
completely distinguished by the definition. Of the things which
differ from the *definiendum*, some are further away (namely, those
which do not even share in the same genus), and others are closer
and belong to the same genus. Now the genus itself distinguishes it 30
from items in a different genus, while the *differentiae* distinguish it
from items in the same genus. That is why the genus is taken first in
definitions, since it distinguishes items which differ most from one

[60] Retaining *legoito* (Wallies emends to *legoi to*).
[61] See Eudemus, F 26 Wehrli; cf. the scholium to Aristotle, 146a24-7 [= F 27 Wehrli]:
'Eudemus, in the first book of his *On Expression* shows at some length that the "is" in
simple propositions (such as "Socrates is", "Socrates is not") is predicated and is a
term.' (Thus the final paragraph of this section refers back to 15,14-22.)
[62] With sections 2.4.1-4 compare *in Top.* 7,10-15,14.
[63] For Aristotle's definition see also *Top.* 100a25-7; *SE* 164b27-165a2; *Rhet.*
1356b16-18; cf. Kapp; Frede (1974b), pp. 110-22; Barnes (1981), pp 21-5.
[64] With this account of definition by genus and differentia cf. e.g. Alexander, *in Top.*
421,3-34.

another. Well, then, having taken the genus of the syllogism,
17,1 Aristotle next shows the appropriate and peculiar essence of the
syllogism by taking the *differentiae* of utterances and compounding
them with the genus.

By 'certain things being posited', he indicates that some
propositions must be assumed or conceded by whoever is syllogizing
– something which is not the case with every utterance. For what is
5 posited in a prayer or a command or a request[65] or an invocation?[66]
Some people think that 'posited' does not mean simply 'assumed' but
makes clear what sort of thing must be assumed.[67] For that the
propositions assumed for a syllogism must be predicative[68] is – they
say – shown by the word 'posited' (it is these propositions which
Aristotle has defined); for he will prove that hypothetical
propositions, in and of themselves, do not produce syllogisms.[69] This
10 – they say – is why he says 'posited' and not 'assumed'.

Furthermore,[70] that there must be not just one posit or one
proposition but at least two,[71] is made clear by the plural 'things
posited'.[72] For the 'single-assumption' arguments, as the more
recent thinkers[73] call them, are not syllogisms. A syllogism by its
very name betokens a sort of compounding of utterances. For the
prefix *sun-* means a conjunction or compounding or collection of the
15 things it is added to. Thus *suntrekhein* ['run in company'] signifies a
compounding or concourse of runners; *summakhein* ['fight
alongside'], a combination of fighters; *sumpalaiein* ['wrestle with'], a
group of wrestlers; *suzêtein* ['investigate with'], a group of
investigators. So too *sumpsêphizein* ['compute'] signifies a compounding of counters. And thus, a syllogism is a compounding of
utterances.[74]

---

[65] Adding *ê en têi erôtêsei* after *entolê* (see Introduction, p. 16 n. 83).

[66] For the five species of *logos* which the later Peripatetics distinguished see e.g.
Ammonius, *in Int.* 2,9-3,6; 5,1-23; 64,26-65,2; *in An. Pr.* 26,30-3; Boethius, *Syll. Cat.*
797BC. The ideas derive ultimately from Aristotle, *Int.* 17a4. For full details see
Schenkeveld.

[67] So Alexander himself, *in An. Pr.* 348,29-32; *in Top.* 8,8-14; the interpretation is
rejected by Ammonius, *in An. Pr.* 27,6-14; cf. Philoponus, *in An. Pr.* 33,6-10.

[68] See above, 11,17-20 and note.

[69] See Aristotle, *An. Pr.* 50a16-28.

[70] 17,10-18,7 = *FDS* 1051.

[71] And also at most two: e.g. Aristotle, *An. Pr.* 41b36-42a40; Alexander, *in An. Pr.*
257,6-12.

[72] cf. Alexander, *in An. Pr.* 257,8-13; *in Top.* 8,14-9,19; Ammonius, *in An. Pr.*
27,14-33; Philoponus, *in An. Pr.* 33,10-23. That a syllogism requires at least two
premisses is explicit in Aristotle: *An. Pr.* 34a16-19; 40b30-7; 53b16-23; *An. Post.*
73a7-11.

[73] See above, 3,3 note.

[74] i.e. *sullogismos* is derived from *sun-* and *logos* (cf. Alexander, *in Top.* 9,17-19;
Ammonius, *in An. Pr.* 26,2-6; Philoponus, *in An. Pr.* 2,14; 64,11-15). The etymology is
false: *sun-* is rather compounded with *logismos*, 'calculation'.

The so-called single-assumption arguments[75] are sometimes thought to be syllogisms inasmuch as when you hear them you add 20 the second premiss because it is well known. For
> You are breathing,
> Therefore: you are alive,

seems to be a syllogism because the hearer himself adds the second premiss:
> Everyone who is breathing is alive,

which is well known. Were this not well known, no one would concede the conclusion
> Therefore: you are alive,

on the basis of
> You are breathing,

– rather, they would demand a reason. A syllogism is supposed to be the assembling of a conclusion from the premisses,[76] and this cannot 25 be done from a single premiss.[77]

Even if something quite certainly follows from some single item by necessity, it does not thereby follow syllogistically. For it is not the case that, because a syllogism has a conclusion which follows necessarily from the suppositions, then if one thing follows necessarily from another it follows syllogistically as well. For necessity is of wider extension than the syllogism.[78] Thus in 30 implications and relations and in sound continuous[79] or conditional propositions, the consequent follows the antecedent by necessity, but they are not thereby syllogisms. In the case of
> If it is day, it is light,

its being light follows by necessity from its being day – but not syllogistically. Similarly, to err follows from to steal, and to wrong from to assault; but these are not therefore syllogisms. 18,1

It is the proper characteristic of a syllogism that it proves necessity from a plurality of items. That is why even if there is a

[75] On which see below 21,25; Alexander, *in Top.* 8,14-9,19; 13,25-8; 574,10-15; Sextus, *PH* II 166-7; *M* VIII 441-3; Apuleius, *Int.* 184,19-23; Ammonius, *in An. Pr.* 27,14-33; Philoponus, *in An. Pr.* 33,10-23; Boethius, *Syll. Cat.* 821BC; scholium to Aristotle, 147b47-148a2. See Mates, p. 66; Mueller (1969), pp. 175-7; Frede (1974a), pp. 118-19; (1974b), p. 114; Maróth, pp. 84-5. (17,18-22 = *SVF* III Ant 27.)

[76] cf. Ammonius, *in An. Pr.* 26,6.

[77] What, then, is the status of 'conversions'? Within Aristotelian syllogistic, 'B holds of some A' follows from 'A holds of every B'; and this appears to be a single-assumption argument. The ancient texts give no satisfactory explanation of this: see Barnes (1990a), III.8.

[78] Aristotle, *An. Pr.* 47a22-3; cf. Alexander, *in An. Pr.* 344,9-13.27-31; 379,20-1; *in Top.* 9,5-8. See Lee, p. 98; Maconi, p. 95; Barnes (1990a), III.6.

[79] 'Continuous (*sunekhês*)' was the word used by 'the earlier thinkers' (i.e. probably by the early Peripatetics) for conditional propositions: Alexander, *in An. Pr.* 262,32-5; 390,3-4; Galen, *Inst. Log.* iii 3; cf. Bochenski (1947), p. 108; Frede (1974a), p. 16. (The idea is that a conditional proposition links two things together and so makes them continuous, whereas a disjunction separates them.)

plurality of expressions for what is posited, still, if the rest[80] signify the same as the first, there will be no syllogism from them in such a case. For an argument of this sort is virtually a single-assumption argument – e.g.

5   It is day.
        But it is not the case that it is not day.
        Therefore: it is light.

For 'It is not the case that it is not day' differs from 'It is day' only in expression.[81]

2.4.2 The conclusion

This, then, is what 'being posited' means. As for 'something different from the suppositions comes about by necessity', this separates

10   syllogisms from inductive arguments; for it means that the conclusion necessarily follows from the suppositions – something which holds neither of paradigmatic nor of inductive arguments, even though in them too you posit some thing or things.[82]

Aristotle[83] was quite right to add that the conclusion must be something different from what has been posited.[84] It is useless[85] – it destroys any syllogistic utility – to infer what is agreed and

15   supposed. No syllogistic utility is provided by the argument:

        If it is day, it is light,
        But it is day,
        Therefore: it is day[86]

– nor generally by those which the more recent thinkers call non-differently concluding arguments.[87] (These include the duplicated arguments,[88] such as

        If it is day, it is day.
        But it is day.

---

[80] Reading *talla* for *tauta*.

[81] But at *in Top.* 12,31-13,10, Alexander argues that 'P' and 'Not-not-P' do not mean the same thing primarily (*proêgoumenôs*). On double negations, or *huperapophatika*, see Diogenes Laertius, VII 69; cf. O. Becker, p. 29; Frede (1974a), p. 72.

[82] See below, 43,17-44,2.

[83] 18,12-24 = *FDS* 1171; 18,12-18 = *SVF* II 261.

[84] cf. Ammonius, *in An. Pr.* 27,34-28,20.

[85] See above, 2,34 note.

[86] Reading *hêmera* for *phôs* with B and the Aldine (so Wallies, in his *corrigenda*: *in Top.* p. 711); cf. Frede (1974a), p. 184 (Lee, p. 99 n. 8, offers an alternative).

[87] On these arguments see Alexander, *in An. Pr.* 164,30; *in Top.* 10,8-13; 566,25-7; Galen, *PHP* V 224; Apuleius, *Int.* 184,23-31; Ammonius, *in An. Pr.* 28,5-9; 32,12-14; scholium to Aristotle, 294b23-9. See Frede (1974a), p. 184 n. 21.

[88] On these arguments see below, 20,10-12; Alexander, *in Top.* 10,7-10; Apuleius, *Int.* 184,23-31; Ammonius, *in An. Pr.* 27,35-28,5; 32,13; Philoponus, *in An. Pr.* 33,23-6; Boethius, *Syll. Cat.* 821C-822A. (On 'duplicated' propositions add: Sextus, *PH* II 112; *M* VIII 93-5, 108-9; Diogenes Laertius, VII 68.) See Frede (1974a), p. 50 n. 5; (1974b), pp. 116-18.

Therefore: it is day.)
This sort of thing may indeed have a syllogistic figure and a
syllogistic combination, but it is certainly not a syllogism. For 20
syllogisms are instruments, and they are introduced for some useful
purpose – for proving something. Hence what is not useful is not a
syllogism.

We shall see that arguments of this kind are useless if we run
through the species of syllogism[89] and ask in which of them it could
be appropriate to infer one of the suppositions. Is it appropriate in
demonstrative syllogisms? – No: they attempt to reveal what is
unclear by way of what is clear and known, what is posterior by way 25
of what is primary. In dialectical syllogisms? – No: what an
interlocutor is unwilling to concede they attempt to prove by way of
what is reputable and conceded by him, bringing him to a
contradiction. In eristic syllogisms? – No: their purpose, too, is to
bring the respondent to a contradiction or an apparent contradiction
on the basis of what he grants. They do not conclude to what he 30
grants: they conclude, on the basis of what he grants, to what he is
unwilling to grant. Clearly, then, they will infer something different 19,1
from what is granted. Now if a genus exists in its species,[90] and if
the syllogism is the genus of its species, and if in none of the species
is what is inferred the same as what is assumed, then this will not
be so of syllogisms in general.

As[91] for disjoint syllogisms constructed from contradictories,[92]
they do not infer their conclusions *qua* the same as the
re-assumption or (as the more recent thinkers put it) the 5
co-assumption.[93] If you say:

---

[89] On the kinds of syllogism see above, 7,9 and note. For the form of argument
which Alexander uses here see Aristotle, *Top.* 121a27-39; Alexander, *in Top.*
302,23-304,6.
[90] cf. e.g. Alexander, *in Top.* 321,26-8; *DA* 90,2-9. Alexander's view on universals is
controversial: see e.g. Lloyd (1981), pp. 49-61; Tweedale; Sharples (1990), pp. 101-3.
[91] 19,3-12 = *SVF* II 261.
[92] With the following paragraphs cf. Alexander, *in Top.* 10,30-13,10; Lee, pp. 101-3.
By a 'disjoint' syllogism Alexander means a two-premissed argument in which one
premiss is a disjunction ('Either P or Q') and the other premiss is one of the disjuncts
(i.e. 'P', or 'Q'). Disjunction is construed exclusively: Either P or Q – but not both (but
see below, 66,10 note). Hence the syllogism yields the conclusion 'not-Q' (or: 'not-P'). A
disjoint syllogism is 'constructed from contradictories' if the two disjuncts are
contradictories of one another. See further below, notes 99 and 102.
[93] 'Co-assume', *proslambanein*, is a standard term in Stoic logic (e.g. Diogenes
Laertius, VII 76; cf. Frede (1974a), p. 118 n. 1 – the verb is also found in Aristotle: e.g.
An. Pr. 40b36); 're-assume', *metalambanein*, was the corresponding Peripatetic term
(Alexander, *in An. Pr.* 263,26-36; Ammonius, *in Int.* 3,19-20; [Ammonius], *in An. Pr.*
68,7-13; Philoponus, *in An. Pr.* 243,8-10 – who notes, however, that *proslambanein*
had come into general use). *Metalambanein* derives from Aristotle (see e.g. *An. Pr.*
41a39). It was used in a variety of other senses (see e.g. Alexander, *in An. Pr.* 262,5-9;
386,5-30). See also Volait, pp. 86-9; Ross, p. 373; and also – for its use in the
grammarians – Sluiter, pp. 111-17.

Either it is day or it is not day,

and then co-assume one of the disjoints – either the negative:

But it is not day,

or the affirmative:

It is day,

– you do indeed deduce either:

Therefore: it is not day,

or:

Therefore, it is day.

10 And this does seem to be the same as what was co-assumed – either as:

But it is not day,

or as:

But it is day.

It is not, however, inferred *qua* being the same as the co-assumption, but rather *qua* contradictory of the other disjoint. In syllogisms of this sort it so happens that this contradictory is the same as the co-assumption. But there is a world of difference between taking as the conclusion from the outset something which 15 is the same as one of the suppositions and taking as the conclusion something *qua* something different which then turns out to be the same.

Now inferences of this sort never occur unless the contradictory of one disjoint[94] is the same as the co-assumption; and so in these cases too,[95] it is taken *qua* different – since being this particular proposition is indeed different from being the contradictory of the other disjoint. (They are the same in expression but not in force.[96]) 20 And so it is in these cases – as[97] the Stoics too must admit, since they say that in disjoint or disjunctive syllogisms it is by the co-assumption of one of the disjuncts that the contradictory of the remaining disjunct[98] follows.[99] But if this is so, there will no longer be a syllogism, according to them, where one element in the disjunction is co-assumed and you infer not the contradictory but 25 something which is the same as the co-assumption. Hence either the

---

[94] Reading *heterôi* for *hepomenôi*.

[95] i.e. 'What is true in general of arguments of the form "Either P or Q; P: therefore, not-Q", is also true of the special case of such arguments in which "Q" is "not-P".' (But it is difficult to find this in the text; and the repetition of *kai tote* at 19,17 and 19 suggests the possibility of textual corruption.)

[96] cf. Alexander, *in Top.* 12,31-13,10: in the co-assumption, 'It is day' is used to affirm that it is day; in the conclusion 'It is day' is used to deny that it is not day. Hence, according to Alexander, 'It is day' has different senses (or different primary senses) in these different contexts.

[97] 19,20-3 = *SVF* II 261.

[98] Omitting *tês sullogistikês sumplokês*.

[99] This is the fourth of Chrysippus' five indemonstrable syllogisms: see e.g. Sextus, *PH* II 158; Galen, *Inst. Log.* vi 6; Frede (1974a), p. 152.

conjunction[100] in question is not syllogistic (if it infers the same
disjunct as the one co-assumed) or else, if it is syllogistic, then
according to them too what is inferred has not been taken *qua* the
same as the co-assumption.

Even if it happens to be the case that one item is both the
contradictory of one of the disjoints and also the same as the other, it   30
does not thereby follow that it is the same thing for it to be the same as
the one and to be the contradictory of the other. For if these
characteristics were the same as one another, then in *all* cases the
contradictory of one disjoint would thereby also be the same as the
other; but since they are different in most cases, then where they *do*   20,1
hold of the same thing at the same time, they do not do so in virtue of
being the same. Hence if you take one of the disjoints *qua* contradictory of the one, you do not take it *qua* the same as the other.
Thus[101] in disjoints which are not constructed from contradictories –
say, in those constructed from contraries – the conclusion is not the
same even in expression as either of the suppositions, because in
these cases it does not happen that the contradictory of the one is the   5
same as the other.[102] In the argument:

> Either it is day or it is night,
> But it is not day,
> Therefore: it is night,

'It is night' is not the same as either of the assumptions, neither as
what they call the 'tropic' (that is, the whole disjunction, 'Either it is
day or it is night')[103] nor as the co-assumption (the co-assumption is
'But it is not day'). 'It is night' is different from each of these.[104]   10

The[105] arguments which they call duplicated[106] are not syllogistic –

---

[100] i.e. the conjunction or combination of the two premises.

[101] 20,2-10 = *SVF* II 265.

[102] The illustrative argument which Alexander produces is not an instance of the
fourth Chrysippean indemonstrable (above, n. 99); hence it is not, strictly speaking, a
'disjoint' syllogism in the sense in which Alexander has up to now been
understanding that expression (above, n. 92). Rather, the illustrative argument has
the form: either P or Q; not-P; therefore, Q. (This is the fifth of Chrysippus' five
indemonstrables: see e.g. Sextus, *PH* II 158; Galen, *Inst. Log.* vi 6; Frede (1974a), pp.
152-3.)

[103] For this (Stoic) use of *tropikon* see e.g. Alexander, *in An. Pr.* 262,29-31;
263,11-12; rival explanations of the term in Galen, *Inst. Log.* vii 1; [Ammonius], *in
An. Pr.* 68,6-7; Philoponus, *in An. Pr.* 243,4-8. See Frede (1974a), p. 101 n. 25.

[104] The gist of Alexander's argument is this: 'An argument of the form "P or not-P;
P; therefore, P" is valid not in virtue of the fact that it exhibits *that* form, but rather in
virtue of the fact that it exhibits (is a special case of) the form "P or Q; P; therefore,
not-Q". Hence the conclusion of the argument really has the form "not-Q", and hence
is not formally the same as the co-assumption, "P".' (See the summary version of this
material at Alexander, *in Top.* 11,23-7.) All Alexander's ingenuity is wasted: in the
end, he (and Aristotle) must either modify their definition of the syllogism or else
reject disjunctive arguments from contradictories.

[105] 20,10-16 = *SVF* II 261.

[106] See above, 18,17 note.

for example:
> If it is day, it is day.
> But it is day.
> Therefore: it is day.

First, they do not offer any syllogistic utility. For[107] even if it is true that a thing follows from itself,[108] a conditional of this sort is not thereby useful for syllogisms – no more than one which does not allow a co-assumption, such as 'If you are a horse, you are an animal'.[109]

Secondly, if it is non-syllogistic to co-assume the consequent of a continuous proposition, and if in continuous propositions of this sort the antecedent is the same as the consequent, then the co-assumption is no more of the antecedent than of the consequent.[110]

Again, if it is non-syllogistic to co-assume both of them – both the antecedent and the consequent – then in this way too arguments of this sort will be refuted. For where the antecedent is the same as the consequent, the co-assumption is either of both or of neither. (Or[111] is it rather of the consequent – and in this way is more like it?)

Again, if it is non-syllogistic to assume the starting-point,[112] then

---

[107] The text of 20,12-22 is odd; and although the general train of Alexander's thought seems reasonably plain, we are not sure what words he actually wrote. Here we transpose *ou gar ... zôon ei* (20,16-18) to follow *parekhetai* (20,13).

[108] i.e. if every conditional of the form 'If P, then P' is true – as it is on some, but not on all, ancient accounts of conditional propositions: see Sextus, *PH* II 110-12.

[109] But such conditionals may, of course, be 'useful' in reduction to the impossible. (Note that there is indirect evidence, from Avicenna, of some ancient dispute over the truth-value of conditionals with impossible antecedents: see Maróth, pp. 128-9.)

[110] i.e. 'From a continuous proposition and its consequent (from "If P, Q" and "Q") nothing follows. But in duplicated arguments the antecedent is the same proposition as the consequent. Hence in duplicated arguments nothing follows from the conditional and its antecedent.' (This must be what Alexander means.)

[111] Placing *ê mallon ... ginetai* (20,21-2) in parentheses. We tentatively paraphrase this obscure paragraph as follows: 'Nothing follows from a conditional together with *both* its antecedent *and* its consequent. Nothing follows from a conditional together with *neither* its antecedent *nor* its consequent. But in duplicated arguments the antecedent and the consequent are the same. Hence either you co-assume both or you co-assume neither. Hence nothing follows from the premises of a duplicated argument. Or else perhaps there *is* a difference between antecedent and consequent; but in that case the co-assumption is actually more like the consequent than like the antecedent, and so (once again) nothing follows.' (Compare *in Top.* 10,28-30, which appears to be a shortened and simplified version of the present text.) This interpretation raises two questions. First, why suppose that nothing follows from a conditional together with *both* its antecedent *and* its consequent? – Because such arguments have redundant premises, and arguments with redundant premises are not syllogisms (see below, 23,1). Secondly, why might the co-assumption be more like the consequent than like the antecedent of the conditional? – Perhaps because the antecedent is thought of as including the word 'if': the co-assumption and the consequent are each simply 'P', whereas the antecedent is 'if P'. (cf. [Ammonius], *in An. Pr.* 68,8-13.)

[112] i.e. to 'beg the question': see esp. Aristotle, *An. Pr.* 64b28-65a37 (cf. Alexander,

in this way too we may fault an argument which infers something
which is the same as one of the suppositions – for it co-assumes what
it purports to prove.

Again, Aristotle himself announced, at the beginning of the study,   25
what its end and aim are, namely demonstration and demonstrative
knowledge.[113] Hence whatever makes no contribution to these
things will not be appropriate to the study before us.

Again, it would be absurd to deny the name of induction to an
inductive argument in which one of the assumptions or suppositions
is inferred and yet to claim that duplicated arguments are
syllogisms.

2.4.3 *Necessitas consequentiae*[114]

As for 'comes about by necessity', this does not mean that the   30
conclusion is necessary, as some have thought (this is so only when
the premisses are necessary), but rather that the conclusion follows
by necessity from the suppositions, whether it is actual[115] or   21,1
contingent or indeed necessary.[116] For even if a conclusion is
contingent, still in syllogistic combinations it too follows from the
premisses by necessity. Aristotle's expression does not mean that
the proposition which is concluded must be necessary: rather, it   5
marks a certain relation between the conclusion and the premisses.
If you assume the premiss:
> Every man is lying down,
and co-assume the premiss which says:
> Everyone lying down is asleep,[117]
then:
> Every man is asleep
will follow by necessity – yet it will not be necessary that every man
is asleep.

2.4.4 Non-syllogistic arguments

As to why he added 'inasmuch as they are the case'[118] to the   10
definition of the syllogism, he himself explained this when he said:
'By "inasmuch as they are the case" I mean that it comes about

---

in An. Pr. 257,1-4; *in Top.* 10,14-16; 566,25-31; Philoponus, *in An. Pr.* 451,15-453,33).
  [113] *An. Pr.* 24a10-11; above, 9,5-23.
  [114] See Patzig, pp. 16-36.
  [115] For our use of the word 'actual' here see Introduction, p. 30.
  [116] cf. Ammonius, *in An. Pr.* 29,20-34.
  [117] Note that in presenting this argument Alexander has reversed the order of the
premisses: see Patzig, pp. 59; 76-7.
  [118] For further comments on this clause see below, 68,27-69,4; Alexander, *in An. Pr.*
343,21-344,6; 350,11-16 (cf. Barnes (1980a), pp. 168-73).

because of them.' This itself might still seem less than plain. For 'because of them' betokens an explanation, and yet there can be syllogisms which do not proceed by way of explanations – for example, syllogisms by way of signs which prove what is primary
15   from what is posterior.[119] This feature – viz. being syllogized by way of explanations – is a proper characteristic of demonstrations.[120] For although the premisses must indeed be explanatory of the conclusion if there is to be a syllogism, what is meant by the premisses need not always be explanatory of what is meant by the conclusion. (For you can also syllogize what is prior by way of what
20   is posterior – proving that she has given birth from the fact that she is lactating, or that there was a fire from the ashes – and in general, syllogisms by way of signs are of this sort: for the posterior is not explanatory of the prior.) This[121] is why he also explained 'it comes about because of them', by saying that they 'need no external term for the generation of the necessity', i.e. that the terms laid down are sufficient in themselves for the conclusion.[122]
25   By this addition he shows at the same time that the so-called single-assumption arguments are not syllogisms.[123] For these need some external term and premiss for their conclusion – a term and premiss which those to whom the argument is addressed add for themselves, inasmuch as it is well known. In general,[124] if something is deduced, yet not from the suppositions but by the co-assumption of some other premiss, then this will be called
30   necessary but it is not thereby a syllogism. The arguments which the Stoics say conclude unmethodically are of this sort.[125] Thus you might say:

[119] For sign-inferences see Aristotle, *An. Pr.* 70a2-b38; cf. Burnyeat.

[120] See Aristotle, *An. Post.* 71b22; above, 14,13.

[121] 21,21-22,26 = *FDS* 1087.

[122] The paragraph is obscure. Alexander means to distinguish two ways in which the premisses of a syllogism may be explanatory of its conclusion. One way is reasonably plain: for 'P, Q; therefore, R' to be a demonstrative syllogism, it is necessary that the states of affairs referred to by P and Q should explain the state of affairs referred to by R. The other way is harder to grasp, and Alexander does nothing to elucidate it. In the second way, the premisses of *every* syllogism must explain, or be *aitia* for, the conclusion. At *Phys.* 195a16-21 (= *Metaph.* 1013b17-23) Aristotle asserts that the premisses are *aitia* for the conclusion inasmuch as they are 'that from which' the conclusion comes about. In his commentary, Alexander claims that the premisses are not the matter or 'material cause' of the conclusion (rather, they are the matter of the syllogism as a whole); but that they should be regarded as the *efficient* cause, *aition poiêtikon*, of the conclusion (*in Metaph.* 351,9-15; cf. Simplicius, *in Phys.* 320,1-10, quoting Alexander's lost commentary). It is a plausible guess that our passage in *in An. Pr.* alludes to this claim.

[123] Above, 17,19 and note.

[124] 21,28-22,3 = *SVF* II 260.

[125] On unmethodical arguments see also Alexander, *in An. Pr.* 344,9-346,6 (cf. below 68,21-4); *in Top.* 14,17-15,14; Galen, *Inst. Log.* xix 6 (cf. xvi-xviii); [Ammonius], *in An. Pr.* 70,11-13; Philoponus, *in An. Pr.* 36,5-13 (cf. 321,7-322,18). See Mueller

The first is greater than the second.
But the second is greater than the third.
Therefore: the first is greater than the third.
This follows necessarily, but not syllogistically – not unless you   22,1
co-assume a premiss from outside which says:
> What is greater than something greater is also greater than
> what is smaller than it.

The same sort of argument occurs[126] in the first book of Euclid's
Elements,[127] viz:
> This is equal to this.
> But this is equal to this.
> Therefore: this is equal to this.   5

This is indeed true – but there is need of a universal premiss if it is
to be deduced syllogistically. The premiss is this:
> Things equal to the same thing are also equal to one
> another.[128]

The argument in Plato's *Republic*[129] is similar:
> If he was the son of a god he was not avaricious.
> But if he was avaricious he was not the son of a god.
> Therefore: he was not both.

This too is not deduced by way of the suppositions but by the   10
co-assumption of a universal premiss. The premiss is this:
> When from each of two things[130] there follows the
> contradictory of the other, they cannot both hold of the same
> thing at the same time.

For if with this premiss, which is universal, you co-assume:
> From each of *being the son of a god* and *being avaricious*
> there follows the contradictory of the other,

you get as conclusion:
> They do not both hold of the same thing.   15

For from *being the son of a god* there follows the contradictory of
being avaricious (i.e. its negation), and conversely, from *being
avaricious* there follows the negation of *being the son of a god*.

In general,[131] the arguments which the more recent thinkers say
conclude unmethodically are of this sort. For example:

(1969), pp. 175-8; (1974), pp. 59-67; Frede (1974a), pp. 121-4; (1974b), p. 102; Lee, pp. 108-14; Maróth, pp. 178-85; Barnes (1990a), IV.

[126] Deleting *theôrêma*.

[127] For other references by Alexander to Euclid see *in An. Pr.* 260,23-261,2; 268,7-8.

[128] This proposition is the first of Euclid's 'common notions'; it is explicitly invoked in Euclid's proof at *Elements* I 1.

[129] See *Rep.* 408C (but Alexander offers a feeble interpretation of the text). For syllogizing interpretations of Platonic arguments see e.g. anon, *in Theaet.* 66,12-43; Albinus, *Didasc.* 158-60; Galen, *Inst. Log.* xviii 2-4; cf. Moraux (1973/84), II, pp. 487-90; O'Meara, p. 42 n. 33.

[130] Omitting *tôn antikeimenôn* – but see Lee, p. 110 n. 22.

[131] 22,17-19 = *SVF* II 260.

It is day.

But you say that it is day.

Therefore: you are telling the truth.

20 This is not a syllogism. But it will be one if you add the universal premiss:

> Anyone who says that what is the case is the case, is telling the truth,

and add to this:

> Someone who says that it is day when it is day says that what is the case is the case.

The conclusion from the suppositions is:

> Therefore: someone who says that it is day when it is day is telling the truth.

25 Hence it is because of single-assumption arguments and arguments which conclude unmethodically that 'inasmuch as they are the case' is added – and also because of arguments which do not have canonical[132] premisses and which must be transformed in order for there to be a syllogism. For example, the argument which runs:

> If a non-substance is destroyed, a substance is not destroyed.
>
> But if the parts of a substance are destroyed, the substance is destroyed.
>
> Therefore: the parts of substances are substances.

(Aristotle refers to this argument at the end of the book.[133]) The
30 conclusion does not come about 'inasmuch as they are the case' – rather, the premisses must be transformed.

23,1 The[134] added phrase will also rule out, as he said,[135] arguments which contain a superfluous addition,[136] among which are those sophisms which make the non-explanatory explanatory.[137]

---

[132] *kurios*: i.e. the propositions presented as premisses are not premisses in the strict sense.

[133] See *An. Pr.* 47a22-31; cf. Alexander, *in An. Pr.* 346,10-14.

[134] 22,30-23,1 = *FDS* 1118.

[135] Reading *eipen* for *eipon*: the reference is to Aristotle, *SE* 168b22-6.

[136] For arguments with superfluous or redundant premisses, which were deemed not to be syllogisms, see Aristotle, *Top.* 161b28-30 (cf. *An. Pr.* 47a16-20); Alexander, *in Top.* 8,29-9,5; 13,28-14,2; 568,18-23; Sextus, *PH* II 156-67; *M* VIII 438-43; Boethius, *Syll. Cat.* 822C. See Barnes (1980a), pp. 164-75.

[137] See Aristotle, *SE* 167b21-36; 168b22-6; *Top.* 162a32-4; *An. Pr.* 65a38-b40; cf. e.g. Philoponus, *in An. Pr.* 456,24-457,7; anon., *Logica* 62; [Alexander], *in SE* 50,8-52,28. A standard example. Suppose that, in a reduction to the impossible of the claim that all white things are coloured, you argue as follows: 'All white things are coloured; all winged things are white; all crows are winged: therefore, all crows are white'. Your argument will be rejected with a cry of *'ou para touto'*: the conclusion does not *depend* on the premisses (the first premiss is redundant). But in a syllogism the premisses must explain the conclusion. Hence your argument treats what is not explanatory as explanatory.

2.4.5 'Positing'

Some[138] people try to quibble at the term 'posited', holding that it is not used as it should be. They say that position is properly ascribed to bodies which occupy places, but that utterances are incorporeal, 5
and that – according to Aristotle himself[139] – in definitional utterances one should not use words in metaphorical senses. These people seem not to understand the reason why in definitional utterances one should not use words in metaphorical senses. It is because the utterances then become less plain. Hence it is metaphors of this sort and in these circumstances which should be guarded against. But when through common usage a metaphor is 10
better known than the strict sense, there is no longer anything wrong in using it. And the metaphor in question is ubiquitous in common usage. (That is why Plato can use it as though it were obvious when, in the *Theaetetus*, he says: 'Posit a wax tablet in the soul.'[140])

2.4.6 Perfect syllogisms[141]

I call a syllogism perfect if it needs nothing else apart from the 15
assumptions in order for the necessity to be evident; <and imperfect if it needs one or more items which are necessary by way of the terms supposed but have not been assumed by way of premisses>. [1.1, 24b22-7]

If you look at it carelessly, you will think that the definition he has already given[142] is a definition of *perfect* syllogisms; for in it he said that syllogisms need no term for their necessity to come about, and now he calls a syllogism imperfect 'if it needs one or more items ...'. 20

---

[138] 23,3-6 = *FDS* 691.

[139] See *An. Post.* 97b37-9; cf. e.g. *Top.* 123a33-7; 139b32-140a2; *Meteor.* 357a24-32; Alexander, *in Top.* 425,16-426,5; Philoponus, *in An. Post.* 416,13-31.

[140] See *Theaetetus* 191C8-9 (Alexander's citation is not exact – but the crucial word *thes* is in Plato's text); cf. e.g. *Philebus* 33D2. As Alexander rightly says, the metaphorical use of 'posit' ('suppose') is as common as the strict or 'literal' use.

[141] See Mignucci (1969), pp. 191-2; Flannery; Patzig, pp. 43-61, and esp. 69-83 (for a history of the interpretations of perfection). Note that Ammonius (*in An. Pr.* 32,30-3) and Philoponus (*in An. Pr.* 36,19-37) give a different account from Alexander's: they stress that in imperfect syllogisms the necessity is not *evident*. Note, too, that some Peripatetics held that syllogisms in *all* figures were perfect: see esp. Themistius, *Max.*; Ammonius, *in An. Pr.* 31,14-32,7; scholium to Aristotle, 156b43-157b9. This view was championed by Boethus (see Moraux (1973/84), I, pp. 165-8, and later defended by Porphyry, Iamblichus and Maximus. Themistius opposed Maximus: the dispute was put to imperial arbitration, and the Emperor Julian decided for Maximus. Ammonius (*in An. Pr.* 31,22-3 = F 20 Graeser) says that 'Theophrastus seems (*phainetai*) to have taken the view opposed to Aristotle'; but see e.g. Bochenski (1947), pp. 64-5. (See also below, 30,6 note; 31,9 note.)

[142] i.e. at *An. Pr.* 24b18-22, the immediately preceding sentence.

But in that case, imperfect syllogisms will not be syllogisms. But the syllogisms of the second and third figures are imperfect, and he insists that they too are syllogisms. Again, at the beginning of the book he spoke of imperfect syllogisms as syllogisms; for he proposed to investigate 'what sort of syllogisms are perfect and what sort
25 imperfect',[143] suggesting that imperfect syllogisms are indeed syllogisms.

But this is not what is said here. In the definition of the syllogism imperfect syllogisms too are included; for Aristotle does not mean that the things which he says imperfect syllogisms need should be assumed from outside – rather, he means that they are present in the suppositions but stand in need of proof. For he says of them that
30 they 'are necessary by way of the terms supposed but have not been assumed by way of premisses'. And if the items from which the conclusion derives are present in the suppositions, then both in perfect and in imperfect syllogisms the conclusion will be deduced
24,1 'inasmuch as they are the case'; and hence imperfect syllogisms too will be syllogisms. (Arguments[144] which conclude unmethodically[145] are not even imperfect syllogisms; for in them the item which explains the deduction is added from outside.)

Imperfect syllogisms which need a single conversion in order to be reduced to one of the perfect and indemonstrable syllogisms in the
5 first figure need one item; and those which are reduced to a perfect syllogism by two conversions need more items, as he will later show.[146] Again, syllogisms which are proved by reduction to the impossible are also imperfect.

Thus arguments which need the addition of some account from outside in order for their conclusion to be deduced are not syllogisms at all (arguments which conclude unmethodically are of this sort), whereas arguments in which what is needed is present potentially
10 in the suppositions but which need to be helped and unveiled are indeed syllogisms but they are imperfect syllogisms (such are the non-indemonstrable arguments of the second and third figures).

Why do the assumptions in impossibles[147] not come from outside? No doubt the assumptions do indeed come from outside and are not even potentially present in the suppositions (as converses are); but
15 the assumptions do not syllogize the point at issue but rather something else. For the syllogism yields something which is rejected inasmuch as it is impossible and which explains why we may posit

[143] *An. Pr.* 24a12-13.
[144] 24,1-12 = *FDS* 1100.
[145] See above, 21,31 and note.
[146] i.e. in his account of second and third figure syllogisms in *An. Pr.* 1.5-6.
[147] If the text is right, 'impossibles' here must be shorthand for 'reductions to the impossible'.

the point at issue. That is why we say that it is proved not by a syllogism but from a hypothesis – the syllogism yields something else.[148]

2.5 Kinds of proposition

2.5.1 Universal propositions

For one thing to be in another as in a whole and for the other to   20
be predicated of all the one are the same thing. <We say that
one thing is predicated of all another when it is not possible to
take any of it of which the other is not said. And similarly for of
none.> [1.1, 24b26-32]

As his account proceeds, he will make use of the phrases
'such-and-such holds of every so-and-so', 'is in as in a whole', 'holds
of none' and 'is in none'. So first he makes these known to us. He
tells us what 'to be in as in a whole' and 'of every' mean, saying that
they are the same as one another and are used for universal   25
affirmative propositions; and he tells us what 'of none' and 'in none'
mean, saying that these too are always the same as one another and

---

[148] Alexander's later accounts of reduction to the impossible are clearer than this brief sketch: see below, 31,10-19; 77,20-5; 93,25-30; 112,25-31; *in An. Pr.* 259,8-260,6; 317,31-318,10; 386,5-30 – and for an example of his perfectly competent *use* of reduction see e.g. below 79,27-80,24. (For Aristotle's treatment of reduction, on which Alexander draws, see *An. Pr.* 41a23-32; 61a18-33; cf. e.g. Łukasiewicz, pp. 54-5; Patzig, pp. 144-56). The problem Alexander is here trying to solve is this: 'You hold that reduction to the impossible is a syllogistic procedure; and yet a reduction surely introduces something from outside. Therefore syllogisms may depend on external propositions' (cf. below, 84,19-31; Philoponus, *in An. Pr.* 37,16-38,29). Alexander replies that a reduction does indeed introduce something external, but that what a reduction syllogizes is not the point at issue but something else – and the reduction introduces nothing external to *this* item. An example will show more clearly what Alexander means. Suppose we want to prove *Baroco* by reduction to the impossible (see below, 83,24-84,3; and cf. Appendix 2, p. 211). We assume
    (1) M holds of every N,
and
    (2) M does not hold of some O.
(These are the premisses of *Baroco*.) Now hypothesize:
    (3) N holds of every O.
From (1) and (3) we can infer, by *Barbara*, that
    (4) M holds of every O.
But (4) is impossible, since it contradicts (2). Hence we must reject the hypothesis, (3), and thus posit its contradictory,
    (5) N does not hold of some O.
Here the external item introduced by the reduction is the hypothesis, (3): it is external to the premisses of *Baroco*, inasmuch as it is neither identical with nor derivable from them. The reduction is the argument (1)-(5). It is not, as a whole, a syllogism. It also contains an item external to *Baroco*. This item is indeed used in a syllogism. It is used in the instance of *Barbara* contained in (1)-(5); and in this syllogism it is not, of course, external.

are used for universal negative propositions.

Thus he says that 'of every' holds 'when it is not possible to take any of it of which the other is not said', i.e. when none of the subject can be
30   taken of which the predicate is not said. For every predicative proposition consists of a subject term and a predicate term,[149] and the predicate is truly said of every one of the subject when none of the subject can be taken of which the predicate is not said. For example,
25,1   animal is said of every man – for no man can be taken of which animal is not said. This being so, man is in animal as in a whole, i.e. it is included in it as in a whole;[150] for what is in something as in a whole is in a sense part of the universal: 'as in a whole' signifies that none of what is said to be in something as in a whole falls outside that which it
5   is said to be in as in a whole. For it is not only what is completely co-extensive with something else which is said to be in it as in a whole: parts too are in things as in a whole. What is said of every so-and-so may be of wider extension (as for example animal extends further than man); and it may also be of equal extension (as with risibility and man).[151]
10   Now in such cases we say 'of every' when we start from the predicate (for it is this which is 'of every'); and we say 'as in a whole' when we start from the subject (for it is this which is in something 'as in a whole').[152]

Note that he does not present universals in the same way here and in the *Posterior Analytics*.[153]

After giving an account of 'of every', he says 'And similarly for of none'. By this he does not mean that 'of every' and 'of none' are the
15   same (they are contraries), but rather that it is possible to define 'of none' on the basis of what has been said about 'of every'.[154] For if what has been said is presented the other way about, we shall get 'of none'. For when none of the subject can be taken of which the predicate is
20   said, 'of none' can truly be said. For example, 'Neigher holds of no man': there is no man of whom neigher is predicated. Thus neigher holds of no man and man s in no neigher. (Both of these formulations are used for universal ne$_{\downarrow}$ ative propositions.)

[149] See above, 14,25-15,4.

[150] For 'as in a whole' see Introduction, p. 28.

[151] Contrast Philoponus, *in An. Pr.* 39,15-24, who maintains that 'A is in B as in a whole' implies that A has a *smaller* extension than B.

[152] See above, 10,2-9; below, 53,19-25; 54,2-29; Ammonius, *in An. Pr.* 33,28-34,5; Philoponus, *in An. Pr.* 12,5-12. See e.g. Mignucci (1969), pp. 216-17; 224-7.

[153] See *An. Post.* 73b26-7; above, 12,2-3. (The words at 25,11-13 are exactly the same as those at 12,2-3: it is difficult to avoid the suspicion that their second occurrence is not due to Alexander.)

[154] Omitting *eipein peri tou kata mêdenos* (with the Aldine).

2.5.2 Modality

> Now every proposition is either of holding or of holding by
> necessity or of holding contingently. [1.2, 25a1-2]

25

With 'every proposition' one has to understand 'predicative'. For
Aristotle is here dealing only with propositions and syllogisms of
this sort – they are the ones of which he has given an account.[155]
Now in every predicative proposition a term is predicated of a term
either affirmatively or negatively, i.e. as holding of the subject or not   26,1
holding of it. Of those terms which hold of something, some hold
always while others sometimes hold and sometimes do not hold. If
what is said to hold holds always and is taken as holding always,
then the proposition is a true necessary affirmative. A true   5
necessary negative is a proposition in which what by nature never
holds of something is taken never to hold of it. If the predicate does
not always hold of the subject, then if it holds of it at the present
moment, the proposition which marks this is a true actual[156]
affirmative; and in the same way, a true actual negative is a
proposition which says that what does not now hold does not hold. If   10
the predicate does not hold of the subject at the present moment,
although it is possible for it to hold, and if it is taken in this way, i.e.
as being possible, then the proposition is a true contingent
affirmative; and a proposition which says of something which either
holds or does not hold but can both hold and not hold, that it is
contingent for it not to hold, is a true contingent negative.[157]

---

[155] See above, 11,17-20; 17,5-8.   [156] For our use of 'actual' see Introduction, p. 30.
[157] (1) Aristotle normally operates with three (or four) different modalities:
necessity, possibility, contingency (or 'two-sided' possibility) and, as an optional
extra, impossibility. It is *contingent* that P if and only if it is possible that P and also
possible that not-P (see e.g. *Int.* 23a7-26; *An. Pr.* 32a18-b2; cf. A. Becker, pp. 11-16;
Hintikka (1973), pp. 27-30, 47-51). See also below, 41,10 note. (2) The later
Peripatetics regularly gloss these modalities in temporal terms (see e.g. Ammonius,
in Int. 153,13-15; 215,11-14), so that 'Necessarily P' is equivalent to 'Always P' and
'Possibly P' to 'Sometimes P'. Hence 'Contingently P' becomes equivalent to
'Sometimes P and sometimes not-P', and 'Impossibly P' to 'Never P'. Traces of these
equivalences are to be found in Aristotle, but it is disputed how thoroughly
Aristotelian they are (see e.g. Hintikka (1973), pp. 93-113; Barnes (1977)). (3)
Alexander's account in the present text (cf. e.g. *in An. Pr.* 183,19-24) is clearly based
on some idea of temporal equivalences; but it is muddled. He preserves the equations
between 'Necessarily P' and 'Always P' and between 'Necessarily not-P' (i.e.
'Impossibly P') and 'Never P'. But for 'Contingently P' he offers the curious 'Possibly P
and now not-P' (which he finds in Aristotle at *An. Pr.* 29b29-32; cf. *in An. Pr.*
119,22-8). For 'Contingently not-P' he offers the odder 'Possibly P and possibly not-P
and (either now P or now not-P)'. And, what is oddest of all, the accounts he gives of
'Contingently P' and 'Contingently not-P' evidently do not run parallel. We can find
no way of explaining – let alone of justifying – this muddle. In addition, Alexander
glosses the non-modal 'P', or 'Actually P', in temporal terms: 'P' is equivalent to 'Now
P and not always P'. This has some strange consequences. Thus 'Necessarily P' does
not entail 'P'; 'P or not P' is not logically true. It also fails to consist with Aristotle's
remark at *An. Pr.* 34b7-18 (cf. *An. Post.* 73a29; 75b25-6), according to which 'you must

15   Such propositions are false when they mark something as having a mode which it does not in fact have. For since propositions make clear that what is meant by them holds, the propositions themselves, if they are assimilated to the mode of what they mean, correspond to the way in which those items hold.

Further, everything which holds of something either is inseparable from it and holds of it in its own right or else is
20   separable. If it is inseparable, the proposition which means this is necessary, and if it is separable, contingent. If a contingent proposition means what is already present, it is actual; if it means either what has been separated or what is not yet present but can hold, then it is contingent in the specific sense.[158]

2.5.3 Quality and quantity

Of these some are affirmative and others negative, in respect of each adjunct. [1.2, 25a2-3]

25   Having mentioned three kinds of proposition – necessary, actual and contingent – he says that in respect of each of these kinds some propositions are affirmative and others negative. For there are necessary affirmatives and necessary negatives, as we said, and it is the same with the actual and the contingent. Hence there are six kinds of proposition.

'In respect of each adjunct' means 'in respect of each different type
27,1   of predication', i.e. 'in respect of each addition of a mode'.[159] He claims that propositions take their necessity, actuality and contingency not from what underlies and is meant by them, but from the addition which is annexed or co-predicated, and which says
5   that this holds of this by necessity or that it holds or that it holds contingently.[160] For in this way there will be some true and some false necessary propositions – and similarly for the actual and contingent. For there would be no false utterances if something

take "holds of every" in an unqualified way and without limiting it in time (e.g. to now or to this time)' (cf. Hintikka (1973), pp. 68-9; 136-8).
[158] With the analysis of the modalities offered in this paragraph compare e.g. Alexander, *in Top.* 257,22-3. The analysis is problematical in itself; and it appears to yield results which are inconsistent with those yielded by the earlier temporal analysis. (But note Ammonius, *in Int.* 153,13-15: 'what is necessary in the unqualified and proper sense is that which (a) always holds of the subject in such a way as (b) not even to be able to subsist separately from it'. Here Ammonius combines Alexander's first account, in (a), with his second, in (b).)
[159] On 'modes' or *tropoi* see Introduction, p. 29.
[160] i.e. Alexander distinguishes between (a) propositions which say that P, where in fact it is necessary that P; and (b) propositions which have the form 'Necessarily P'; and he holds, correctly, that when Aristotle talks about 'necessary propositions' in the context of his syllogistic he has (b) and not (a) in mind. Cf. Ammonius, *in Int.* 88,12-28; 215,7-28; Philoponus, *in An. Pr.* 43,18-44,1; Barnes (1991).

were only called an utterance if it signified the nature of the objects
and were of the same kind as the things it signified. But we say that
assertoric utterances admit both truth and falsity. Thus, just as we
say that some affirmations[161] are true and others false (namely,
those which do not describe their subjects as they are), so we will   10
also say that some necessary propositions are false. False necessary
propositions will be those which say that what is not necessary is
necessary. These adjuncts and modes must therefore be annexed to
the propositions.

Again, of affirmatives and negatives, some are universal, some
particular, some indeterminate. [1.2, 25a3-5][162]   15

With these differences added to the propositions mentioned before,
there are eighteen kinds of predicative proposition in all. Three
necessary affirmatives, universal, particular and indeterminate; the
three negatives which are opposite to these; similarly three actual
affirmatives and three actual negatives; and the same for the   20
contingent. Hence there will be in all three times six propositions
differing from one another in form. From them predicative
syllogisms are constructed.

So much for the kinds and number of propositions. Next he sets
out to discuss their conversions. For most of the syllogisms[163] in the
second and third figures, which are all imperfect, require one or   25
more propositional conversion to prove them syllogistic, as will be
shown.

2.5.4 Modes[164]

It seemed to me worth asking why, when he is dealing in these books
with syllogisms and figures, he also introduces material differences
among propositions.[165] For the fact that a predicate belongs in this
way rather than in that way is a material difference. Differences of
this sort among propositions will seem to bear not on an argument's   28,1
being a syllogism *simpliciter* but on its being this or that kind of
syllogism – demonstrative, say, or dialectical.[166]

---

[161] Alexander must mean: 'some actual [i.e. non-modal] affirmative propositions'.
[162] cf. 24a17.
[163] Not all, since some can only be reduced by using reduction to the impossible.
[164] cf. Barnes (1990a), III.3-4; (1991).
[165] Note that 27,1-5 has effectively answered this question, by distinguishing
between propositions which say that P, where it is necessary that P (where necessity
introduces a 'material' difference) and propositions which have the form 'Necessarily
P' (which introduces a formal difference). The present section breaks the flow of the
argument: Alexander perhaps incorporated it into his commentary at a late stage.
[166] See above, 7,9 and note.

Or are these differences among propositions in general necessary
5 for the method and study of syllogistic? For since propositions which
differ in respect of the modes we have mentioned do not convert in
the same way, and since most of the syllogisms in the figures other
than the first are proved to be deductive by means of conversions, it
is indeed necessary for him to divide propositions according to the
modes. For it is by converting in one way in the case of the necessary
and the actual and in another way in the case of the contingent, that
10 the propositions will produce syllogisms. Moreover, when propositions which differ in respect of these modes are mixed[167] with one
another, they produce different syllogisms: for this reason too, the
difference among propositions in respect of these modes is necessary
for the study of syllogistic.

Thus, ignoring the material aspect, he annexes the modes
themselves to the propositions and produces universal proofs for
them; and he thereby shows that the difference among the
15 syllogisms depends not on there being this or that matter, but
rather on the annexed mode. So the proofs, being universal, are a
proper object of syllogistic study.

Aristotle mentions these modes insofar as they are useful for
syllogistic method – as is clear from the fact that there are
20 differences among propositions in respect of other modes too. If 'well'
or 'badly' or 'at length' or 'briefly' or 'fast' or 'slowly' is annexed, these
are modes and differences among propositions (e.g. in 'Socrates
talks well' or 'at length' or 'concisely').[168] But Aristotle does not
mention any of these when he makes his division of propositions,
since they do not bear on the generation or differentiation of
syllogisms.

25 Now these different modes are useful for the generation and
construction of syllogisms, but not for the generation of the *species* of
syllogism. For the different kinds of syllogism (i.e. the demonstrative, the dialectical and the sophistical) depend not on this
division but on the one which Aristotle discusses in the studies
30 appropriate to them. For there he says much about this theory and
makes it splendidly plain.[169]

---

[167] For such 'mixing' see 123,28-124,7: *mixis* was the standard term for 'mixed'
modal syllogisms (cf. the title of Alexander's work on the subject: Introduction, p. 3).

[168] cf. Ammonius, *in Int.* 214,31-215,3 (see Barnes (1991), XI). For other modes in
Alexander see *in An. Pr.* 270,10-28; 329,30-330,5; 411,35-7 (with reference to
Aristotle, *Int.* 22a13, where 'truly' is implicitly taken as a mode).

[169] See above, 7,9 note (and cf. 14,18-21).

3

Conversions

3.1 Conversions in general[1]

And in the case of propositions of holding, it is necessary for the 29,1
universal privative to convert in its terms ... [1.2, 25a5-6]

Next he discusses the conversions of propositions. The exposition of
this topic is of use to him in relation to the imperfect syllogisms, 5
which, as we said,[2] are constructed in the second and third figures;
for most of these are shown to be syllogistic by means of one or more
conversion.

There[3] are several sorts of conversion. Thus conversion is
performed on syllogisms, and syllogisms are said to convert – an
argument which converts from a syllogistic argument is itself said to
be syllogistic. These arguments convert together with an opposition. 10
For when we assume the opposite of the conclusion and co-assume
one of the premisses, we deduce syllogistically the opposite of the
other premiss. For what converts in this way from a syllogistic mode
is itself syllogistic. Aristotle will instruct us about the conversion of
syllogisms in the second book of the study before us.[4] 15

There is conversion together with an opposition among
propositions too. For the proposition saying 'What is not an animal
is not a man' converts from 'Man is an animal'.[5]

There is also conversion among propositions when an affirmation

---

[1] cf. e.g. below, 45,14-46,16; Alexander, *in Top.* 191,6-12; 582,23-6; and esp. *Conv.*;
also Galen, *Inst. Log.* vi 3-7; Apuleius, *Int.* 181,19-183,6; Ammonius, *in An. Pr.*
35,7-36,15; Philoponus, *in An. Pr.* 39,32-42,34; Boethius, *Int. Syll. Cat.* 785B-790C
(cf. *Syll. Cat.* 804A-809A). See Lee, pp. 79-94; Maróth, pp. 140-3.

[2] See above, 27,22-6 (or perhaps 23,21-24,7, if the previous section is a later
addition).

[3] 29,7-13 = *FDS* 1163.

[4] See *An. Pr.* 2.8-9. On conversion of syllogisms see also Alexander, *Conv.* 60;
Galen, *Inst. Log.* vi 5; Patzig, pp. 152-3.

[5] cf. below, 46,6-8; Alexander, *in Top.* 190,26-193,7 (on Aristotle, *Top.* 113b15-26,
whence Alexander's example in *in An. Pr.* is taken); *Conv.* 60-1; Galen, *Inst. Log.* vi 4;
[Ammonius], *in An. Pr.* 68,28; Lee, pp. 86-7.

is true together with[6] the corresponding negation. In this sense a contingent affirmative is said to convert from a contingent negative.
20 For example, if it is true (as a contingency) that it is contingent that every man is walking, then it is also true that it is contingent that no man is walking.

Conversion of terms when the items are true together is also called conversion of propositions. Conversion of terms occurs when we interchange and make the subject term the predicate term and
25 what was the predicate[7] the subject, preserving the quality of the converted proposition. The interchange of terms in the manner described is called conversion *simpliciter*[8] – for example:

Every man is an animal.
Every animal is a man.

Here the terms have been converted. When in addition to the conversion, the propositions which are converted, being assumed in the same way,[9] are also true together, then the propositions are said to convert from themselves.

3.2 Non-modal conversions

3.2.1 General remarks

30 It is this sort of propositional conversion which he now discusses, and he shows which of the propositions we have mentioned convert from one another and which do not. It will be shown that propositions convert from one another if their opposites convert from one another and that they do not convert if their opposites do
30,1 not convert.[10] Thus particular affirmatives are contradictorily opposed to universal negatives and particular negatives to universal affirmatives. Now universal negatives convert from themselves, as
5 Aristotle will show: given that a universal negative is true, then the proposition assumed in the same way but with its terms reversed is also true. For example, 'No man is a horse' is true, and 'No horse is a man' is true.[11]

---

[6] The verb *sunalêtheuein* is used in two ways: 'x is true together with y' sometimes means 'When y is true, x is true' (e.g. Ammonius, *in Int.* 161,11-16); more often, however, it means 'x is true if and only if y is true' (e.g. Ammonius, *in Int.* 272,3). The ambiguity leads to confusion and obscurity in some passages: see Lee, pp. 88-92.

[7] Reading *teôs* for *pôs*. cf. below, 75,13; 110,28.29.

[8] Or *anastrophê*: see Alexander, *in Top.* 264,19; Ammonius, *in Int.* 194,15; Philoponus, *in An. Pr.* 42,20; Sextus, *M* VIII 108; Galen, *Inst. Log.* vi 3 – and esp. *Simp. Med. Temp.* XI 463-6K; 498-500K. See Lee, pp. 80-1.

[9] i.e. having the same quantity and quality.

[10] cf. Alexander, *Conv.* 63.

[11] Some people denied that universal negatives converted and produced putative counterexamples: see Philoponus, *in An. Pr.* 48,18-49,5, and esp. Alexander, *Conv.* 69-74 (cf. Themistius, *Max.* 186). If the conversion is rejected, then the second figure

Particular affirmatives, which are opposite to universal negatives, also convert. For, given that a particular affirmative is true, then the proposition assumed in the same way but with the terms reversed is also true. For example, 'Some man is musical' is true, and so also is 'Some musical is a man.' So these too convert from themselves.

Universal affirmatives do not convert from themselves. For it is not the case that, if the proposition that every man is an animal is true, then the proposition which says that every animal is a man is thereby also true (were that so, they would convert from themselves). But the particular affirmative which says that some animal is a man does convert from it – hence the particular affirmative converts both from itself and from the universal affirmative.

Just as the universal affirmative does not convert from itself, neither does the opposite of the universal affirmative – i.e. the particular negative – convert from itself. For it is not the case that if it is true that some animal is not a man, it is also true that some man is not an animal. (If some propositions of this type can be assumed and found to be true together with their converses, this does not disprove what we have just said. For in all such cases, in order to reject a universal claim it is sufficient to prove that it is not so in some instances. For items which are not true together in all instances do not derive their convertibility from their own nature but from the special nature of their matter.[12])

Aristotle discusses these propositional conversions: he attempts to show that the conversions hold not only by appealing to the obvious but also by invoking certain universal arguments. He does not discuss indeterminate propositions because they are not useful for

10

15

20

25

30

---

syllogisms *Cesare* and *Camestres* cannot be reduced to *Celarent* and must therefore be treated as perfect (Alexander, *Conv.* 69; Themistius, *Max.* 180): see above, 23,14 note. Themistius explicitly and Alexander implicitly ascribe the rejection to the Megaric philosopher Eubulides; and Alexander explicitly says that he defended, against Aristotle, the thesis that particular negatives convert (see below, 30,26 note). Eubulides is known from Greek texts as an enemy of Aristotle's (e.g. Diogenes Laertius, II 109: see Giannantoni II B, 8-11); but the two Arabic texts provide the only evidence thus far discovered that Eubulides attacked Aristotle's *philosophical* position rather than his life and person. (It must be added that the attacks show no logical refinement at all.) The two texts also provide evidence that thinkers outside Aristotle's immediate circle knew the contents of his *Analytics*.

[12] cf. Alexander, *Conv.* 61; Boethius, *Syll. Cat.* 805B-806A; *in Cic. Top.* 1133BC. In *Conv.* Alexander goes on to remark that 'Eubulides argued against Aristotle's view that particular negatives do not convert from any proposition, saying that they convert sometimes from particular negatives and sometimes from universal affirmatives' (66: on 66-8 Alexander rightly scouts this suggestion). See above, 30,7 note.

syllogisms and because they are equivalent to particular propositions.[13]

3.2.2 Universal negatives

31,1   First, then, let the proposition AB be a universal privative. Now if A holds of no B, B will hold of no A. <For if of some, e.g. of C, it will not be true that A holds of no B. For C is something of B.> [1.2, 25a14-17]

Theophrastus and Eudemus gave a simpler proof that universal
5   negatives convert from themselves. (By 'universal privative' Aristotle means universal negative.) They conduct their proof in this way. Suppose that A is said of no B. If it is said of no B, then A is disjoined and separated from B; but what is disjoined from something is disjoined from something disjoined from it; therefore B is disjoined from every A, and if this is so, it is said of none of it.[14]

10   This is the way in which they argue. Aristotle, however, seems to use a reduction to the impossible to prove this conversion. We[15] have a reduction to the impossible when we hypothesize the opposite of what we wish to prove, co-assume one of the items agreed and supposed, and reject syllogistically something which is evident.[16] For the hypothesis because of which what is evident and agreed is
15   rejected is proved to be false by way of such a reduction, and when this has been proved false, its opposite is found to be true, since in every case one part of a contradictory pair is true and the other false. And this opposite is the point at issue which is to be proved.

Geometers make most[17] use of this method, but logicians use it
20   too; and Aristotle seems to use it here. For he says that 'if A holds of

---

[13] 'B holds of A' is equivalent to 'B holds of some A'; 'B does not hold of A' to 'B does not hold of some A'. (For 'B holds of A' will be true if either all As are B or some As are B. But if all As are B, then some As are B. Hence 'B holds of A' is true if and only if some As are B.) This view (which finds support at e.g. *Int.* 17b29-37; *An. Pr.* 26a29-30; 29a27-9) is a commonplace in the commentators: e.g. below, 62,24; 94,20; 111,30-112,2; Alexander, *in Top.* 288,13-289,8; Apuleius, *Int.* 177,15-17; Ammonius, *in Int.* 100,21-3; 106,13-16; Philoponus, *in An. Pr.* 79,4-5; and see esp. Ammonius, *in Int.* 111,10-120,12, which argues at length for the equivalences (cf. Boethius, *Int. Cat. Syll.* 776C-778A; *Syll. Cat.* 802C-803B) against unnamed adversaries. See also Brunschwig (1968); Bäck.

[14] F 13 Graeser: cf. below, 34,13-15; Alexander, *in An. Pr.* 124,18-22; 132,24-32; 220,12-15; *Conv.* 65; Ammonius, *in Int.* 185,14-18; Philoponus, *in An. Pr.* 48,11-18. See Maier IIa, pp. 20-1; 44 n. 1; Bochenski (1947), pp. 54-6. Note that the idea of 'separation' was later adopted by Boethus (and hence Maximus) in connexion with the thesis that all syllogisms are perfect: Themistius, *Max.* 190-1; scholium to Aristotle, 157a13-24. (See above, 23,14 note.)

[15] 31,11-20 = *FDS* 1184.

[16] Reading *enargôn sullogistikôs* for *enargôs [enargôn M] sullogistikôn* (cf. Philoponus, *in An. Pr.* 90,20).

[17] Reading *pleista* (LM, Aldine) for *pleistoi*.

no B, B will hold of no A', which is what he wishes to prove. If
someone should not concede this, clearly he will say that its opposite
is true, i.e. that B holds of some A. For 'of no' and 'of some' are
contradictorily opposed, as Aristotle has shown in *On Interpreta-*
tion.[18] Hypothesizing that B holds of some A, he takes some of A of   25
which B holds, namely C, which is a part of A, and by means of this
he proves that A will hold of some B.

He proved the point at issue in a very brief compass; and that is
why some think he conducted the proof by taking particular
affirmatives to convert – and then accuse him of using reciprocal
proof.[19] For, on the one hand, when he wants to prove that universal   30
negatives convert, he invokes the particular affirmative (so they
say) and its conversion. On the other hand, when a little later on he   32,1
proves that particular affirmatives convert, he invokes the
conversion of universal negatives. But such a method of proof is
agreed to be unsound.

But Aristotle does not proceed as they think he does. It is agreed
that he proves that particular affirmatives convert by means of the   5
conversion of universal negatives; but he does not here prove that
universal negatives convert by assuming that particular affirmatives convert. He proves the point at issue, but he does not use
the particular conversion as something agreed and supposed. He
proves it by means of items already proved and supposed, i.e. 'of
every' and 'of none' and 'in as in a whole' and 'in none'. These are the 10
items he invokes in his proof of the conversion of actual universal
negatives.[20]

If it is supposed that A holds of no B, he says that it follows from
this that B holds of no A. For if B holds of some A (this is the opposite
of what was supposed, and one of the two must be true), let it hold of
C; for let C be some of A of which B holds. Now C will be in B as in a   15
whole and will be some of B, and B will be said of every C, since 'in as
in a whole' and 'of every' mean the same. But C was some of A; C,
therefore, is also in A as in a whole. But if it is in A as in a whole, A

---

[18] See *Int.* 17b16-20.
[19] The same charge is reported and rejected below, 100,24-6; cf. Alexander, *Conv.*
64-5; Philoponus, *in An. Pr.* 49,6-31. Bochenski (1947), p. 55, guesses that the charge
may have been levelled by Theophrastus, who therefore elaborated his new proof of
the conversion. (On reciprocal proof see Barnes (1990c), ch. 3.)
[20] i.e. the conversion can be proved on the basis of the definitions of 'of every' and 'of
no': it depends on what the mediaevals called the *dictum de omni et nullo*. See also
below, 54,2-29; 55,1-3; 61,3-5; 69,16-20; Alexander, *in An. Pr.* 126,1-8, where perfect
syllogisms are put on the same basis. (Cf. e.g. Philoponus, *in An. Pr.* 188,20-1;
198,19-20; 201,18-19; Boethius, *Syll. Cat.* 809C-810C.) Thus according to Alexander –
and almost all the later commentators – Aristotle makes his syllogistic depend on the
dictum, which is itself a 'dialectical' or 'topical' rule. Łukasiewicz, pp. 46-7, dismisses
Alexander's interpretation; but see e.g. Smith (1989), p. 111. On the later controversy
over the relation between syllogistic and topics see Stump.

will be said of every C. But it was supposed that C was some of B.
Therefore A will be predicated of some of B. But it was supposed
20   that A is said of no B – and 'of none' meant that there is no B of
which A is predicated.[21]

That he does not conduct the proof by assuming particular
affirmatives to convert is clear from the very expression he uses. He
did not say: 'For if B holds of some A, A holds of some B' – this would
25   be to conduct the proof by means of the particular affirmative. Thus
when he later proves that particular affirmatives convert, he
invokes the conversion of universal negatives by saying: 'For if of
none, A will hold of no B' – there he uses the conversion as
something agreed.[22] But here he does not assume the conversion of
particular affirmatives as something agreed. Rather, he sets out
30   some of A (namely C) and conducts the proof in terms of this – and B
is no longer said of *some* of this.[23] That is why we should say that for
the proof Aristotle used not the particular conversion but rather 'of
every' and 'in as in a whole'.

Or is it better and most faithful to the text to say that the proof
proceeds by means of exposition and perception, and not by the
33,1   method described, i.e. not syllogistically? For the method of
exposition depends on perception and is not syllogistic.[24]

As C, the item set out, we take something which is perceptible and
is a part of A. For if B is said of a perceptible individual, C, which is a
part of A, then this same C will also be a part of B, since it is in it.
5   Hence C will be a part of both and in both. So A, insofar as it is
predicated of C, which is a part of itself, will also be predicated of
some B, since C is a part of B, being in it. For example, if it is
supposed that man holds of no horse, then if someone refuses to
concede that horse holds of no man,[25] he will say that it holds of
10   some man. If this man – call him Theo – is taken, it will turn out
that man does hold of some horse, since Theo was assumed to be

---

[21] If B holds of some A, then there is something – call it C – such that B holds of
every C and A holds of every C. (If B holds of some A, then consider the ABs, i.e. the
things which are both A and B: A holds of all of them, and so does B.) Hence, by a
syllogism in *Darapti*, we have it that A belongs to some B – which contradicts the
supposition that A belongs to no B. See Patzig, pp. 161-3, who finds this thought in
Aristotle, at *An. Pr.* 43b43-44a2 (and who maintains that 31,6-34,22 is 'one of the
finest parts of <Alexander's> commentary').

[22] See *An. Pr.* 25a20-2.

[23] *sc.* 'but of *all* of it'.

[24] On 'exposition' or *ekthesis* see below, 67,11-12; 89,12-13; 96,17; and esp.
99,27-100,14; 103,25-104,9; 112,33-113,2; Alexander, *in An. Pr.* 121,15-123,24; see
e.g. Ross, p. 318; Kneale, p. 77; Mignucci (1969), pp. 261-2; Lee, p. 93 n. 24; Smith
(1982); and esp. Thom, pp. 164-76. (See also Appendix 2, p. 211.) With Alexander's
account in the next paragraph compare *Conv.* 63-4; see Łukasiewicz, pp. 59-67;
Patzig, pp. 156-68.

[25] Omitting *toutôi* (with L). M offers *to*, the Aldine *touto*, for *toutôi*: either reading
will give the same sense as our preferred text.

both a man and a horse. But this is impossible, since it was agreed that man holds of no horse.

When in the third figure, he explicitly uses proof by exposition,[26] he uses it as a perceptual and not a syllogistic proof. And this is why he uses it here too: we do not yet know anything about syllogistic proofs. 15

Now by using this proof you can also show that particular affirmatives convert inasmuch as this too follows from what has already been said. Hence some deem him to conduct the proof by means of the conversion of particular affirmatives. But he does not do this: he does not invoke the conversion of particular affirmatives. For 20 he assumes that A holds of some B not because it converts but because C, which is a part of A, is also a part of B. Thus he continues: 'For C is something of B.' The particular conversion follows from this; but he did not invoke it. After all, it is possible to use the same proof to show that particular affirmatives convert from universal affirmatives.[27] But this does not mean that Aristotle is using it here. 25

That proof by means of exposition is something other than proof by means of conversion he has shown most evidently in the case of the third figure.[28] For he takes the combination in which both extremes are predicated of all the middle term, and first proves the syllogistic conclusion by conversion of one of the premisses. Then, after this, he 30 conducts a proof by means of exposition, suggesting that it is a different proof and distinct from proof by means of conversion. And 34,1 the proof he uses here in the case of the conversion is very similar to the proof by exposition which he uses there.

This, then, is the proof in the case of universal negatives. Aristotle conducts it without using either reciprocal proof or syllogistic 5 reduction to the impossible. The latter would not have been timely, and even if a proof by way of the impossible fits what he says, it does not follow that he actually used it to prove the point at issue. For the expository mode of proof is different from the reductive.

A[29] proof of the point at issue by way of the impossible comes about in the third figure: hypothesize that B holds of some A, i.e. of every C (where C is something of A), and co-assume the premiss 'A holds of 10 every C', which is obvious: then it can be deduced in the third figure that A holds of some B. But this is impossible, since it was supposed to hold of none. However, a proof through the third figure is untimely here.[30] So it is better to say that his remarks show that B must be disjoined from A if A is disjoined from B – this is what Theophrastus 15

[26] For *Darapti* see Aristotle, *An. Pr.* 28a22-6; below, 99,19-100,26.
[27] So Alexander, *Conv.* 63.
[28] See *An. Pr.* 28a22-6; below, 99,19-100,26.
[29] This paragraph and the next are repetitive and inconsistent: they probably represent an early version of Alexander's commentary.
[30] Later commentators did find a reduction in the text (e.g. Philoponus, *in An. Pr.* 47,14-15).

assumes without proof, as being obvious.

It is also possible to prove it through a syllogism in the first figure (just as Aristotle invokes reduction to the impossible³¹). If it is denied that universal negatives convert, then suppose that A holds of no B, and – if it does not convert – let B hold of some A. We get, in
20   the first figure, that A does not hold of some A – which is absurd.³² But it is untimely to prove something by a syllogism when we do not yet know about syllogisms. Hence we should use the method of proof which Aristotle set out.³³

3.2.3 Other propositions

<If A holds of every B, then B will hold of some A. For if of none, A will hold of no B. But it was supposed to hold of every B. – Similarly if the proposition is particular. For if A holds of some B, then it is necessary for B to hold of some A. For if of none, then A will hold of no B.> [1.2, 25a17-22]

Having proved the negative conversion, he invokes what he has proved for what he will prove next. For he proves that particular
25   affirmatives convert by invoking the conversion of universal negatives. If A holds of some B, then B holds of some A; for if of none (this is the opposite of 'of some'), then A will hold of no B, since universal negatives have been proved to convert. But it was supposed that A holds of some B. Therefore B will hold of some A.³⁴
30   That particular affirmatives convert from universal affirmatives is proved in the same way: if A holds of every B, then B holds of some
35,1   A. For if of none, we have a universal negative, which has been proved to convert from itself. Hence A will hold of no B. But it was supposed to hold of every B.

He does not mean that universal affirmatives never convert from

³¹ The Greek seems to mean something like this: 'We can also prove the conversion by using a reduction which involves a first figure syllogism – just as Aristotle proves the conversion by using a reduction which involves a third figure syllogism.' But Alexander expressly denies that Aristotle uses a reduction. Perhaps, then, the text means rather this: 'We can also prove the conversion by using a first figure syllogism, invoking a reduction of the sort which Aristotle uses elsewhere.' But it is hard to believe that the Greek can convey this sentiment.

³² 'This is perhaps the neatest example of an argument by substitution derived from an ancient source' (Łukasiewicz, p. 10).

³³ With the paragraph cf. Alexander, *Conv.* 65.

³⁴ Note that Alexander inverts Aristotle's order of exposition, taking the particular-particular conversion before the universal-particular conversion. So too at *Conv.* 63, where the universal-particular conversion is proved from the particular-particular conversion together with the law of subalternation. (If A holds of every B, then A holds of some B. If A holds of some B, then B holds of some A. Hence if A holds of every B, B holds of some A.) So too e.g. Boethius, *Int. Syll. Cat.* 786D-787A.

themselves – they do convert in certain material instances (e.g. in the case of co-extensional terms and properties).[35] But since they do not always convert, whereas particulars always do (for the particular is   5 true even when the universal converts), for this reason he says that particulars convert from universals.[36] For conversions – and in general deductions in the figures – do not depend, as I have already said,[37] on the peculiarities of matter (which is different in different cases) but on the nature of the figures themselves. That is why proofs in their case are universal.

> <If A does not hold of some B, it is not necessary that B should not hold of some A. E.g. if B is animal and A man: man does not hold of every animal, but animal holds of every man.> [1.2, 25a22-6]

That particular negatives do not convert he proved by way of a   10 material instance. For if there are any occasions or cases where it does not convert, universality is lost. Although it is true that
> Man does not hold of every animal (or: does not hold of some animal),

the proposition saying that
> Animal does not hold of every man (or: does not hold of some man)

is not true. For if its opposite is assumed, nothing impossible follows, as it does – so we have proved – with propositions which do   15 convert. 'Of every' is opposed to 'not of some'. If we assume that B holds of every A, it will follow that A holds of some B. It was supposed not to hold of some B. But it is not impossible that what holds of some should also not hold of some. Thus man, which does not hold of some animal, also holds of some animal.[38]

3.3 Modal conversions[39]

3.3.1 Necessary propositions

3.3.1.1 Necessary universal negatives

> The case will be the same for necessary propositions. [1.3,   20 25a27-8]

[35] On this argument see Barnes (1990a), III.7.
[36] Reading *autêi* (with B and the Aldine) for *hautêi* (Wallies: LM have *heautêi*). 'Particular affirmatives always convert from universal affirmatives; for even when "A holds of every B" yields "B holds of every A", it also – and thereby – yields "B holds of some A".'
[37] See above, 30,21-6.
[38] With this paragraph compare Alexander, *Conv.* 65-6; and see above, 30,26 note.
[39] On the issues raised in this section see esp. Wieland.

He says that necessary propositions convert in the same way as actual propositions, and here too he first proves that universal privatives convert from themselves, thus:

25   For if it is necessary for A to hold of no B, it is necessary for B to hold of no A; for if it is contingent that it holds of some, then it will be contingent that A holds of some B. [1.3, 25a29-31]

36,1 Actual universal negatives have been proved to convert; and since necessary universal negatives differ from actual universal negatives inasmuch as they hold by necessity, he conducts the proof with reference to the point at which what is now being proved differs from what has already been proved (i.e. with reference to the necessity). Let it be the case that B does not hold of no A by necessity
5   but that it is contingent that it holds of some A (this is what rejects or contradicts the necessary universal negative, as has been proved in the discussion of affirmation[40]). Then it will be contingent, he says, that A holds of some B. But it was supposed that A holds by necessity of no B.

      Here again he seems to have used the conversion of contingent particular affirmatives in his proof for necessary universal
10   negatives, even though he has not yet discussed conversions of contingent propositions.[41] Or should we rather say this? He holds it to be agreed that contingent particular affirmatives are opposite to necessary universal negatives (they are contradictories), and therefore assumes this. Having assumed it, then since what holds of some (if it does not hold by necessity) is said to be contingent or to
15   hold of it contingently, and since he has proved that actual particular affirmatives convert from themselves, it is them which he invokes. Thus he rejects the necessity by saying that it is contingent that A holds of some B; and he invokes the fact that what holds of some – when it holds – converts:[42] if it is contingent that it holds of some, then either it already holds of it or else it can hold of it at some time; and whenever it holds, it converts. In this way what by

---

[40] Reading *kataphaseôs*, with LM and the Aldine, for *antiphaseôs*: we follow the majority reading, for there is nothing else to go by. Alexander does not appear to be referring to a work of Aristotle's (but Philoponus, *in An. Pr.* 52,4-56,5, reads the point into *Int.* 22a24-33); perhaps Alexander refers to a work of his own – a section of his lost commentary on *Int.* or an otherwise unknown essay?

[41] For the charge see Alexander, *Conv.* 76-7; Philoponus, *in An. Pr.* 52,27-9. A. Becker, p. 90, argues that the text of *An. Pr.* does contain the 'vicious circle' which Alexander and Philoponus try to explain away; and he infers that *An. Pr.* 25a29-34 was interpolated by a later hand. Ross, pp. 294-5, agrees that there is a vicious circle, but he thinks that 'the reasoning is so natural' that Aristotle himself is probably responsible for it.

[42] Alexander's syntax is uncertain here (if indeed the text is not corrupt): we take *tôi ... antistrephein* to depend on *prosekhrêsato*, understood from 36,15.

necessity holds of none will at some time hold of some, which is   20
impossible. That 'contingent' is said of what holds but does not hold
by necessity he says a little later on when he distinguishes kinds of
contingency: he says that it signifies both what is necessary and also
what is not necessary but actual[43] – and this is the sense in which he
now uses it. And the opposite of what by necessity holds of none is
what contingently holds or will hold of some.[44]

What is necessary either is necessary *simpliciter* or is called   25
necessary with a qualification[45] – e.g.

> Man holds by necessity of every grammarian so long as he is a
> grammarian.

This proposition is not necessary *simpliciter*. (Theophrastus showed
the difference between them.[46]) For there are not always
grammarians, and men are not always grammarians. Since they
differ in this way, we must recognise that Aristotle is here   30
discussing what is necessary *simpliciter* and in the strict sense – it
is necessary propositions of this sort which convert.

3.3.1.2 Other propositions

If A holds by necessity of all or of some of the Bs, then it is   37,1
necessary for B to hold of some of the As. <For if it is not
necessary, A will not hold of some B by necessity.> [1.3,
25a32-4]

That necessary particular affirmatives convert both from necessary

---

[43] See *An. Pr.* 25a38-9 (cf. e.g. *Int.* 23a6-11; *Metaph.* 1019b30-3).

[44] (1) Philoponus elaborates the following argument on Aristotle's behalf (*in An. Pr.* 56,15-57,13):

> Suppose that necessarily A holds of no B and that it is not necessary that B holds
> of no A. Then it is possible that B holds of some A. Then at some time, t, B does
> hold of some A. Then at t A holds of some B. Then it is possible that A holds of
> some B. Hence it is not necessary that A holds of no B. But this contradicts the
> supposition.

Philoponus' reduction is sound, and it does not invoke the conversion of 'Possibly some A is B' in any vicious fashion. (2) Alexander *appears* to argue thus:

> Suppose that necessarily A holds of no B and that it is not necessary that B holds
> of no A. Then it is possible that B holds of some A. Then B holds of some A. (For
> here 'Possibly P' has the force of 'P'.) Then ...

This is unsound; for it says nothing of the cases in which 'Possibly P' does *not* have the force of 'P'. (Thus A. Becker, pp. 84-6, who finds the error again in 37,26-41,29 – and also, presumably, at 37,15-18.) But this is an uncharitable interpretation of Alexander. If we disregard, as a trifling slip, the words *hoion te* ('... or else it *can* hold of it ...') at 36,18, then we may find the sound Philoponan argument in Alexander's text. (No doubt Philoponus himself found it there.) And a similar defence can be made in the other two passages where Becker finds the same error.

[45] For the distinction see also Alexander, *in An. Pr.* 140,14-141,6; 155,20-5; 156,27-157,2; 201,21-4; cf. e.g. Ammonius, *in Int.* 153,13-26; 240,7-13. The ultimate source is Aristotle, *An. Pr.* 30b35-40.

[46] F 14 Graeser: see Bochenski (1947), pp. 73-4.

universal affirmatives and from necessary particular affirmatives, he
5   proves in the same way as he did in the case of universal privatives. If
A holds of every or of some B by necessity, and B does not hold of some
A by necessity, it will be contingent that B holds at some time of no A;
for the negation of 'It is necessary for it to hold of some' is 'It is not
necessary for it to hold of some', which is equivalent to 'It is
contingent that it holds of none'. ('It is not necessary for it to hold of
some' and 'It is contingent[47] that it holds of none' are the same.) But
10   when B holds of no A, A will hold of no B (this has been proved).
Hence, A will not hold by necessity either of every or of some B.[48]
(Aristotle omitted 'of every' and was content to take it that A no longer
holds of *some* B by necessity.[49] For instead of saying 'For if it is
contingent[50] for it to hold of none', he simply said 'For if it is not
necessary'.)
It is clear that he has not conducted the proof with contingent
15   negatives; for he holds that they do not convert. Rather, he brings it to
an actual negative, thus[51] subtracting the necessity. (He makes this
clear by no longer using 'contingent', but simply 'For if it is not
necessary'.) For he is supposing that actual negatives convert. (It is
clear from this that in the previous proof too he used 'It is contingent
20   that it holds of some' for an actual proposition; for there 'For if it is
contingent that it holds of some' should be understood to be used
instead of 'For if it holds contingently of some'.[52])

<The particular privative does not convert for the same reason
as we gave earlier.> [1.3, 25a34-6]

He says that no proposition converts from a necessary particular
negative, because none converted from an actual particular
negative; i.e. because it is proved in the same way – by way of terms
and material instances – that they do not convert. The refutation
uses the same terms:
        By necessity man does not hold of some animal,
25   and
        By necessity animal holds of every man.

---

[47] Reading *endekhetai* (with LB[2]: *endekhesthai* M) for *anankê*.
[48] See above, 36,11 note, for the argument.
[49] And rightly, since from 'It is not necessary for A to belong to some B' we may
infer 'It is not necessary for A to belong to every B'.
[50] Reading *endekhetai* for *anankê*. Note that Philoponus, *in An. Pr.* 57,24-58,27,
knows – and rejects – a variant reading in Aristotle's text: *endkhetai mêdeni* for *mê
anankê*.
[51] Reading *tautêi* for *tautês* (*aphelôn* here has the same sense as *anelôn* at 36,16).
[52] Above, 36,20-3.

3.3.2 Contingent propositions[53]

3.3.2.1 Contingent affirmatives

> As for contingent propositions, since being contingent is meant
> in several ways <(we say that the necessary and the
> non-necessary and the possible are contingent), in affirmatives
> the case will be similar in respect of conversion in all instances.
> If it is contingent for A to hold of every or of some B, then it will
> be contingent for B to hold of some A. For if of none, then A of
> no B (this has been proved earlier).> [1.3, 25a37-b3]

He showed us the homonymy of 'contingent' in *On Interpretation*
too.[54] For we use 'contingent' both of what is necessary, when we say   38,1
that it is contingent that animal is said of every man, and of what is
actual, if we say of what holds of something that it is contingent that
it holds. Here in saying 'the non-necessary' Aristotle means what
holds; for what holds differs in this way from what is necessary
while sharing with it the fact of holding at the present time. (Note   5
the expression: what holds contingently is the same as what is
signified by an actual proposition.) 'Contingent' is also said of what
is possible. He will explain what this means a little later on when he
refers to 'those which are said to be contingent inasmuch as they
hold for the most part and by nature – this is the way in which we   10
determine the contingent ...'.[55]
Now given that 'contingent' is homonymous and is predicated of
these several cases, he says that however the contingency is taken
(whether as necessary or as actual or as possible) contingent
affirmative propositions convert in the same way: particular
affirmatives convert from universal affirmatives, and similarly   15
particular affirmatives convert from particular affirmatives, i.e.
from themselves. He proves this by invoking what he has previously
said and proved. If it is contingent that A holds of every or of some B,
then it will be contingent that B holds of some A; for if it is
contingent that B holds of no A, then we have a universal negative,
and this has been proved to convert from itself. If contingency
signifies what is possible, then the negative which is assumed and   20
hypothesized is a necessary universal (for 'It is not contingent that it
holds of some' has this character), and this has been proved to
convert. If it signifies what is actual, then the proposition
hypothesized is an actual universal negative, and this too has been

---

[53] The lines of *An. Pr.* to which Alexander now turns are extraordinarily difficult:
see e.g. Maier IIa, p. 25 n. 1; A. Becker, pp. 59-65; 83-91; Ross, pp. 295-8; Hintikka,
pp. 35-8.
[54] See *Int.* 23a7-20. On the present passage see Sharples (1982).
[55] Aristotle, *An. Pr.* 25b14-15.

proved to convert. And if 'It is contingent that A holds of every or of some B' signifies what is necessary, it has been proved in this case too that its opposite, a contingent universal negative, will be such that at some time it holds of no B (for this is the way in which what is contingent is true); and it has been laid down that actual negatives convert.[56] (This was how he conducted the proof in the case of necessary universal and particular affirmatives.[57])

3.3.2.2 Contingent negatives

<In negatives it is not the same. With those which are said to be contingent inasmuch as it is by necessity that they do not hold or inasmuch as it is not by necessity that they do hold, the case is indeed similar. E.g. if someone were to say that it is contingent for man not to be a horse or that it is contingent for white to hold of no cloak. ... For if it is necessary for it to hold of some, then white will hold of some cloak by necessity – this was proved earlier. (Similarly too for particular negatives.)> [1.3, 25b3-14][58]

He says that the conversions will hold in the same way in the case of all the affirmatives, but that this is no longer so in the case of negatives. Rather, where contingency signifies what necessarily does not hold or what holds not by necessity (he means actual negatives in saying 'or inasmuch as it is not by necessity that they do hold') – when contingency is taken in these senses, the

[56] (1) Alexander argues as follows. If it is not contingent that B holds of some A, then it is contingent that B holds of no A. Then, since 'contingent' is ambiguous, there are three cases to consider. 'It is contingent for A to hold of some B' means either 'Possibly A holds of some B' or 'A holds of some B' or 'Necessarily A holds of some B'. The two latter propositions have already been proved to convert, and the first is readily proved to convert too. Hence in whatever way 'contingent' is construed, contingent particular affirmatives convert. Thus Alexander's argument rests on the thought that 'contingent' is *ambiguous*. But Aristotle does not hold, and it is not true, that 'contingent' is ambiguous; and Alexander's argument is thus based on a misconception. (2) Given that 'It is contingent that P' means 'Possibly P and possibly not-P', then the conversion can be shown as follows. Suppose that it is not contingent that B holds of some A. Then either it is necessary that B holds of some A or it is necessary that B does not hold of some A. Hence either it is necessary that B holds of some A or it is necessary that B holds of no A. Hence (by the conversions already established) either it is necessary that A holds of some B or it is necessary that A holds of no B. Hence it is not contingent that A holds of some B. But it is laid down that it is contingent that A holds of some B. (3) *Aristotle's* text remains obscure. When he says 'For if of none ...' he ought to mean (as Alexander sees) 'For if it is contingent that B holds of no A'; but it is hard to see how this hypothesis, which is not the negation of 'It is contingent that B holds of some A', can ground the proof.
[57] See above, 36,16-21; 37,15-18.
[58] Note that Alexander's text of Aristotle differs from the modern text at a crucial point in this passage (see Appendix 1). In consequence, his interpretation of Aristotle will not match our text.

conversions are the same. And this is reasonable enough. For in them only the name is changed and what is signified is the same as in the cases which have already been proved. In the case of contingencies of this kind, universal negatives convert from universal negatives, and no proposition converts from particular negatives.

    Of his examples,

        It is contingent for man not to be a horse
signifies a necessary negative, whereas
        It is contingent for white to hold of no cloak
signifies an actual negative. The conversions which he sets down are plain. He said 'For if it is necessary for it to hold of some, then white will hold of some cloak by necessity', since necessary particular affirmatives must be opposed to contingent universal negatives, and the actual proposition supposed was expressed in terms of contingency. Its opposite, then, will contain necessity in its expression, but what is signified by it will be an actual particular affirmative; for this is opposite to an actual universal negative. And if we take a particular affirmative which is necessary in the strict sense, this too has been proved to convert.

    He says 'Similarly too (*sc.* it will hold) for particular negatives'; for no proposition converts from contingent particular negatives, when they signify either what is necessary or what is actual.

    But as for those which are said to be contingent inasmuch as they are for the most part and by nature <– this is the way in which we determine the contingent – here the case will not be similar for negative conversions. Rather, the universal privative proposition does not convert whereas the particular does convert. This will be evident when we discuss the contingent.> [1.3, 25b14-19]

The third sense of the contingent was the possible. Here in saying what it is, he speaks of 'those which are said to be contingent inasmuch as they are for the most part and by nature'. He set down only this sort of contingency[59] – what holds for the most part and is by nature (for what is by nature holds for the most part), since only this sort is useful for syllogistic purposes. The possible also covers what holds in equal part and what holds for the lesser part, but syllogisms with matter of this kind are of no use. For no art and no science deals with this sort of contingency and possibility. For in the case of such matter the opposite will hold no more and no less than what is proved syllogistically to hold – and in the case of what holds

[59] Perhaps we should read *dunatou* for *endekhomenou*?

for the lesser part, it is actually the opposite which holds more than
what is deduced – as Aristotle himself will say when he discusses
syllogisms of the contingent.[60] Thus he deals only with the kind of
contingency and possibility which holds for the most part and which
is by nature or according to nature (which itself holds for the most

30   part). For some natural events are indeed proved on such a basis,
and there are some arts concerned with what is in this way
contingent – for instance, the conjectural arts.[61] A doctor assumes

40,1   that someone who is ill in such-and-such a way is for the most part
unwell from surfeit, and that someone who is unwell from surfeit is
for the most part cured by venesection; and he deduces that it is
contingent that someone who is ill in this way will be cured by
venesection. Taking this to be so, he performs a venesection.[62] For

5   this reason, there is syllogistic utility in these things.
    In the case of what is said to be contingent in this sense, he says
that negative conversions are no longer the same as those he proved
in the case of necessary and actual propositions. For in the latter
cases, universal negatives convert from themselves and nothing
converts from particular negatives. But in the former case he says

10   that contingent universal negatives do not convert with themselves
(but do convert with particulars: this is what he means), and that
particular negatives convert from themselves. Thus it is the other
way about here in comparison with the former modes. He says that
he will explain the reason for such conversions when he discusses
the syllogisms which come about from contingent propositions.[63]

15   For the moment, in addition to what we have said, let it be
clear that 'It is contingent that it holds of none or not of some'
has an affirmative figure. <For 'It is contingent' is ranked in
the same way as 'is', and 'is' (where it is co-predicated) always
and in every case makes an affirmation – e.g. 'It is not good' or

---

[60] See *An. Pr.* 32b18-22 (cf. e.g. *An. Post.* 87b19-27; *Metaph.* 1027a19-26;
Alexander, *in An. Pr.* 164,17-165,15 (cf. 168,31-169,10); Philoponus, *in An. Pr.*
61,16-62,4). For syllogisms involving what holds 'for the most part' see also *An. Pr.*
43b32-6; *An. Post.* 96a8-19; cf. Maier, IIa, p. 138 n. 1; A. Becker, pp. 76-83; Ross,
p. 328; Mignucci (1969), pp. 303-4; Barnes (1969), pp. 133-5; (1975), pp. 184, 229; and
esp. Mignucci (1981).
[61] For which see, elsewhere in Alexander, *in An. Pr.* 165,8-15; 300,3; *in Top.*
32,12-34,5; *Quaest.* 61,1-28. The distinction is a commonplace (e.g. Philodemus, *Rhet.*
v 34-vi 19; Sextus, *M* II 13) and goes back by way of Aristotle (e.g. *EN* 1112a34-b8) to
Plato (*Philebus* 55E-56C). The rules or general principles of an art guarantee success
in the sense that if you apply them correctly you will achieve your end. An art is
conjectural if it can only guarantee success *for the most part*.
[62] Medicine was a stock example of a conjectural art (e.g. Galen, *Meth. Med.* X 206K;
Opt. Sect. I 114-15K); cf. the reference to the art of medicine at Alexander, *in An. Pr.*
165,10 (and see Aristotle, *Metaph.* 1027a23-4).
[63] See *An. Pr.* 36b35-37a31; Alexander, *in An. Pr.* 219,35-221,13.

'It is not white' or generally 'It is not such-and-such' (this too will be shown in what follows).> [1.3, 25b19-25]

Aristotle says here that those propositions in which 'to be contingent' is co-predicated are affirmations (just like those propositions in which 'is' is predicated without 'to be contingent'). 20
This is true, and he stated and proved it in *On Interpretation*.[64] Yet the fact that contingent negatives are actually affirmations is not a sufficient explanation of why they convert in the same way as the other affirmations, i.e. of why particulars convert both with universals and with particulars. If this were sufficient the same 25
would have to hold of necessary negative propositions; for he showed that propositions in which necessity is co-predicated are also affirmations.[65] But even though they have this character, he proved that necessary universal negatives convert from themselves – although they are affirmations (for necessary negatives, although they are affirmations *simpliciter*, are called necessary negatives as a whole); and no proposition converted from necessary particular negatives. Thus he was not giving an explanation of the fact that 41,1
contingent universal negatives do not convert when he said what he posits here; rather he hypothesized it as something to be made evident later on, and he intimates to us that we must regard them as affirmations and investigate their conversions in this light.

He will give the true explanation of why they must convert like 5
affirmations when he proceeds further. For since contingent universal negatives and contingent universal affirmatives convert from each other and are true together if their terms are preserved in the same order (in the case of what is called contingent in this way), because of this the conversions of contingent universal negatives are like the conversions of affirmatives. For what contingently holds of none also contingently holds of all, and what contingently holds of 10
all also contingently holds of none.[66] This is not so for other propositions but only for those which are contingent in this sense. Thus it is because universal negatives are in this respect equivalent

[64] See Aristotle, *Int.* 21a34-22a13 (cf. *An. Pr.* 32a31-b3; 51b3-52b34) and the long discussion in Ammonius, *in Int.* 221,11-229,11 (esp. 227,3-25, on *An. Pr.* 25b19-25). See also Philoponus, *in An. Pr.* 53,15-56,5 (cf. 62,28-63,3) for a dispute over the matter (cf. Maier IIa, p. 27 n. 1).

[65] i.e. at *Int.* 21a34-22a13.

[66] See Aristotle, *An. Pr.* 32a29-b1; cf. e.g. Alexander, *in An. Pr.* 158,24-161,2; 218,20-4. The conversion was rejected by Theophrastus and Eudemus (whom the later Platonists followed): Alexander, *in An. Pr.* 199,7-10; [Ammonius], *in An. Pr.* 45,42-46,1 [= Eudemus, F 13 Wehrli]; 49,7-12 [= F 14 Wehrli] (all placed under Theophrastus, F 16 Graeser). The conversion depends on Aristotle's 'two-sided' conception of contingency (above, 26,14 note): in effect, Theophrastus and Eudemus jettisoned the two-sided conception, and thus rejected the conversions associated with it (cf. below, 41,23 note). See e.g. A. Becker, pp. 14-15; Bochenski (1947), pp. 74-6; Barnes (1969), p. 135.

to universal affirmatives – and are in any case affirmations – that they convert in the same way, and not because they have 'contingent' co-predicated.

For given that the negation is equivalent to the affirmation, if the
15   universal negative converted, then contingent universal affirmatives would also convert with themselves. But this is false. For suppose someone were to say that, if it is contingent that A holds of no B and also of every B, then it is also contingent that B holds of no A: then inasmuch as it would also be contingent that it holds of every A, contingent universal affirmatives would convert from themselves, which is not true. For if it is contingent that every man
20   is walking, it is not thereby contingent that everything which walks is a man.

This, then, is why Aristotle denies that contingent universal negatives convert from themselves.[67] But Theophrastus says that in fact they convert in the same way as other negatives.[68] I shall discuss the difference between them in more detail when I talk about contingent propositions.[69]

25   And in respect of conversions the case will be similar to that of the others. [1.3, 25b25]

Having said that contingent negatives are affirmatives, he says that in respect of conversion they will behave in the same way as the others, *sc.* as the affirmatives.[70] Contingent particular negatives[71] convert both from contingent universals and from contingent particulars. For this is how the affirmatives convert.

---

[67] Alexander has in effect summarized the argument of *An. Pr.* 36b35-37a31: cf. *in An. Pr.* 221,16-227,9.

[68] F 15 Graeser; cf. Alexander, *in An. Pr.* 219,35-221,5 [= Eudemus, F 16 Wehrli]; anon, *in Int. An. Pr.* 100 Mynas [= Eudemus, F 15 Wehrli]; cf. A. Becker, pp. 65-7; Bochenski (1947), p. 74 (see above, 41,10 note).

[69] i.e. at *in An. Pr.* 219,35-221,5.

[70] So too Philoponus, *in An. Pr.* 63,19-64,7; Ross, pp. 299-300. For a contrary view see Maier, IIa, p. 27 n. 1; see also Mignucci (1969), pp. 209-10.

[71] Reading *apophatikêi* (Aldine) for *kataphatikêi*.

4

The First Figure

4.1 Introductory

4.1.1 General remarks

> Having determined these issues, let us now say by what means 41,30
> and when and how every syllogism comes about. We must
> discuss demonstration later. [1.4, 25b26-8]

After these preliminary remarks he proposes to discuss the issues to   42,1
which they were preliminary.

As to by what means syllogisms come about, they come about by
means of premisses. Since syllogisms come about by means of a
particular compounding of premisses, he added 'when' and 'how' to
'by what means'. 'When' signifies the combinations and figures: in
the figures and combinations in which syllogisms come about the   5
premisses must share a term. It also signifies the quality of the
premisses: syllogisms do not come about from all compounded
premisses (they do not come about from two negatives or from two
particulars, as he will show).[1]

'How' means the combinations in each figure[2] and the modes of
the syllogisms. For if a syllogism is to come about from the
premisses, they must be compounded not in any way whatsoever but   10
in the appropriate order. For syllogisms come about by means of
certain kinds of premisses and in figures (which he will discuss), and
in these figures they come about according to a particular
conjunction of the premisses with each other. For in each figure
there are both non-syllogistic and syllogistic combinations,
depending on the particular compounding of the premisses.

Thus: 'By what means?' – By means of premisses. 'When and   15
how?' – From premisses of such-and-such a sort, compounded in
such-and-such a way – where 'when' makes clear that one must take
such-and-such a sort of premisses and 'how' a compounding of
such-and-such a type.

---

[1] See Aristotle, *An. Pr.* 41b6-31; cf. Alexander, *in An. Pr.* 266,8-270,8.
[2] Reading *skhêma* for *skhêmatôn*.

<We must discuss syllogisms before demonstration because
syllogisms are more universal: a demonstration is a syllogism,
but not every syllogism is a demonstration.> [1.4, 25b28-31]

Here he plainly presents the reason why, after having proposed to
discuss demonstration, he first deals with syllogisms: it is because
20   syllogisms are 'more universal'. And he tells us in what sense they
are universal by showing that there is no conversion: 'a
demonstration is a syllogism, but not every syllogism is a
demonstration.' Since syllogisms stand in this relation to
demonstrations they are primary with regard to them. This indeed
is the explanation of the titles *Prior* and *Posterior Analytics* which
25   have been given to these studies, as we have said.[3] For in order to
define demonstrations and to place them in the genus of syllogisms,
one must learn first what a syllogism is, and by what means it comes
about, and when, and how these means must relate to each other.

He has added 'every syllogism',[4] although he discusses only
predicative syllogisms, because he thinks that only these are
30   syllogisms in the strict sense, as he will show later on. For he thinks
that no syllogism from a hypothesis syllogizes the point at issue.[5]

4.1.2 Syllogisms and justification

43,1   Now when three terms so stand to one another that the last is
in the middle as in a whole ... [1.4, 25b32-3]

Now comes his account of the syllogistic figures – the figures in
which all syllogisms, both perfect and imperfect, have their
5   construction; and he first discusses what is called the first figure, in
which the perfect syllogisms are generated.

A syllogism is a type of justification;[6] for when you syllogize
something, you justify and prove it by means of certain things – that
is to say, when you syllogize, you justify a disputed point by means
of things which have been justified. But not all justifications are
10   syllogisms. So we could do worse, perhaps, than say a few things
about justification; for in this way syllogistic justification will be

[3] See above, 6,32-7,11.

[4] i.e. in *An. Pr.* 25b27, in the previous lemma.

[5] See *An. Pr.* 50a16-b4; Alexander, *in An. Pr.* 386,5-30 (cf. above, 24,18 note); on
syllogisms 'from a hypothesis' in Aristotle see Striker; Lear, ch. 3. Alexander is no
doubt alluding, generally, to 'hypothetical' syllogisms: a hypothetical syllogism is a
syllogism in which at least one premiss is a hypothetical proposition (on hypothetical
propositions see above, 11,20 note). For the stock contrast between categorical and
hypothetical syllogistic see e.g. the little essay in [Ammonius], *in An. Pr.* IX 22-XI 36;
cf. e.g. Mueller (1969); Frede (1974b); Barnes (1983), (1985); Maróth.

[6] cf. Aristotle, *An. Pr.* 68b8-14.

better known.[7]

Now anyone who justifies something or wishes to make it known, justifies it on the basis of some other item or items. Nothing is proved and justified on its own basis, otherwise everything would be justified. Since, then, justification is based on some other item, either you prove the point at issue on the basis of what is whole and universal and inclusive (the point at issue is either some part of that 15 by means of which the justification is effected or, more generally, is something of it; and it is proved by means of it), or you prove the whole on the basis of its parts or a part on the basis of some part falling under the whole.

When a part is proved or justified on the basis of a part, such a proof (and the justification so conducted) is called a paradigm.[8] For instance, someone opposes Dionysius' demand that the Syracusans give him a bodyguard on the grounds that if he gets it he will aim at 20 a tyranny; and he justifies this by observing that when Pisistratus got the bodyguard he demanded from the Athenians, he became a tyrant; and that Theagenes did the same to the Megarians. Each of the items − both what is being proved and that by means of which the proof is effected (and the demand opposed) − are parts of a whole: the whole being the fact that all those who demand a bodyguard aim at tyranny.[9] So he produces a justification[10] by way 25 of the one part, which he uses to establish the other; and the argument proves an unknown and disputed part by means of a known and justified part.

When the whole is justified and proved on the basis of the parts, such a proof is called an induction.[11] For instance: men move their

---

[7] Aristotle says that 'a justification is a sort of demonstration; for we take something to be justified *par excellence* when we deem it to have been demonstrated' (*Rhet.* 1355a4-6: cf. Grimaldi, pp. 349-56; Sprute, pp. 58-67); and he analyses justifications by way of the part/whole relation (*Rhet.* 1357b26-30; cf. *An. Pr.* 49b37-50a1; 64a15-17, b11-13; 69a13-16; see Introduction, p. 28, on 'in as in a whole', and in general Barnes (1988)). Usually he distinguishes *two* varieties of justification: syllogisms (the rhetorical version of which is the enthymeme) and inductions (the rhetorical version of which is the paradigm) see *Rhet.* 1356a35-b10; *An. Pr.* 68b8-14; *Top.* 103b3-7; *SE* 165b27-8 (followed by Alexander, *in Top.* 62,6-13; Apuleius, *Int.* 185,10-20). But at *An. Pr.* 69a16-19 he implicitly marks *three* varieties of justification, inasmuch as there he distinguishes between inductions and paradigms; and the later tradition generally adopts this three-fold division (e.g. Alexander in the present passage; Galen, *Simp. Med. Temp.* XI 470K; *Sem.* IV 581K; Ammonius, *in An. Pr.* 28,21-29,19; Philoponus, *in An. Pr.* 34,12-30; David, *in Porph. Isag.* 88,12-89,10). Note that here Alexander, following Aristotle, confounds the notion of an argument with the notion of a proof: see esp. 44,14, where syllogisms are simply said to be *proofs*.

[8] The definition and the example of Dionysius (for whom see Diodorus Siculus, XIII 91-5) are taken from Aristotle, *Rhet.* 1357b25-1358a2 (cf. 1393a25-1394a18).

[9] See Plato, *Rep.* 566B.

[10] Reading *ho de* [with the MSS: *ho dê* Wallies] *pistin* [*piston* MSS].

[11] cf. e.g. Aristotle, *Top.* 105a13-16; 108b10-11; see Ross, pp. 481-5; Hintikka

lower jaw, as do horses, dogs, cows and sheep; therefore every animal does.[12] Induction is a path by way of known and justified
44,1   particulars toward the universal which is unknown. Both these things (induction and paradigm) contain plausibility but not necessity.[13]

Aristotle discusses these types of justification at greater length in the second book,[14] showing how they differ from syllogistic justification, that they too are useful, and how[15] they are subsumed
5   under syllogistic justification. Thus for present purposes what we have said about them is enough.

When a part is justified from the whole, such a justification is called a syllogism; and this is the most compelling[16] type of justification. For anything which applies to or holds of a universal and a totality, by necessity also holds of what is within it and is
10   included in it. If you assume that all justice is noble and that everything noble is good, then it is by means of the whole and the universal – that is, by means of the fact that everything noble is good – that you prove justice to be good, this being a part of the fact that everything noble is good, since justice is indeed noble. (Aristotle has already given an account of what a syllogism is.[17])

4.1.3. Problems

15   Now since a syllogism is a proof, by means of agreed items, of something disputed, and since what is disputed and proposed for proof is called a problem, let us say a little about problems.[18] Problems belong to the genus of propositions;[19] for problems and assumptions and agreements and conclusions and axioms are all the same in genus – they are all propositions, differing from one another in aspect.[20] When a proposition is put forward for proof as not being
20   known, it is called a problem; when it is assumed in order to prove

---

(1980); Burnyeat, pp. 200-1.
    [12] The example is a stock one: e.g. Sextus, *PH* II 185; Apuleius, *Int.* 185,10-20; Ammonius, *in An. Pr.* 28,32-29,2; Philoponus, *in An. Pr.* 34,21-6. The usual point of the example is that the induction is misleading – for the crocodile does not move its lower jaw (Herodotus, II 68; Aristotle, *HA* 492b23-6; *PA* 691b5-16).
    [13] See above, 18,8-12; cf. Apuleius, *Int.* 185,10-20; Ammonius, *in An. Pr.* 28,23-5; Philoponus, *in An. Pr.* 34,10-14.
    [14] Paradigms at *An. Pr.* 68b38-69a19, inductions at 68b13-37.
    [15] Reading *kai pôs* for *pôs*.
    [16] *anankastikôtatos*: cf. Aristotle, *Top.* 105a16-19 (cf. *An. Pr.* 68b35-7); Alexander, *in Top.* 86,21-87,6; cf. Long, pp. 137-9.
    [17] i.e. at *An. Pr.* 24b18-22.
    [18] cf. Aristotle, *Top.* 101b16-36 (cf. Alexander, *in Top.* 40,13-41,16): a 'problem' has the form of a question: 'Is it the case that P, or not?' (see e.g. below, 46,25).
    [19] On *protasis* as a genus see above, 11,4 note.
    [20] cf. Apuleius, *Int.* 183,22-6; Ammonius, *in Int.* 10,2-4; *in An. Pr.* 26,34-27,4; Philoponus, *in An. Pr.* 11,25-36; 22,4-15; *in Cat.* 11,20.

something else, it is an assumption[21] or an agreement (as Plato calls it[22]) or a proposition in the special sense;[23] it is an axiom if it is true and known through itself; and if it has been proved, it is a conclusion (for anything which has been proved is a conclusion from the items by means of which it was proved).

Thus problems belong to the genus of propositions, and every proposition consists of a subject term and a predicate term – the subject being that about which something is said, the predicate that 25 which is said about it;[24] and again, the subject is that to which the quantitative determination of the proposition is annexed ('every' or 'no' or 'some' or 'not every')[25] and the predicate is that to which is annexed 'is' or something equivalent to 'is' which includes 'is' potentially in itself.[26] Well then, since there are two terms in a problem – the subject, and the predicate, which must be proved to 30 hold or not to hold of the subject – there must be some third term to prove it, a term which, when it is co-assumed, will either bring the 45,1 terms in the problem together or else separate and part them. This term which is co-assumed from outside must stand in a certain relation to the two terms in the problem. When it is taken, it becomes a middle term for them both, dividing the problem and making the one proposition two. It is itself introduced into each of the two 5 premisses, being compounded with each of the terms of the problem in turn, now with the subject and now with the predicate. You can recognize the middle term, which has been introduced from outside, inasmuch as it is taken twice and is present in both the premisses.

A conjunction of propositions of this sort is called a combination: there is a combination when two propositions share one term, which 10 is a middle term. For when propositions differ from one another, then either they share nothing at all with each other (e.g. 'Everything just is noble' and 'Every pleasure is good'), or else they share something; and if they share something, then either they share one term or else they share the two terms.

---

[21] cf. e.g. *in Top.* 23,21.
[22] See *Theaetetus* 155AB; cf. Maróth, pp. 25-32.
[23] i.e. a premiss: see Introduction, p. 22.
[24] See above, 14,27-15,4.
[25] For the four 'quantitative determinations' or quantifiers see e.g. below, 65,26-7; 100,11-14; Galen, *Inst. Log.* ii 5; Ammonius, *in Int.* 89,2-36. The quantifiers are taken to modify the subject term (cf. Alexander, *in An. Pr.* 297,22-3; Philoponus, *in An. Pr.* 277,29-31; *in An. Post.* 155,24-5): the predicate term is not quantified (see below, 58,29 note). See also Introduction, pp. 28-9.
[26] On the copula see above, 15,23-16,17 and notes. For the thought that it is annexed to the predicate see above, 16,8-10 (cf. e.g. Alexander, *in An. Pr.* 406,32-5). Ammonius says, more persuasively, that 'is' is added to 'the terms' and serves to 'bind them together' (*in Int.* 165,10-16).

4.1.4 Propositions which share two terms[27]

Now it is among propositions which share the two terms that
15   oppositions and conversions of propositions are found.[28] For when
they share their terms in such a way that the terms preserve the
same order in both propositions but differ either in quality or in
quantity or in both, then we find the oppositions, i.e. the different
types of opposition.[29]

     When their terms are supposed in the same way and the quantity
20   is the same in both, but they differ in quality, then if they are
universal they are contraries. For universal affirmatives and
universal negatives, when they have the same terms in the same
order and differ only in respect of being affirmative and negative,
are contraries. When both are particular, they are called
subcontraries (these seem to stand in opposition to one another but
25   are not in fact opposed[30]). When their quality and also the order of
their terms are the same but they differ in quantity, then they are
subalterns (and these are not in any way opposed). Universal
affirmatives stand in this relation to particular affirmatives, and
universal negatives to particular negatives. When they differ both
30   in quantity and in quality and have the same terms ordered in the
same way, then they are contradictories. Universal affirmatives and
particular negatives stand in this relation to one another, as do
46,1 universal negatives and particular affirmatives – these are
contradictorily opposed to one another.

     When propositions share their two terms with one another but the
terms in them are not in the same order but are taken inversely – it
is among propositions which share in this way that propositional
5   conversions are found.[31] For the conversion of propositions is a
matter of their sharing their two terms, inversely posited, and in
addition being true together. When they differ in quality, such
propositional conversions require an opposition – and they are
called 'conversions with opposition'. When they are the same in
quality, the conversions which are taken in this way and are true
10   together come about without an opposition. Of those which convert
in this way, some preserve their quantity as well as their quality –

[27] On this and the following section see Lee, pp. 65-74.
[28] On the *koinônia* of terms see e.g. Ammonius, *in An. Pr.* 36,8; Philoponus, *in An.
Pr.* 42,22; Boethius, *Syll. Cat.* 798C-799A. Galen calls such pairs of propositions
sunoroi or 'co-terminal': *Inst. Log.* vi 3.
[29] On the different types of opposition, which produce the so-called 'square of
opposition', see Introduction, pp. 26-7; cf. e.g. Apuleius, *Int.* 179,16-181,17;
Ammonius, *in Int.* 91,4-93,18. The terminology is Aristotelian, apart from the words
'subcontrary' and 'subaltern', which we find as logical terms first in Alexander.
[30] Note that Aristotle counts them as opposites at *An. Pr.* 59b8-11; but at 63b23-30
he remarks that they are opposites only *kata tên lexin*, in expression.
[31] See above, 29,1-30,6.

as was proved in the case of universal negatives, both actual and necessary (and similarly for particular affirmatives). Others have the same quality but disagree in quantity, namely those which convert with universal affirmatives (they are particular affir- matives), and similarly those which convert with contingent 15 universal negatives (it is contingent particular negatives which convert with them).

4.1.5 Combinations and figures[32]

These are the different ways in which propositions may share their two terms. When they share one term, they make combinations, as I have already said;[33] and the different ways in which the middle term is shared in relation to the extremes – the terms in the problem 20 – determine the different syllogistic figures. For this middle term, which is taken twice and connected with each of the extremes (which were the parts of the problem) may be so taken that it actually holds a middle position between them, being predicated of the subject in the problem and being subject for the predicate. Thus consider the problem: Is it the case that every just thing is good, or 25 not? If we introduce a term, noble, from outside and predicate it of just (which was subject) and make it subject for good (which was predicate), then we get the following combination:

Everything just is noble.
Everything noble is good.

When the middle term has this position, and when the premisses share the middle term in this way, we call this the first figure: when there is a combination in which the middle term, which is taken 30 twice, is predicated of one of the terms in the problem and made subject for the other, then this is called the first figure.[34]

Or again, the middle term may be predicated of both the terms in the problem, as in the following combination. Suppose we are investigating whether men are neighers or not. We take a third term, rational, and predicate it of both the others – both of man and of neigher (affirmatively of man and negatively of neigher). This 47,1 makes the following combination:

Every man is rational.
No neigher is rational.

This way of sharing the middle term in relation to the extremes

---

[32] On the definition of the figures see esp. Patzig, pp. 88-108.
[33] Above, 45,8-10.
[34] cf. e.g. below, 53,2-8; Alexander, *in An. Pr.* 349,5-7. Note that Alexander's definition is subtly but significantly different from Aristotle's at *An. Pr.* 25b32-5: in effect Alexander excludes, while Aristotle implicitly leaves room for, a fourth figure (below, 47,12 note). See esp. Łukasiewicz, pp. 27-8.

makes what is called the second figure.

    There is also a third way in which the middle term may be shared
5   in relation to the extremes, different from the ways so far
mentioned. This occurs when the term taken as middle is subject for
both the terms in the problem. Imagine that we are investigating
whether or not any substance is animate. We take animal as middle
term, and make it subject for both terms (both for substance and for
animate). Then we get:

        Every animal is a substance.

        Every animal is animate.[35]

10 In this combination the middle term is subject for both. Such a
conjunction of middle and extreme terms makes what is called the
third figure.

    There are only these three figures;[36] for (1) it is in general the way
of taking the middle term which generates the combinations and the
figures, and (2) it is impossible for the middle term to be connected
to the two extremes by any relation among three terms other than
15 those already described, and (3) every simple syllogism depends on
three terms and two premisses, as Aristotle will prove.[37]

4.2 Why is the first figure first?[38]

Since in each figure there are some syllogistic and some
non-syllogistic combinations, he will discuss these and show how
many syllogisms there are in each figure and what they are. And
20 first, as I said, he discusses the first figure.

    It is reasonable for that figure to be first in which the middle term
is middle not only in its relation to the extremes but also in order
and in position;[39] for since the middle term explains the generation
of the figures, it is reasonable that it should also be authoritative in
the matter of their order. And so he places before the others the
figure in which the same term is actually middle in all respects.

25   Again, the syllogisms which come about in this figure are perfect,

[35] Omitting *tis ara ousia empsukhos estin.*
[36] See Aristotle, *An. Pr.* 1.23 (esp. 41a2-20); Alexander, *in An. Pr.* 256,32-258,25;
Conv. 56-7; Albinus, *Didasc.* 158H; Galen, *Inst. Log.* xii 1; Ammonius, *in An. Pr.*
7,6-14. On the history of the fourth figure see Thouverez; on the logical and exegetical
problems connected with it see e.g. Patzig, pp. 109-27; Rescher; Ebert (1980); Thom,
pp. 24-7.
[37] See *An. Pr.* 41b36-42b26; Alexander, *in An. Pr.* 271,16-272,10.
[38] With this section compare Philoponus, *in An. Pr.* 65,4-66,26 (cf. 86,4-13);
Themistius, *Max.* 181-2; scholium to Aristotle, 151a46-b4. And see below, 94,5-17, on
the third figure.
[39] 'Order', *taxis*, sometimes refers to the role of a term as subject or predicate of a
proposition, and sometimes to the relative position of a word in a (standard) formula
or diagram; and exactly the same is true of 'position' or *thesis*. We cannot tell which
term here refers to which feature.

while those in the other figures are imperfect and are helped by this figure.[40] And the perfect is prior to the imperfect.

Moreover, the two figures owe their generation to the first.[41] For there are two premisses in the first figure, one on the major term and the other on the minor. (The major term is the term predicated in the problem – and also in the conclusion[42] – being called major because it has a wider extension than the term of which it is predicated. Actually, this is not always so: sometimes it has an equal extension. But that they are sometimes equal is a feature common to subject and predicate alike, whereas when they are not equal, it is a proper characteristic of the predicate that it is said to extend more widely and of the subject that it is said to extend less widely – I mean, in true propositions; for it is never the other way about.[43] Now each takes its name from its proper characteristic, even when they are equal: the predicate is called major even when it is equal, because it is its proper characteristic sometimes to be major and never to be minor. The subject is called minor, since this is its proper characteristic: it is never major in extension.) Well then, there are two premisses in the first figure. One of them contains the middle term connected to the predicate and major term, and for this reason is itself called major. The other contains the middle term connected to the subject and minor term, and for this reason it too is called minor. Now it is the conversion of each of these two premisses which generates each of the other two figures.[44] Hence for this reason too it is first in relation to them: it actually generates the others.

In syllogisms the universal is more authoritative (for proving something from a universal is the proper characteristic of syllogistic justification[45]), and the major premiss in the first figure is universal if

---

[40] cf. Aristotle, *An. Post.* 79a29-32; below, 53,8-10.

[41] On the 'generation' of the figures see below, 71,12-21; 94,10-17; 95,14-24; 97,14-30; cf. e.g. Alexander, *in An. Pr.* 136,1-2; Boethius, *Syll. Cat.* 812D-813B; Themistius, *Max.* 180-3. (Note that, according to Themistius, *Max.* 184, Aristotle, Theophrastus and Eudemus did not discuss the generation of the figures: the topic was introduced by 'the more recent Peripatetics'.) See Lee, pp. 120-3; Maconi, pp. 96-8; Lloyd (1990), pp. 21-3.

[42] See below, 60,16-18; 75,10-19; cf. e.g. Philoponus, *in An. Pr.* 67,18-30.

[43] What Alexander says holds only of true universal affirmatives: if it is true that A holds of every B, then the extension of 'A' is at least as great as that of 'B'. This is not so for any other type of proposition, and the standard explanation of 'major' and 'minor' in terms of relative extension will not in general work. See e.g. Patzig, pp. 97-100.

[44] By 'conversion' here Alexander means conversion *of terms* (see above, 29,23-9): 'Man holds of every animal; animal holds of no stone' is a first figure combination. Convert the first proposition and you get the second figure combination 'Animal holds of every man; animal holds of no stone'. Convert the second proposition and you get the third figure combination 'Man holds of every animal; stone holds of no animal'. The conversions are not logical derivations: they are mere interchanges of terms.

[45] See above, 44,6-7.

15 the combination is syllogistic. Hence the conversion of the premiss which is major and more authoritative will generate the more authoritative and first of the remaining figures. But when this premiss is converted, the middle comes to be predicated of both extremes. It is therefore reasonable that the middle and second figure should be the one in which the middle is predicated of both extremes.[46] The third and last figure comes about by the conversion 20 of the minor premiss in the first figure: when it is converted, the middle comes to be subject for both extremes.

Again, the first figure is also first for the following reason.[47] In this figure all problems can be deduced – universal affirmative and universal negative and particular affirmative and negative. Hence for this reason too it is rightfully first, being complete and perfect in 25 every way. In the remaining two figures not everything can be deduced. Every proposition has two features, quality and quantity. In quantity, the universal is more valuable, in quality the affirmative.[48] Each figure excels the other in one respect: the second excels the third, inasmuch as universals can be deduced in it, and 30 they are superior in quantity (nothing affirmative is proved in this figure); the third excels the second, inasmuch as affirmatives can again be deduced in it, and they are more valuable in quality 49,1 (nothing universal is deduced in the third figure). Now it is universality rather than affirmativeness which is the proper characteristic of syllogisms; for the generation of syllogisms depends on universals, and it is by the universal that they differ from other sorts of justification. Reasonably enough, then, the figure which excels in the proper characteristic of syllogisms, i.e. which possesses this characteristic, is ranked before the figure which proves no 5 universal conclusion. (In the same way, the second indemonstrable syllogism excels the third and is ranked before it.[49])

Again,[50] some syllogisms are demonstrative, some dialectical, some sophistical.[51] The demonstrative are the most valuable, the dialectical hold the second rank, and the sophistical the third. Now the first figure is more appropriate for demonstrative syllogisms. 10 For those who demonstrate in the strict sense conclude to universal affirmatives (demonstrations come about by means of them), and these are proved through the first figure alone.[52] For this reason too, then, it is rightfully first. The second figure is more appropriate for dialectical syllogisms; for dialecticians, I suppose, always attempt to

---

[46] See below, 71,11.
[47] Later this is called the chief reason: below, 69,23-5 (cf. Apuleius, *Int.* 183,15-21).
[48] cf. Aristotle, *An. Post.* 85a13-86b39; Barnes (1975), pp. 175-80.
[49] i.e. *Celarent* is ranked before *Darii*: below, 51,12-16.
[50] On this paragraph see Patzig, pp. 154-5, who calls it 'logically grotesque'.
[51] On the species of syllogisms see above, 7,8 note.
[52] cf. Aristotle, *An. Post.* 79a17-32.

refute what has been posited by their partners and hence deduce
negatives – and to these the second figure is dedicated. Sophists
request and deduce indeterminate propositions. Inasmuch as the   15
indeterminate is equivalent to the particular,[53] and all propositions
deduced in the third figure are particular, this will be the
appropriate figure for them.

4.3 First figure syllogisms in general

4.3.1 General rules[54]

So much for the quality of the figures and their order and the reason
for their order. In the first figure, the major term must be predicated 20
of the middle and the middle of the last and minor term: the minor
and last term – either the whole or a part of it – must by necessity be
in the middle term as in a whole,[55] if there is to be a syllogism. If the
terms stand in this relation to one another, then the minor premiss
(i.e. the premiss on the minor extreme) will be either a universal
affirmative or a particular affirmative – but in any case an   25
affirmative. For if this premiss is not affirmative in the first figure, it
is impossible for there to be a syllogism. The major premiss, for its
part, is necessarily universal, if there is to be a syllogism in the first
figure. For since the minor is in the middle term as in a whole[56] and
may be a part of it (even if it is sometimes taken as equal to it), and
the middle term may be major in extension compared to the minor,   30
then if the major extreme is predicated not of all the middle but of a
part of it, the minor term is not necessarily encompassed by it. For
the major may be predicated of some other part of the middle, if it is   50,1
particular, and not of that part which is either the whole minor term
or a part of it. Someone who has part of his face wounded is not
necessarily wounded in the eye, but someone who is wounded over
his whole face has his eye wounded, since the eye is in the face as in
a whole: similarly in the case of the combination before us – an   5

[53] See above, 30,31 note.
[54] Compare e.g. Apuleius, *Int.* 185,23-186,10; and esp. Philoponus, *in An. Pr.*
69,30-71,17, who makes a more elaborate and systematic attempt to formulate rules
for all syllogisms (cf. Lee, pp. 119-20).
[55] 'A is in B as in a whole' means 'B holds of every A' (above, 24,21-25,11). Hence
'The whole of A [or: a part of A] is in B as in a whole' makes no immediate sense.
Nonetheless, it is reasonably clear what Alexander means. 'The whole of A is in B as
in a whole' simply means 'A is in B as in a whole', and hence is equivalent to 'B holds
of every A'. 'A part of A is in B as in a whole' means 'B holds of all of a part of A', i.e. 'B
holds of every D, where D is a part of A', i.e. 'B holds of every D, where A holds of
every D'. Hence (by the equivalence explained above, 32,20 note), 'A part of A is in B
as in a whole' is equivalent to 'B holds of some A'.
[56] i.e., since either the whole of the minor or a part of the minor is in the middle as
in a whole ...: see above, 49,19-22.

extreme which encompasses the whole of the middle also co-
encompasses all its parts, while an extreme which encompasses a
part of it does not necessarily thereby encompass the part which is
either the whole minor term or a part of it. So the major premiss will
by necessity be universal, either affirmative or negative; and in the
first figure the major premiss will have its quantity determined (it is
10   universal) and its quality indeterminate, while with the minor it will
be the other way about – its quality will be determined (it will always
be affirmative) and its quantity indeterminate (there will be a
syllogism both when it is a universal affirmative and when it is
particular).

Hence the major premiss in the first figure will be either a
universal affirmative or a universal negative, and the minor either a
15   universal affirmative or a particular. Since we thus have four
propositions – two of them universal (either affirmative or negative)
and two affirmative (either universal or particular) – there are four
conjunctions when they are conjoined. Hence there are four syllogisms in the first figure: either the affirmative minor premiss will be
universal and be connected to a major which is itself also universal
20   and affirmative; or, remaining a universal affirmative, it will be
compounded with a major which is a universal negative; or it will be a
particular affirmative and be connected to a major which is in one
case a universal affirmative and in the other a universal negative.

In the first figure the conclusion will always have its quality from
the major premiss; for whatever quality the major premiss has –
25   whether it is affirmative or negative – the conclusion will be the
same.[57] On the other hand, it will have its quantity from the minor
premiss; for if the minor is universal the conclusion too will be
universal, and if it is particular the conclusion too will be particular.

Thus the conclusion is determined by what is indeterminate in
each premiss – and this is itself evidence of the fact that syllogisms
30   depend on what has been posited, i.e. on what is conceded. For it is
what can also *not* be conceded which is conceded; whereas what is
51,1   necessary – i.e. what is such that if it is rejected no syllogism will
come about – is not posited and conceded. Thus that syllogisms
depend on what has been posited is clear from the fact that the
conclusion is similar to what has been conceded and not to what holds
by necessity. Moreover, if the conclusion were similar to what is
5   determined in the premisses, one and the same thing would always
be deduced (namely a universal affirmative, an affirmative because of
the minor and a universal because of the major); and it would not be
possible to prove anything else syllogistically in the first figure.

[57] See Apuleius, *Int.* 186,5-10.

Further, in this way it turns out that the conclusion is similar to the inferior assumption.[58]

4.3.2 Ranking[59]

When both premises are universal and affirmative, the conclusion too is such. And it is reasonable for this syllogism to hold the first 10 rank; for in its conclusion it possesses both what is superior in quantity and what is superior in quality.[60] When the major premiss changes to a universal negative, we get the syllogism which holds the second rank. For this syllogism again possesses what is superior in the proper characteristic of syllogisms (but not both types of superiority); for it is universal. If the minor premiss changes and 15 becomes particular, then since the major is a universal affirmative and the minor a particular, the conclusion will be affirmative. This syllogism is third in rank; for it excels the next syllogism by being superior in quality: it is affirmative, whereas the other is negative. When the minor premiss is a particular affirmative and the major is a universal negative, the conclusion is a particular negative. This 20 syllogism is the last in the first figure, being excelled by its predecessors – by one with respect to quantity, by one with respect to quality, and by one with respect to both.

4.3.3 The number of combinations[61]

The syllogistic combinations in the first figure are this many, and they are found in this way, if we take combinations of determinate premises. But if we also count in the combinations of indeterminate 25 premises,[62] two other syllogisms will be found in the first figure,

---

[58] This is the earliest formulation of the *peiorem*-rule (*peiorem semper conclusio sequitur partem*); cf. e.g. Philoponus, *in An. Pr.* 71,12-17; Thom, pp. 183-5; Lee, p. 119. (Note that Theophrastus and Eudemus introduced a corresponding *peiorem* rule in modal logic: Alexander, *in An. Pr.* 124,8-30; 126,29-127,2; 173,32-174,19; Philoponus, *in An. Pr.* 123,12-17; 129,16-19; [Ammonius], *in An. Pr.* 38,38-39,2; 40,2-40 (texts collected in F 24-5 Graeser; F 11 Wehrli). See Bochenski (1947), pp. 78-87.)

[59] cf. below, 76,29-77,31; 95,25-31; 96,22-97,11, on the ranking of syllogisms in the second and third figures.

[60] See above, 48,25-8.

[61] See Philoponus, *in An. Pr.* 68,8-69,29.

[62] Since indeterminates are equivalent to particulars (above, 30,31 note), it might be thought that indeterminate combinations should *not* be added (see Apuleius, *Int.* 193,9-16). There is some support for this view in Aristotle (see esp. *An. Pr.* 26a28-30; 29a27-9), and it is the view which Alexander takes below, 111,30-112,2 (cf. 94,20). But at 61,1-3 he says that particular and indeterminate premises produce *similar* conclusions (not *the same* conclusions); and in Philoponus it is clear that the indeterminates provide new and distinct combinations of premises (e.g. *in An. Pr.* 79,4-9).

when the minor is assumed as an indeterminate affirmative and connected either to a major which is a universal affirmative (the conclusion of this combination will be an indeterminate affirmative) or to a major which is assumed as a universal negative (the
30 conclusion will be an indeterminate negative). For it is impossible for there to be a syllogism if the major is assumed as indeterminate. And it seems that the conclusion is always similar to the inferior of the premises assumed, both in respect of quantity and in respect of quality.[63]

The syllogistic combinations in the first figure are this many. The combinations in the first figure – and also in the other two figures –
35 will be thirty-six in all, if you count in the indeterminates. In each figure the one premiss can be compounded in six ways with the
52,1 other, which itself can similarly be taken in six ways. For if the major is a universal affirmative, there will be six combinations, the minor being taken either as a universal affirmative or as a universal negative or as a particular affirmative or as a particular negative or
5 as an indeterminate, affirmative or negative. And if, again, the major is a universal negative, there will again be six further combinations, since the minor can be compounded with it in the six ways we have just mentioned. If the major is taken as an indeterminate affirmative, the minor will again be compounded with it in six ways. Similarly and in the same number of ways, if the
10 major is taken as an indeterminate negative. In the same way, if the major is taken as a particular, whether affirmative or negative.

The major changes in six ways and itself becomes sometimes a universal affirmative, sometimes a universal negative, sometimes an indeterminate affirmative or negative, and sometimes a
15 particular affirmative or negative. Hence inasmuch as in each different case the minor can be compounded with it in six ways, the conjunctions of premisses in this figure will be six times six in all. (They are the same in the other two figures as well.) However, if the indeterminates are set aside, the conjunctions will be four times four in all, which make sixteen. If the four syllogistic combinations are subtracted, the remaining non-syllogistic combinations are
20 twelve. Combinations are called syllogistic and reliable if they do not alter together with differences in the matter – i.e. if they do not deduce and prove different things at different times, but always and in every material instance preserve one and the same form in the conclusion.[64] Combinations which change and alter configuration together with the matter and acquire different and conflicting conclusions at different times, are non-syllogistic and unreliable –

[63] See above, 51,7-8.
[64] For the error illustrated here see Introduction, pp. 12-13.

just as a man is unreliable if he is not stable and firm in his
judgment.[65]

4.3.4 Aristotle's general comments

He discusses the first figure first and indicates what it is by way of 25
examples, saying:

> Now when three terms so stand to one another that the last is
> in the middle as in a whole and the middle is or is not in the
> first as in a whole, <it is necessary for there to be a perfect
> syllogism of the extremes.' I call a term middle when both it is
> in another and another is in it – it is middle by position too.>
> [1.4, 25b32-6]

These are examples, one the first and the other the second
syllogism. He next gives the account of the first figure, which he is 53,1
discussing, in his remarks about the middle term: the first figure is
that in which the middle term 'both ... is in another and another is
in it'. For in this figure the middle is predicated of one of the terms
and is subject for the other. He does not give a general account of the 5
middle term but one which holds for the first figure. In general, the
middle term in a combination is the one which is taken twice, which
occurs in both premisses, and which the premisses in the
combination share with each other.[66]

The expression he uses also makes clear the reason why this is the
first figure. (He says: 'it is necessary for there to be a perfect 10
syllogism of the extremes.') For it is reasonable that the figure with
the perfect syllogisms should be the first figure.[67]

He does not mean that combinations in which the middle term
'both ... is in another and another is in it' and in which the middle
holds the middle position, are always syllogistic or that a perfect
syllogism always comes about from them. For in that case all the
combinations in this figure would be syllogistic. Rather, he means 15
that this is so when the terms stand in the way he has just
described. He sets down this way by saying: 'so ... that the last is in
the middle as in a whole and the middle is or is not in the first.' For
when the premisses stand in this way, there is then a perfect

---

[65] The terms 'reliable' and 'unreliable' are not used in this logical sense by Aristotle,
and Alexander's explanation perhaps implies that they are new (or at least
unfamiliar). Galen knows them: *Inst. Log.* xi 6.
[66] On the middle term see above, 44,29-45,10; 46,21-32.
[67] See above, 47,24-7.

syllogism of the extremes in relation to one another. (Here he calls the conclusion a syllogism.[68])

20 He begins his exposition of the syllogisms now with 'as in a whole' and now with 'of every', since each of these items is a sort of principle and is primary.[69] 'As in a whole' is primary and a principle in relation to us. For things which are 'as in a whole' and subjects are better known to us than things said with a wider extension; for they are closer to perceptible things. On the other hand, 'of every' is primary

25 by nature; for it is more common and more general, and common items are primary by nature and thus are also principles.[70]

4.4 Combinations of universal premises

4.4.1 *Barbara* and *Celarent*

> If A is said of every B and B of every C, <then it is necessary for A to be predicated of every C. For we have earlier said what we mean by 'of every'.> [1.4, 25b37-40]

He uses letters in his exposition in order to indicate to us that the

30 conclusions do not depend on the matter but on the figure, on the conjunction of the premises, and on the modes.[71] For so-and-so is deduced syllogistically not because the matter is of such-and-such a

54,1 kind but because the combination is so-and-so. The letters, then, show that the conclusion will be such-and-such universally, always, and for every assumption.

He has told us that for one thing to be in another as in a whole and for the other to be said of all the one are the same.[72] So, having used

5 'as in a whole' in setting out the figure, he now uses 'of every' instead. Both of these formulae occur in universal affirmative propositions. He draws our attention to the account he gave of 'of every' ('when it is not possible to take any of the subject of which the predicate is not said') in order to indicate that in these deductions there is no need for anything external to make the necessity evident,

10 but that the suppositions are sufficient. For 'of every', which is

---

[68] For the word *sullogismos* used in the sense of 'conclusion' see e.g. Galen, *Inst. Log.* i 5; cf. Patzig, pp. 95-6.
[69] See above, 25,9-11 note.
[70] On the primacy of universals in Alexander see Tweedale.
[71] For other comments on Aristotle's use of letters see below 77,32-78,5; 98,20-3; Alexander, *in An. Pr.* 125,26-8; 379,14-380,27; 414,9-10; 415,10-12; *in Top.* 2,16-29; *Conv.* 61; Philoponus, *in An. Pr.* 46,25-47,11; Boethius, *Syll. Cat.* 810CD. Cf. Bochenski (1956), p. 157; Łukasiewicz, pp. 7-10 (but the letters should not be construed as variables: Frede (1974b), p. 113).
[72] See *An. Pr.* 24b26-8; above, 24,26-25,11.

supposed and taken in the premises, is sufficient for the proof of the deduction.[73]

This[74] is why syllogisms of this kind are perfect and indemonstrable in the strict sense.[75] Let A be the major extreme, B the middle term, and C the minor extreme. If C is in B as in a whole, B is said of every C. For these formulae convert from each other. Therefore it is not possible to take any of C of which B is not said. 15 Again, if B is in A as in a whole, A is said of every B. Hence it is not possible to take[76] any of B of which A is not said. Now, if nothing of B can be taken of which A is not said, and C is something of B, then by necessity A will be said of C too. The deduction in syllogisms of this sort is thus directly obvious, being justified by means of the 20 suppositions – by means of 'of every' and 'of none' – and not needing anything else from outside.

He[77] uses 'of every' and 'of none' in his exposition because by means of these formulae the deduction becomes known, and because when they are stated in this way the subject and the predicate are better known, and because 'of every' is primary by nature in relation to 'in it as in a whole', as I have already said.[78] (But syllogistic usage 25 is normally the other way about. Virtue is not said of every justice, but the other way about – 'All justice is virtue'. This is why we have to train ourselves in both types of formulation, so that we can follow both normal usage and Aristotle's exposition.[79])

Similarly, if A is said of no B <and B of every C, A will hold of 30 no C.> [1.4, 25b40-26a2]

Having set out the first syllogism in the first figure, which deduces a universal affirmative from two universal affirmatives, he next mentions the second, which deduces a universal negative from a universal negative major and a universal affirmative minor. He says 55,1 that in this case too the deduction is known by way of 'of none' and 'of every'.[80] This[81] is why this syllogism, too, is both indemonstrable

---

[73] See above, 32,11 note.
[74] 54,11-12 = *FDS* 1101.
[75] Why 'in the strict sense [*kuriôs*]'? Alexander does find a sort of proof for these syllogisms, based on the *dictum de omni et nullo*; presumably he holds that this proof is not a demonstration in the strict sense – perhaps because it cannot be expressed within categorical syllogistic.
[76] Reading *labein*, with M and the Aldine. Wallies omits the verb.
[77] On this paragraph see Łukasiewicz, p. 17; Mignucci (1969), pp. 185-6; Thom, p. 20; and esp. Patzig, pp. 8-12 (but the construal which he canvasses at p. 15 n. 24 will hardly fit the text) and Ebert (1977).
[78] See above, 53,24-6.
[79] See Introduction, pp. 30-1.
[80] See above, 32,11 note.
[81] 55,3 = *FDS* 1101.

and perfect. For if B is said of every C, there will be nothing of C of
5   which B is not said. Therefore C is something of B. Now if A is said of
no B, there will be nothing of B of which A is predicated. But C was
something of B. Therefore A is said of no C.

4.4.2 Non-syllogistic combinations[82]

> But if the first follows all the middle and the middle none of the
> last, there will not be a syllogism <of the extremes. For
> nothing necessary follows inasmuch as they are the case. For it
> is possible for the first to hold of all and also of none of the last.
> Hence neither the particular nor the universal is necessary.
> And if nothing is necessary by way of these items, there will
> not be a syllogism. Terms for holding of every: animal, man,
> horse. For holding of none: animal, man, stone.> [1.4, 26a2-9]

10 He calls being predicated 'following'; for the predicate follows what
falls under it.[83]
   Having discussed the syllogistic[84] combinations of the first figure
in which both premisses are universal, he sets down the
non-syllogistic combinations in which the premisses are universal.
There are four combinations in the first figure, given that both
15 premisses are universal. Two of them are syllogistic and reliable
(these he has set out); two are non-syllogistic – the one with a
negative minor and an affirmative major (which he mentions here)
and the one in which both premisses are negative. The reason why
the combination set out here is non-syllogistic is that the minor has
been assumed as negative; for we have already said that it is
20 impossible for there to be a syllogism in the first figure where the
minor proposition is negative.[85]
   He sets down material instances to prove that, when the
premisses stand thus, nothing necessary can be deduced (which is
the proper characteristic of a syllogism[86]). For he will prove that in
some material instances it is possible for a universal affirmative to
be deduced, and in other material instances a universal negative[87] –
25 and this is the most obvious sign that this combination has no
syllogistic force, since contraries and opposites are proved in it and
they cancel one another. For nothing can be deduced syllogistically

---

[82] On Aristotle's ways of showing that a combination is non-syllogistic see Patzig,
pp. 168-92; Lear, pp. 54-75.
[83] cf. Alexander, *in An. Pr.* 326,31-2; Philoponus, *in An. Pr.* 302,17-19; and note
Aristotle's use of *hepesthai* at e.g. *An. Pr.* 43b3; 44a13. See Barnes (1983), pp. 309-13.
[84] Reading *sullogistikón* for *sullogismón tôn*.
[85] See above, 49,22-50,7.
[86] See above, 18,8-12.
[87] For the confusion exhibited here see Introduction, pp. 12-13.

in a combination in which universal affirmatives and universal negatives can be proved. What is deduced syllogistically must be the same in every material instance and must be either a universal affirmative, or a universal negative, or a particular affirmative or negative; but both affirmatives are cancelled by the universal negative and both negatives by the universal affirmative. This is what he means when he says 'Hence neither the particular nor the universal is necessary'. 30

56,1

He does not mean that if you prove a contradictory pair to be deducible in some combination then you cancel the possibility that something may be syllogistically deduced in it. For if a universal affirmative and a particular negative are deduced, there is nothing to prevent a particular affirmative from being deduced syllogistically since this is cancelled by neither of the suppositions. And if the other contradictory pair is proved, it is still possible for a particular negative to be deduced syllogistically. We will say more about this shortly;[88] for the moment let us add the reason why the combination set out here is non-syllogistic. 5

If C is in no B, B is said of no C. Therefore, it will not be possible to take anything of C of which B is said. Thus C has been separated from B and is in no way linked to it. A is supposed to be said of every B. But what is said of all of something may actually have a wider extension than it (it is for this reason that the predicate term is called 'major').[89] You may take A in such a way as to encompass all of B and yet have some parts which fall outside the compass of B. Thus A may either encompass or not encompass C with those parts of itself which fall outside B. So, depending on the difference of matter, opposites are true when premises are conjoined in this way, and such conjunctions are non-syllogistic. Let A be animal, B man, and C horse: animal holds of every man, man of no horse, and animal of every horse. It is by the part which falls outside man that animal includes horse – the sharing of the middle term is not the explanation. If stone is posited instead of horse, the premises are true in the same way: animal is said of every man, man of no stone.[90] Therefore the combination is unreliable; for it does not itself impose a form on the matter but changes together with the differences in the matter and deduces nothing necessary from the suppositions.[91] 10 15 20 25

Having said 'for it is possible for the first to hold of all and also of

[88] See below, 89,29-91,33.

[89] See above, 47,29-48,6.

[90] Omitting *kai to zôion kat' oudenos lithou*, which Wallies adds to the text on the authority of the Aldine.

[91] With this argument compare below 61,24-9; 62,16-21; 64,15-22; 67,17-22; 81,28-82,1; 85,27-9.

30   none of the last', he continues: 'Hence neither the particular nor the universal is necessary.' For, as we have said, it is not only the universal affirmative which is cancelled by the universal negative

57,1 but also the particular affirmative (since they are contradictories); and again, it is not only the universal negative which is cancelled by the universal affirmative but also the particular negative. Hence in proving that contraries are deduced, he has proved that no particular is deduced with syllogistic necessity.

5   Nor when the first holds of none of the middle and the middle of none of the last will there be a syllogism in this case either. <Terms for holding: science, line, medicine. For not holding: science, line, unit.> [1.4, 26a9-13]

He has moved on to the combination of two negative universals in the first figure, and he proves that this too is non-syllogistic. Again, he sets down terms such that, in the different cases, A evidently

10 holds of every C and also of no C. The reason why nothing is deduced syllogistically in this combination is that the middle bears no relation to either of the extremes (it is as if a middle had not been taken at all – and syllogisms depend on the middle term); and when it stands thus, C may fall under A and also not fall under A. If A is

15 science, B line, and C medicine, both universal negative premisses are true and science will hold of all medicine. But if unit or stone is posited instead of medicine, the premisses are true in the same way, but science will hold of no unit and of no stone.

4.4.3 Concluding remarks

20 Thus when the terms are universal it is clear ... in this figure ... [1.4, 26a13]

We have said that there are four combinations in the first figure when the premisses are taken universally, and that two of them are syllogistic and two non-syllogistic.

... and that if there is a syllogism, it is necessary for the terms

25 to stand as we have said, <and that if they stand in this way there will be a syllogism.> [1.4, 26a14-16]

He converts his statement: if there is a syllogism in the first figure with universal premisses, then the terms must have the position and the mutual order which he has described; and if the terms stand thus and in this position, then there must be a syllogism.

58,1 Now if there is to be a universal affirmative conclusion, then it is clear that it must come about in the first figure from premisses of this sort supposed in the way we have shown – for no universal affirmative is deduced in any other figure. But how is this still true in the case of universal negative conclusions? For it will seem not to be necessary that if a universal negative conclusion has come about syllogistically, then the terms stand as we have described them in the second combination of the first figure. For the same conclusion can be proved syllogistically when the terms stand otherwise: universal negatives are proved in the second figure, and in two ways. Hence it will seem untrue that 'if there is a syllogism, it is necessary for the terms to stand as we have said'.

Thus if what Aristotle says is to be true, we must understand 'in this figure'. He said earlier 'when the terms are universal, it is clear ... *in this figure* ...'.[92] Hence what he goes on to say also refers to the syllogisms in this figure.

One may also say that what he has said does actually fit the syllogisms which deduce a universal negative in the second figure. For there too, even if the order in the premisses is not the same – the terms stand to one another in a different relation and not as they do in the first figure –, nonetheless there too they stand in this relation potentially. At any rate, it is in virtue of an analysis into the first figure by way of conversions of their premisses that these combinations are proved to be syllogistic. Hence here too the terms do stand to one another in the way he described in the case of the second combination of the first figure. For the syllogisms which deduce a universal negative in the second figure are reduced to this combination, as he will later prove.[93]

4.5 Combinations of universal and particular premisses

4.5.1 *Darii* and *Ferio*

If one of the terms is universal and one particular in relation to the other ... [1.4, 26a17]

'In relation to the other' is not, in my view, idly added to 'and one particular'. For it is possible that in one and the same premiss one of the terms is universal and the other particular – the subject, if taken as a whole, being universal, and the predicate, part of which is said of the subject, being particular. Not every animal is said of man: a part of animal is said of every man in the proposition which says 'Every man is an animal' – some animal is said of man. Again, 'Animal is said of some animate' has one of its terms universal and

---

[92] *An. Pr.* 26a13-14 (see also below, 60,9).
[93] See *An. Pr.* 27a5-14; cf. below, 78,21-2; 79,7-8.

the other particular.[94] (That is why the converses of such propositions
are particular.) Thus it was in order to make it clear that the
universality and particularity of the terms occur in the conjunction of
5   the premisses and not in a single premiss nor yet in a converse of a
premiss, that he added 'in relation to the other': i.e. 'when one term is
predicated universally, and this is predicated particularly of something else'; or, more simply, 'when the same term is universal in
relation to one term and particular in relation to the other in the
conjunction described'. For it is when it is taken particularly in this
10   way that we get a combination or conjunction of premisses.

Having discussed combinations in the first figure with two universals, he turns next to combinations in which one premiss is
particular and the other universal, showing which and how many
they are and which of them are syllogistic. First, he sets them out. Of
15   these combinations, two again are reliable, viz. the combination of a
universal affirmative major premiss and a particular affirmative
minor, and the combination of a particular affirmative minor and a
universal negative major. He mentions both of them together when
he says:

   … when the universal is posited on the major extreme (whether
   it is predicative or privative) and the particular on the minor is
20   predicative, it is necessary for there to be a perfect syllogism.
   [1.4, 26a18-20]

When the major is universal and affirmative, what is deduced will
be a particular affirmative; and if the major is assumed as a
universal negative, a particular negative will be deduced. Inasmuch
as one premiss must be assumed as particular, and the major must
certainly be universal, the minor will be particular; and he has said
25   that it will also be predicative.

---

[94] A puzzling passage; for in what sense can we talk about the *terms* in a
proposition being universal or particular? It might seem that Alexander is supposing
that the proposition 'Every man is an animal' predicates *some* animal of *every* man, so
that man is universal and animal particular. And it might then further seem that
Alexander is here admitting – or even insisting – that the predicate as well as the
subject bears a quantifier. But quantification of the predicate was rejected by
Aristotle (*Int.* 17b12-16; *An. Pr.* 43b17-22; *An. Post.* 77b30), and the commentators
followed him: e.g. Alexander, *in An. Pr.* 297,4-23 (cf. above, 44,28 note); Philoponus,
in An. Pr. 277,26-32; and esp. the long essay in Ammonius, *in Int.* 101,14-108,36, on
which see Mignucci (1983). Rather, Alexander has the following simple fact in mind:
in some cases where A holds of every B, only some As are Bs, and in other cases all As
are Bs. In the former cases A is 'particular', in the latter 'universal'. (And this has
nothing to do with quantifying the predicate.)

But when it is on the minor or the terms stand in any other way, it is impossible. [1.4, 26a20-1]

Having referred to the major premiss and said that there will be a syllogism when it is privative, he continues 'But when it (*sc.* the privative) is (*sc.* posited instead) on the minor' – so that it is a particular negative and the major is universal, either affirmative or negative. 'Stand in any other way' means 'If the major is instead assumed as a particular and the minor as a universal'. For when they stand so, there is no syllogism.

'But when it is on the minor' may also have the force of 'when the universal is instead assumed on the minor' – and to judge by what comes next, this is indeed rather what he is saying.[95] Then 'or the terms stand in any other way' will be said in reference to the minor premiss – 'if this is not assumed instead as a universal but remains particular and is assumed as a negative'.

I call the major extreme the one in which the middle is, and the minor the one under the middle. [1.4, 26a21-3]

Everything he says must be understood to be said of the first figure. For what he says here is this: 'In the first figure, the major term is the one which the middle is in and the minor the one under the middle.' For in this figure, as we saw, the middle term is subject for one term and predicate of the other. In the second figure both the major and the minor are in the middle term – the middle is under no term. Conversely, in the third figure the middle is not only under the major but also under the minor – no term is in the middle term.[96]

He has shown plainly that the term predicated in the conclusion is the major term in the premisses and that the major premiss is major because of it.[97]

For let A hold of every B and B of some C. <Then if being predicated of every is what we said at the beginning, it is necessary for A to hold of some C.> [1.4, 26a23-5]

This is the combination of the third indemonstrable, which has a particular affirmative conclusion. If B holds of some C, then something of C is in B as in a whole.[98] But A is said of every B.

---

[95] i.e. *An. Pr.* 26a30-1; below, 63,11-12 (cf. Philoponus, *in An. Pr.* 77.22-9).
[96] See above, 46,21-47,12. On the unannounced use of 'under [*hupo*]' here see Patzig, pp. 98-9.
[97] See above, 47,30-48,10.
[98] For the locution 'some C is in B as in a whole' see above, 49,22 note. Note that Alexander again tacitly invokes the thesis that if A holds of some B, then there is some D such that A holds of every D and B holds of every D (above, 32,20 note).

Therefore there is nothing of B of which A is not said. But C is something of B. Therefore A will be said of it.

> <And if A holds of no B and B of some C, it is necessary for A not to hold of some C. For we have also defined what we mean by 'of none'. Hence there will be a perfect syllogism.> [1.4, 26a25-8]

25   Similarly with the fourth indemonstrable, which has a universal negative major premiss and a particular affirmative minor. For if something of C is in B as in a whole, and B is in no A, then A will not hold of some C. For something of C is under B; but nothing of B can be taken of which A is said. Hence A will not be said of that item of C
61,1   which is something of B.

> <Similarly too if BC is indeterminate ...> [1.4, 26a28-9]

Deductions similar to these[99] are found if we make the minor premiss an indeterminate affirmative and keep the major either as a universal affirmative or as a universal negative.

5   All the syllogisms thus far described are perfect; for in all of them the deduction is evident, invoking only 'of every' or 'of none', which are supposed.[100]

4.5.2 Non-syllogistic combinations

4.5.2.1 Major particular, minor universal

> If the universal, either predicative or privative, is posited on the minor extreme, there will not be a syllogism, <whether the indeterminate or particular is affirmative or negative>. [1.4, 26a30-3]

He is discussing combinations which have one premiss universal and the other particular. He first discussed those in which the
10   universal is on the major premiss and the particular, which is affirmative, on the minor, proving that such combinations are syllogistic. He then added the combinations in which the minor premiss is indeterminate instead of particular, everything else remaining the same, and found two syllogisms when the minor is taken in this way. Now he turns to the complementary cases – I
15   mean the combinations which have a universal minor premiss. When this is universal, the major premiss is either particular or

---

[99] See above, 51,25 note.
[100] See above, 32,11 note.

indeterminate, and if it is particular or indeterminate, then – as we have already said[101] – all the conjunctions are non-syllogistic. Thus he sets out these conjunctions or combinations and proves that they are non-syllogistic. Once again, he sets down material instances in which contraries are found to be deduced.   20

He said 'the particular' instead of 'the major'[102] – for the major premiss is particular.

I.e. if A holds or does not hold of some B <and B holds of every C. Terms for holding: good, disposition, sagacity. For not holding: good, disposition, ignorance.> [1.4, 26a33-6]

If the major premiss is particular, whether affirmative or negative, the conjunction is non-syllogistic. For if A is said of some B, and B of   25 every C, there will be nothing of C of which B is not said; hence C is something of B. But since A is said of some B, it may be said of that part of B which is C, and it may also be said of some other part; for B is predicated of C with a wider extension.[103] Therefore A will neither hold nor not hold of C by necessity. For example, suppose that A is good, B disposition, and C sagacity: good is said of some disposition,   62,1 disposition of all sagacity, good of all sagacity. But if C is ignorance (here he takes ignorance as a disposition,[104] i.e.[105] as folly or vice), good, the major extreme, will hold of no ignorance and of no folly, although disposition, which was the middle term, is universally   5 predicated of them. Hence the combination is unreliable.

If A does not hold of some B, the proof is similar and uses the same terms. For as A holds of some B, so it may also not hold of some – good will hold of some disposition in this way, because it does not hold of some.

Again, if B holds of no C and A holds of some B or does not hold   10 (or does not hold of every), <in this case too there will not be a syllogism. Terms: white, horse, swan; white, horse, raven. The same terms serve if AB is indeterminate.> [1.4, 26a36-9]

'Does not hold of some' and 'does not hold of every' both mean particular negatives, differing only in expression.[106] (To 'does not hold' you must add 'of some', which goes with both verbs.)

---

[101] See above, 49,26-50,8.
[102] Retaining Wallies' *tou* for the MS reading *to, pace* Ross, p. 303. The MS reading is ungrammatical.
[103] See above, 56,8-27.
[104] For this sense of 'ignorance' see Aristotle, *An. Post.* 79b23-5; cf. Barnes (1975), p. 145.
[105] Reading *kai* for *hê*.
[106] This was affirmed by Aristotle (*An. Pr.* 62a9-10) and denied by Theophrastus,

He proves that conjunctions which have a universal negative minor
15 and a particular major are not deductive.[107] By following the same
path as before,[108] we will find that A sometimes holds of every C and
sometimes holds of none. Let A be white, B horse, and C swan: white
holds of some horse and also does not hold of some horse; horse of no
swan; white of every swan. For white is of wider extension than horse
20 and is predicated of it; and in that part by which it exceeds horse it
now encompasses C, which is swan, of none of which horse holds. And
if we make C raven instead of swan, horse will hold of no raven, and
nor will white.

If the major premiss is taken as indeterminate, whether affirmative or negative, the proof will be given by the same terms – for
indeterminates are taken as equivalent to particulars.[109]
25 Note that when the minor is a universal affirmative and the major
is particular, the combination is non-syllogistic because of the major's
being particular; whereas when the major is particular or indeterminate and the minor is a universal negative, the combination is
non-syllogistic on account of both premisses – on account of the major,
because it is particular, and on account of the minor, because it is
30 negative.

4.5.2.2 Minor particular and negative

63,1 When the term on the major extreme is universal, either
predicative or privative, and the term on the minor is privative
and particular, there will not be a syllogism (whether it is
assumed as indeterminate or as particular). I.e. if A holds of
5 every B, and B does not hold of some C (or if it does not hold of
every C). <For the first will follow all and also none of that of
some of which the middle does not hold. Suppose the terms to be
animal, man, white. Then of the whites of which man is not
predicated, take swan and snow. Then animal is predicated of
all the one and of none of the other. Hence there will not be a
syllogism.> [1.4, 26a39-b10]

'Does not hold of some' and 'does not hold of every' are again the
same.[110]

---

who suggested that 'not of every' implies that the predicate holds of *several* of the
subject and that 'not of some' implies that it holds of one (scholium to Aristotle,
145a30-7 = F 5 Graeser – but the sense of the passage is uncertain); cf. Bochenski
(1947), p. 43.
   [107] 'Deductive' translates *sunaktikos* (from *sunagein*, 'to deduce'): it is here used as
a synonym for 'syllogistic'.
   [108] See above, 61,24-9.
   [109] See above, 30,31 note.
   [110] See above, 62,11-12.

Having first proved non-syllogistic the combinations in which the major is particular, he now proves non-syllogistic those in which the major remains universal, whether affirmative or negative, and the 10 minor is a particular negative. (He thereby shows what he meant when he said above: 'But when it is on the minor or the terms stand in any other way.'[111]) These combinations are non-syllogistic because of the minor, which is negative.

His proof[112] that these combinations are non-syllogistic uses the part of C of which it is supposed that B does not hold. For taking 15 this, he proves, again by setting down terms, that A holds of all and also of none of it. He intended in this way to give an appropriate proof of the fact that the combination set out is non-syllogistic; for if the proof used every C, it would no longer be suitable in the same way. When B held of no C, the combination was proved to be non-syllogistic inasmuch as A could hold both of all and also of none 20 of that of none of which B held:[113] in the same way, when B is supposed not to hold of some C, the combination would be proved non-syllogistic, if it were proved that A could hold of all and also of none of that part of C of which B does not hold.[114]

Again, since the minor is a particular negative, the same premiss can also be a particular affirmative in the same respect;[115] for 25 nothing prevents that which does not hold of some so-and-so from holding of some of it as well. But when the minor is a particular affirmative, there is a syllogism if the major is universal, whether affirmative or negative − a syllogism which is either a particular affirmative or a particular negative, as has been proved[116] (for each of the premisses possesses its proper characteristic, the minor being 30 affirmative and the major universal). And since this combination is syllogistic, it was not possible for him to take terms both for which A 64,1 holds of every C and also for which it holds of no C. Hence, since it is supposed that B does not hold of some C, then if it also holds of some C, it will not be possible to take terms for which A holds of every C and also for which it holds of no C. For in that case we should also disprove and reject the syllogistic combinations in which B holds of

---

[111] *An. Pr.* 26a20-1; see above, 59,28-60,6.

[112] On this see Maier, IIa, p. 87; Ross, p. 304; Patzig, pp. 177-80.

[113] See *An. Pr.* 26a2-9; above, 55,20-56,1.

[114] Alexander's thought seems to be this: since 'B does not hold of some C' only concerns *some* C (*some* white things), a disproof of the combination which invoked *all* C would be too general and hence not appropriate. This is a confused thought; and it is intended to justify a procedure which is unjustifiable. (Aristotle's argument fails because, in Alexandrian terms, he does not take *that* part of C of which B does not hold: he takes two *different* parts of C.)

[115] Alexander must mean: 'The particular affirmative, "B holds of some C", may be true when the particular negative premiss is true.'

[116] i.e. *Darii* and *Ferio*: Aristotle, *An. Pr.* 26a17-29. (Note that here 'syllogism' is used in the sense of 'conclusion': see above, 53,19 note.)

5 some C and A of every B, and in which B holds of some C and A of no
B. For in the case of the combination which deduces an affirmative,
it is impossible to take terms for which A holds of no C, since it holds
syllogistically of some C; and in the case of the combination which
syllogizes a particular negative, it is impossible to take terms for
which A holds of every C, since it is syllogistically proved that A does
10 not hold of some C. Each of these combinations would be rejected if,
in the case of the combination before us, terms were found for A's
holding of every C and also for A's holding of no C.[117]

For this reason, since it is not possible, he does not give the proof
in terms of C *simpliciter*, but rather takes from C those parts of
which B does not hold (for it is supposed that B does not hold of some
C); and by setting down material instances he proves that there are
15 parts of C (of which B does not hold) of all of which A holds, and
parts of none of which A holds.

It is also possible to prove that the conjunction we have set out[118]
is non-syllogistic by predicating B universally and negatively of the
parts of C, assuming the minor as a universal negative. For suppose
that A is said of every B and B of none of the parts of C which have
20 been taken: since A may have a wider extension than B (for it is
possible that A is such as to exceed B), it may include the parts of C
of which B does not hold, and also not include them.[119] Such a
combination is unreliable.[120]

The terms which Aristotle sets down are animal for A, man for B,
and white for the whole C, of some of which man holds and of some
25 of which man does not hold. Next, since BC is a particular negative
and it is impossible to prove and deduce a universal negative of C
when the terms are so taken (or a universal affirmative if AB is
taken as a universal negative), let us take some parts of white, of
none of which man is said – let them be swan and snow. (Man is said

---

[117] This is false: the valid combinations would be rejected only if we could find
terms to verify 'A belongs to every B and B does not belong to some C *and B belongs to
some C*' as well as 'A belongs to every C' or 'A belongs to no C'.
[118] Reading *ekkeimenên* for *eirêmenên* (Wallies, from the Aldine: the MSS have
antikeimenên).
[119] See above, 56,8-27.
[120] Alexander's procedure in this paragraph is correct, but his exposition is
compressed. The argument depends on the fact that 'B does not hold of some C' is true
if and only if there is some D such that C holds of every D and B holds of no D. (See
above, 32,20 note, for the corresponding fact about 'B holds of some C'.) Hence if a
syllogism of the form 'P, B does not hold of some C: therefore, Q' is valid, then so too is
the corresponding syllogism of the form 'P, B holds of no D: therefore, Q'. Hence a
counterexample to the latter will refute the former. According to Alexander, this
train of reasoning, although probative, was not Aristotle's (see below, 65,16-32:
Alexander implies that some critics had both ascribed it to Aristotle and found it
wanting). Later Philoponus expresses the line of thought more clearly – and reads it
into Aristotle (*in An. Pr.* 82,21-7; cf. 82,34-83,4; and note *metalambanein* at
109,20-1).

neither of swan, which is white, nor of snow.) Now animal is said of
every swan but of no snow. In this way such a combination is proved   65,1
unreliable and non-syllogistic in terms of a part of C to which B does
not belong.

(As for conjunctions with two particulars,[121] when he sets down
the terms by which he proves that such conjunctions are
non-syllogistic, he no longer argues in terms of a part of C of some of
which it is supposed that B does not hold, but rather in terms of the   5
whole of C; for a conjunction with two particulars is non-syllogistic,
both if B does not hold of some C while also holding of some C and
also if B holds of no C. Now inasmuch as there is no syllogistic
combination to set alongside such a conjunction of premises, it is
possible to take the whole of C and obtain terms both for A's holding
of every C and also for its holding of none. And if something holds of
the whole of C, clearly it also holds of each of its parts – and hence of   10
the part of which B does not hold.)

<Again, let A hold of no B and let B not hold of some C; and let
the terms be inanimate, man, white. Then of the whites of
which man is not predicated, take swan and snow. Inanimate
is predicated of all the one and of none of the other.> [1.4,
26b10-14]

The refutation is similar if AB is taken as a universal negative. Let
the terms be inanimate for A, man for B, white for C; and let us
again take swan and snow as whites of which man is not predicated.
For inanimate holds of all snow and of no swan. (The same terms,
swan and snow, were used to prove that the combination is   15
non-syllogistic when the major is a universal affirmative.)

He does not, as some think, invoke a universal negative in setting
out the terms, transforming the particular negative of the minor
proposition into a universal negative. (Nor, if someone does invoke
it, should one therefore deem him not to prove the given   20
combination to be non-syllogistic.) For you invoke what is universal
if you prove 'of every' and 'of none' for all C rather than for some part
of C.[122]

Again, if it were not possible to take any parts of the last term of
which the middle did not hold universally, then the objectors would
be right in objecting to the transformation. This would be the case if
C were indivisible and did not have parts. But if it is indivisible, it   25
cannot be true that the middle does not hold of some of it. For if the
determinations – namely 'of every' and 'of none' and 'of some' and

---

[121] Aristotle, *An. Pr.* 26b21-5; below, 68,9-21.
[122] See above, 64,15-24 and note.

'not of some'[123] – are annexed to the universal, as has been shown in
On Interpretation,[124] it is clear that the last term is universal and
not indivisible;[125] and sometimes there will be not only some thing
but some things of which it is predicated, if the middle has been
30   taken not to hold of some of it – as in the examples Aristotle sets
down. If it is of this sort, then both the exposition[126] and the
transformation into the universal are correct, and the proof by way
of the universal that the given combination is non-syllogistic is
sound.

4.5.2.3 The indeterminacy of particulars[127]

<Again, since 'B does not hold of some C' is indeterminate and
it is true both if it holds of none and if it does not hold of all
(because it does not hold of some), and since there is no
syllogism if terms are taken such that it holds of none (this has
been said earlier), it is evident that there will not be a
syllogism inasmuch as the terms stand in the way we are
considering. For then there would be one in this case too.>
[1.4, 26b14-20]

66,1   He also proves in the following way that the two combinations set
out here are non-syllogistic. 'Again, since "does not hold of some" is
said indeterminately ....' For 'does not hold of some' is true both if it
holds of none and also if it holds of some. Here he calls propositions
indeterminate if they do not have their truth determined. Thus it is
5   true to say that hot does not hold of some snow – and hot holds of no
snow. In the same way it is true that man does not hold of some
horse, because man holds of no horse. Theophrastus, too, in his *On
Affirmation*, mentions this sort of indeterminacy. He calls
indeterminate 'Some of these are ...' and 'One of them is ...': 'Some of
these are ...' because it is true both if all are and also if some are and

---

[123] See above, 44,27 note.

[124] See Aristotle, *Int.* 17a37-b12; cf. e.g. below, 100,11-14; Boethius, *Int. Syll. Cat.*
778B.

[125] Alexander argues that since the quantifiers are annexed to the term C, then C
must be a general and not a singular term. The argument thus seems to turn on the
vexed question of the place of singular terms in Aristotelian syllogisms (on which see
Łukasiewicz, pp. 4-7; Patzig, pp. 4-8; Ackrill; Thom, pp. 174-6). But in fact
Alexander's point requires less than he supposes: it is enough for the argument to go
through that 'B does not hold of some C' does not *exclude* the possibility that there is
more than one C. (Moreover, Alexander could safely allow that C may sometimes be a
singular term – as in fact he does, e.g. at *in An. Pr.* 350,30-352,26.)

[126] By 'exposition' (*ekthesis*) Alexander probably refers to Aristotle's device of
taking parts of C: cf. 67,11; 89,13.15. But note that at 65,17 Alexander has used
ekthesis of the setting down of terms (i.e. as equivalent to *parathesis*).

[127] On this see Łukasiewicz, pp. 67-72; Patzig, pp. 180-3; Brunschwig (1969);
Thom, pp. 59-62. See Introduction, p. 29.

some are not, 'One of them is ...' because this too is true if both are   10
and also if only one of them is.[128]

Now particular negatives are not determinate but are true both
for negatives which are particular in the specific sense and for
universal negatives. For inasmuch as what is called subaltern[129] to
something is true together with it, and particular negatives are
subaltern to universal negatives, the particular negative is true
when the universal negative is true even if it is assumed in its own   15
right. Now suppose we assume that B does not hold of some C: even
if it is not possible to obtain suitable terms for every such
combination, yet it is enough to set down a single case, given that its
truth is indeterminate, to prove the conjunction non-syllogistic.
When it is true because it holds of none, and we set down suitable
terms, then the conjunction will be proved non-syllogistic for
negatives which are particular in this way, inasmuch as A holds of   20
every C and also of no C.[130] (This has been proved, when the minor
is a universal negative, by means of the terms animal, man, horse,
and stone.[131]) And if the combination with a particular negative
minor is proved to be non-syllogistic in the case of one material
instance, it is universally non-syllogistic. For if it were syllogistic,
then you should not have been able to disprove and refute it by   25
setting down material instances when the particular negative is
taken to be true in this way (i.e. inasmuch as it falls under the
universal negative) – for it is no less true then than when it is taken
in its own right.[132]

Aristotle made this clear by saying 'For then there would be one in
this case too.'

In the following expression you must take the connective 'for'
instead of 'and'. In this way the phrase becomes plainer and more   67,1
congruous: '*For* it will be proved in the same way as it would be if a

---

[128] Theophrastus, F 4 Graeser – see Brunschwig (1982). (The other three texts
which Graeser assigns to F 4 make a perfectly different point, namely that
Theophrastus called particular propositions indeterminate because they do not refer
to any one individual. Like Aristotle, Theophrastus evidently used the word
'indeterminate' in different senses.) Note that in saying that 'One of them is ...' is
indeterminate, Theophrastus in effect construes disjunctions as *inclusive*. ('x or y is F'
will be true if both x and y are F.) The later Peripatetic tradition construed
disjunctions as exclusive: e.g. Galen, *Inst. Log.* iv 1-4; Alexander, *in Top.*
174,5-176,26; cf. Maróth, pp. 55-69 (see above, 19,23 note).

[129] See above, 45,26.

[130] Omitting *tôi* before *mêdeni*.

[131] See Aristotle, *An. Pr.* 26a2-9; above, 55,21-56,27.

[132] Alexander's exposition is cumbersome. The point is this. Given that 'B holds of
no C' entails 'B does not hold of some C', then if we can infer Q from P together with 'B
does not hold of some C' we can infer Q from P together with 'B holds of no C'. But no
syllogistic conclusion follows from 'A holds of every B' together with 'B holds of no C'.
Hence no syllogistic conclusion follows from 'A holds of every B' together with 'B does
not hold of some C'.

universal privative had been assumed.'[133]

He calls 'not of some' indeterminate not in the sense that the proposition is indeterminate[134] (for it is determinate, since it is particular and the particular is as determinate as the universal) but rather in the sense that the truth which is signified by it is not determinate. For it may be true both if it holds of none of that of some of which it is assumed not to hold, and also if it holds[135] of some, as I have already said.

In the case of this figure, since the particular negative is true in an indeterminate way (being true both in its own right and because of the universal), he has proved that it is non-syllogistic in both cases – both if it is assumed in its own right and if it holds because of the universal. If in its own right, by exposition (i.e. by taking a term of some of which B does not hold); if because of the universal, by taking the terms he gives here. For the middle, which was taken not to hold of those items which are in the last term as in a whole, is taken not to hold of them when they are separated from the whole and taken by themselves.[136] In the second and third figures he is content to prove similar conjunctions non-syllogistic solely by the indeterminacy of the particular negative.[137]

The explanation of why the combination with a particular negative minor is non-syllogistic is this. Part of C is separated from B; and A includes all B. Because of B, A will not include the part of C which lies outside B; yet there are parts of A which exceed B (since A is major in relation to B), and with these parts it may encompass the part of C – in the case of some material instances – and also, conversely, not encompass the same part.[138]

When the major is a universal negative, the terms with which he refuted this conjunction were inanimate, man, swan, and snow.[139]

And it will be proved in the same way if the universal is posited as privative. [1.4, 26b20-1]

The phrase means either 'For it will be proved in the same way ...' or 'Thus ... in the same way ...', so that he uses 'and' either instead of

[133] See below, 67,27-68,6, which is an expansion of this little paragraph. The second of the two accounts which Alexander gives in the later paragraph is plainly the correct interpretation of Aristotle's meaning.

[134] i.e. unquantified.

[135] Omitting *mê*: see 66,2-3.

[136] This sentence applies to the first of the two cases distinguished in the previous sentence ('If in its own right, ...').

[137] See Aristotle, *An. Pr.* 27b20-3, 27-9; 28b24-31; below, 87,5-88,14; 104,25-105,8; cf. Alexander, *in An. Pr.* 203,15-35.

[138] See above, 56,8-17.

[139] See *An. Pr.* 26b11-13.

'for' or instead of 'thus'.[140]

For it will be proved that the combination which has a particular negative minor is non-syllogistic in the same way as the combination with a universal negative minor. But he has already 30 proved the latter case.

Or else he uses the proof by way of the indeterminate separately 68,1 for each conjunction – for the one in which the major is a universal affirmative and the minor a particular negative, and for the one which has a universal negative major and a particular negative minor. *Thus*, after he has first given an account of the combination 5 which has a universal affirmative major, he says that it will be proved in the same way if the major, being universal, is transformed into a negative.

4.6 Combinations of particular premisses

Again, if both the intervals[141] are particulars, either predicatively or privatively <(or one is said predicatively and the other privatively), or one indeterminate and the other determinate, or both indeterminate, in none of these cases will there be a syllogism. Terms common to all cases: animal, white, horse; animal, white, stone.> [1.4, 26b21-5]

He proves that the combinations are also non-syllogistic if both premisses are particular, whichever quality they have, whether 10 both are affirmative or both negative or the major affirmative and the minor negative or conversely. Nor are they syllogistic when the premisses are indeterminate, whether both are affirmative or both negative or the major negative and the minor affirmative or conversely. The terms are common to all eight combinations. For holding: animal, white, horse. For not holding: animal, white, stone. 15 The reason why all such conjunctions are non-syllogistic is clear. For inasmuch as nothing is assumed universally, the middle term does not share with the other two terms in virtue of the same part but may be posited in virtue of different parts, so that it is hardly even a middle term for them. Reasonably enough,[142] nothing is deduced syllogistically from two particular propositions, since it is supposed 20 that a syllogistic justification justifies by means of a universal and proves one of the items under it.[143]

---

[140] See above, 66,29-67,2. For comparable comments on aberrant particles in Aristotle see Alexander, *in An. Pr.* 129,9; 203,3-5; 221,6; cf. e.g. Ammonius, *in Int.* 257,10-13.

[141] *Diastêmata*: i.e. the premisses.

[142] 68,19-69,9 = *FDS* 1090 (68,21-69,4 = *SVF* II 260).

[143] See above, 44,6-13. For the fact that every syllogism must have at least one universal premiss see Aristotle, *An. Pr.* 41b6-22; Alexander, *in An. Pr.* 266,8-267,27.

As for those who think that something can be deduced syllogistically from two particulars[144] – for example, those who in proof of this adduce the arguments which the Stoics say conclude unmethodically[145] and who also collect certain other examples – either they must disprove the examples cited by Aristotle to show that such conjunctions are non-syllogistic, proving that they are[146] false (and then they would be saying something), or else they must recognize that setting down even one example is sufficient to prove the combination non-syllogistic.

Besides, in the examples they adduce, the conclusion does not follow by necessity from what is assumed and posited, i.e. it does not follow inasmuch as they are the case,[147] but rather inasmuch as in these cases the universal premiss is true: although they get the conclusion from this universal premiss, they leave it out when they assume the premisses and they divide the minor into two.[148]

69,1 Of the arguments which they call unmethodically concluding, all those which have two particular premisses deduce in this way; and it is easy to prove this for the examples they adduce. And the other examples which they mistakenly take hold of in their effort to prove that such combinations are syllogistic are also not difficult to refute.

4.7 Additional syllogisms

5 Thus it is evident from what has been said that if there is a particular syllogism in this figure, it is necessary for the terms to stand as we have said; <for if they stand in any other way, there is not.> [1.4, 26b26-8]

He has proved that in the particular syllogisms (there were two of these) the major must be universal and either affirmative, in which case the conclusion is affirmative, or negative, in which case the conclusion is negative; and the minor must be a particular affirmative in both syllogisms.

---

[144] On these people see Barnes (1990a), IV.5. Note that [Ammonius], *in An. Pr.* XII.10-16, also allows that there may be syllogisms with two particular premisses.

[145] See above, 21,32 note. For the view that unmethodically concluding arguments, all or some of them, have *particular* premisses see Alexander, *in An. Pr.* 345,18-20; Philoponus, *in An. Pr.* 321,12-14; [Ammonius], *in An. Pr.* 70,20-2; 71,3-4. See Barnes (1990a), V.2-3.

[146] Reading *auta* for *autên*.

[147] See Aristotle, *An. Pr.* 24b20; cf. above, 21,10 note.

[148] Alexander's general view is this: corresponding to every unmethodical argument, 'P₁, P₂, ..., Pₙ: therefore Q', there is a categorical syllogism, 'U, P*: therefore Q', where U is a universal proposition and P* is some sort of amalgamation of the premisses of the unmethodical argument. Thus Alexander represents his opponents as starting from this syllogism, omitting U, and dividing P* into P₁ and P₂. See the examples above, 21,25-22,24; cf. the other references in 21,10 note, and see esp. Barnes (1990a), V.8-11.

It is clear too that all the syllogisms in it are perfect <(for they are all perfected by means of the initial assumptions) ...> [1.4, 26b28-30]

He defined a perfect syllogism as one which 'needs nothing else apart from the assumptions in order for the necessity to be 15 evident'.[149] He says that all the syllogisms which have been proved in this figure are perfect, since they all are perfected by means of what was initially assumed and posited and need nothing else. The items assumed initially are those by means of which the necessity is evident – namely, 'of every', which is equivalent to 'in as in a whole', and 'of none' or 'in no'.[150] 20

... and that all problems are proved by means of this figure ... [1.4, 26b30-1]

This is the main reason why this figure is the first.[151] This is why Aristotle, having said this, continues: 'I call this the first figure',[152] suggesting that he has given the reasons why this figure is rightly 25 called the first.

Aristotle[153] has proved that the four syllogisms which have been set out are the primary syllogisms in the first figure. To these four Theophrastus adds five more, which are no longer perfect or indemonstrable. Aristotle, too, will mention these, some at a later point in this book and some at the beginning of the next, i.e. the 70,1 second, book. Three of them, which come about from the first three indemonstrables by conversion of the conclusion, he will mention at the beginning of the second book, where he is investigating whether it is possible for there to be several conclusions from the same suppositions.[154] The other two he will mention in this book, where 5 he says that of the non-syllogistic combinations those similar in form are perfectly[155] non-syllogistic, while in non-syllogistic combinations which have a universal negative and are dissimilar in form something can be deduced with the minor term said of the major.[156] These two conjunctions are in the first figure, one with a universal affirmative major and a universal negative minor and the 10 other with a particular affirmative major and a universal negative minor. (The remaining combinations are either syllogistic or similar

[149] Aristotle, *An. Pr.* 24b23-4.
[150] See above, 32,11 note.
[151] See above, 48,21-49,6.
[152] *An. Pr.* 26b33.
[153] 69,26-9 = *FDS* 1101.
[154] *An. Pr.* B 1, 53a3-14.
[155] Reading *teleon* for *teleioi* with Wallies (see his *corrigenda* on p. 426).
[156] *An. Pr.* 29a19-27.

in form or do not have a universal negative minor.) Theophrastus
calls one of them the eighth and the other the ninth. When both
15   their premisses are converted, a particular negative conclusion is
deduced with the minor term said of the major. If particular
negatives converted, then each of the two combinations would be
syllogistic necessarily and primarily, proving the point at issue by
conversion of the conclusion. But since they do not convert, the
combinations are non-syllogistic with regard to the point at issue –
20   but something else can be deduced syllogistically by means of them.
We will say something about these syllogisms when we come to the
passages in question.[157]

[157] See below, 109,4-111,27, on *An. Pr.* 29a19-27. (Alexander's commentary on *An.
Pr.* B – and hence his discussion of 53a3-14 – is lost). On the 'additional' syllogisms
see e.g. Volait, pp. 30-6; Bochenski (1947), pp. 56-61; Rose, pp. 57-79; 109-32; Patzig,
pp. 112-14; Thom, pp. 52-5 (also Appendix 2, pp. 213-15). (1) Aristotle says at *An. Pr.*
53a3-14 that whenever the conclusion of a syllogism converts, then there is a further
syllogism to hand. He thus recognizes – but only implicitly and in entirely general
terms – *eight* further syllogisms; for we may convert the conclusions of *Barbara*,
Celarent and *Darii* in the first figure, of *Cesare* and *Camestres* in the second figure,
and of *Darapti*, *Disamis* and *Datisi* in the third figure. Let us call these new
syllogisms Group A. (2) At *An. Pr.* 29a19-27 Aristotle remarks that, of the
combinations which he has rejected as non-syllogistic, some will in fact yield a
conclusion in which the minor term is predicated of the major: the combinations are
those which consist of a universal negative and a universal or particular affirmative.
Aristotle thus recognizes – but only implicitly and in entirely general terms – five
further syllogisms, namely *Fapesmo* and *Frisesomorum* in the first figure, *Firesmo* in
the second figure, and *Fapemo* and *Frisemo* in the third figure. (There are, in all,
twelve combinations – four in each figure – which contain a universal negative and a
universal or particular affirmative. Seven of these combinations are recognised as
syllogistic in *An. Pr.* 1.4-6.) Let us call these new syllogisms Group B. (3)
Theophrastus added five syllogisms to the first figure (F 17 Graeser: in addition to the
present text see below, 109,29-110,21; Alexander, *Conv.* 60; Apuleius, *Int.* 193,7-13
[but the text is corrupt: see the discussion in Sullivan, pp. 155-7]; Martianus Capella,
IV 411; Boethius, *Syll. Cat.* 813BC, 814C-816C [Boethius mentions Eudemus – and
Porphyry – alongside Theophrastus]; scholium to Aristotle, 188a4-12). The five are
Baralipton, *Celantes* and *Dabitis*, from Group A, and *Fapesmo* and *Frisesomorum*,
from Group B. Theophrastus seems to have described these syllogisms in detail and
to have shown how they can be reduced to the four direct syllogisms in the first figure.
No text hints that Theophrastus made any additions to the other figures. Later
logicians refer to these syllogisms as 'reflected' (*kat anaklasin* or *antanaklômenoi*:
Boethius, *Syll. Cat.* 815A; Philoponus, *in An. Pr.* 79,10); the terminology was in use
before the time of Apuleius, who translates it by *reflexim*, and it may go back to
Theophrastus. (4) According to Apuleius, 'Ariston and some of the more recent
Peripatetics' added a further five syllogisms (*Int.* 193,16-20; see Sullivan, pp. 165-6).
(Note that the best MSS give *Aristoteles* instead of *Aristo*. At *Int.* 193,24 the MSS
again give *Aristoteles*; but here the text should not be changed to *Aristo*: see Moraux
(1973/84), I, pp. 190-1.) They are the so-called subaltern moods, i.e. *Barbari*,
Celaront, *Celantos*, *Cesaro*, and *Camestrop*. (Any combination which yields a
universal conclusion will also yield the particular proposition which falls under the
universal.) Call them Group C. Apuleius regards the addition of Group C as 'very
silly'. (5) At *Inst. Log.* xi 3-7 Galen enumerates certain additional syllogisms. (The
text is desperate: we follow here the version suggested by Jonathan Barnes and
Michael Frede in their forthcoming edition.) To the first figure Galen adds the five

Theophrastean syllogisms (three from Group A, two from Group B) and the two Aristonian syllogisms (from Group C). To the second figure he adds *Cesaro* and *Camestrop* from Group C (he omits *Celantop*). To the third figure he adds *Daraptis* from Group A. (6) At *in An. Pr.* 109,4-111,27 Alexander adds *Firesmo* to the second figure and *Fapemo* and *Frisemo* to the third, all from Group B. (7) Philoponus accepts the three first figure syllogisms from Group A (*in An. Pr.* 79,10-20); he accepts the five syllogisms from Group B (*in An. Pr.* 112,21-113,20); and he implicitly endorses all eight syllogisms from Group A (*in An. Pr.* 388,18-399,9). (8) The general disregard for Group C is not, perhaps, surprising; for (as Apuleius in effect remarks) the subaltern moods do not add anything to the probative power of categorical syllogistic. But why are Group A syllogisms not added to the second and third figures? The explanation is to be found in Galen; for he observes that the reflected form of *Cesare* is simply *Camestres*, and *vice versa*, and that the reflected form of *Disamis* is simply *Datisi* and *vice versa* (*Inst. Log.* xi 7). (Convert the conclusion of *Cesare* and you get: B holds of no A; B holds of every C: therefore, C holds of no A. And this is *Camestres*, with the premisses in reversed order.) It is, then, strange that Galen allows the reflected form of *Darapti*; for *Daraptis* is in fact identical with *Darapti*, as Apuleius observes (*Int.* 189,23-5). Here Galen seems to be following Theophrastus (see below, 95,30 note).

5

The Second Figure

5.1 General remarks

When the same item holds of all the one and of none of the other, or of all or none of each, <I call this the second figure.> [1.5, 26b34-6]

70,25 Having spoken of the first figure and the combinations in it, and having shown which of them are syllogistic and which non-syllogistic, he moves to the second figure; and he will discuss its combinations in the same way. The second figure, as we have said,[1] is the one in which the common or middle term is predicated of both terms in the problem at issue. He shows this by saying 'When the

30 same item holds of all the one and of none of the other, or of all or none of each'; for this is equivalent to 'When the same term (that is,

71,1 the middle term, which is taken twice) holds of all of one of the extremes – i.e. is predicated of all of it – and of none of the other – i.e. is predicated of none of it – or is said of all or none of each of the extremes.' Again, with this figure as with the first,[2] he set down

5 examples to make evident how the middle term stands, viz. that it is predicated of both extremes. The examples which he uses betoken the combinations of two universal premisses. He discusses them first, as he did in the first figure too. And he mentioned all combinations of universal premisses in saying 'When the same item

10 holds of all the one and of none of the other, or of all or none of each.'

Now, we have said that this is the second figure, and for what reasons.[3] It is clear that by the conversion of the major premiss in the first figure, the middle term comes to be predicated of both extremes.[4] For when it is converted, the middle comes to be

15 predicated of the term for which it was subject (it was the subject for the major extreme); and it is also predicated of the minor. Therefore

---

[1] Above, 46,32-47,4.
[2] See above, 52,30.
[3] Above, 48,12-18.
[4] On the 'generation' of the second figure see above, 47,27 note.

it comes to be predicated of both terms once the major has been converted. And as predicated, it has a superior place in the second figure since being predicated is more important than being subject.[5] Reasonably, therefore, this is the second figure, since the middle (because of which syllogisms come about), having lost the position appropriate to it (which it had in the first figure), has the nobler of the   20
two remaining positions.

A combination is syllogistic in the second figure when the major premiss is universal. When it is particular there will be no syllogism in the second figure – and with good reason. For the syllogistic   25 combinations in the second figure preserve the proper characteristic of the proposition by the conversion of which the second figure was generated from the first.[6] The second premiss, the minor, must be either particular or universal (it is syllogistic both when it is universal and when it is particular). And it must by necessity be opposite in quality to the major, i.e. dissimilar in form: if the latter is   30 affirmative, it must be negative; if negative, affirmative. For if they are similar in form a syllogism does not come about in the second figure: neither from two negatives (because in no figure is such a combination syllogistic), nor from two affirmatives, as will be proved. The syllogistic premisses standing thus, in this figure too there will   72,1 be four syllogistic combinations: if the major premiss is affirmative, it is connected either to a universal or to a particular negative minor; if the major is assumed as negative, the minor is either a universal or a particular affirmative.   5

I say that in it the middle term is the one predicated of both ...
[1.5, 26b36-7]

This is actually the account of the second figure: it is the figure in which the middle is predicated of both the extremes for which the deduction must be made.

... and the major extreme is the one supposed on the middle. The middle is posited outside the extremes and first in   10 position. [1.5, 26b37-9]

By the diagram of the terms[7] and the expression[8] he uses he has made clear to us that it is when the major premiss in the first figure

---

[5] See above, 48,25-7.

[6] cf. below, 95,14-19; Themistius, *Max.* 182-3.

[7] For other references to diagrams see e.g. below, 78,4; Alexander, *in An. Pr.* 301,9-19; 381,8-12; Philoponus, *in An. Pr.* 65,20-3; 87,8; Boethius, *Syll. Cat.* 814B. For illustrative examples see [Ammonius], *in An. Pr.* VIII.20-1, 24-5; X.10-XI.1; 39,9 app. crit. See Rose, pp. 133-6.

[8] Reading *lexeôs* (with LM and the Aldine) for *taxeôs*.

is converted that the second figure comes about. For the position and
order of the terms which he describes – the fact that the middle is
put first in order and the major supposed after it – make clear that it
15   is the major premiss which was converted.[9]

5.2 Major and minor terms

... and the major extreme is the one supposed on the middle.
[1.5, 26b37-8][10]

People investigate whether by nature there are major and minor
extremes in the second figure, and how we can judge which they
are.[11] For if it is indifferent, then it will be possible to call major
whichever sort of term we like to connect in position to the middle
20   term. This will be so because the conclusions in this figure are
negative, and universal negatives convert from one another. Hence
for this reason one term will be no more major than the other in
universal negations – since the predicate is major and these terms
are counterpredicated each of the other with an equal extension. In
the case of affirmatives, the major is the term predicated
25   universally, since it has a wider extension. (That is why they do not
convert.) Hence being major holds of it by nature. But in the case of
universal negatives this is no longer the case.
     Now Herminus takes the following view.[12] If in the second figure
the two terms of which the middle is predicated are co-generic, then
the major extreme is the one which is nearer to their common
73,1   genus.[13] Suppose the extremes are bird and man: bird is closer than

---

[9] In the 'diagram' for first figure syllogisms the terms are arranged thus:
     A – B – C.
For the second figure the corresponding diagram is:
     B – A – C
Hence it is clear that the major premiss (represented by 'A – B') has had its terms
converted. (See below, 98,2-12.)

[10] It is curious that Alexander makes no comment at all on this phrase; nor does he
discuss the next phrase in *An. Pr.* ('and the minor is the one further from the middle'),
which his own text of Aristotle apparently lacked.

[11] See Philoponus, *in An. Pr.* 67,18-68,8; 87,10-19, who concludes that it is
convention and not nature which determines the major and minor terms in the
second and third figures (cf. Themistius, *Max.* 181-2). See Łukasiewicz, pp. 30-2 (who
remarks that 'what John Philoponus writes on this subject deserves to be regarded as
classic'); Mignucci (1969), pp. 219-21; and esp. Patzig, pp. 118-27.

[12] On Herminus' view see Moraux (1973/84), II, pp. 383-5. Bochenski (1947), p. 64
n. 218 observes that 'this is one of the most instructive passages we possess about the
Peripatetic cast of mind'.

[13] Herminus' view presupposes that every term which may appear in a syllogistic
proposition has a unique and fixed position in some 'division' of terms: it represents a
node in a Porphyrean tree. The 'distance' between one term and another, given that
they appear in the same tree (i.e. are co-generic), is then determined by the number of
nodes between them. Then take a middle term, B, and two extreme terms, A and C.

man to their common genus, animal, and is produced by the primary division. Hence bird is the major extreme. And in general, when the terms are co-generic, the one related in this way to the common genus is major.

If both terms are equally distant from the common genus, as man and horse are, then one must look at the middle term which is 5 predicated of them and see of which it is predicated because of itself and of which because of another term. If it is predicated of one because of itself and of the other because of another term, then you should compare the term because of which it is predicated of something else with the term of which[14] it is predicated in its own right.

If the former term – the term because of which it is predicated of something else – is closer to their common genus, then you should call major the term of which the middle is predicated because of the 10 term nearer to the common genus. For example, suppose the extremes are horse and man, and rational is predicated of them (negatively of horse, affirmatively of man). Now rational is not denied of horse in its own right but because horses are non-rational, whereas rational is affirmed of man in his own right; and non-rational is closer than man to their common genus, animal.[15] 15 Thus horse will be the major extreme in relation to man, even though man is equally distant from their appropriate genus, because the term because of which the predicate is predicated of it is

---

There are two possibilities. (1) A and C appear in the same tree. Then there must be some term, D, higher in the tree under which both A and C fall. (A cannot fall under C, nor C under A; or at least, this is apparently excluded by the fact that the first two syllogisms in the second figure have universal negative conclusions.) Again, there are two possibilities. (i) A and C are not equidistant from D. Then the term closer to D is the major term. (ii) A and C are equidistant from D. Then we must consider the terms because of which B is predicated of A and of C. Suppose that B is predicated of A because of E and of C because of F. Then if E is closer to D than F is, A is the major term; and if F is closer, C is major. (What if E and F are equidistant from D? Herminus tacitly excludes this case by supposing that either E will be identical with A or F will be identical with C; i.e. either B is predicated of A because of itself or it is predicated of C because of itself.) (2) A and C appear in different trees, T and T*. Then consider the highest genus in each tree, G and G*. There are, again, two possibilities. (i) The distance between A and G is not the same as the distance between C and G*: then the term nearer its own highest genus is the major term. (ii) A and C are equidistant from G and G*. Then – as in case (1)(ii) – consider E and F. If E is closer to G than F is to G*, then A is major; if F is closer, C is major. Numerous comments might be made on this elaborate suggestion; but the matter does not merit detailed discussion. For, as Alexander rightly says (74,5-6), the whole thing is 'a waste of time'.

[14] Reading *tôi hou* for *tôi di' hon*.

[15] The transmitted text of this sentence has Herminus contradict himself in an obvious (and wholly irrelevant) fashion. The text is surely corrupt, but no convincing emendation suggests itself. We add *ekeino de* before *enguterô* in line 14 and delete *ho hippos êper anthrôpos* in line 15. We do not suppose that Alexander wrote these precise words; but we do suppose that they give the sense of what he wrote.

major. For rational is denied of horse *qua* non-rational, not *qua* horse, whereas rational is affirmed of man in his own right.

20   If the extreme terms are not co-generic but belong to different genera, then one should posit as major the one which is closer in its own genus. For example, if something is predicated of colour and of man, colour is the major extreme. For colour is closer to quality than man is to substance – man is an indivisible species whereas colour is not. If, again, they are both equally distant from their appropriate

25   genera, then you should ascend to the predicate and seek of which of them it is predicated because of itself and of which because of another term. And if the term because of which it is predicated of something else is closer to its own genus, then you should deem the major extreme to be the one of which the middle is predicated because of that term. For example, suppose the terms are white and man, both being indivisible species (the one of quality and the other of substance), and suppose that rational is predicated affirmatively of man and negatively of white. Now it is affirmed of man *qua* man

74,1 but denied of white not *qua* white but *qua* inanimate. Then since inanimate, because of which rational is denied of white, is more common and more universal and closer to inanimate substance than man is to animate substance, then for this reason white is the major term in relation to man.

5   Now to say all this, and to seek to prove that the major extreme in the second figure is major *by nature*, is not only a waste of time – it is not even true. For, first, if we examine not the terms taken, in and by themselves, but rather those terms in virtue of which the predicated term does not hold of them, then the major term will always be in the negative proposition. For it will be either equal or

10   major in relation to the middle term, either having been taken in this way from the beginning or becoming such because of the term because of which the middle term is denied of it, so that[16] it is major in relation to the middle term which is denied of it. For the middle term will not hold of that of which it is supposed not to hold, because its opposite and co-ordinate holds of the subject; and what is opposite to the middle term and co-ordinate with it is equal to it. It will fail to hold either because of this term itself or because of

15   something else which is of wider extension than the middle term – as when rational is denied of something because of inanimate. It is equal when it holds because of non-rational – for rational is equal to non-rational, because of which rational is negatively predicated of horse. Thus the middle term is either equal to that of which it is negated or minor in relation to it – when rational is denied of something because of inanimate. For inanimate is equal to animate,

---

[16] Reading *hôste* for *houtôs*.

under which rational falls – and rational is major in relation to the   20
other term, of which it is affirmed. Now since the term predicated
affirmatively is major in relation to its subject, the term of which the
middle is denied is also major in relation to the term of which the
middle is affirmed – since the reason why it is denied is equal or
major in relation to the middle itself, which is major in relation to its
subject in the affirmative proposition. Hence the negative
proposition will always be major in relation to the affirmative.[17] But
Aristotle says that the negative can be posited on the minor term as   25
well – thus the second syllogism in this figure has a negative
minor.[18]

Again, why will it only be in the case of negatives that we
transform the issue and seek the term because of which the middle
is negatively predicated? The same thing will be sought in the case
of affirmation. For even if rational is said of man in his own right, it   30
is not said of man primarily or *qua* man but *qua* rational. Hence if it
is said of horse because of non-rational and of man because of
rational, and if rational is equal to non-rational (since they arise   75,1
from the same division), then the method before us will not yet have
yielded the major term.

For these reasons one should not judge which is the major premiss
in the second figure in this way. For, in general, inasmuch as both
the affirmative and the negative may be on the major term in this   5
figure, then whatever term is found to be major by the method we
have described will make the combination syllogistic whether it is
taken as major or as minor. But in that case it will no longer be the
major term in this figure. (We are not seeking the major term
simpliciter but the major term in this figure.)

Yet we should not simply say that the term predicated in the   10
conclusion of the syllogism is the major term, as some people
think.[19] For it is not clear which this term is: sometimes it will be
the one and sometimes the other – it is not determined (inasmuch as
universal negatives convert), and what is now major will later be
minor, and it will be up to us to make the same term both major and
minor.[20] Thus in negatives there is by nature no major term, nor   15
should one take the major simply from the conclusion. For it will not

---

[17] Alexander's argument is convoluted. It may be summarized as follows. Consider
the term, D, because of which B holds of no C. Either D is identical with not-B, in
which case it is on a level with B, or it holds of every B, in which case it is above B. But
B holds of every A. Hence B is above A. Hence C is always major in relation to A.

[18] i.e. *Camestres*.

[19] So later e.g. Philoponus, *in An. Pr.* 67,27-30; cf. above, 47,30; Alexander, *in An.
Pr.* 341,15-19.

[20] Thus the combination 'A holds of every B, B holds of every C' will yield 'A holds of
no C' (by *Celarent*) and also 'C holds of no A' (by *Celantes*). Hence we cannot say which
of A and C is 'the predicate in the conclusion'; for there are two conclusions.

be determined which this term is. Moreover, the conclusion has as predicate the term taken as major in the premisses, so that the conclusion does not show the major term – rather, the reason why a term is predicated in the conclusion is that it is taken as the major term.[21]

20   Yet we cannot say that there is no major term in the figure. For it is determined that in it the major premiss must be universal if there is to be a syllogistic conjunction,[22] and the major premiss is the one containing the major term. Now we must deem to be major and posit as primary the term which we want to prove and deduce in the problem, i.e. the term which we have predicated in it. For everyone

25   who syllogizes first defines for himself what he wants to prove and so obtains premisses appropriate to it.[23] He does not hit on the conclusion by chance. Now it is the term predicated in the problem set up for proof which should be posited as the major term. For even if it converts, and for this reason the same term becomes subject, nonetheless it was and remains predicated in the problem which is

30   set up for us to prove. (That is why if we get a different conclusion we convert it.) Hence for us, who prove and syllogize and order the terms, this is the major term; for it is not in their own natures that terms are major and minor in negatives but rather with reference to our purpose in the conclusions – and it is clear that the term predicated in the problem is also predicated in the conclusion.[24]

5.3 Second figure syllogisms

76,1   Now there will not be a perfect syllogism in this figure, but there will be a potential one both when the terms are universal and when they are not universal. [1.5, 27a1-3]

He called perfect syllogisms those in which the necessity is evident

5   from the suppositions (the syllogisms in the first figure have been shown to be such) and imperfect syllogisms those which need some external item or items – items which are necessary because of the terms laid down but have not been taken in a premiss.[25] The syllogisms in this figure and in the third are of this sort. For three of the syllogisms in this figure need conversion in order for their

10   necessity to become evident; and while the fourth is not proved by conversion, the necessity of its deduction is proved by reduction to the impossible.

[21] This is not Alexander's normal view: see above, 47,29-48,6.
[22] See above, 71,22-6.
[23] See esp. Kapp for this way of looking at syllogisms. But it is not the only way in which Alexander (or Aristotle) regards them.
[24] See above, 47,30.
[25] See Aristotle, *An. Pr.* 24b22-6; above, 23,17-24,12.

The sentence 'But there will be a potential one both when the terms are universal and when they are not universal' means that in this figure too it is possible to get a syllogism both when both premisses are universal and also when they are not both universal.[26] (In the latter case, clearly only one of them is particular, namely the minor. For there is no syllogism if both premisses are particular, nor – as we have said[27] – if the major is particular.)

When they are universal, there will be a syllogism when the middle holds of all the one and of none of the other, on whichever the privative may be; and in no other case. [1.5, 27a3-5]

We have said[28] that if we are to produce a syllogistic combination, the premisses in this figure must be dissimilar in form with regard to quality. When both premisses are universal and are also dissimilar in form, there will be a syllogism – whether the major is negative and the minor affirmative or conversely. For both combinations of this sort are syllogistic, deducing a universal negative.

As we have already said,[29] there are four syllogistic combinations in this figure, as there are in the first: two with universal premisses and two in which one, the minor, is particular.

The order of these syllogisms is as follows.[30] First are the two which deduce a universal negative from universal premisses. (No affirmative is deduced in this figure, because nothing is deduced from premisses similar in kind.) These are first, because the universal is more valuable than and prior to the particular.[31] Of these two, the first will be the one which has the major premiss universal and negative and the minor universal and affirmative. For this syllogism needs a single conversion to make its necessity evident: by converting the major premiss it is reduced to the second indemonstrable, as will be proved.[32] The syllogism with the major premiss universal and affirmative will be ranked after this; for it

---

[26] By 'a potential one' Aristotle here means 'a potentially perfect syllogism': see *An. Pr.* 41b33 (cf. 28a16), with Philoponus, *in An. Pr.* 255,27-9 (cf. Alexander, *in An. Pr.* 271,2-6, who takes the word to mean 'potentially evident'); Patzig, p. 46. Here, however, Alexander appears to take 'there will be a potential one' to mean 'it is possible to get a syllogism' (so too Philoponus, *in An. Pr.* 87,30-88,2).

[27] Above, 71,22-6.

[28] Above, 71,28-33.

[29] Above, 72,1-5.

[30] cf. Apuleius, *Int.* 190,15-191,5; Philoponus, *in An. Pr.* 88,26-33; 94,3-7; see above, 51,8-24, on the order of syllogisms in the first figure, and below, 95,25-31 and 96,22-97,11, on the order in the third figure.

[31] See above, 48,27.

[32] See Aristotle, *An. Pr.* 27a5-9; below, 78,12-22.

needs two conversions to prove that the major extreme holds of the minor extreme. Thus since it needs more help than the syllogism before it, it is reasonable to rank it after it, being more imperfect than it.[33] It will be shown that in this syllogism two propositions are converted.[34]

10   As we have said,[35] the two syllogisms which deduce particular negatives must have their major premisses universal – the minor in both cases is particular. The syllogism in which the major is universal and negative and the minor a particular affirmative will be third. Its necessity becomes evident by the conversion of the
15   major premiss; for if this is converted we get the fourth indemonstrable in the first figure. (If the converse has not been explicitly assumed in the premisses, it is there potentially.[36]) For this reason, this syllogism is less imperfect than the one after it, which has the major premiss universal and affirmative and the minor particular and negative. This cannot be proved by conversion,
20   but needs more help. Its necessity is proved by reduction to the impossible, and in this proof we introduce from outside a premiss which is not disclosed by what has been laid down. Nevertheless, the point at issue is not deduced by using other terms or by proving something else. For, as will be shown, the syllogism deduces the opposite, and, since this is evidently impossible, by rejecting it we
25   justify the point at issue which is its opposite.[37] On the other hand, syllogisms which deduce by way of conversions syllogize the point at issue itself. As the syllogism in question needs so much help, it stands to reason that it is more imperfect and has the last place among the syllogisms of this figure. For the three syllogisms before it which are proved by conversion can also be proved by reduction to
30   the impossible, whereas the fourth cannot be proved by conversion and is justified as a syllogism only by reduction to the impossible.

While examining the combinations in this figure – which and how many they are and which are syllogistic and which non-syllogistic –
78,1   Aristotle sets out the combinations by way of letters, as he did in the first figure.[38] The letters he uses are not A, B, C, as in the first figure, but M, N, O: as middle term he takes M, which is predicated of both the other terms and has first position in the diagram;[39] as

---

[33] On degrees of imperfection see Patzig, pp. 48-9 (on degrees of perfection see below, 113,8 note).

[34] See Aristotle, *An. Pr.* 27a9-14; below, 78,25-79,25.

[35] See above, 71,29.

[36] See above, 58,13-22.

[37] This account of reduction to the impossible is compact to the point of unintelligibility; for a fuller and clearer account see below, 83,24-84,3, to which Alexander refers us (cf. above, 24,18 note).

[38] See above, 53,30 note.

[39] On logical diagrams see above, 72,11 note.

major extreme N, which is laid down next after the middle; and as   5
last and minor O.

By saying 'on whichever the privative may be; and in no other
case' he makes it clear that if there is no privative premiss, there
will not be a syllogistic combination in this figure. And, as he proves,
there are twelve non-syllogistic combinations in this figure apart
from the indeterminate ones, since there are sixteen combinations
in all.

5.4 Combinations of universal premisses

5.4.1 *Cesare* and *Camestres*

> Let M be predicated of no N and of every O. Since the privative   10
> converts, <N will hold of no M. But M was supposed to hold of
> every O. Hence N of no O (this has been proved earlier).> [1.5,
> 27a5-9]

It has been proved above that actual universal privatives convert
from themselves.[40] Thus since the major premiss has been assumed
as a universal negative (for it is supposed that M holds of no N), then
if it is converted, N will hold of no M. But it is supposed that M holds   15
of every O. With such premisses we get the second syllogism of the
first figure, which deduces a universal negative, 'N holds of no O'.
Thus this will also be deduced from the combination set out here.
Let M be animal, N inanimate, O man. If animal is said of no
inanimate, by conversion inanimate is said of no animal. But animal   20
is said of every man. Therefore inanimate is said of no man. This is
the first syllogism of the second figure and it is perfected with such
help.[41]

> Again, if M holds of every N and of no O, O will hold of no N.
> <For if M holds of no O, O holds of no M. But M held of every N.
> Therefore O will hold of no N. For we have got the first figure
> again. And since the privative converts, N will hold of no O.
> Hence there will be the same syllogism.> [1.5, 27a9-14]

We ought first to infer the conclusion which should be proved in this   25
conjunction (namely, that N holds of no O – for it is supposed that N
is the major term, and so we must predicate it in the conclusion),
and then to turn to the proof of how this conclusion is deduced. But
Aristotle[42] omitted the final conclusion, and instead gives the   79,1

---

[40] See Aristotle, *An. Pr.* 25a14-17; above, 31,4-34,23.
[41] On proofs by conversion see esp. Patzig, pp. 137-44.
[42] Reading *ho de* (conjectured by Wallies, *index verborum* s.v. *hode*) for *hode*.

demonstration by which the following conclusion will be proved: he says that O will hold of no N. And he proves that this is the first conclusion to result from this combination. For since it is supposed that the minor premiss, MO, is a universal negative, and since

5 universal negatives convert, O will hold of no M. But it was supposed that M holds of every N. From this it is deduced that O holds of no N. (The major was a universal affirmative.) With these suppositions we again get the second indemonstrable in the first figure; for O holds of no M, M holds of every N, and from this it can be deduced that O holds of no N. Thus by converting the minor

10 premiss he proves what he said would be the conclusion. But since this was not the point at issue to be proved (for it was supposed in the combination that the major term is N and the major term must be predicated in the conclusion), he converts the conclusion, which is a universal negative, and thus proves that N holds of no O – and this was what he had to prove to be deducible. Thus we needed two

15 conversions for the proof of the point at issue: we converted both the minor premiss and the conclusion which then resulted. Let M be animal, N man, O inanimate. Animal holds of every man, animal of no inanimate. Proof: inanimate holds of no animal, animal of every man, inanimate of no man, and therefore man of no inanimate.[43]

20 He added 'Hence there will be the same syllogism' to show that the conclusion that N holds of no O will be proved by the same syllogism by which it was proved that O holds of no N. This was proved to be deducible through the second syllogism in the first figure, by converting the universal negative. Hence the former conclusion is also proved by this syllogism. For it is supposed to be agreed that the universal negative, which was the conclusion,

25 converts from itself, and no other syllogism is needed for this.[44]

It is also possible to prove these by reduction to the impossible.
[1.5, 27a14-15]

He says that by using reduction to the impossible[45] you can also prove that the combinations just mentioned are syllogistic and deduce a universal negative conclusion.

30 The first syllogism we will prove in the following way. Suppose the premisses that M holds of no N and that M holds of every O. I say that N holds of no O. For if this is impossible, let N hold of some O, which is the opposite of 'of none'. But either the latter or the former must be deduced. For in every case one part of the contradictory pair

---

[43] On this paragraph see Patzig, pp. 140-1.

[44] Other interpretations of Aristotle's phrase are possible: see Ross, p. 308; Patzig, p. 186 n. 18.

[45] On proofs by reduction to the impossible see above, 24,18 note.

holds. Since, then, it is supposed that N holds of some O, it is clear   80,1
that O will hold of some N, because particular affirmatives convert
from themselves. But it is also supposed that M holds of every O. Thus
we get the combination: M holds of every O, O holds of some N.
Therefore M holds of some N, which is impossible. For it is supposed   5
that M holds of no N. Now if this impossibility follows because it was
hypothesized that N holds of some O, then the hypothesis is
impossible and false. But if it is false, its opposite is true. But the
opposite of 'N holds of some O' is 'N holds of no O'. Therefore N holds of
no O, which we aimed to prove.

Or is it better to prove it in the following way?[46] I say that N holds of   10
no O in the combination set out. For if someone says that this is false
let its opposite, that N holds of some O, be hypothesized. But it is also
supposed that M holds of no N. Then it can be deduced in the first
figure that M does not hold of some O. But it was supposed that M
holds of every O. Therefore something impossible has been deduced,
namely that M does not hold of some O, on the hypothesis that N   15
holds of some O. Therefore[47] the hypothesis is false. Therefore its
opposite, that N holds of no O, is true.

Again, suppose the second combination: M holds of every N; M
holds of no O. I say that N holds of no O. For if of some and if it is also
supposed that M holds of every N, then M will hold of some O, which is
impossible. For M held of no O. Therefore the hypothesis on which   20
this has been deduced, i.e. the hypothesis which posits that N holds of
some O, is false. Therefore its opposite, that N holds of no O, is true.

If we convert the hypothesis and produce 'O holds of some N' and
co-assume 'M holds of no O', again something impossible is deduced,
namely that M does not hold of some N. For it was supposed to hold of
every N.

Thus it is evident that there is a syllogism when the terms stand   25
thus <– but not a perfect one. For the necessity is perfected not
only from the initial assumptions but also from other items.>
[1.5, 27a15-18]

After he has proved by conversion and reduction to the impossible
that these two combinations in the second figure are syllogistic, he
remarks that the syllogisms are not perfect inasmuch as they
needed a demonstration from outside in order to make their   30
necessity evident.

---

[46] The first reduction uses *Darii*, the second *Ferio*; Alexander presumably thinks
that the second is better because it does not require us to convert the hypothesis.
Both proofs are, of course, equally 'good'.
[47] Reading *ara* for *gar*.

5.4.2 Non-syllogistic combinations

81,1   If M is predicated of every N and O, there will not be a
syllogism. <Terms for holding: substance, animal, man. For
not holding: substance, animal, number. (Substance is the
middle.)> [1.5, 27a18-20]

Having proved the syllogistic combinations with two universal
premisses in the second figure, he sets down the non-syllogistic
5   combinations and shows that they are non-syllogistic, setting down
material instances to prove that in them the major extreme may
hold of all and also of none of the minor. The remaining
combinations with two universal premisses are the ones which are
similar in form, i.e. the combination with two universal affirmatives
and the combination with two universal negatives.

First, then, he tackles the combination with two universal
10   affirmatives, in which M holds of every N and O. For the case that N
holds of every O, he sets down the terms substance for M, animal for
N, man for O. For substance holds both of every animal and of every
man. And animal, which was N, holds of every man, which was
supposed for O.

For the case in which N holds of no O he posits number for O.
15   What he says would be more evident if stone had been posited. For
the premisses are again true in the same way (substance holds both
of every animal and of every stone), and animal holds of no stone.

Either he took number to stand for unit – for they say[48] that units
are substances. (They say that units are not quantities inasmuch as
they are neither continuous nor determinate.[49] They are substances
inasmuch as they are capable of receiving contraries[50] – for a
20   beginning and an end are contraries, and numerical units possess
both.) But if a unit is what is undivided in quantity, a point what is
undivided in magnitude, and an instant what is undivided in time,[51]
then they will have one genus[52] – they will be quantities. Further,
the unit is a part of number. For numbers are compounded from
units.[53] But what is a part of a quantity is a quantity.
25   It is better to say that he uses the example rather loosely – in
other cases too we shall find him using examples without deliberate

[48] Who? According to Philoponus, the view is Pythagorean (*in An. Post.* 301,26-8);
but Alexander's 'they' are no doubt earlier scholars who have in mind Aristotle's own
remark that 'a unit is a substance without position' (*An. Post.* 87a36).
[49] Quantities are either continuous or determinate: Aristotle, *Cat.* 4b20.
[50] This is the proper characteristic of substances: *Cat.* 4a10-11.
[51] See e.g. Aristotle, *An. Post.* 77a22-3 (units); *Metaph.* 1016b24-6 (points); *Phys.*
233b33 (instants).
[52] Reading *hen genos* for *en genei* (Wallies' emendation of *en genesi*, which the MSS
present).
[53] See e.g. Aristotle, *Metaph.* 1053a30; cf. *Cat.* 4b23 for number as a quantity.

precision – since[54] the doctrine is Pythagorean. For according to the Pythagoreans numbers are substances since they are principles of substances.[55]

The reason why there is no syllogistic combination from two universal affirmatives in the second figure is that the middle is predicated of both extremes, and the predicate is the major term. 30 Thus, being major in relation to both, it may be predicated of one extreme term in virtue of one of its parts, and of the other in virtue of another. And in this way there is nothing which the extremes share with each other, if they each share with the middle term in virtue of different parts of it. For the extremes must share in one and the same thing if there is to be a syllogism.[56]   82,1

<Nor when M is predicated of no N and of no O. Terms for holding: line, animal, man. For not holding: line, animal, stone.> [1.5, 27a20-3]

He proves in the same way that the combination with two universal negatives is non-syllogistic, setting down terms for holding of all and of none: line for M, animal for N, man and stone for O. For line holds of no animal, of no man, and of no stone, and animal holds of every 5 man and of no stone. We have already said for what reason nothing is deduced from two negative premisses.[57]

After this he continues as follows: if there is a syllogism with a universal conclusion in the second figure,[58] it must have premisses dissimilar in form of the sort we have described[59] – one a universal negative, the other a universal affirmative. Otherwise there will be 10 no syllogism. For it has been proved that, apart from these, the conjunctions of universal premisses in this figure are non-syllogistic.

5.5 Combinations of universal and particular premisses

5.5.1 *Festino*

If the middle is universal in relation to one term ... [1.5, 27a26]

[54] We follow LM and the Aldine: after *paradeigmasin* B has *all'hôsper* with *te* written above -*per* and Wallies prints *allôs te*.
[55] So Philoponus, *in An. Pr.* 92,9-12 (for the evidence about Pythagorean number metaphysics see Burkert (1972), pp. 28-52). Cf. Aristotle, *An. Pr.* 27b6-8; below, 86,5-6.
[56] For the style of argument see above, 56,27 note.   [57] See above, 57,10-14.
[58] Alexander is paraphrasing *An. Pr.* 27a23-5. In modern texts Aristotle continues as follows: '... if there is a syllogism when the terms are universal', i.e. 'if there is a syllogism with universal *premisses*'. It is unlikely that Alexander should have misunderstood this, so we suppose that he had a different text before him.
[59] See above, 71,29-31.

Having discussed the combinations with two universal premisses,
15   and having proved some of them to be syllogistic and the others
non-syllogistic, he now discusses those which are compounded from
a universal and a particular. He shows which they are, and which of
them are syllogistic and which non-syllogistic. He shows that here
too the combinations dissimilar in form are syllogistic – provided
that the universal is preserved for the major premiss. There are two
20   syllogistic combinations: one in which the major is a universal
negative and is compounded with the minor which is a particular
affirmative; the other in which the major is a universal affirmative
and the minor a particular negative.

> For if M holds of no N and of some O, it is necessary for N not to
> hold of some O. <For since the privative converts, N will hold
> of no M. But M was supposed to hold of some O. Hence N will
> not hold of some O. For we get a syllogism by way of the first
> figure.> [1.5, 27a32-6]

25   He proves this combination to be syllogistic by invoking the
conversion of the universal negative MN. For if M holds of no N, N
holds of no M. But it is supposed that M holds of some O. We get the
combination of the fourth syllogism in the first figure (N holds of no
M, M of some O), from which it was deduced that N does not hold of
30   some O. This then will also be the conclusion in the second figure
combination before us.
83,1   It is also possible to prove it by reduction to the impossible. For
suppose that M holds of no N and of some O: I say that N does not
hold of some O. For if this is not so, then its opposite, that N holds of
every O, is the case. But it is also supposed that M holds of no N. It
5   will be deduced, according to the second syllogism in the first figure,
that M holds of no O, which is impossible – for it is supposed that M
holds of some O. The hypothesis by means of which this was deduced
is therefore false. Its opposite, therefore, is true. And opposed to 'N
holds of every O' is the proposition stating that N does not hold of
some O.

5.5.2 *Baroco*

10   Again if M holds of every N and not of some O, it is necessary
for N not to hold of some O. For if it will hold of every O, <and
M is predicated of every N, it is necessary for M to hold of every
O. But it was supposed not to hold of some.> [1.5, 27a36-b1]

He does not reduce this syllogism to one of the indemonstrables by conversion and thus prove it as he proved the three before it in the second figure. The reason is that it is not possible to conduct such a proof for the present combination. For if we convert the major, 15 which is a universal affirmative, it no longer remains a universal, since a universal affirmative converts with a particular affirmative; and neither in the first figure nor in the second is there a syllogistic combination in which the major is particular. Nor in general is there a syllogistic combination in which the two premisses are particular. (The major becomes particular through the conversion, and the 20 minor was taken as a particular at the beginning.) For this reason, then, it is not possible to use conversion of the major premiss. And it is impossible to convert the minor, which is a particular negative: for particular actual negatives do not convert with particular negatives.[60] So he uses reduction to the impossible to prove that the 25 combination under consideration is syllogistic. For if it is not true in the case of the supposed premisses that N does not hold of some O, then its opposite will be true. This is that N holds of every O. But it is supposed that M holds of every N. Thus we get the combination in the first figure with two universal affirmatives, from which it will be 84,1 deduced that M holds of every O. But this is impossible; for it is supposed that it does not hold of some O. What was hypothesized, that N holds of every O, is therefore false. Its opposite, that N does not hold of some O, is therefore true.

And if M holds of every N and not of every O, <there will be a 5 syllogism that N does not hold of every O. The demonstration is the same.> [1.5, 27b1-3]

He[61] conducted the proof in terms of 'does not hold of some'. And since 'does not hold of some' is equivalent to 'not of every', differing only in expression,[62] he now makes the transformation and instead of supposing that M does not hold of some O, he posits that M does not hold of every O. He says that there will be the same syllogism, and by way of the same proof, if the particular negative is 10 transformed into this expression. For the conclusion too will differ in expression in the same way – it will be deduced that N does not hold of every O.

This is an argument of the sort which the more recent thinkers call subsyllogistic:[63] it takes something equivalent to the syllogistic

[60] See below, 103,15-19, on *Bocardo*.
[61] 84,6-19 = *FDS* 1084 (84,11-19 = *SVF* II 264).
[62] See above, 62,12 note.
[63] The 'more recent thinkers' are Stoics; and subsyllogistic arguments had been discussed by Chrysippus. See Galen, *Inst. Log.* xix 6 ('the arguments called subsyllogistic <are expressed> in formulations equivalent to the arguments said to be syllogistic'); and for examples of such arguments see Alexander, *in An. Pr.*

premiss and deduces the same thing from it. ('Does not hold of some' has been transformed into 'does not hold of every', which is equivalent to it.) The more recent thinkers deny[64] that such arguments are syllogisms, since they look to the words and the expression.[65] Aristotle, however, looks to the meanings (when the same things are meant) rather than to the words and says that the same syllogism is deduced when the expression of the conclusion is transformed in this way – granted that the conjunction is in general syllogistic.

15

It is worth observing how a reduction to the impossible, which takes an external hypothesis in order to prove the point at issue, can be syllogistic;[66] for a syllogism is an argument which needs nothing external for the generation of the necessity (as Aristotle said when he defined the syllogism[67]). Perhaps in a reduction to the impossible the point at issue is in fact proved and justified by means of the suppositions, while the hypothesis proves something else and is assumed with a different conclusion in view. This conclusion is proved to be impossible by means of the suppositions and nothing else; when it is rejected, the hypothesis is rejected together with it; and when the hypothesis is rejected, the point at issue is justified. It is the items by means of which the hypothesis is proved to be impossible which prove that what is called the conclusion[68] follows by necessity from the premisses which have been assumed. Here the conclusion was that N does not hold of every O; and this was proved by the suppositions that M is predicated of every N and not of every O.

20

25

30

Note the following point. In the *second* figure, in the syllogistic combination which contains the particular negative, the major must be a universal affirmative and the minor a particular negative. It is only when the terms stand thus[69] that the proof by means of the impossible can proceed – and it is only in this way that this combination is proved to be syllogistic. If the terms are taken the other way about, proof by means of the impossible no longer has any force; and that is why the combination is no longer syllogistic when it is taken in this way.[70] Now in the *third* figure, the sixth syllogistic combination also has a particular negative for one of its premisses

85,1

5

373,16-35; Diogenes Laertius, VII 78. See Kneale and Kneale, p. 158; Frede (1974b), p. 102; Barnes (1990b).

[64] The negative particle *ou* is omitted by LM and the Aldine, and von Arnim prints *oun* in its stead (*SVF* II 264). But the Stoics did not regard subsyllogistic arguments as genuine syllogisms, and the negative particle is required.

[65] For this common criticism of Stoic logic see e.g. Alexander, *in An. Pr.* 372,29-30; 373,16-30; Galen, *Inst. Log.* iii 5.

[66] See above, 24,18 note.

[67] *An. Pr.* 24b18-22; above, 21,10-23,2.

[68] i.e. the conclusion of the syllogism whose validity the reduction is establishing: not the conclusion of the hypothetical argument.

[69] Retaining *ekhontôn* (Wallies emends to *ekhousôn*).

[70] See Aristotle, *An. Pr.* 27b4-6; below, 85,17-29.

and a universal affirmative for the other; and it too is proved by reduction to the impossible. But here things are the other way about. For in this figure the major premiss must contain the particular 10 negative and the minor the universal affirmative, inasmuch as in this figure the major premiss must always be negative and the minor affirmative if there is to be a syllogism. When the combination is of this sort, it is proved to be syllogistic by means of the impossible.[71] If the premisses are the other way about, the conjunction is non-syllogistic, as we shall affirm and prove shortly.[72]

5.5.3 Non-syllogistic combinations

5.5.3.1 Major universal, minor particular

5.5.3.1.1 Aristotle's proofs

If it is predicated of every O and not of every N, there will not be 15 a syllogism. [1.5, 27b4-5]

He has shown which conjunctions are syllogistic when the premisses are dissimilar both in quality and in quantity. Now he sets down the non-syllogistic combinations and shows which they are when the premisses are dissimilar in both the ways mentioned.

We said that if there is to be a syllogism in the second figure, then 20 the major premiss must contain the universal.[73] So every combination not of this sort is unreliable and non-syllogistic.

He proves the combination before us to be non-syllogistic by way of the following terms: for 'N holds of every O', animal, substance, raven (animal does not hold of every substance and holds of every raven; and substance holds of every raven); for 'N holds of no O', 25 animal, white, raven (animal does not hold of every white and holds of every raven; and white holds of no raven).

The combination is non-syllogistic because there are parts of the major which[74] fall outside and do not share in the middle term, and with these it may non-syllogistically include the minor term and also not include it.[75]

Nor when of no O and of some N. <Terms for holding: animal, 86,1 substance, unit. For not holding: animal, substance, science.> [1.5, 27b6-8]

---

[71] *Bocardo*: Aristotle, *An. Pr.* 28b15-20; below, 103,9-25.
[72] Below, 104,13-106,2, on *An. Pr.* 28b22-4.
[73] See above, 71,22-6.
[74] Retaining *kata ta moria* (*kata ha moria* [*sic*] Wallies), and adding *ha* after *autou*.
[75] See above, 56,27 note.

In this combination too the major premiss is again particular. Terms
for 'N holds of every O': animal, substance, unit (animal is middle).
Animal holds of some substance and of no unit; and substance of
5   every unit. (He uses a doctrine of the Pythagoreans, who think that
units are substances – a little earlier he used number in the same
way.[76] But the proof is the same if you take stone instead of unit.)
Terms for not holding: animal, substance, science. Animal holds of
some substance and of no science; and substance of no science.
10   The reason why this combination is non-syllogistic is the same.

Thus when the universal is opposite to the particular, <we
have said when there will be a syllogism and when not. When
the premisses are similar in form – i.e. both privative or
affirmative – there will in no case be a syllogism.> [1.5,
27b9-12]

For the cases where the premisses are dissimilar in form[77] both in
quality and in quantity (he means difference in quality when he
says 'Thus when the universal is opposite to the particular'), he has
15   proved which combinations are syllogistic and which non-syllogistic.
The combinations in which the major premiss is a universal
negative and the minor a particular affirmative, and in which the
major is a universal affirmative and the minor a particular negative
– these are both syllogistic. The others are non-syllogistic.
Next he proves that, just as the combinations of universals similar
20   in form are non-syllogistic, so too it is with the combinations which
have one premiss universal and the other particular (where the
universal is no longer opposite to the particular). For the
combinations in the second figure which are similar in form are all
of them non-syllogistic, however they stand with regard to quantity.
He makes clear which combinations are similar in form – namely
25   those which are similar in quality – by saying 'i.e. both privative or
affirmative'. He takes as the first combination of premisses similar
in form the one which has a universal negative major and a
particular negative minor.

<Let them first be privative, and let the universal be supposed
on the major extreme.> I.e. let M hold of no N and not of some
O. Now it is possible for N to hold of every O and also of no O.
<Terms for not holding: black, snow, animal.> [1.5, 27b12-16]

---

[76] Aristotle, *An. Pr.* 27a20; above, 81,17-28.

[77] 'Dissimilar in form [*anomoioskhêmôn*]' means 'different in quality' (see
Introduction, p. 27): either Alexander uses the word loosely here, or else he wrote
anomoiôn (as he does in the parallel sentence at 85,17).

He undertakes to refute the conjunction and prove it non-syllogistic   87,1
by setting down terms; for it is possible to find terms for this
combination to prove that N holds of every O and also of no O.[78] For
'N holds of no O' he takes the terms black, snow, animal; for black
holds of no snow (which is the major extreme, answering to N), and
does not hold of some animal (which is the minor extreme,   5
answering to O); and snow holds of no animal.

<It is not possible to take terms for holding if M holds of some
O and not of some O. For if N holds of every O and M of no N, M
will hold of no O; but it was supposed to hold of some. Thus in
this case it is not possible to take terms – it must be proved
from the indeterminacy. For since 'M does not hold of some O'
is true even if it holds of none, and since there was no syllogism
when it held of none, it is evident that there will not be one in
the present case either.> [1.5, 27b16-23]

Then he turns to take terms for 'N holds of every O' (for this is how
the combination was to be proved non-syllogistic). He first draws our
attention to the fact that if the particular negative, MO, is taken to
be true in one way, then it is possible to obtain terms for 'N holds of
every O', but that if it is taken in another sense it is impossible. For
particular negatives, just like affirmatives, are true both inasmuch   10
as the universal propositions over them are true and also inasmuch
as their subcontraries are true.[79] The proposition saying that M
does not hold of some O is true even if M holds of no O; for it is
ranked under this proposition and follows it and is subaltern to it. It
is also true if the proposition saying that M holds of no O is false and
the proposition positing that M holds of some O is true. (This is   15
subcontrary to the proposition saying that M does not hold of some
O; for they both fall under the universals which are contraries of
each other.[80])
    Since, then, particular negatives are true in two ways, if the
premiss saying that M does not hold of some O is taken as true
because M also holds of some O, we will not be able to obtain terms
proving that N holds of every O. The reason for this is that we have   20
proved that the combination saying that M holds of no N and of
some O is syllogistic and deduces a particular negative; for it is
necessary for N not to hold of some O.[81] But if a particular negative
is deduced syllogistically and by necessity when M does not hold of

---

[78] Deleting *to asullogiston* at 86,30.
[79] On the indeterminacy of particular negatives see above, 66,1-67,24 (where the
argument is closely parallel to that of the present section).
[80] On subcontraries see above, 45,24-5.
[81] i.e. *Festino*: Aristotle, *An. Pr.* 27a32-6; see above, 82,25-83,8.

some O in such a way that it also holds of some O, then it is clear
25   that we will not obtain terms which predicate N of every O. For in
this way, we should reject the fact that a particular negative is
deduced by necessity in the combination in which M holds of no N
and of some O, since we are now assuming that M does not hold of
some O in such a way that it also holds of some O.

This is the reason why it is not possible to take terms for 'N holds
30   of every O', if we take MO to be true in this way. Aristotle proves by
means of the impossible that if it is supposed that the particular
negative MO is true in this way, it will be impossible for N to hold of
88,1 every O. For if it is supposed that N holds of every O, then as it is
supposed that M holds of no N, we get in the first figure that M holds
of no O. But this is impossible; for it was hypothesized that M does
not hold of some O in such a way that it also holds of some O. So if we
take the particular negative in this way, it is not possible to obtain
terms for 'N holds of every O'.

5   But 'M does not hold of some O' is true not only when M also holds
of some O, but also when it holds of none; for the truth of particular
negatives is indeterminate. Thus if 'M does not hold of some O' is
taken as true in such a way that it holds of none, i.e. if we take a
material instance in which M holds of no O (for the particular
10   negative is no less true in this case), then we will obtain terms to
prove that N holds of every O. For we have proved that nothing is
deduced from two universal negative premises.[82] Terms for 'N
holds of every O': line for M, animal for N, man for O. Line holds of
no animal and does not hold of some man (since it holds of no man);
and animal holds of every man.

<Again, let them be predicative and let the universal be
supposed in the same way. I.e. let M hold of every N and of
some O. ...> [1.5, 27b23-5]

15   He uses the same proof when both premises are affirmative, the
major MN being universal and the minor MO particular. He obtains
terms for holding of none, positing white for M, swan for N, stone for
O. White holds of every swan and of some stone, and swan of no
20   stone. But not for holding of all – if the particular affirmative has
been assumed in such a way that it is true together with the
particular negative. For, as has been proved, if the minor is again a
particular negative and the major a universal affirmative, a
particular negative conclusion can be deduced syllogistically in this
figure.[83] Thus since 'not of some' is true in this combination, it is

[82] See Aristotle, *An. Pr.* 27a20-3; above, 82,1-7.
[83] i.e. *Baroco*: Aristotle, *An. Pr.* 27a36-b1; above, 83,13-84,3.

impossible to obtain terms for 'N holds of every O'. For in that case 25
the syllogistic combination will be cancelled and disproved: if it
holds of all, it will also hold of that of some of which it was proved
syllogistically not to hold. So if the particular affirmative is true in
this way, it will again not be possible to obtain terms for 'N holds of
every O'. For if N holds of every O, and M of every N, M will hold of
every O; but it was supposed that it does not hold of some. For the 30
particular affirmative MO was true in this way.

But the truth of particular affirmatives is indeterminate; for they
are true not only when their subcontraries are true as well, but also
when the universal affirmatives under which they fall are true. So
when it is assumed to be true in this way, i.e. because of the
universal under which it falls, the combination will be disproved in 89,1
the case of such terms – as it has already been disproved. For it was
proved that nothing is deduced in this figure from two universal
affirmatives.[84] Hence for this reason nothing will be deduced, if the
one premiss is taken as a universal affirmative and the other as a
particular affirmative. For the particular affirmative is true in both 5
cases, both when the universal affirmative is true and also when its
subcontrary is true. And to prove that a combination is non-
syllogistic, it is sufficient to find some cases and some material
instances which prove that it holds of all and also of none. Terms for
'N holds of every O': substance, animal, man. Substance holds of
every animal and of some man (since it holds of every man).

He invoked the indeterminacy of particular propositions earlier, 10
in the first figure, when he proved that the combination with a
universal negative major and a particular negative minor is
non-syllogistic.[85] But there he also refuted the combination by
exposition, while here he was content with the indeterminacy of the
particular. However, in the case of the conjunctions we have just 15
mentioned, you can also prove through terms and by exposition that
they are non-syllogistic.[86]

If both premisses are negative, take as terms science, vice,
disposition. For science belongs to no vice and does not belong to
some disposition. And for those parts of disposition of which science
does not hold, take courage and cowardice. (For the virtues are not
sciences.) Thus vice holds of no courage and of all cowardice. If it is 20
assumed that virtue holds of no vice and does not hold of some
disposition, and if for those parts of disposition of which virtue does
not hold medicine and cowardice are taken, then vice holds of all
cowardice and of no medicine.

---

[84] See Aristotle, *An. Pr.* 27a18-20; above, 81,3-82,1.

[85] Aristotle, *An. Pr.* 26b14-20; above, 66,1-29.

[86] i.e. Aristotle's argument at *An. Pr.* 26b10-16 (see above, 64,1-65,22) can be
applied to the present case.

If both premisses are affirmative, let the terms be disposition,
science, quality. For disposition holds of every science and of some
quality. And for those parts of quality of which disposition holds,
25   take self-indulgence and grammar. For science holds of all grammar
and of no self-indulgence. The same argument holds also if
substance is taken to hold of every animal and of some white. Take
swan and snow for those whites of which substance holds. For
animal holds of every swan and of no snow.

5.5.3.1.2 The view of Herminus[87]

Aristotle, then, disproved the combinations we have just described
30   in this way: they are non-syllogistic inasmuch as one can obtain
material instances for 'N holds of every O' and also for 'N holds of no
O'. He thinks that this is sufficient proof that the combinations are
non-syllogistic.

Some think that you can disprove the combinations in question if
you prove that N holds of no O and also of some O, since these are
90,1   contradictories. Some of the earlier thinkers say this, and so does
Herminus. (Herminus says that if you can prove that a pair of
contradictories can be deduced, it is reasonable to call the
combination no less non-syllogistic than one in which contraries can
be deduced. For contradictories, like contraries, cannot hold at the
same time.) As terms for 'holds of some', they set down inanimate,
animate and fleshly body.[88] For inanimate holds of no animate, and
5   does not hold of some fleshly body – or simply body –; and animate
holds of some fleshly body – or simply body. But this is not at all
sound, nor is it sufficient for the disproof of a combination.

It will be conceded that neither of the contradictories can be
deduced syllogistically, because they cancel each other. However,
one may say that – as far as these suppositions go – a particular
negative can still be deduced. For the particular negative is
10   cancelled by neither of the contradictories in question. The items set
down to refute a non-syllogistic combination must not only not be
able to hold at the same time as each other: they must also cancel
everything which can be proved syllogistically. But how is the
particular negative disproved, if you do not obtain a material
instance for 'holds of every'?[89]

---

[87] On this section see Patzig, p. 177; Moraux (1973/84), II, pp. 385-94.

[88] i.e. they accept Aristotle's terms for 'N holds of no O' and supply their own terms
for its contradictory, 'N holds of some O'.

[89] The essence of Alexander's point is this. You may show by material instances
that a combination is compatible both with 'A holds of no C' and with 'A holds of some
C'. But this leaves open the possibility that the combination entails 'A does not hold of
some C'. This is correct – but Alexander mars it by making his characteristic error
(see Introduction, pp. 12-13).

Further, in combinations which are agreed to be syllogistic you can find contradictory pairs being deduced. Either, then, we will call these combinations non-syllogistic as well, or else the present combination is not non-syllogistic on that count. For example, in the first figure, where the combination of a universal negative major and a particular affirmative minor with a particular negative conclusion is syllogistic, you can obtain terms for holding of none and also for holding of some. For holding of none:[90] man holds of no horse, horse holds of some quadruped, man holds of no quadruped. For holding of some: snow holds of no swan, swan of some white, snow of some white. (In the combination with a universal affirmative major one can take terms for holding of all and also for not holding of some. For holding of all: substance, animal, man. For not holding of some: substance, animal, white.) Moreover, if we take the combination before us, i.e. the one with a universal negative major, and hypothesize that A holds of some C,[91] nothing impossible meets us;[92] hence 'holds of some' is not cancelled. But it has been proved that A holds of no C.[93]

But surely, they say, proof by means of the impossible will be rejected if opposites can be proved in a syllogistic combination? For we shall no longer deduce only the proposition whose opposite is impossible – we shall also deduce something else, the opposite of which can also be proved. But if this is so, then proof by means of the impossible will no longer have any standing. For if in the combination which deduces a particular affirmative in the first figure it is also possible to deduce both a universal affirmative and a particular negative, but neither of these can be proved by reduction to the impossible by assuming and hypothesizing the opposite of the particular affirmative,[94] then the deduction[95] will be disproved as being useless.

Again, it seems that the conclusion of every syllogistic combi-

---

[90] Adding *tou men mêdeni* before *anthrôpos*.

[91] Reading *to A tini tôi G* (with M and the Aldine) for *to prôton tini tôi tritôi*.

[92] Take as premisses 'A holds of no B' and 'B holds of some C', and hypothesize the contradictory of the putative conclusion, viz. 'A holds of some C'. Then you will be able to infer 'B does not hold of some C'. But this is not 'impossible', i.e. it is consistent with 'B holds of some C'.

[93] The train of thought is obscure. We guess that 'the combination before us' is 'A holds of no B, B holds of some C' (from which, as *Ferio*, we may deduce 'A does not hold of some C'). Alexander's point is this: the combination is compatible with 'A holds of some C'. Yet we have shown that you can deduce 'A holds of no C' from the combination. Hence you can get contradictories from it. (Of course, we have not shown that 'A holds of no C' can be *deduced* from the combination. But Alexander thinks that we have.)

[94] Removing Wallies' parentheses at 91,1 and 3.

[95] Alexander must mean the reduction to the impossible; and perhaps we should emend *sunagôgê* to *apagôgê*.

5   nation can also be proved by means of reduction to the impossible.
But this is not possible in a combination in which opposites are
deduced. For in the case of such a combination neither of the
opposites is impossible. Either, then, no syllogistic conjunction
deduces syllogistically, or else the opposite cannot also be true.

But this is not what we have said. Hence proof by means of the
10   impossible is not rejected. For the only thing deduced syllogistically is
that of which the opposite is impossible. Nonetheless it is not
impossible that there should be other propositions, distinct from
what can be proved syllogistically and opposite to one another, and
that in certain material instances there should be a deduction – but
no longer a syllogistic deduction – from such propositions: if they are
hypothesized, nothing impossible turns out to be deduced. For in the
deduction of the particular affirmative it is impossible to obtain terms
15   for its opposite, i.e. for holding of none. However, it is not impossible
to obtain terms for holding of all and for not holding of some: neither
of these is opposite to 'of some', nor is it proved to be syllogistically
deduced. Neither[96] when the universal affirmative nor when the
particular negative is hypothesized does it follow that anything
impossible is deduced. It is only if the opposite of the particular
affirmative is hypothesized that something impossible follows. For
20   this was what followed syllogistically.

The proof, then, which Herminus uses is not sufficient to disprove a
combination and to assert that it is non-syllogistic. Hence Aristotle is
right to refute the non-syllogistic combinations by setting down only
what holds of all and of none. For here nothing can be proved
syllogistically inasmuch as, whatever you assume to be syllogistically
25   deduced, you will find that its opposite, which cancels it, is true in the
case of some material instances. In general, consider syllogistic
combinations with a particular conclusion. Particulars are true in an
indeterminate way; for a particular is true both with the universal
under which it falls and with its own subcontrary. Thus we can
assume it to be true in either way: sometimes we will obtain terms
30   which prove the universal under which the particular we have
assumed falls; sometimes we will obtain the subcontrary of the
particular which we have assumed and deduced, which does not in
any way cancel its particular subcontrary.

5.5.3.2 Minor universal, major particular

92,1   If the universal is on the minor extreme, and M holds of no O and
not of some N ... [1.5, 27b28-9]

Having proved non-syllogistic the combinations in the second figure

---

[96] Omitting the *gar* which Wallies adds.

which are similar in form and have a particular on the minor and a
universal on the major, he now takes up those which are similar in   5
form and have, conversely, a particular on the major and a universal
on the minor; and he proves them to be non-syllogistic by setting
down terms. These combinations in this figure are non-syllogistic on
two counts: both because of the similar form of the premisses and
because the major is assumed as particular. And that these are not[97]
syllogistic he proves simply by setting down terms, this time not   10
invoking the indeterminacy of the particular. For in whatever way
the major, being particular, is true – whether because of the universal
or in its own right (inasmuch as the particular affirmative which is
subcontrary to it is true) –, the combination will be non-syllogistic
inasmuch as there is no syllogism in this figure when the premisses   15
are similar in form.

As terms for 'N holds of every O' he sets down white, animal, raven:
animal holds of every raven. For 'N holds of no O': white, stone, raven
– for stone holds of no raven. (White holds both of some animal and of
some stone, but of no raven.)

<If the premisses are predicative ...> [1.5, 27b32-3]

He conducts the proof similarly when both premisses are taken as
affirmative and the major as particular. For not holding, the terms   20
are white, animal, snow. Animal holds of no snow, while white holds
of some animal and of all snow. For holding: white, animal, swan.
Animal holds of every swan, while white holds of some animal and of
every swan.

5.6 Combinations of particular premisses

Nor if it holds of some of each, or does not hold, <or of some of
one and not of some of the other, or of all of neither, or
indeterminately.> [1.5, 27b35-8]

He has discussed all the combinations which have one universal and   25
one particular premiss, and has proved that only two among them
are syllogistic. (Those which have a universal major and a minor
opposite in quality have been proved to be syllogistic,[98] and all the
others – six in number – to be non-syllogistic.[99]) He now turns to
combinations of two particulars. He discusses them all at the same   30
time and proves all of them to be non-syllogistic by means of the

---

[97] Retaining *mêde* (*mêdenos* Wallies).
[98] Aristotle, *An. Pr.* 27a26-b2.
[99] Aristotle, *An. Pr.* 27b3-36.

same examples, just as he did in the first figure.[100] And he counts the indeterminates along with the particulars as being, like them, non-syllogistic – they are equivalent to them[101] and are refuted by the same terms.

93,1   Having said, 'Nor if it holds of some of each or does not hold (*sc.* of some of each)', he adds 'or of all of neither'. This differs only in expression from 'does not hold of some of each'. For both expressions betoken particular negatives.[102]

5   Terms for holding of every: white, animal, man. For holding of no: white, animal, inanimate. For white holds of some animal and of some man, and also does not hold of some; and it holds of some of one of them and does not hold of some of the other; and it holds of each indeterminately, and also does not hold (and complementarily); and indeterminately of the one and as a determinate particular of the

10   other. And animal holds of every man. Again, white similarly holds of animal and inanimate – through all the particular and indeterminate permutations; and animal holds of no inanimate.

5.7 Concluding remarks

Thus it is evident from what we have said that if the terms stand to one another in the way we have said, there is a syllogism by necessity, and that if there is a syllogism it is

15   necessary for the terms to stand in this way. [1.5, 28a1-3]

We must again[103] understand 'in the second figure'. For it is not the case *simpliciter* that if there is a universal negative or a particular negative syllogism, the premises must stand in this way. For there are syllogisms of these sorts in the first figure[104] and not only in the second figure.

<...   they are all perfected when certain items are co-assumed
20   which> either inhere by necessity in the terms or are posited as hypotheses <– i.e. when we prove by means of the impossible ...> [1.5, 28a5-7]

What 'inhere by necessity in the terms' (or in the premises supposed) are the converses, which we have invoked for the perfecting of those syllogisms where the proof is by way of

---

[100] Aristotle, *An. Pr.* 26b21-5; above, 68,9-21.
[101] See above, 30,31 note.
[102] See above, 62,12 note.
[103] i.e.'as we did at *An. Pr.* 27a23': see above, 82,8, where the point is not explicit but is implicit in Alexander's paraphrase. (See above, 58,10 and 60,9, on the first figure, and below, 108,22 on the third.)
[104] i.e. *Celarent* and *Ferio* (and also, in the third figure, *Bocardo* and *Ferison*).

conversion. For the converses of the premisses inhere in the 25
premisses which are assumed.[105]

What are 'posited as hypotheses' are the hypotheses we use for the
proof of imperfect syllogisms in reductions to the impossible, as
Aristotle has made clear. For we take as an hypothesis the opposite
of what we are proving and thus produce a syllogism and a
deduction of the impossible. Then by means of this we reject the
hypothesis and establish its opposite, which was the point at issue. 30

<... there is no affirmative syllogism in this figure, but ... all of
them ... are privative.> [1.5, 28a7-9]

It is clear too that all the conclusions in this figure are negative.

[105] cf. above, 58,13-22.

6

The Third Figure

6.1 General remarks

94,1   When one term holds of all and the other of none of the same
        term, <or both of all or none, I call this the third figure.> [1.6,
        28a10-12]

He turns to the third figure, and makes clear what it is and what
position the middle term has in it. He does this, again,[1] by example,
taking the combinations of universal premisses in this figure. In it
5   the middle is subject for both the terms. This, as we said,[2] is the
third figure.
        It is third, and comes last in order, being ranked thus for several
reasons. (1) The middle term, which is the reason why the extremes
share something in common, is ranked last in order in this figure.[3]
(2) No universal is deduced in it.[4] (3) Sophistical syllogisms, which
conclude to indeterminates and particulars, occur in this figure
10 especially, and sophistical syllogisms are the last sort of syllogism.[5]
(4) The second and third figures being each generated from the first,
the third is generated from the inferior premiss. For each of the two
premisses in the first figure, when converted, produces one of these
figures, as we have already said – when the major is converted, the
15 second figure is generated and when the minor the third.[6] Hence if it
is generated from the inferior premiss in the first figure (for the
minor is inferior *qua* minor[7]), then the figure itself will reasonably
be last.
        In this figure, as in the one before it, there are sixteen
combinations in all, not counting the combinations of indeterminate
20 propositions. (We have omitted them as being equivalent to the

---

[1] See above, 52,30, for the same procedure in the second figure.
[2] Above, 47,4-11.
[3] See above, 47,21-4.
[4] See above, 49,1.
[5] See above, 49,14-18.
[6] On the generation of the figures see above, 47,27 note.
[7] The same point, implicitly, at 48,15.

particulars.[8]) But there are more syllogistic combinations in this figure – there are six, whereas each of the earlier figures contained four syllogistic combinations.

The reason is this. In the third figure the minor premiss must again[9] by necessity be affirmative if there is to be a syllogism (if it is negative, there is no syllogism in the third figure); but so long as it is 25 affirmative, there is a syllogism no matter how the major is assumed, provided only that we ensure that the premisses are neither both negative nor both particular. For in no figure is there a syllogism from two particulars or from two negatives.[10] (The major and the minor premisses will be grasped in the same way in this figure as they are in the second.[11]) Now if these conditions are 30 observed, there are six syllogistic combinations. Hence this is the number of syllogistic combinations in this figure. If the minor is a universal affirmative, there will be four syllogistic combinations, the major being taken either as universal, whether affirmative or 95,1 negative, or as particular, whether affirmative or negative; and if the minor is a particular affirmative, there are two further syllogistic combinations, the major being universal and either affirmative or negative.

The reason why there are more syllogistic combinations in the 5 third figure is this. In the other figures more features were determined, and these had to be preserved in order for there to be a syllogistic conjunction. Both in the first and in the second figure two features were determined. In the first figure, the major premiss was determined (it had to be universal) and so was the minor (it had to be affirmative).[12] In the second figure the major was determined (it had to be universal), and it was also determined that the two 10 premisses must not be similar in form (it is the proper characteristic of the second figure that nothing is deduced from two affirmatives).[13] But in the third figure only the minor premiss is determined – it must be affirmative. (The fact that the premisses may not be both particular or both negative is common to the three figures and not a proper characteristic of the third.) And what is less determined is more general and has a wider extension.

Given that the first figure has both its premisses determined, the major in quantity (it is universal) and the minor in quality (it is affirmative), it stands to reason that the other figures (I mean the 15 second and the third) should preserve the proper characteristic of

---

[8] See above, 30,31 note; 51,25 note.
[9] i.e. as well as in the first figure: above, 49,25.
[10] See above, 71,32-3.
[11] i.e. the major premiss is the premiss containing the major term, and the major term is the term which is predicate in the problem: see above, 75,19-84.
[12] See above, 49,19-50,14.
[13] See above, 71,22-33.

20 the premiss by the conversion of which each of them was generated.[14] The second figure was generated by conversion of the major, and it preserves the proper characteristic of that premiss in syllogistic combinations[15] – in the second figure, too, the major premiss is universal in the syllogistic conjunctions. The third figure was generated by conversion of the minor and retains its proper characteristic[16] – for in this figure the minor is again determined, as we said, inasmuch as it is affirmative.

6.2 Third figure syllogisms

25 Of the six syllogisms in this figure, the first in order[17] deduces a particular affirmative from two universal affirmatives by conversion of the minor premiss. It can also be generated by converting the major, but in that case the conclusion too will have to be converted.
30 For this reason, some add this syllogism, as being different from its predecessor, and say that there are seven syllogisms in this figure.[18] This conjunction is first because each of its premisses is both universal and affirmative.

One might raise the following question. In the second figure there

[14] Reading *ta alla skhêmata, to te deuteron ... kai to triton* for *tôn allôn skhêmatôn, tou te deuteron ... kai tou tritou.*

[15] See above, 71,24-6.

[16] See above, 94,15.

[17] On the order of the syllogisms in the third figure see below, 97,11 note. Compare above, 51,8-24 and 76,29-77,31, on the order in the first and second figures.

[18] What is 'this syllogism' which some people added to the third figure? (1) Alexander's text here, and also his ensuing discussion, indicates that it is *Darapti*, i.e. that some people thought that the form 'A holds of every B, C holds of every B: therefore, A holds of some C' actually marked out *two* syllogisms. And Alexander further implies that this view was based on the fact that the form can be reduced to *Darii* in two ways, either by converting the major premiss or by converting the minor premiss. (2) From other sources we learn that Theophrastus added a 'second *Darapti*' to the third figure (Apuleius, *Int.* 189,19-27 = F 19 Graeser); he was followed by Galen (*Inst. Log.* xi 7) and later by Porphyry (Boethius, *Syll. Cat.* 813C, 819B). See Bochenski (1947), pp. 61-4; Sullivan, pp. 102-3. It seems clear from these texts that the syllogism in question was *Daraptis* ('A holds of every B, C holds of every B: therefore, C holds of some A'), which may be derived by converting the conclusion of *Darapti*. (See above, 70,21 note.) It is a puzzle why *Daraptis*, which is a mere notational variant on *Darapti* should have been added to the third figure, when *Cesares* and *Camestre* (which are, in the same way, notational variants on *Cesare* and *Camestres*) were – for that very reason – not added to the second. (As Apuleius puts it: 'It does not matter from which premiss you make the particular affirmative, since it does not matter which you propound first.' Bochenski and Sullivan attempt, vainly, to defend Theophrastus here.) (3) It is tempting to suppose that Alexander's remarks reflect his understanding of the Theophrastean position, and that he thought that *Daraptis* simply was a second *Darapti* inasmuch as it is a mere notational variant on *Darapti*. We might further imagine that Theophrastus argued that *Darapti* is genuinely different from *Daraptis* because the proof of the former is different from the proof of the latter. But this – as Alexander plainly shows – is such a bad argument that we might well be reluctant to ascribe it to Theophrastus.

were two syllogistic conjunctions having a universal negative as one
premiss and a universal affirmative as the other, inasmuch as now
the major and now the minor, being universal negatives, convert.[19]   96,1
Why, then, in the third figure are there not said to be two syllogistic
conjunctions with two universal affirmatives, even though here too
now the minor and now the major may be converted? Well, in the
second figure, inasmuch as the premisses are dissimilar in form, the   5
universal negatives are different, so that by necessity a different
premiss – now the major and now the minor – is converted: it is not
up to us to convert whichever we wish. But in the third figure, when
the two premisses are universal affirmatives, it is not the way in
which the premisses are posited which explains why now one and
now the other of them converts; for this is similar and the same.   10
Rather, the choice is up to us, and it does not depend on the
combination. This is why, although each of the premisses can be
converted in the same way inasmuch as they are posited in the same
way, we take the premiss whose conversion yields the least
laborious proof, and we determine the syllogistic status of the
combination by way of this premiss.

Again, the differences among the syllogisms in each figure depend
on the differences in the combinations and not on differences in the   15
proofs. Thus the same conjunction can be proved syllogistic both by
conversion and by reduction to the impossible – and also by
exposition. But this does not mean that there are several syllogisms,
because there is one combination for which the different proofs are
made. Hence if there is one combination of two universal
affirmatives in the third figure, there is also one syllogism, even if   20
there are different proofs inasmuch as now one and now the other of
the premisses can be converted.

After this comes the syllogism which deduces a particular
negative from a universal negative major and a universal
affirmative minor. This has both premisses universal, but not both
affirmative. It too is proved to be deductive by conversion of the   25
minor.

The third deduces a particular affirmative from a universal
affirmative major and a particular affirmative minor. It too is
proved by conversion of the minor. It is prior in rank to the syllogism
after it, which deduces a particular affirmative from similar
premisses, because it is proved by *one* conversion to deduce the point   30
at issue, whereas the syllogism after it, with a particular affirmative
major and a universal affirmative minor, is proved by two
conversions to deduce the point at issue. (You must convert both the
major, which is a particular affirmative, and the conclusion.)

---

[19] i.e. *Cesare* and *Camestres*: *An. Pr.* 27a5-14; above, 78,10-79,25.

97,1   The fifth deduces a particular negative from a universal negative
major and a particular affirmative minor. It is proved by conversion of
the minor. It comes after the others because it deduces a negative and
it too has one particular premiss.

Sixth rank is held by the syllogism which deduces a particular
negative from a particular negative major and a universal affir-
5   mative minor. This syllogism is no longer proved by conversion, but
rather by reduction to the impossible – like the fourth syllogism in the
second figure, which has a universal affirmative major and a
particular negative minor.[20] For this reason, just as that syllogism
was last in the second figure, so this is last in the third.

10   This is the ranking of the syllogisms in this figure, but Aristotle did
not follow it in his presentation – he changed it.[21]

The following point stands to reason. In the second figure the
syllogisms proved by means of conversion are proved by the conver-
15   sion of the major premiss. For the second syllogism, which has a
universal affirmative major and a universal negative minor, and
which comes about[22] by conversion of the negative, in fact makes
what is supposed as the minor into the major, as far as the proof goes.
That is why we need to convert the conclusion too in this case, in order
that the term which was supposed in the premisses as major may be
20   predicated in the conclusion.[23] In the third figure, on the other hand,
it is the minor which is converted. For in this figure, in the
combination of a particular affirmative major and a universal
affirmative minor, the particular affirmative, which is supposed as
major, is converted, and as far as the syllogism goes it in fact becomes
the minor. That is why, once again, in this combination too we had to
25   convert the conclusion too in order that the term supposed as major
might be kept as predicate in the conclusion. For as far as the
syllogism by means of conversion goes, it became the minor.

This, as I said, stands to reason. For each of these figures is
generated from the first figure by the conversion of a premiss; and
when this premiss is again converted, the figures are analysed into

---

[20] i.e. *Baroco*: Aristotle, *An. Pr.* 27a36-b3; above, 83,12-84,3.

[21] Alexander follows Theophrastus in placing *Datisi* before *Disamis* and *Ferison*
before *Bocardo* (see Philoponus, *in An. Pr.* 105,28-106,2; Boethius, *Syll. Cat.*
819A-821A; scholium to Aristotle, 155b8-19: = F 21 Graeser; cf. Bochenski (1947),
p. 65; Sullivan, pp. 123-6). The later tradition generally took the Theophrastean line
(e.g. Apuleius, *Int.* 190,25-191,5; Martianus Capella, IV 413). Galen (*Inst. Log.* x 1-6)
follows Aristotle in placing *Disamis* before *Datisi*, but like Theophrastus he has
Ferison before *Bocardo*.

[22] Or 'is generated': see below, 97,30 note.

[23] See above, 78,25-79,19. Here Alexander seems to treat the *proof* of *Camestres* as
consisting simply in the application of *Celarent*, which yields the conclusion 'O holds
of no N'. The conversion of this conclusion is then superadded to the proof proper.

and reduced to the first figure – and by the analysis they are proved 30
to be syllogistic.[24]

... I say that in it the middle is that of which both are
predicated, ... [1.6, 28a12]

This is an account of the third figure, in which both extremes are
predicated of the middle.

... the major is the extreme further from the middle, <and the 98,1
minor is the one nearer.> [1.6, 28a13-14]

Since the major premiss in the first figure was converted, the middle
term came to be posited before the major extreme in the second
figure.[25] In the same way, since the third figure has been generated
by converting the minor premiss in the first figure, the middle term 5
in the third figure comes to have position after the minor extreme.
For by the conversion of each premiss the middle term falls in the
position near the extreme with which it is combined in the converted
premiss. In the third figure the middle term comes to be near the
minor extreme and becomes subject for both terms: for the minor
because of the conversion of the minor premiss, for the major 10
because it was supposed from the beginning in the first figure to be
its subject. Being subject for both, it reasonably holds the last
position.[26]

6.3 Combinations of universal premisses

6.3.1 *Darapti*

... but there will be a potential one both when the terms are
universal and when they are not universal in relation to the
middle. [1.6, 28a16-17]

'Not universal' does not mean 'neither of them being universal' (for it 15

[24] On the generation of the figures see above, 47,27 note. Here Alexander, in trying
to correlate generation with analysis, conflates figures with syllogisms: the figures,
properly speaking, are generated but not analysed or proved (it makes no sense to
speak of proving a *figure*); the syllogisms, properly speaking, are analysed or proved
but not generated (cf. Themistius, *Max.* 184).
[25] See above, 72,15 note.
[26] Alexander tacitly alludes to the standard diagrams (see above, 72,11 note). In
the first figure the terms are set out thus:
    A – B – C.
By converting the minor premiss, i.e. by inverting the order of B and C, we get:
    A – C – B.
And A, the major term, is further from B than C is.

is impossible, as we have already said,[27] to get a syllogism from two particular propositions). It means 'not both being universal'.

> If they are universal, then when both P and R hold of every S, <P will hold of some R by necessity. For since the predicative converts, S will hold of some R. Hence since P holds of every S and S of some R, it is necessary for P to hold of some R. For we get a syllogism by way of the first figure. It is also possible to effect the demonstration by means of the impossible and by exposition. For if both hold of every S, then if something of S – say N – is taken, both P and R will hold of this. Hence P will hold of some R.> [1.6, 28a17-25]

20 In this figure he again uses letters[28] – this time P, R, S, where P signifies the major extreme, R the minor, which should be subject in the conclusion, S the middle term. First he sets out the combination of two universal affirmative premisses. To prove that this is 25 syllogistic, he converts the minor premiss RS, which is a universal affirmative, and assumes RS as a particular affirmative; and in this way he reduces it to the third syllogism of the first figure, which deduces a particular affirmative from a universal affirmative major and a particular affirmative minor.

As I said,[29] it is also possible to prove that the same thing is deduced by converting the major premiss, if we also convert the 99,1 conclusion. For if P holds of every S, S holds of some P. But it is also supposed that R holds of every S. It follows that R holds of some P. Now if we convert this too, P will be said of some R. And this was to be proved. Aristotle does not set this proof down, because it is inferior to the one which we have already discussed, since it needs two conversions.

5   He also uses reduction to the impossible to prove that in this combination a particular affirmative can be deduced. For hypothesize the opposite of 'P holds of some R' – i.e. 'P holds of no R'. It is also supposed in the combination that R holds of every S. It is deduced that P holds of no S according to the second syllogism in the first figure, which deduces a universal negative from a universal negative major and a universal affirmative minor. But it is 10 impossible for P to hold of no S; for it was supposed in the combination before us that it holds of every S. Therefore the hypothesis on which the impossible conclusion depended is false. But if the hypothesis positing that P holds of no R is false, then its 15 contradictory opposite, which posits that P holds of some R, is true.

27 Most recently at 94,27-8.
28 See above, 53,30 note.
29 See above, 95,25-31.

He says that it is possible to prove that the conclusion is a particular affirmative by reduction to the impossible; but he refrains from setting down the proof itself since it is already familiar – he used it in the second figure.[30] But he does add a third kind of proof, which can also be invoked to prove that in the combination before us 20 it can be deduced that P holds of some R. He calls this a proof 'by exposition', and he shows in outline what the method of exposition is.[31] Since it is supposed that both P and R hold of every S, if instead of S we take one of the items under S, it is clear that both P and R hold of this, since they hold of everything under S. In this way, it 25 will be proved that P holds of some R. He takes N: given this, he says, P will hold of some R.

But it seems that in this way nothing is gained with regard to proving the point at issue. For what is the difference between assuming that both P and R hold of every S, and taking it that they hold of some part of S, viz. N? The case remains the same if N is 30 taken; for the combination is the same, whether they are each predicated of every N or of S. Or is this not the proof he uses? For the method of exposition proceeds by perception. He does not tell us to take something of S, of all of which both P and R are said (if we did that we would gain nothing), but to take something which falls within our perception and which is evidently both in P and in R. For 100,1 example, suppose that animal is taken for P and holds of every man, which is S, and rational is taken for R and also holds of every man. Then if we take some perceptible item of S – i.e. some man, say Socrates –, then inasmuch as it is evident and perceptible that he is 5 both animal and rational, it becomes obvious that P, i.e. animal, shares in and holds of some R, i.e. rational.[32]

That proof by exposition is perceptual is indicated first by the fact that if it is not taken in this way, there will be no proof. Next, there is the fact that in the case of N, which is something of S, Aristotle no longer says that both P and R hold of every N,[33] but simply posits 10 that P and R hold of it. Note also that he does not convert either premiss. For in the case of things which are perceptible and one in number, neither 'of every' nor the determinations in general are appropriate; for the determinations of propositions have their place with universals, and individuals are not universal.[34]

Proof by exposition is peculiar to the third figure because in this 15 figure there is a single subject for both extremes.[35] For exposition

---

[30] See Aristotle, *An. Pr.* 27a36-b3.
[31] See above, 32,32-34,2.
[32] On this paragraph see Łukasiewicz, p. 63; Patzig, pp. 159-60.
[33] Deleting *to ekkeimenon*, which Wallies emends to *tôi ekkeimenôi*.
[34] See above, 65,27 note.
[35] Excising *ditton to meson esti <kai>*.

needs to be done from what is both a middle term and a subject.[36]
(Some people think that if they take some one item, which is
perceptible, then with respect to this item they will find the
predicates either linked with or separated from each other.[37]) But if
an item is taken from several subjects, it will not be one thing,
20   inasmuch as something different will be taken from each –
especially if the predicate is predicated affirmatively of one term
and negatively of the other. And in this way there is no evident and
perceptible sharing of the terms.

It can also be shown by the fact that everything deduced in this
figure is particular; for if you take some one item, i.e. something
perceptible, that is sufficient for conclusions of this sort.
25   Aristotle's proof that actual universal negatives convert is
patently of this type and not, as some think, by way of the particular
affirmative.[38]

6.3.2 *Felapton*

And if R holds of every S and P of none, <there will be a
syllogism that P does not hold of some R by necessity. There is
the same mode of demonstration, the premiss RS being
converted. It can also be proved by way of the impossible, as in
the earlier cases.> [1.6, 28a26-30]

He has turned to the second combination, which has a universal
negative major and a universal affirmative minor. This too he
30   proves syllogistic by conversion of the minor, RS, which is a
universal affirmative. He takes RS as a particular affirmative and
reduces the syllogism to the fourth syllogism in the first figure. (This
was the syllogism which deduces a particular negative conclusion
from a universal negative major and a particular affirmative
minor.[39])

It is clear that one can also prove this syllogism by reduction to
101,1 the impossible, as he says; and it is plain what impossibility is
deduced. For if you hypothesize that P holds of every R, then since R
was supposed to hold of every S, it will be deduced that P holds of
every S – but it was supposed to hold of no S.

---

[36] Aristotle also uses exposition for a *second* figure syllogism, viz. *Baroco* with two
necessary premisses (*An. Pr.* 30a5-14); but Alexander argues that this is a different
type of exposition (*in An. Pr.* 121,15-123,9).
[37] Who are these people and what is their view? The style of reference leads us to
think that Alexander is mentioning a rival interpretation of exposition; but we are
unable to find anything here incompatible with what Alexander himself says. (It is
possible that Alexander has Boethus in mind: see Themistius, *Max.* 191-2 – but the
text is obscure.)
[38] See above, 31,27-32,32.
[39] *Ferio*: Aristotle, *An. Pr.* 26a25-8.

And, once again, you can also prove it by invoking exposition, although Aristotle does not mention this. If we take some perceptible 5 item of S, then inasmuch as it is obviously in R and participates in it but does not share with P, it will be evident that P does not hold of some R. For it will not hold of what has been taken and set out, and this is some item of R.

6.3.3 Non-syllogistic combinations

If R holds of no S and P of every S, <there will not be a syllogism.   10
Terms for holding: animal, horse, man. For not holding: animal,
inanimate, man.> [1.6, 28a30-3]

Having set out the syllogistic combinations with two universal premises, he now mentions those which are non-syllogistic. First he sets down the combination with a universal negative minor and a universal affirmative major. He shows that it is non-syllogistic by setting down terms, proving that if this combination is supposed, P   15 may hold of every R and also of no R. Animal, which is P, holds of every man, which is S; horse, which is R, holds of no man; and animal holds of every horse, i.e. P of every R. Again, animal holds of every man; inanimate, which is R, of no man; and animal of no inanimate, i.e. P of no R. The reason why the combination is   20 non-syllogistic is again the same as in the first figure where the major is a universal affirmative and the minor a universal negative.[40]

Nor when both are said of no S <will there be a syllogism.
Terms for holding: animal, horse, inanimate. (Inanimate is the
middle.)> [1.6, 28a33-6]

He also proves non-syllogistic the combination with two universal negative premises, which is the remaining combination of   25 universal premises. Terms for 'P holds of every R': animal, horse, inanimate. Neither animal nor horse holds of inanimate, which is S; and animal holds of every horse, i.e. P of R. For holding of none: man, horse, inanimate. Again, neither man nor horse holds of   30 inanimate, which is S; and man does not hold of horse.

Thus it is evident in this figure too ... [1.6, 28a36]   102,1

He draws our attention to the point (which has already been made) that in this figure two combinations of universal premisses will be

---

[40] See Aristotle, *An. Pr.* 26a2-9; above, 56,7-27.

syllogistic (he says which they are[41]) and two will be non-syllogistic.

6.4 Combinations of universal and particular premisses

6.4.1 *Disamis* and *Datisi*

5   If one term is universal in relation to the middle and the other
         particular, <then if both are predicative, it is necessary for
         there to be a syllogism, whichever of the terms is universal. For
         if R holds of every S and P of some S, it is necessary for P to hold
         of some R. For since the affirmative converts, S will hold of some
         P. Hence since R holds of every S and S of some P, R will hold of
         some P. Hence also P of some R.> [1.6, 28b5-11]

Having discussed the combinations of universal premisses in the
third figure, he turns to those with only one universal. For this sort
of combination too, he proves which of them are syllogistic and
which non-syllogistic. He says first that there will be a syllogism if
10   both premisses are affirmative, whichever is universal, the major or
the minor. Hence there are again two syllogistic combinations here,
when both premisses are affirmative and one is universal.
    First he sets out the one having the minor, RS, as a universal
affirmative and the major, PS, as a particular affirmative.[42] (*We*
15   ranked this combination fourth, inasmuch as it needs two
conversions.[43]) If the particular affirmative, PS, which was the
major, is converted, we get 'S holds of some P'. It is also supposed
that R holds of every S. By the third syllogism in the first figure it is
deduced that R holds of some P. But since P is supposed as major
and must be predicated in the conclusion, the conclusion too will be
20   converted. It was deduced that R holds of some P. Therefore P will
hold of some R. Thus it needed the conversion of the conclusion as
well, and not only of the premiss PS. Aristotle makes this clear by
adding 'Hence also P of some R' after he has proved that by the
syllogism we get the conclusion that R holds of some P.

25   Again, if R holds of some S and P of every S, <it is necessary for
          P to hold of some R. There is the same mode of demonstration.
          It is also possible to demonstrate by means of the impossible
          and by exposition, as in the earlier cases.> [1.6, 28b11-15]

Now he takes the premisses the other way round. He has kept them
both as affirmative but has made the major universal. He proves

[41] At *An. Pr.* 28a37-b4.
[42] On Aristotle's proof of *Disamis* see Patzig, pp. 141-2.
[43] See above, 96,28-34.

that this combination too is syllogistic by converting the minor
premiss, which is a particular affirmative, and by reducing the   30
combination to the third indemonstrable in the first figure, which
has a universal affirmative major and a particular affirmative
minor. (*We* ranked this combination third, since the point at issue   103,1
becomes evident and is proved by one conversion and not by two, as
was the case with the previous combination.[44]) He remarks of this
combination too that one can prove it by reduction to the impossible
and also by exposition. By adding 'as in the earlier cases' he made   5
clear that not only proof by means of the impossible but also proof by
exposition is common to all the syllogisms in this figure.[45]

6.4.2 *Bocardo*

If one is predicative and the other privative <and the
predicative is universal, then when the minor is predicative
there will be a syllogism. For if R holds of every S and P does
not hold of some S, it is necessary for P not to hold of some R.
For if of every, and R of every S, then P will hold of every S. But
it did not hold. It is also proved without the reduction if
something of S is taken of which P does not hold.> [1.6,
28b15-21]

From premisses similar in form he moves on to premisses dissimilar
in form and the combinations constructed from them, first   10
preserving one of the premisses as a universal affirmative. He shows
which of these conjunctions are syllogistic combinations. Thus, if the
minor is universal and affirmative, it is clear that the major will be
particular and negative and the combination syllogistic. For if R
holds of every S and P does not hold of some S, it can be deduced that   15
P does not hold of some R. The proof can no longer proceed by
conversion; for the particular negative does not convert, and if we
convert the universal affirmative we will produce two particulars –
and from two particulars nothing necessary can be deduced in any
figure.[46] Rather, he proves by reduction to the impossible that we   20
get a particular negative conclusion with this combination. For if,
when the premisses are supposed in the way we have said, someone
should not concede that P does not hold of some R, then let the
opposite be hypothesized, i.e. let P hold of every R. But it is supposed
that R holds of every S. Thus it will be deduced that P holds of every
S. But this is impossible; for it was supposed that P does not hold of   25
some S.

[44] See above, 96,26-32.
[45] It is hardly true that Aristotle 'made this clear'; but see below, 106,21.
[46] Compare the similar remarks about *Baroco*, above 83,12-24.

He says that you can prove this same conclusion to be deducible even without reduction to the impossible, 'if (he says) something of S is taken of which P does not hold'. He means again the method of exposition. Quite rightly he has not taken one of the Ss of which R holds but rather one of them of which P does not hold. For, since R
30   holds of every S and P does not hold of some, R will certainly hold of any item of S of which P does not hold; but it is not necessary for P not to hold of any item of S of which R holds – for it is possible to take something of S of which P will hold. (It was supposed not that it holds of no S but that it does not hold of some S; and what does not
104,1 hold of some may also hold of some.) But if you take one of the Ss[47] (an individual thing) of which P does not hold, then since this is certainly in R (for R was said of every S), P will not hold of some R.

It is possible to conduct the proof for this combination if you take
5   not some perceptible and individual item of S but rather some of S of none of which P will be predicated. For then P will be predicated of none of it and R of all, and it has been proved that such a combination deduces syllogistically that P does not hold of some R.[48]

Note that he uses the method of exposition for negatives too.
10   *We* made this the final syllogistic combination since it is not possible to prove its conclusion by conversion.[49]

6.4.3 Non-syllogistic combinations

When the major is predicative, there will not be a syllogism <– i.e. if P holds of every S and R does not hold of some S. Terms for holding of every: animate, man, animal. It is not possible to take terms for holding of none if R holds of some S and does not hold of some. For if P holds of every S and R of some S, then P will hold of some R. But it was supposed to hold of none. We must take terms as in the earlier cases. For 'does not hold of some' is indeterminate, and it is true to say of what holds of none that it does not hold of some. But if it holds of none, there was no syllogism. So it is evident that there will not be a syllogism>. [1.6, 28b22-31]

He is still discussing combinations of premisses dissimilar in form where the affirmative is universal. He has proved that if the
15   affirmative, being universal, is on the minor premiss, there is a syllogism, and he has justified this by means of a reduction to the impossible. Now he takes the converse case, in which the universal affirmative is on the major premiss and the particular negative on

---

[47] Reading *ti* for *touto* (the Aldine prints *ti toiouto*).
[48] i.e. *Felapton*: Aristotle, *An. Pr.* 28a26-30; above, 100,28-101,8.
[49] See above, 97,3-9.

the minor, and he proves that this combination is non-syllogistic, showing its unreliability by setting down terms. (This is how he usually shows combinations to be unreliable.) He proves that the 20 major extreme may hold of all and also of none of the minor.

As terms to prove that P holds of every R in this combination he set down animate for P, man for R, animal for S. For animate holds of every animal, man does not hold of some animal, and animate 25 holds of every man.

But he says that it is not possible to take terms for 'P holds of no R', if the particular negative which says that R does not hold of some S is taken as true in such a way that R also holds of some S. (This is the case with the terms he set out: man, which does not hold of some animal, also holds of some animal.) Now when the particular 30 negative is true in such a way that the particular affirmative is true together with it, it will not be possible to take terms for 'of no R'. The reason, again,[50] is that, if the major is supposed as a universal affirmative and the minor as a particular affirmative, it can be 105,1 deduced syllogistically that P holds of some R; and this conjunction is present potentially when the particular negative is taken as true in its own right, i.e. in the way I have just described. And since, when the premisses are posited in this way, it can be deduced syllogistically that P holds of some R, then it is impossible to obtain 5 terms by means of which we may prove that P holds of no R. For in that case the syllogistic combination would be rejected. This is what Aristotle shows when he says 'For if P holds of every S and R of some S, then P will hold of some R'.

Having shown this, he continues: 'But it was supposed to hold of none.' He does not mean that it was somehow supposed in the 10 premisses that P holds of no R; for what he wanted to prove was that terms cannot be taken for 'P holds of no R'. What he means is rather this: if someone hypothesizes that P holds of no R, when it is supposed that P holds of every S and that R does not hold of some S in such a way as also to hold of some S, then he will make an impossible hypothesis. For P will hold syllogistically of some R. And if this is so, it is impossible for it to hold of none. It is possible to 15 assume the hypothesis that P holds of no R and to prove it impossible by a proof which he himself ordinarily uses. For if P holds of no R and if R holds of some S (because it is supposed that R does not hold of some S in such a way as also to hold of some S), then it comes about syllogistically that P does not hold of some S – and this is impossible. For it was supposed in the combination that P holds of 20 every S.

Thus when the particular negative is taken to be true in this way,

[50] See above, 66,1-67,24; 87,5-88,14.

you can neither obtain terms for 'P holds of no R', nor prove the combination to be non-syllogistic. But since particular negatives are true not only when their subcontraries are true but also when the
25   universal negative is true (the truth of particular negatives is indeterminate, as we said earlier[51]), then when the particular negative is taken as true in such a way that the universal under which it falls is also true, the combination is non-syllogistic; for it consists of a universal affirmative major and a potentially universal negative minor, and he has proved that this combination is
30   non-syllogistic by setting down terms.[52] It is clear, then, that the present combination will also be non-syllogistic, inasmuch as in some cases the particular negative is true together with the universal negative.

If the terms are animal, inanimate, man, then animal holds of every man, inanimate will not belong to some man (since in fact it
106,1   holds of no man), and animal holds of no inanimate. Hence in this way we can obtain terms for 'of no R', just as we did for 'of every R', and we can prove the combination non-syllogistic.

6.4.4 *Ferison*

If the privative is the universal term, <then when the major is privative and the minor predicative, there will be a syllogism. For if P holds of no S and R holds of some S, P will not hold of some R. For again there will be the first figure, the premiss RS being converted.> [1.6, 28b31-5]

He is still discussing premisses dissimilar in form and combinations
5   which contain only one universal. Having discussed those in which the universal is affirmative, he now discusses those which have the negative universal (and the particular, of course, affirmative). In combinations of such premisses he says that if the major is a universal negative, there will be a syllogism, but not in the converse case.
10   He proves that there is a syllogism when the major is a universal negative and the minor a particular affirmative, setting out the combination with letters. If P holds of no S and R of some S, P will not hold of some R. For when the minor premiss, RS, is converted,
15   we get the first figure and its fourth syllogism, which deduces a particular negative from a universal negative major and a particular affirmative minor.
We said that this syllogism was the fifth, inasmuch as it is proved by way of conversion, whereas the syllogism which Aristotle placed

[51] See above, 66,1-10.
[52] See Aristotle, *An. Pr.* 28a30-3; above, 101,11-22.

fifth cannot be proved by conversion.[53] For proof by conversion is more authoritative and more appropriate than proof by means of the impossible, as Aristotle himself will say.[54] It is possible to use 20 reduction to the impossible and the method of exposition for this syllogism too; but he does not say so since it is well known and has already been said.[55]

6.4.5 More non-syllogistic combinations

When the minor is privative, <there will not be a syllogism. Terms for holding: animal, man, wild. For not holding: animal, science, wild. (Wild is middle in both cases.)> [1.6, 28b36-8]

He has turned to the combination in which the minor premiss is a universal negative and the major a particular affirmative, and he proves that it is non-syllogistic by setting down terms. For 'of every', 25 he sets down animal, man, wild: animal (which is P) holds of some wild (which is S); man (which is R) holds of no wild; and animal holds of every man. For 'of none': animal, science, wild. Again, animal holds of some wild, science (supposed for R) of no wild, and 30 animal of no science. The reason is that the minor is negative.

Nor when both are posited as privative <and one is universal   107,1
and the other particular>. [1.6, 28b38-9]

He assumes both premisses as negative with one of them universal, and he proves that the combinations of these premisses are non-syllogistic, whichever is the universal. Now, if the minor is a universal negative, the terms he sets down for 'of every' are animal, 5 man, wild. For animal does not hold of some wild, man holds of no wild, animal of every man. For 'of none': animal, science, wild. For animal does not hold of some wild, science holds of no wild, and animal of no science.

When the major, <for not holding: raven, snow, white. It is not possible to take terms for holding if R holds of some S and does not hold of some S. For if P holds of every R and R of some S, P

---

[53] See above, 96,34-97,3.

[54] Aristotle nowhere says exactly this. Alexander is probably thinking of *An. Post.* 87a1-30, where Aristotle argues that a direct proof of a proposition is 'superior' to a proof by reduction to the impossible (see Barnes (1975), pp. 180-1). (But note that Themistius, *Max.* 192, says that Aristotle makes the point in the second book of *An. Pr.*)

[55] Aristotle has not in fact said this; but Alexander wrongly takes him to have done so at *An. Pr.* 28b15 (see above, 103,4-7).

holds of some S. But it was supposed to hold of none. It must be proved from the indeterminacy.> [1.6, 29a2-6]

10   He is trying to prove that the combination in which the major is a universal negative and the minor a particular negative is non-syllogistic. Now for 'P holds of no R' the terms he sets down are raven, snow, white; for raven holds of no white, snow does not hold of some white, raven holds of no snow.

15   He says again that it is not possible to take terms for 'P holds of every R' when R does not hold of some S in such a way that it also holds of some S. (This was the case with the terms he set down, snow and white.[56]) The reason is this. We again get a syllogistic combination which has a universal negative major and a particular affirmative minor; and as we have proved,[57] this deduces a particular negative, the opposite of which is impossible. Thus if we
20 hypothesize that P holds of every R, then given that R does not hold of some S in such a way that it also holds of some S, our hypothesis will be impossible. For it will be cancelled, since it was proved syllogistically that P does not hold of some R. But since the truth of particulars is indeterminate, if we take the particular negative to be true inasmuch as the universal negative is true, we will then obtain
25 terms for 'of every', and we will prove that the combination is non-syllogistic. For it is potentially the same as the combination of two universal negatives.[58] Aristotle proved by reduction to the impossible that it is not possible to obtain terms for 'P holds of every R', given that the particular negative RS is true in its own right. For if it is hypothesized that P holds of every R and it is also the case
30 that R holds of some S, then P will also hold syllogistically of some of the Ss. But this is impossible – for it is supposed that P holds of no S.

6.5 Combinations of particular premisses

108,1   And if each holds of some of the middle, ... [1.6, 29a6-7]

He proves that all combinations of two particulars are non-syllogistic, if they are assumed both as affirmative, or both as negative, or as dissimilar in form, or both as indeterminate, or the
5 one as indeterminate and the other as particular. He proves that all these conjunctions are non-syllogistic by way of the same terms, setting them down and showing that P will hold of no R and also of every R when the combinations are assumed in these ways. For holding of every: animal, man, white. For you can assume animal
10 and man each to hold of some white, and each not to hold of some, or

---

[56] See also above, 104,25-9.
[57] i.e. *Ferison*: Aristotle, *An. Pr.* 28b31-5; above, 106,4-21.
[58] See Aristotle, *An. Pr.* 28a33-6; above, 101,24-30.

one to hold of some and the other not to hold of some, and also indeterminately; and animal holds of every man, however the premisses are taken. For holding of none: animal, inanimate, white. For again you can assume animal and inanimate each to hold of some white and each not to hold of some – and also in the complementary cases, and indeterminately: when any of these combinations is true, animal holds of no inanimate.   15

6.6 Concluding remarks

Thus it is evident in this figure too when there will be a syllogism and when there will not ... [1.6, 29a11-12]

He has shown in this figure, as in the one before it, how many and which are the syllogistic combinations and why. And he has also shown which are the non-syllogistic conjunctions.   20

... and if there is a syllogism, it is necessary for the terms to stand thus. <It is evident too that all the syllogisms in this figure are imperfect ... and that it is not possible to syllogize a universal, whether privative or affirmative, by means of this figure.> [1.6, 29a13-18]

Here too[59] we must understand 'in this figure'. For what he first said, namely 'that when the terms stand as has been said there is a syllogism', is true without qualification; but 'if there is a syllogism, it is necessary for the terms to stand thus' is not true without   25 qualification – rather, if there is a syllogism in this figure. For it is possible to syllogize particular affirmatives and particular negatives even if the terms are not taken in this way: it is possible to prove a particular affirmative by the first figure (in which the terms stand in a different way) and a particular negative both in the first and in the   30 second. It is evident too, as he adds, that the syllogisms in this figure are all imperfect, like those of the second figure, and that no universal is deduced in the third figure.

[59] See above, 93,16 note.

7

Further Reflections

7.1 Syllogisms with non-standard conclusions[1]

109,1   It is clear too that in all the figures, when there is no syllogism, if both the terms are predicative or privative nothing necessary comes about at all; <but if they are predicative and privative, then if the privative is taken as universal there is always a syllogism of the minor extreme in relation to the major. E.g. if A holds of every or of some B and B of no C. For if the premisses are converted, it is necessary for C not to hold of some A. Similarly in the other figures too: there is always a syllogism by means of conversion.> [1.7, 29a19-27][2]

5   After he has set out all the combinations in the three figures and has shown in each figure which conjunctions are syllogistic and which non-syllogistic, he discusses the non-syllogistic conjunctions and records the following facts about them. The non-syllogistic combinations in each figure which are similar in form not only do not prove the point at issue – they do not prove or deduce anything else either. But as for the non-syllogistic combinations in each figure

10   which are dissimilar in form and have a universal negative – although they are non-syllogistic in relation to proving the point at issue, it is possible to syllogize and prove something else from them.

In the first figure the combinations similar in form are the two particular affirmatives, the negatives (universal and particular), and the complementary cases;[3] in the second figure all affirmatives

---

[1] On this section see 70,21 note.

[2] On this paradoxical text see esp. Patzig, pp. 93-6 (cf. pp. 56, 110, 128 n. 14).

[3] Alexander should describe *six* cases here: (1) the combination of two particular affirmatives, which we suppose him to intend by the inaccurate phrase 'the two particular affirmatives' (there are not two affirmative *combinations*); those (2) of two universal negatives, and (3) of two particular negatives, which we take to be intended by the phrase 'the negatives (universal and particular)'; and those of (4) a particular affirmative major and a universal affirmative minor, (5) a universal negative major and a particular negative minor, and (6) a particular negative major and a universal negative minor – which must somehow be encompassed by the phrase 'the complementary cases' (for which see above, 108,14). It is extremely difficult to believe

184

and all negatives; in the third figure the particular affirmatives and   15
all negatives. These conjunctions of premisses, then, prove nothing
syllogistically at all.

Of conjunctions dissimilar in form (i.e. differing according to their
quality) and having a universal negative, the following were
non-syllogistic: in the first figure, the combination of a universal
affirmative major and a universal negative minor and that of a
particular affirmative major and a universal negative minor; in the   20
second figure, the combination having a particular affirmative
major and a universal negative minor; and in the third figure those
having an affirmative major, either universal or particular, and a
universal negative minor.

It has been proved that these combinations do not syllogize the   25
point at issue.[4] Yet something else can be syllogized from them,
either by converting both premisses and interchanging the terms[5]
(in the first figure), or by converting only one premiss (in the other
two figures), so that the minor extreme becomes the major and is
predicated in the conclusion.

Take first the non-syllogistic combination in the first figure with   30
'A holds of every B' and 'B holds of no C'. In this combination there is
no deduction from A to C. This is why the combination is
non-syllogistic, being of no use with regard to the point at issue. Yet
something can be deduced syllogistically from the minor to the   110,1
major term. For if both premisses are converted, we get 'C holds of
no B' and 'B holds of some A' (since the universal affirmative
converts with the particular). From these premisses it can be
deduced that C does not hold of some A, where C takes the place of
the major term in the conclusion and A that of the minor, conversely   5
to how they were supposed. (The particular negative does not
convert, so that we cannot convert and have the conclusion we
proposed. In that case the conjunction would deduce the point at
issue, though not indemonstrably.) From this combination, then,
this is what can be proved and this is the way in which it is proved.

The other combination – with a particular affirmative major and a   10
universal negative minor – also proves by conversion of both
premisses that C does not hold of some A, taking the terms
conversely to how they were supposed.

These are the last two syllogisms of the five which Theophrastus –
who says that there are nine syllogisms in the first figure – adds to
the four laid down in the first figure.[6] They are last because they do   15

---

that the text yields these six cases: either Alexander has made a trivial error or else
his scribes have miscopied.

[4] See Aristotle, *An. Pr.* 26a2-9, 36-9; 27b6-8; 28a30-3, 36-8.

[5] i.e. making the major term minor and the minor major.

[6] Theophrastus, F 17 Graeser (see above, 70,21 note).

not prove the point at issue at all, unlike the three before them in which the conclusion is converted. (The remaining three, which come about by conversion of the conclusions of the first, second, and third syllogisms in the first figure, are also mentioned by Aristotle, at the
20   beginning of the second book of the *Prior Analytics*.[7] We will remark on them again in our notes there. In Theophrastus they are ranked before the other two.)

The non-syllogistic conjunction in the second figure with a particular affirmative major and a universal negative minor is indeed non-syllogistic with regard to proving that something is deduced from
25   the major to the minor term; but it deduces something from the minor to the major if the universal negative minor is converted and the minor term takes instead the major place. For if the order is changed[8] and the minor converted, then the premiss which was the minor is the major and a universal negative and the premiss which was the major is the minor and a particular affirmative, the terms remaining in the
30   same order. From these premisses it can be deduced that the term originally hypothesized as minor does not belong to some of the one originally posited as major.

Again, the two combinations in the third figure – one with a
111,1 universal affirmative major and a universal negative minor and the other with a particular affirmative major and a universal negative minor – are non-syllogistic with regard to the point at issue. Again, both of them syllogize a particular negative from the minor to the
5   major term, again by conversion of the affirmative major premiss.

These and thus many are the conjunctions in combinations which are non-syllogistic with regard to the point at issue but syllogistic with regard to something else. They all deduce their conclusions in the first figure. Aristotle shows how the deduction comes about and what is deduced in one of the combinations in the first figure: he omits the other combinations which syllogize something in a way similar to
10   the one he mentions. He makes only this one clear because these syllogisms are generated and proved in the same way in all the figures. This is so because they all yield the fourth indemonstrable.

<It is clear too that if an indeterminate is posited instead of a particular predicative, it will effect the same syllogism in all the figures.> [1.7, 29a27-9]

One might ask why he says 'an indeterminate ... instead of a particular predicative' and not 'and negative' as well. Either, then,
15   he means to refer to the latter in referring to the former, or else it is

[7] See Aristotle, *An. Pr.* 53a3-14: Alexander's commentary on the second book of *An. Pr.* has not survived.
[8] i.e. the order of the *terms* in the premiss (see above, on *taxis*), not the order of the

because in syllogistic combinations the particular affirmative has a certain advantage over the particular negative. For in those syllogistic combinations in which the particular premiss is affirmative, the point at issue is proved probatively – either indemonstrably, as in the first figure, or by conversion of a premiss, as in the second and third figures. But in those syllogistic   20
combinations in which the particular is negative, the point at issue is proved only by reduction to the impossible, as in the fourth syllogism of the second figure and the sixth of the third. (The particular negative occurs only in these syllogisms.) Perhaps, then, this is why he mentions the affirmative – because it has a certain advantage. For even in reductions to the impossible we do not use   25
the particular negative for the syllogism of the falsehood – rather, it is used to prove the impossibility of the conclusion.

It is clear too that if an indeterminate is posited instead of a particular predicative, it will effect the same syllogism in all the figures. [1.7, 29a27-9]

We have said that indeterminate propositions are equivalent to   30
particulars.[9] For even if they sometimes cover the universal case, nonetheless, they are not equivalent to universals. For it is not the case that if an indeterminate is true, the universal is always true. But the particular *is* always true – just as, conversely, when a particular is true, so also is the indeterminate. Hence, if an   112,1
indeterminate is assumed, then since it is equivalent to a particular, it will produce the same syllogism as the particular produced when it was posited.

7.2 Reduction

7.2.1 All syllogisms reduced to the first figure

It is evident too that all the imperfect syllogisms are perfected by means of the first figure. <For they are all brought to a conclusion either probatively or by means of the impossible, and in both ways we get the first figure – when they are perfected probatively, because they are all brought to a conclusion by means of conversion and conversion produces the first figure; when they are proved by means of the impossible, because when the falsity is posited the syllogism comes about by means of the first figure. (E.g. in the last figure, if A and B

premisses (*pace* Volait, pp. 30-3), to which Alexander (rightly) shows himself indifferent.
[9] See 30,31 note.

hold of every C, A holds of some B. For if of none and B of every C, then A of no C. But it held of every C. Similarly in the other cases too.)> [1.7, 29a30-9]

5   He has proved above that the syllogisms of both the second and the third figures, which are imperfect, are all perfected by means of the first figure, and now he brings the fact to our attention. For they were perfected either by conversion – those in the second, by conversion of the major premiss, those in the third, by conversion of 10   the minor – or by reduction to the impossible. And those which are perfected by conversion were reduced to the first figure, while those which are perfected by reduction to the impossible were proved to deduce the point at issue insofar as it was proved in the first figure that an impossibility follows from the hypothesized premiss.

He says that those proved by conversion are proved 'probatively' because in them, once the conversion is made, it is the point at 15   issue[10] which is primarily proved. With 'because they are all completed by means of conversion', we must understand 'those which are proved probatively'; for they are not all proved by conversion.

Those which are proved by way of the impossible assume a hypothesis and produce a syllogism and a proof of something else and not primarily of the point at issue; rather, with them, the point 20   at issue is proved accidentally. Reduction to the impossible comes about by way of the first figure both in the case of syllogisms in the second figure and in the case of those in the third. He shows this by taking one of the combinations of the third figure which is also proved by conversion.[11] This is the combination which deduces a particular affirmative from two universal affirmatives – which is proved to be syllogistic, as we have said,[12] both by conversion and 25   also by reduction to the impossible. For if it is supposed that A and B hold of every C, then A holds of some B. For if not, hypothesize the opposite – which is that A holds of no B. But it was supposed that B holds of every C. We get the second combination in the first figure, which deduces a universal negative, 'A holds of no C'. Since this is 30   impossible (for it is supposed that A holds of every C), the hypothesis from which this followed and which posited 'A holds of no B' is rejected, and it is established that A therefore holds of some B. And just as in the case before us the reduction to the impossible has come about by means of the first figure, so it does too in all the other syllogisms of both the second and the third figures.

---

[10] Reading *prokeimenou* for *keimenou*.
[11] Removing the commas after *gignetai* (112,20) and *edeixen* (112,21) and adding a comma after *tritôi* (112,21).
[12] *Darapti*: see above, 98,20-99,15 (on *An. Pr.* 28a18-23).

That proof by exposition is perceptual and not syllogistic is clear   113,1
from the fact that he does not mention it here as coming about by
means of a syllogism.[13]

7.2.2 All syllogisms reduced to *Barbara* and *Celarent*[14]

It is also possible to reduce all the syllogisms to the universal
syllogisms in the first figure. [1.7, 29b1-2]

He[15] first proved that all the syllogisms in the second and the third   5
figures reduce to the first figure and are perfected by it; for in this
sense the latter are perfect and indemonstrable. Here, since the first
two syllogisms in the first figure are more perfect,[16] containing two
universal premisses, he proves that all the syllogisms can be
reduced to them. He thus sets us an exercise,[17] and at the same time   10
shows that it is possible, on the basis of combinations which are
syllogistic *par excellence* and by general agreement,[18] to justify the
view that the others are indeed syllogisms. There are two remaining
syllogisms in the first figure (those with particular affirmative
minors), four in the second figure, and six in the third. Thus he
reduces all these twelve to the first two in the first figure.   15

<For the second figure syllogisms are evidently perfected by
them (though not all in the same way: the universals by
conversion of the privative, each of the particulars by means of
reduction to the impossible).> [1.7, 29b2-6]

The first two syllogisms in the second figure have an evident
reduction.[19] They were proved when their universal negative was
converted, and by this conversion we got the second syllogism in the
first figure with a universal negative major and a universal
affirmative minor. The two syllogisms which deduce a particular   20
negative are reduced to first figure syllogisms by reduction to the
impossible. In the case of the syllogism which deduces a particular
negative from a universal negative major and a particular
affirmative minor,[20] we hypothesize the opposite of what is deduced
(which is a particular negative), i.e. a universal affirmative, and we

---

[13] See above, 33,1 note.
[14] On this section see Volait, pp. 48-53.
[15] 113,5-7 = *FDS* 1101.
[16] 'Degrees of perfection' are not found in Aristotle: see Patzig, pp. 48-9 (on degrees
of imperfection see above, 77,9).
[17] *gumnasion*: for a comparable comment see e.g. Ammonius, *in Int.* 251,31.
[18] Reading *homologoumenôs sullogistikôn* for *homologoumenôn*.
[19] *Cesare, Camestres*: Aristotle, *An. Pr.* 27a5-14; above, 78,11-79,25.
[20] *Festino*: Aristotle, *An. Pr.* 27a32-6 (where it reduces to *Ferio* by conversion);
above, 82,25-83,8.

25   co-assume the major, which is a universal negative. In this way we
      get, in the first figure, a universal negative major and a universal
      affirmative minor, which we hypothesized. The conclusion is a
      universal negative, which is impossible – for the middle term, which
      was deduced to hold of none of the last term, holds of some of it. And
      in this way the third syllogism in the second figure is reduced to the
30   second in the first.
          The fourth, which has a universal affirmative major and a
      particular negative minor,[21] is reduced to the first syllogism in the
      first figure, which has two universal affirmatives, as has been
      proved. For if it is not true that the major does not hold of some of
      the minor, then suppose it to hold of all. But the middle is supposed
      to hold of all the major. Thus there are two universal affirmatives in
35   the first figure, and from them it will be deduced that the middle
      holds of all the minor. But it was supposed not to hold of some of it.

          <The particular syllogisms of the first figure are indeed
          perfected by means of themselves; but it is also possible to
          prove them by means of the second figure by reducing them to
          the impossible. E.g. if A holds of every B and B of some C, then
          A of some C. For if of none and of every B, then B will hold of no
          C – we know this by means of the second figure. The
          demonstration will be similar in the case of the privative
          syllogism. For if A holds of no B and B of some C, A will not
          hold of some C. For if it holds of every C and of no B, B will hold
          of no C. (This was the middle figure.) Hence since all the
          syllogisms in the middle figure are reduced to the universal
          syllogisms in the first figure, and the particular syllogisms in
          the first figure to the syllogisms in the middle figure, it is
          evident that the particular syllogisms will be reduced to the
          universal syllogisms in the first figure.> [1.7, 29b6-19]

114,1   Having proved that all the syllogisms in the second figure reduce to
      the two in the first figure with two universal premisses, he next
      discusses the two in the first figure which have a particular
      affirmative minor and a universal major (in the one case affirmative
5   and in the other negative). He says that for the proof of their
      necessity they are self-sufficient and need nothing else since they
      are perfect, but that they can in fact be reduced to the two
      syllogisms in the first figure with two universals, if they are first
      reduced by reduction to the impossible to the first two in the second
      figure.
          The third, which deduces a particular affirmative, he reduces to

      ---

      [21] *Baroco*: Aristotle, *An. Pr.* 27a36-b1; above, 83,12-84,3.

the second in the second figure, which has a universal affirmative   10
major and a universal negative minor. For it is supposed that A
holds of every B and that B holds of some C. The conclusion is that A
holds of some C. If this is not so, then its opposite, that A holds of no
C, is the case. But it was supposed that A holds of every B. This is
the combination of the second syllogism in the second figure which,
by conversion of the negative premiss, was reduced to the second   15
syllogism of the first figure. (Its conclusion was also converted.) So if
the third syllogism in the first figure has been reduced to the second
in the second and the second in the second to the second in the first,
then the third in the first reduces to the second in the first.

The fourth syllogism, which has a particular negative conclusion,   20
he reduces by reduction to the impossible to the first in the second
figure, which has a universal negative major. For if it is not true
that A does not hold of some C, it will hold of every C. But it is
supposed that it also holds of no B. This is the combination of the
first syllogism in the second figure, which is itself reduced by
conversion of the universal negative to the second in the first. The   25
fourth in the first will therefore also reduce to the second in the first.

Having reduced the two syllogisms in the first figure which
deduce a particular to the two[22] which deduce a universal by
reducing them to the first two in the second which had been reduced
to the latter, he next attempts to reduce the six syllogisms in the   30
third figure to the same two, and says:

> The syllogisms in the third figure, when the terms are
> universal, are perfected immediately by means of those
> syllogisms; ... [1.7, 29b19-21][23]

What he means is this: in the third figure the first two syllogisms
contain two universal premisses – one of them has two affirmatives,   115,1
the other a universal negative major.[24] He says that these can be
immediately reduced to and perfected by the syllogisms in question.
This is so because each is immediately reduced to one of them by
reduction to the impossible, the one with two universal affirmatives   5
to the second and the one with a universal negative major and a
universal affirmative minor to the first. For if we hypothesize the
opposite of what is deduced (which is either a particular affirmative
or a particular negative), we have either a universal negative or a

---

[22] Reading *tous* (Aldine edition) for *toutou tous* (Wallies: *toutous* MSS).

[23] With the following paragraphs compare [Ammonius], *in An. Pr.* XIII, a scholium which paraphrases and comments on Alexander.

[24] i.e. *Darapti* (*An. Pr.* 28a17-23 – for the reduction to the impossible by way of *Celarent* see above, 99,4-15); and *Felapton* (*An. Pr.* 28a26-30 – for the reduction to the impossible by way of *Barbara* see above, 100,34-101,3).

universal affirmative; we also have the premiss co-assumed, which
10   is both universal and affirmative (both premisses were universal);
and we get a syllogism in the first figure with two universal
premisses. The deduction is either an affirmative or a negative
universal.

He cannot mean[25] that the reduction proceeds by conversion. For
conversion makes one of the premisses particular. Nor is the fact
that both their premisses are universal in itself sufficient for them
to be reduced to the syllogisms in question. For the reduction must
15   be done by way of conversion, and when the conversion is made, the
premisses no longer remain universal. (In the case of the syllogisms
in the second figure with two universals, he used conversion and by
means of this proved that they reduce to these syllogisms.)

<... and when the terms are taken as particulars, they are
perfected by means of the particular syllogisms in the first
figure – but these were reduced to the former: hence so too are
the particulars in the third figure.> [1.7, 29b21-4]

As for the next three – two of them with a universal major, either
affirmative or negative, and a particular affirmative minor, and the
20   other with a particular affirmative major and a universal
affirmative minor – these no longer seem to derive from two
universals by way of reduction to the impossible. For the premiss
hypothesized in their case must certainly be universal, since it is
taken as opposite to the conclusion, which is particular; but the
co-assumption is particular.

Or does this hold only of the two cases in which the minor is a
25   particular affirmative?[26] For it is this which is assumed together
with the hypothesis, which was universal; and when it is assumed it
produces the first figure – not one of the syllogisms with two
universals but one with one particular premiss. Hence, since they
reduce by reduction to the impossible to the same syllogisms to
which they reduce by conversion, he reasonably used proof by
conversion in their case.[27]
30   It is possible, however, to reduce them by reduction to the
impossible to the syllogisms in the second figure with two universal
premisses; and these are reduced by conversion of the negative

[25] sc. despite the fact that he says 'immediately', which here means not 'by using
one or more conversions' but 'without first being reduced to some other syllogism'.
[26] For the third case, *Disamis*, can be treated by reduction to the impossible using
Celarent since the co-assumption is universal: below, 116,20-9.
[27] *Datisi* is reduced by conversion to *Darii* (*An. Pr.* 28b11-14; above, 102,27-103,3)
and by reduction to the impossible using *Ferio*. *Ferison* is reduced by conversion to
Ferio (*An. Pr.* 28b31-5; above, 106,9-16) and by reduction to the impossible using
Darii.

premiss to the second syllogism in the first figure. For if it is supposed that A holds of every C and B of some C, then I say that A holds of some B. For if not, then A holds of no B. But it is supposed that it also holds of every C. The proof is similar if AC is a universal negative.[28]   35

The reduction by way of the second figure to the first syllogisms in the first figure will seem easier than the proof which reduces them by conversion to the two in the first figure which have a particular minor premiss, inasmuch as these in turn must first be reduced by reduction to the impossible to the syllogisms in the second figure in which both premisses are universal.[29]   116,1

Again, it is possible to say that these syllogisms too are reduced to the first syllogism in the first figure by conversion. In the case of the   5 syllogism with a universal affirmative major, we must hypothesize not the opposite of what is deduced but the converse of the opposite. For if it is supposed that A holds of every C and B of some C, it can be deduced that A holds of some B. If not, then its opposite, that A holds of no B, is the case. But since this converts, B will hold of no A.   10 But it was supposed that A holds of every C. And from this it can be deduced that B holds of no C, which is impossible.

If AC is a universal negative, what is deduced is that A does not hold of some B. For if not, then let its opposite, that A holds of every B, be the case. If this is assumed, and if the universal negative AC is converted so that C is taken to hold of no A, then again we get the   15 second syllogism in the first figure.[30]

But if in a reduction to the impossible you must hypothesize the opposite of what is being proved and co-assume the other supposition, the first syllogism I stated will seem not to satisfy the suppositions, because it hypothesizes not the opposite of what is being proved but the converse of the opposite; nor will the second, because it co-assumed not one of the suppositions but the converse   20 of a supposition.[31]

The syllogism with a particular affirmative major and a universal affirmative minor can be reduced by conversion to the third syllogism in the first figure, which does not contain two universals.[32] However, it can also be reduced by reduction to the impossible to the

[28] i.e. *Datisi* may be treated by a reduction to the impossible using *Cesare*, and *Ferison* by a reduction using *Camestres*.

[29] Thus Aristotle reduces *Datisi* to *Celarent* by way of first *Darii* and then *Camestres*. Alexander reduces *Datisi* to *Celarent* by way of *Cesare* alone.

[30] The combination is: A holds of no C, B holds of some C. Hypothesize that A holds of every B. Convert the first premiss to: C holds of no A. From this and the hypothesis, infer that C holds of no B (by *Celarent*). Convert the conclusion to: B holds of no C — and this is inconsistent with the second premiss of the original combination.

[31] A trifling objection to a sound procedure.

[32] cf. Aristotle, *An. Pr.* 28b7-11; above, 102,6-24.

second syllogism in the first figure which has a universal negative
25   major and a universal affirmative minor, to which the first
syllogism, with two universal affirmatives, was also reduced.[33]
Hence this too, like the first two with two universal premisses, is
also immediately perfected by means of the universal syllogisms in
the first figure. (Those syllogisms reduce by conversion to the third
and fourth[34] just as this reduces to the third.)

30   Now this case was overlooked in what Aristotle said – and still
more the case of the syllogism with a particular negative major and
a universal affirmative minor. For this is not reduced in any way to
the particular syllogisms in the first figure – it is not proved by
conversion at all, as he said when he discussed it,[35] but only by
35   reduction to the impossible, by which it is reduced to the first
syllogism of the first figure.

In this way,[36] then, the syllogisms with two universal premisses
are directly reduced to the syllogisms in question, according to
117,1 Aristotle. The other four, he says, which have a particular premiss,
are reduced by conversions to the two particular syllogisms in the
first figure. These were proved to reduce to the first two syllogisms
by way of the first two in the second figure. Hence the syllogisms in
the third figure will be reduced to them by the same means. For the
5   syllogisms in the third figure reduce by conversion to the particular
syllogisms in the first figure, and the particular syllogisms in the
first figure reduce to the first two in the second figure by reduction to
the impossible, and the first two in the second figure reduce to the
second in the first figure by conversion. Hence the syllogisms in the
third figure with one particular premiss will be reduced to this same
syllogism.

But perhaps, as I said,[37] this is so not for the four syllogisms but
10   only for the three which are proved by conversion. The syllogism
with a particular negative major and a universal affirmative minor
was neither proved by conversion nor reduced to one of the
particular syllogisms in the first figure. Rather, it too was directly
reduced by reduction to the impossible to the first syllogism in the
first figure, as has been proved.[38] But the same is true of one of the

---

[33] See above, 114,33-115,12.

[34] *Darapti* to *Darii* (*An. Pr.* 28a18-22); *Felapton* to *Ferio* (*An. Pr.* 28a26-9).

[35] See *An. Pr.* 28b15-20 – but Aristotle does not say this. Alexander himself does, at 103,16-19. Should we change *eipe* ('he said') to *eipon* ('I said')?

[36] This paragraph does not fit. We suspect that in the original version of Alexander's discussion, 115,17 was immediately followed by 116,36-117,9. When he considered the matter again, Alexander added some new thoughts in 115,17-116,36. Having done so, he re-read 116,36-117,9 which he corrected and supplemented by appending 117,9-25. (See, in general, Introduction, p. 9.)

[37] Above, 116,30-5.

[38] Aristotle, *An. Pr.* 28b15-20; above, 103,9-25.

other three: the syllogism with a universal affirmative minor and a   15
particular affirmative major can indeed be reduced by conversion to
the third syllogism in the first figure – but by reduction to the
impossible it too can be reduced directly to the second syllogism.[39]
And if in this case we must use proof by conversion because it is
more authoritative,[40] then we must do the same in the case of the
syllogisms with two universal premisses. And in that case they too
will no longer be perfected immediately by means of the first two   20
syllogisms in the first figure but will also be reduced to the two
particular syllogisms, the one to the third and the other to the
fourth.

Perhaps, then, with 'when the terms are taken as particulars' we
should understand 'if they cannot be directly perfected by means of
the syllogisms in question' inasmuch as they are reduced to the
particular syllogisms in the first figure. For this is surely missing,   25
and when it is added there is no longer anything to investigate.

7.3 Final remarks

> Thus <we have said how> syllogisms which prove that
> something holds or does not hold <stand – both in their own
> right, when they are from the same figure, and in relation to
> one another, when they are from different figures ...> [1.7,
> 29b26-9][41]

There is a threefold distinction among propositions according to
their modes: some are actual, some necessary, some contingent.[42]
He has discussed the combinations of actual premisses and the   30
syllogisms involving such premisses in each figure; and now that he
is about to move on to the combinations compounded from necessary
premisses and to discuss them, he informs us that his account of the
combinations of actual premisses has been completed.   118,1

When he says 'in their own right, when they are from the same
figure, and in relation to one another, when they are from different
figures', he is referring to the differences among them. The
difference among the syllogisms in each figure in relation to one
another is evident; for one syllogism in the first figure has two
universal affirmatives, another has a universal negative major –   5

[39] See above, 116,20-9.

[40] See above, 106,19 note.

[41] At this point, Alexander's text of *An. Pr.* is significantly different from ours. (He
signals no variant readings: the later commentators do not mention Alexander's
reading.) Moreover, Alexander's double set of comments is inconsistent and
perplexing. Perhaps 118,9-25 represents Alexander's second thoughts, later inserted
into the original text.

[42] On modes see above, 26,2-22; 27,26-28,30.

and so on, in each figure. Again, the difference among the syllogisms
in the different figures in relation to one another is familiar; for the
position of the middle term is not the same in all of them.

> – both in their own right, when they are from the same figure
> ... [1.7, 29b27-8]

10   This depends on 'Thus it is evident'.[43] For it is evident from what he
has said that all syllogisms will be reduced to the first two
syllogisms in the first figure, and how each syllogism is syllogistic in
its own figure, and why each of them is syllogistic. All this has been
proved.

> ... and in relation to one another, when they are from different
> figures ... [1.7, 29b28]

15   This too still depends on 'Thus it is evident'.[44] For it is also evident
from what he has said how the figures, and the syllogisms in the
different figures, differ in relation to one another – the difference
depends on the position of the middle term and on the different ways
in which they are reduced to the first two syllogisms in the first
20   figure. For some are reduced directly and some by reduction to one
another (i.e. the two syllogisms in the first figure and the three in
the third with particular propositions); and of the latter again, some
inasmuch as they are reduced to the first syllogisms in the second
figure (i.e. the two in the first figure), and others inasmuch as they
are reduced to those in the first figure which prove particular
premisses (i.e. the three syllogisms in the third figure which are
25   reduced to these by conversion). The difference in their reductions
shows the differences among these syllogisms.

> <... (either by the middle term> or inasmuch as they are
> reduced to the first figure).

Having said 'either by the middle term', he adds 'or inasmuch as
they are reduced to the first figure'. For they differ in this respect too
119,1   – their reductions are different. For the particular syllogisms in the
first figure are reduced in one way (they are reduced by means of
those in the second) and the syllogisms in the second figure in
another way – and these are themselves reduced in different ways,

---

[43] At *An. Pr.* 29b24; but unless Alexander's text of *An. Pr.* was even further from
ours than we suppose, his construal is impossible.
[44] Again, at *An. Pr.* 29b24; and again, Alexander's construal is impossible.

some by conversion and some by reduction to the impossible. So too with the syllogisms in the third figure: some are reduced by reduction to the impossible and some by conversion first to the 5 particular syllogisms in the first figure.

Appendix 1

Translation of *Prior Analytics* 1.1-7

This Appendix gives a continuous translation of Aristotle, *Prior Analytics* 1.1-7, from which the translated lemmata in the commentary are drawn. The translation is deliberately spare, and at times inelegantly close to the Greek: its purpose is not to ease the understanding of Aristotle's text but to provide an appropriate companion to Alexander's commentary.

We have translated not the standard modern text of Aristotle but rather the text which Alexander had before him – insofar as this text can be reconstructed. Alexander's readings are given explicitly in the citations in the body of his commentary; they can also sometimes be inferred from the tenor of his comments. In addition, there are the lemmata: although their status is uncertain,[1] we here take them to represent Alexander's readings provided that they are consistent with his commentary. In this way, something like two-fifths of the text which Alexander read can be recovered. For the rest, our translation simply follows the Oxford Classical Text of *An. Pr.*, edited by Sir David Ross and Lorenzo Minio-Paluello (Oxford, 1964).

Alexander's text differs from the OCT at a number of places. The notes to our translation signal all these differences, most of which are trifling. In addition, we have drawn attention to a few other interesting textual points. (But it would be rash to use the notes as the basis for any general conjectures about the relationship between Alexander's text and the manuscript tradition of *An. Pr.*[2])

'Alex^l' refers to lemmata in Alexander, 'Alex^c' to citations in the body of his commentary. Other abbreviations are self-explanatory. The sigla for the MSS are those of the OCT for Aristotle[3] and of Wallies' edition for Alexander.

Aristotle *Prior Analytics* 1.1-7

24a10   (1) First, to say about what and of what the inquiry is: it is about demonstration and demonstrative science.[4] Then to determine what a proposition is, and what a term, and what a syllogism, and what sort of syllogisms are perfect and what sort imperfect; and after that, what it is for

---

[1] See Introduction, p. 17.

[2] On this question see Wallies; Ross, pp. 90-2.

[3] We have consulted Williams for corrections and additions to the OCT's critical apparatus.

[4] 24a11: *epistêmên apodeiktikên* Alex^lc; *epistêmês apodeiktikês* OCT, Alex: Aldina.

this to be or not be in that as in a whole, and what we mean by being
predicated of every or of none.   15
  Now a proposition is an utterance affirming or negating something of
something. It is either universal or particular or indeterminate. By
universal, I mean holding of all or of none, by particular holding of some or
not of some or not of all, by indeterminate holding or not holding, without   20
being universal or particular (e.g. that of contraries there is the same
science, or that pleasure is not a good).
  A demonstrative proposition differs from a dialectical proposition in that
a demonstrative proposition is the assuming of one part of a contradictory
pair (for if you are demonstrating you do not request but assume), while a
dialectical proposition is a request for one of a contradictory pair. There will 25
be no difference with regard to there being a syllogism in each case. For
whether you are demonstrating or requesting, you syllogize by assuming
that something holds of something or that something[5] does not hold. Hence
a syllogistic proposition *simpliciter* affirms or negates something of
something in the way already mentioned.[6] It is demonstrative if it is true
and is assumed by way of the initial hypotheses. It is dialectical if it is a   24b10
request for one of a contradictory pair (if you are inquiring) or an
assumption of what is apparent and reputable (if you are syllogizing) – as
has been said in the *Topics*. In what follows we shall say with precision
what a proposition is and how[7] syllogistic and demonstrative and dialectical
propositions differ; but for present purposes let what we have determined   15
be enough.
  I call a term that into which a proposition resolves – i.e. the predicate and
that of which it is predicated (when you add or remove[8] 'is' or[9] 'is not').
  A syllogism is an utterance in which, certain things being posited,
something different from the suppositions comes about by necessity
inasmuch as they are the case. By 'inasmuch as they are the case' I mean   20
that it comes about because of them; and to come about because of them is to
need no external term for the generation of the necessity.
  I call a syllogism perfect if it needs nothing else apart from the
assumptions in order for the necessity to be evident; and imperfect if it
needs one[10] or more items which are necessary by way of the terms   25
supposed but have not been assumed by way of premisses.
  For one thing to be in another as in a whole and for the other to be
predicated of all the one are the same thing. We say that one thing is
predicated of all another when it is not possible to take any of it[11] of which 30
the other is not said. And similarly for of none.

(2) Now every proposition is either of holding or of holding by necessity or of 25a1
holding contingently. Of these some are affirmative and others negative, in
respect of each adjunct. Again, of affirmatives and negatives, some are

  [5] 24a28: *kai ti* Alex[c] (13,27); *ê* codd Arist, Alex[c] (13,17).
  [6] 24a29: *proeirêmenon* Alex[c]; *eirêmenon* OCT.
  [7] 24b13: *tini* Alex[l]; *ti* OCT.
  [8] 24b17: *ê diairoumenou* Alex[c], codd Arist; del OCT.
  [9] 24b18: *ê* Alex[c], OCT; *kai* Arist: ABdΛ.
  [10] 24b25: *henos* Alex[c]; *ê henos* OCT, Alex: Aldina.
  [11] 24b29: *labein* + *tou hupokeimenou* codd Arist; del OCT, non habet Alex[c] (sed cf.
24,29.32; 54,7).

5 universal, some particular, some indeterminate. And in the case of propositions of holding, it is necessary for the[12] universal privative to convert in its terms – e.g. if no pleasure is a good, no good will be a pleasure. Predicative propositions necessarily convert, but to a particular and not to a universal –
10 e.g. if every pleasure is a good, then some good is a pleasure. Of particulars, it is necessary for the affirmative to convert to a particular (if some pleasure is a good, then some good will be a pleasure), but the privative does not necessarily convert (it is not the case that if man does not hold of some animal, then animal does not hold of some man).

15 First, then, let the proposition AB be a universal privative. Now if A holds of no B,[13] B will hold of no A.[14] For if of some, e.g. of C, it will not be true that A holds of no B. For C is something of B.

If A holds of every B, then B will hold of some A. For if of none, A will hold of no B. But it was supposed to hold of every B.

20 Similarly if the proposition is particular. For if A holds of some B, then it is necessary for B to hold of some A. For if of none, then A will hold of no B.[15]

If A does not hold of some B, it is not necessary that B should not hold of
25 some A. E.g. if B is animal and A man: man does not hold of every animal, but animal holds of every man.

(3) The case will be the same for necessary propositions. For the universal privative converts to a universal, and each of the affirmatives to a particular.
30 For if it is necessary for A to hold of no B, it is necessary for B to hold of no A. For if it is contingent that it holds of some, then it will be contingent that A holds of some B.[16]

If A holds by necessity of all or of some of the Bs,[17] then it is necessary for B to hold of some of the As.[18] For if it is not necessary, A will not hold of some B by necessity.

35 The particular privative does not convert for the same reason as we gave earlier.

As for contingent propositions, since[19] being contingent is meant in several ways (we say that the necessary and the non-necessary and the possible are
40 contingent), in affirmatives the case will be similar in respect of conversion in all instances.

25b1 If it is contingent for A to hold of every or of some B, then it will be contingent for B to hold of some A. For if of none, then A of no B (this has been proved earlier).

In negatives it is not the same. With those which are said to be contingent
5 inasmuch as it is by necessity that they do not hold[20] or inasmuch as it is not by necessity that they do hold,[21] the case is indeed similar. E.g. if someone

---

[12] 25a5: *tôn men en tôi huparkhein tên men* Alex[l]; *tên men en tôi huparkhein* OCT; *tên men oun en tôi huparkhein* Alex: Aldina.

[13] 25a15: *tôi* B Alex[cl], OCT; *tôn* B Arist: ABC[2]d, Alex[c]: LM.

[14] 25a15: *tôi* A Alex[cl], OCT; *tôn* A Arist: ABCdΓΠ; *to* B Arist: n[2].

[15] 25a22: *tôi* B Alex[c], OCT; *tôn* B Arist: ABCdΓΠ.

[16] 25a31 *tini tôi* B Alex[l]; *tôi* B *tini* OCT, Alex: Aldina.

[17] 25a32: *tôn* B Alex[l], Arist: A[2]C; *tôi* B OCT, Alex: Aldina.

[18] 25a33: *tôn* A Alex[l], Arist: A[2]C; *tôi* A OCT, Alex: Aldina.

[19] 25a37: *epei* Alex[l]; *epeidê* OCT, Alex: Aldina.

[20] 25b4: *ex anankês mê huparkhein* Alex ut videtur, Arist: A[2]B[2]CdΓΛ; *ex anankês huparkhein* OCT.

[21] 25b5: *mê ex anankês huparkhein* Alex[c], Arist: AB[1]CdΓΛΠ; *mê ex anankês*

were to say that it is contingent for man not to be a horse or that it is contingent[22] for white to hold of no cloak. In the one case it is by necessity that it does not hold, and in the other it is not necessary that it does hold. And the proposition converts in the same way. For if it is contingent for horse to hold of no man, then it may be that man holds of no horse; and if it may be that white holds of no cloak, then it may be that cloak holds of no white. For if it is necessary for it to hold of some, then white will hold of some cloak by necessity – this was proved earlier. (Similarly too for particular negatives.) 10

But as for those which are said to be contingent inasmuch as they are for the most part[23] and by nature – this is the way in which we determine the contingent – here the case will not be similar for negative conversions. Rather, the universal privative proposition does not convert whereas the particular does convert. 15

This will be evident when we discuss the contingent. For the moment, in addition to what we have said, let it be[24] clear that 'It is contingent that it holds of none or not of some' has an affirmative figure. For 'It is contingent' is ranked in the same way as 'is', and 'is' (where it is co-predicated) always and in every case makes an affirmation – e.g. 'It is not good' or 'It is not white' or generally 'It is not such-and-such' (this too will be shown in what follows). And in respect of conversions the case will be similar to that of the others. 20

(4) Having determined these issues, let us now say[25] by what means and when and how every syllogism comes about. We must discuss demonstration later. (We must discuss syllogisms before demonstration because syllogisms are more universal: a demonstration is a syllogism, but[26] not every syllogism is a demonstration.) 30

Now when three terms so stand to one another that the last is in the middle as in a whole and the middle is[27] or is not in the first as in a whole, it is necessary for there to be a perfect syllogism of the extremes. I call a term middle when both it is in another and another is in it – it is middle by position too. Extremes are both that which is in something else and that in which something else is. 35

If A is said of every B and B of every C, then it is necessary for A to be predicated of every C. For we have earlier said what we mean by 'of every'.

Similarly, if[28] A is said of no B and B of every C, A will hold of no C. 26a1

But if the first follows[29] all the middle and the middle none of the last,[30] there will not be a syllogism of the extremes. For nothing necessary follows inasmuch as they are the case. For it is possible for the first to hold of all 5

---

mê huparkhein OCT.

[22] 25b6: *leukon* + *endekhesthai* Alex[c]; non habet OCT.

[23] 25b14: *to polu* Alex[cl], OCT; *to* om Arist: ABd[1], Alex: Aldina.

[24] 25b19: *pros tois eirêmenois estô* Alex[l]; *estô pros tois eirêmenois* OCT, Alex: Aldina.

[25] 25b26: *legômen* Alex[l], OCT; *legomen* Arist: ABCd.

[26] 25b30: *ho de sullogismos* Alex[c]; *ho sullogismos de* OCT.

[27] 25b34: *prôtôi* + *ê* OCT; om Alex[l] bis [52,29 *ê* praebet L, 53,17 *ê* praebet Aldina].

[28] 25b40: *d' ei kai* Alex[l]; *de kai ei* OCT.

[29] 26a2: *akolouthei* Alex[cl], OCT; *huparkhei* codd Arist.

[30] 26a3: *tôi de eskhatôi to meson mêdeni* Alex[l]; *to de meson mêdeni tôi eskhatôi huparkhei* OCT [*huparkhei* om Arist:Λ].

and also of none of the last. Hence neither the particular nor the universal is necessary. And if nothing is necessary by way of these items, there will not be a syllogism. Terms for holding of every: animal, man, horse. For holding of none: animal, man, stone.

10 Nor when the first holds of none of the middle and the middle of none of the last will there be a syllogism in this case either. Terms for holding: science, line, medicine. For not holding: science, line, unit.

Thus when the terms are universal it is clear when there will be a
15 syllogism in this figure and when there will not be one; and that if[31] there is a syllogism it is necessary for the terms to stand as we have said, and that if they stand in this way there will be a syllogism.

If one of the terms is universal and one particular in relation to the other, then when the universal is posited on the major extreme (whether it is predicative or privative) and the particular on the minor is predicative, it is
20 necessary for there to be a perfect syllogism. But when it is on the minor or the terms stand in any other way, it is impossible. (I call the major extreme the one in which the middle is, and the minor the one under the middle.[32])

For let A hold of every B and B of some C. Then if being predicated of
25 every is what we said at the beginning, it is necessary for A to hold of some C.

And if A holds of no B and B of some C, it is necessary for A not to hold of some C. For we have also defined what we mean by 'of none'. Hence there will be a perfect syllogism. (Similarly too if BC is indeterminate, being
30 predicative. For there will be the same syllogism, whether it is assumed as indeterminate or as particular.)

If the universal, either predicative or privative, is posited on the minor[33] extreme, there will not be a syllogism, whether the indeterminate or particular is affirmative or negative. I.e.[34] if A holds or does not hold of some
35 B and B holds of every C. Terms for holding: good, disposition, sagacity. For not holding: good, disposition, ignorance. Again, if B holds of no C and A holds[35] of some B or does not hold (or does not hold of every), in this case too there will not be a syllogism. Terms: white, horse, swan; white, horse, raven. The same terms serve if AB is indeterminate.

26b1 When the term on the major extreme is universal, either predicative or privative, and the term on the minor is privative and[36] particular, there will not be a syllogism (whether it is assumed as indeterminate or as particular).[37] I.e. if A holds of every B and B does not hold of some C (or if it
5 does not hold of every C). For the first will follow all and also none of that of some of which the middle does not hold. Suppose the terms to be animal, man, white. Then of the whites of which man is not predicated, take swan and snow. Then animal is predicated of all the one and of none of the other.
10 Hence there will not be a syllogism. Again, let A hold of no B and let B not hold of some C; and let the terms be inanimate, man, white. Then of the whites of which man is not predicated, take swan and snow. Inanimate is

---

[31] 26a15: *ontos ge* Alex[c] [*ge* om Aldina]; *ontos te* OCT, Alex[l].
[32] 26a22: *to meson* + *on* OCT, Alex[c]: L, Aldina, Alex[l]: Aldina; om Alex[cl].
[33] 26a30: *ton elassona* Alex[l] [*to elasson* Aldina]; *to elatton* OCT.
[34] 26a33: *to men* A OCT, Alex: Aldina; *men* om Alex[l].
[35] 26a36: *tôi* B + *ê* OCT; om Alex[l].
[36] 26b2: *sterêtikon* + *kai* Alex[l]; om OCT, Alex: Aldina.
[37] 26b3: *adioristou te kai en merei lêphthentos* Alex[l], codd Arist; del OCT.

predicated of all the one and of none of the other. Again, since 'B does not hold   15
of some C' is indeterminate and it is true both if it holds of none and if it does
not hold of all (because it does not hold of some), and since there is no
syllogism if terms are taken such that it holds of none (this has been said
earlier), it is evident that there will not be a syllogism inasmuch as the terms
stand in the way we are considering. For then there would be one in this case   20
too. (And[38] it will be proved in the same way if[39] the universal is posited as
privative.)

Again, if both the intervals are[40] particular, either predicatively or
privatively (or one is said predicatively and the other privatively), or one
indeterminate and the other determinate, or both indeterminate, in none of
these cases will there be a syllogism. Terms common to all cases: animal,   25
white, horse; animal, white, stone.

Thus it is evident from what has been said that if there is a particular
syllogism in this figure, it is necessary for the terms to stand as we have said;
for if they stand in any other way, there is not. It is clear, too, that all the
syllogisms in it are perfect (for they are all perfected by means of the initial   30
assumptions), and that all problems are proved by means of this figure
(holding of every and of none and of some and not of some). I call this the first
figure.

(5) When the same item holds of all the one and of none of the other, or of all or   35
none of each, I call this the second figure. I say that in it the middle term is the
one predicated of both, the extremes are those of which this is said, and the
major extreme is the one supposed on the middle.[41] The middle is posited
outside the extremes and first in position.

Now there will not be[42] a perfect syllogism in this figure, but there will be a   27a1
potential one both when the terms are universal and when they are not
universal. When they are universal, there will be a syllogism when the
middle holds of all the one and of none of the other, on whichever the privative   5
may be; and in no other case.

Let M be predicated of no N and of every O. Since the privative converts, N
will hold of no M. But M was supposed to hold of every O. Hence N of no O (this
has been proved earlier).

Again, if M holds of every N and of no O, O will hold of no N. For if M holds of   10
no O, O holds of no M. But M held of every N. Therefore O will hold of no N. For
we have got the first figure again. And since the privative converts, N will
hold of no O. Hence there will be the same syllogism. (It is also possible to
prove these by reduction to the impossible.)   15

Thus it is evident that there is a syllogism when the terms stand thus – but
not a perfect one. For the necessity is perfected not only from the initial
assumptions but also from other items.

If M is predicated of every N and O, there will not be a syllogism. Terms for
holding: substance, animal, man. For not holding: substance, animal,   20
number. (Substance is the middle.) Nor when M is predicated of no N and of

---

[38] 26b20: *homoiôs de* Alex[cl], OCT; *homoiôs gar* cj. Alex.
[39] 26b20: *kai ei* Alex[l], OCT; *kan* Arist: ABd.
[40] 26b21: *meros + êi* Alex[l], Arist: C; om OCT.
[41] 26b38: *keimenon + elatton de to porrôterô tou mesou* OCT; om Alex[l], Arist: B[1].
[42] 27a1: *sullogismos + oudamôs* OCT; om Alex[l].

no O. Terms for holding: line, animal, man. For not holding: line, animal, stone.

Thus it is evident that if there is a universal syllogism,[43] it is necessary for the terms to stand as we said at the beginning. For if they stand in any other way, the necessity does not come about.

If the middle is universal in relation to one term, then if it is universal in relation to the major, either predicatively or privatively, and particular in relation to the minor and in an opposite way to the universal (by 'in an opposite way' I mean that if the universal is privative the particular is affirmative, and if the universal is predicative the particular is privative), it is necessary for there to be a particular privative syllogism. For if M holds of no N and of some O, it is necessary for N not to hold of some O. For since the privative converts, N will hold of no M. But M was supposed to hold of some O. Hence N will not hold of some O. For we get a syllogism by way of the first figure. Again, if M holds of every N and not of some O, it is necessary for N not to hold of some O. For if it will hold of[44] every O, and M is predicated of every N, it is necessary for M to hold of every O. But it was supposed not to hold of some. (And if M holds of every N and not of every O, there will be a syllogism that N does not hold of every O. The demonstration is the same.)

If it is predicated of every O and not of every N, there will not be a syllogism. Terms: animal, substance, raven; animal, white, raven. Nor when of no O and of some N. Terms for holding: animal, substance, unit. For not holding: animal, substance, science.

Thus when the universal is opposite to the particular, we have said when there will be a syllogism and when not. When the premisses are similar in form – i.e. both privative or affirmative – there will in no case be a syllogism. Let them first be privative, and let the universal be supposed on the major extreme. I.e. let M hold of no N and not of some O. Now it is possible for N to hold of every O[45] and also of no O. Terms for not holding: black, snow, animal. It is not possible to take terms for holding if M holds of some O and not of some O. For if N holds of every O and M of no N, M will hold of no O; but it was supposed to hold of some. Thus in this case it is not possible to take terms – it must be proved from the indeterminacy. For since 'M does not hold of some O' is true even if it holds of none, and since there was no syllogism when it held of none, it is evident that there will not be one in the present case either.

Again, let them be predicative and let the universal be supposed in the same way. I.e. let M hold of every N and of some O. Now it is possible for N to hold of every O and also of no O. Terms for holding of none: white, swan, stone. It is not possible to take terms for holding of all (the explanation is the same as before) – it must be proved from the indeterminacy.

If the universal is on the minor extreme, and M holds of[46] no O and not of some N, it is possible for N to hold of every O and also of no O. Terms for holding: white, animal, raven. For not holding: white, stone, raven.

If the premisses are predicative, terms for not holding are white, animal, snow; for holding, white, animal, swan.

Thus it is evident that when the premisses are similar in form and one is

---

43 27a23: *katholou* + *tôn horôn ontôn* OCT; om Alex ut videtur.
44 27a38: *huparxei* Alex[1], Arist: C; *huparkhei* OCT.
45 27b15: *to N tôi X* Alex[1]; *tôi X to N* OCT, Alex: Aldina.
46 27b28-30: *ean ... êi ... huparxêi* Alex[1]; *ei ... esti ... huparkhei* OCT, Alex: Aldina.

universal and the other particular, in no case is there a syllogism.

Nor if it holds of some of each, or does not hold, or of some of one and not of some of the other, or of all of neither, or indeterminately. Terms common to all cases: white, animal, man; white, animal, inanimate.

Thus it is evident from what we have said that if the terms stand to one another in the way we have said, there is a syllogism by necessity, and that if there is a syllogism it is necessary for the terms to stand in this way. It is clear too that all the syllogisms in this figure are imperfect (for they are all perfected when certain items are co-assumed which either inhere by necessity in the terms or are posited as hypotheses – i.e. when we prove by means of the impossible), and that there is no affirmative syllogism by means of this figure but that all of them, both the universal and the particular, are privative.

(6) When[47] one term holds of all and the other of none of the same term, or both of all or none, I call this the third figure; and I say that in it the middle is that of which both are predicated, the extremes are the predicates, the major is the extreme further from the middle, and the minor is the one nearer. The middle is posited outside the extremes and is last in position. There is no perfect syllogism in this figure either, but there will be a potential one both when the terms are universal and when they are not universal in relation to the middle.

If they are universal, then when both P and R hold of every S, P will hold of some R by necessity. For since the predicative converts, S will hold of some R. Hence since P holds of every S and S of some R, it is necessary for P to hold of some R. For we get a syllogism by way of the first figure. It is also possible to effect the demonstration by means of the impossible and by exposition. For if both hold of every S, then if something of S – say N – is taken, both P and R will hold of this. Hence P will hold of some R.

And if R holds of every S and P of none, there will be a syllogism that P does not hold of some R by necessity. There is the same mode of demonstration, the premiss RS being converted. It can also be proved by way of the impossible, as in the earlier cases.

If R holds of no S[48] and P of every S,[49] there will not be a syllogism. Terms for holding: animal, horse, man. For not holding: animal, inanimate, man. Nor when both are said of no S will there be a syllogism. Terms for holding: animal, horse, inanimate. For not holding: man, horse, inanimate. (Inanimate is the middle.)

Thus it is evident in this figure too when there will be a syllogism and when not, the terms being universal. When both the terms are predicative there will be a syllogism that the extreme holds of some of the extreme; and when they are privative there will not be one. When one is privative and the other affirmative, then if the major is predicative and the other affirmative, there will be a syllogism that the extreme does not hold of some of the extreme; if they are the other way about, there will not be.

If one term is universal in relation to the middle and the other particular, then if both are predicative, it is necessary for there to be a syllogism, whichever of the terms is universal. For if R holds of every S and P of some

28a1

5

10

15

20

25

30

35

28b1

5

[47] 28a10: *hotan* Alex[1]; *ean* OCT.
[48] 28A30: *mêdeni* + *tôi* S Alex[1], Arist: Cn[2]; om OCT
[49] 28a31: *tôi* S *huparkhêi* Alex[1] [*tôi* S om Aldina]; *huparkhêi tôi* S OCT.

S, it is necessary for P to hold of some R. For since the affirmative converts, S
10 will hold of some P. Hence since R holds of every S and S of some P, R will hold
of some P. Hence also[50] P of some R. Again, if R holds of some S and P of every
S,[51] it is necessary for P to hold of some R. There is the same mode of
demonstration. It is also possible to demonstrate by means of the impossible
15 and by exposition, as in the earlier cases.[52]

If one is predicative and the other privative and the predicative is
universal, then when the minor is predicative there will be a syllogism. For if
R holds of every S and P does not hold of some S, it is necessary for P not to
20 hold of some R. For if of every, and R of every S, then P will hold of every S. But
it did not hold. It is also proved without the reduction if something of S is
taken of which P does not hold.

When the major is predicative, there will not be a syllogism – i.e. if P holds
of every S and R does not hold of some S. Terms for holding of every: animate,
25 man, animal. It is not possible to take terms for holding of none if R holds of
some S and does not hold of some. For if P holds of every S and R of some S,
then P will hold of some R. But it was supposed to hold of none. We must take
terms as in the earlier cases. For 'does not hold of some' is indeterminate, and
30 it is true to say of what holds of none that it does not hold of some. But if it
holds of none, there was no syllogism. So it is evident that there will not be a
syllogism.

If the privative is the universal term, then when the major is privative and
the minor predicative, there will be a syllogism. For if P holds of no S and R
35 holds of some S, P will not hold of some R. For again there will be the first
figure, the premiss RS being converted.

When the minor is privative, there will not be a syllogism. Terms for
holding: animal, man, wild. For not holding: animal, science, wild. (Wild is
middle in both cases.) Nor when both are posited as privative and one is
29a1 universal and the other particular. Terms when the minor is universal in
relation to the middle: animal, science, wild; animal, man, wild. When the
major, for not holding: raven, snow, white. It is not possible to take terms for
5   holding if R holds of some S and does not hold of some S. For if P holds of every
R and R of some S, P holds of some S. But it was supposed to hold of none. It
must be proved from the indeterminacy.

And if each holds of some of the middle, or does not hold of some, or if one
holds and the other does not hold, or one of some and the other not of all, or
indeterminately – there will not be a syllogism in any of these cases. Terms
10 common to all cases: animal, man, white; animal, inanimate, white.

Thus it is evident in this figure too when there will be a syllogism and when
there will not – that[53] when the terms stand as has been said there is a
syllogism by necessity, and that if there is a syllogism it is necessary for the
15 terms to stand thus. It is evident too that all the syllogisms in this figure are
imperfect (for they are all perfected when certain things are co-assumed),
and that it is not possible to syllogize a universal, whether privative or
affirmative, by means of this figure.

20 (7) It is clear too that in all the figures, when there is no syllogism, if both the

---

50 28b11: *hôste + kai* Alex[c], Arist: BC[2]Λ; om OCT.
51 28b12: *huparkhei + tôi S* Alex[l]; om OCT.
52 28b15: *proteron* Alex[c], OCT; *proterôn* Alex: M, Aldina, Arist: ACd.
53 29a12: *ekhontôn + te* OCT; om Alex[c].

terms are[54] predicative or privative nothing necessary comes about at all; but if they are predicative and privative, then if the privative is taken as universal there is always a syllogism of the minor extreme in relation to the major. E.g. if A holds of every or of some B and B of no C. For if the premisses are converted, it is necessary for C not to hold of some A. Similarly in the other figures too: there is always a syllogism by means of conversion.   25

It is clear too that if an indeterminate is posited instead of a particular predicative, it will effect the same syllogism in all the figures.

It is evident too that all the imperfect syllogisms are perfected by means of the first figure. For they are all brought to a conclusion either probatively or by means of the impossible, and in both ways we get the first figure – when they are perfected probatively, because they are all brought to a conclusion by means of conversion and conversion produces the first figure; when they are proved by means of the impossible, because when the falsity is posited the syllogism comes about by means of the first figure. (E.g. in the last figure, if A and B hold of every C, A holds of some B. For if of none and B of every C, then A of no C. But it held of every C. Similarly in the other cases too.)   30   35

It is also possible to reduce[55] all the syllogisms to the universal syllogisms in the[56] first figure. For the second figure syllogisms are evidently perfected by them (though not all in the same way: the universals by conversion of the privative, each of the particulars by means of reduction to the impossible). The particular syllogisms in the first figure are indeed perfected by means of themselves; but it is also possible to prove them by means of the second figure by reducing them to the impossible. E.g. if A holds of every B and B of some C, then A of some C. For if of none and of every B, then B will hold of no C – we know this by means of the second figure. The demonstration will be similar in the case of the privative syllogism. For if A holds of no B and B of some C, A will not hold of some C. For if it holds of every C and of no B, B will hold of no C. (This was the middle figure.) Hence since all the syllogisms in the middle figure are reduced to the universal syllogisms in the first figure, and the particular syllogisms in the first figure to the syllogisms in the middle figure, it is evident that the particular syllogisms will be reduced to the universal syllogisms in the first figure. The syllogisms in the third figure, when the terms are universal, are perfected immediately by means of those syllogisms; and when the terms are taken as particulars,[57] they are perfected by means of the particular syllogisms in the first figure – but these were reduced to the former: hence so too are the particulars in the third figure. Thus it is evident that all will be reduced to the universal syllogisms in the first figure.   29b1   5   10   15   20   25

Thus we have said how syllogisms which prove that something holds or does not hold stand – both in their own right, when they are from the same figure, and in relation to one another,[58] when they are from different figures (either by the middle term or inasmuch as they are reduced to the first figure).[59]

---

[54] 29a21: *tôn horôn ontôn* Alex[l]; *ontôn tôn horôn* OCT.
[55] 29b1: *anagein* Alex[l]; *anagagein* OCT.
[56] 29b2: *en* + *tôi* OCT; om Alex[l].
[57] 29b21: *epi merous* Alex[c]; *en merei* OCT.
[58] 29b28: *allêlous* Alex[cl], OCT; *allous* Arist: ABd.
[59] 29b28: *heterôn* + *skhêmatôn ê tôi mesôi ê tôi anagesthai eis to prôton* Alex[cl]; om OCT [+ *skhêmatôn* Arist: ABCn²].

Appendix 2

Aristotelian Syllogistic

This Appendix contains, first, a brief outline of Aristotelian syllogistic, and secondly, a list of the syllogistic forms which Aristotle and his successors recognised.

I

The interpretation of Aristotle's syllogistic is controversial, and not only in its details. Here we do not discuss the various rivals: we simply set down a sketch of the system, without argument or defence – and also without any attempt at technical sophistication.[1]

A syllogism, then, is a sort of argument; and an argument may be represented as a sequence of propositions, one the conclusion and the rest the premisses. Any argument, we may say, has the form:

$P_1, P_2, ..., P_n$: therefore, Q

– where the P_is are the premisses and Q is the conclusion. And an argument is valid if its conclusion follows from its premisses.

An Aristotelian syllogism is a valid argument of a particular sort. First, a syllogism is an argument which has exactly two premisses. In other words, it has the form:

P_1, P_2: therefore, Q.

Moreover, the conclusion, Q, must be a different proposition from each of the premisses; and the premisses must be different from each other.

Each of the three component propositions of a syllogism must exhibit a particular structure; for each must be a 'subject-predicate' proposition. A proposition is a 'subject-predicate' proposition if it contains two terms, A and B, one of which (the predicate term) is said of the other (the subject term). Thus 'Horses are animals' predicates animal of horses;[2] and 'Dogs are not cats' predicates cats (negatively) of dogs. If we use '... holds of ——' to

---

[1] For fuller versions of the account we outline, see e.g. Smiley; Corcoran. In adopting this account we implicitly reject the interpretation advanced by Łukasiewicz and elaborated by Patzig: it is nevertheless true, as our notes to the translation suggest, that Łukasiewicz and Patzig have contributed more than any other scholars to our understanding of Aristotle's syllogistic.

[2] Or should we rather say that it predicates 'animal' of horses, or 'animal' of 'horses'? The ancients rarely saw any need for precision on this and allied points; and we shall imitate them. Modern readers will think this a frightful muddle – rightly. But it is a muddle which, or so we think, does not affect the presentation of the syllogistic.

express the predicative tie, we may say that the component propositions of a syllogism all have at their heart the form:

A holds of B

– where A and B are terms, A the predicate and B the subject.

Subject-predicate propositions also have a 'quality' and a 'quantity' and a 'mode'. Their quality consists in the fact that they are either affirmative or negative: either A holds affirmatively of B or A holds negatively of B. Their quantity consists in the fact that they are either universal or particular: either A holds of every B or A holds of some B.[3] Their mode consists in the fact that the predicate is said to be tied to the subject either necessarily or actually or possibly: either A holds necessarily of B or A holds actually of B or A holds possibly of B.

Putting these three features together, we may say that an Aristotelian subject-predicate proposition has a form which could be clumsily represented thus:

δ[A holds +/– of e/s B]

– where δ marks the mode, '+/–' indicates the quality, 'e/s' stands for the quantity ('every', 'some').

In *An. Pr.* 1.4-7 Aristotle investigates syllogisms in which all the component propositions have the neutral mode marked by 'actually'. Hence in the rest of this Appendix we shall ignore modal differences and drop the modal sign from our representation of the form of subject-predicate propositions.

That being so, it is clear that there are exactly four sorts of subject-predicate proposition: universal affirmatives, of the form:

A holds of every B;

universal negatives, of the form:

A holds of no B;[4]

particular affirmatives, of the form:

A holds of some B;

and particular negatives, of the form:

A does not hold of some B.

Three distinct propositions are involved in any syllogism; but the three propositions must be interrelated. In particular, the two premisses must have a term in common (the so-called 'middle' term); and the two terms in the conclusion (the 'extremes') must each appear in one of the premisses. Thus the three propositions of any syllogism exhibit altogether precisely three distinct terms.

It is plain that the middle term may collaborate with the other two terms in the premisses in any one of three different ways: it may be subject for one extreme and predicate for the other; it may be predicate for both extremes; or it may be subject for both. In other words, the premisses may, as a pair, show any one of the following core structures:

I   A holds of B, B holds of C.
II B holds of A, B holds of C.
III A holds of B, C holds of B.

[3] Aristotle sometimes also refers to 'indeterminate' propositions, i.e. to propositions which mark no quantity. Since such propositions are treated as equivalent to particular propositions, we may ignore them here. See 30,31 note.
[4] Note that the word 'no' here combines two functions: it indicates at once the quality – negative – and the quantity – universal – of the proposition.

These three structures determine the three 'figures' of Aristotelian syllogistic: a syllogism belongs to the first figure if its premisses exhibit structure I, to the second figure if its premisses exhibit structure II, and to the third figure if its premisses exhibit structure III.[5]

Since each premiss may have any of four subject-predicate forms, there are sixteen premiss pairings with each structure. Of the sixteen with structure I, four are shown in *An. Pr.* 1.4 to yield conclusions, so that the first figure contains four syllogistic forms. Of the sixteen pairings with structure II, *An. Pr.* 1.5 establishes that four yield syllogistic conclusions, so that the second figure also contains four syllogistic forms. The third figure, analysed in *An. Pr.* 1.6, has six syllogisms.

The first figure syllogisms are 'perfect'; that is to say, their validity is evident. Thus the first syllogistic form in this figure, which is known as *Barbara*[6], looks like this:

(1) A holds of every B
(2) B holds of every C

---

(3) A holds of every C

And it is, or so we are invited to think, evident that (3) follows from (1) and (2).

The syllogisms in the other figures are 'imperfect'; but they can be 'perfected' inasmuch as they can be reduced to first figure syllogisms. Aristotle employs three methods of perfection or reduction – in effect, he has three ways of proving that a given syllogistic form is valid. One method relies on 'conversion', a second on reduction to the impossible, and the third on 'exposition'.

Conversion is an operation on propositions. To convert a proposition of the form 'A holds of B', you interchange the terms A and B to get 'B holds of A'. Aristotle recognises three conversion rules, which he establishes in *An.Pr.* 1.2. They may be set out thus:

(C1) From 'A holds of no B' infer 'B holds of no A'.[7]
(C2) From 'A holds of some B' infer 'B holds of some A'.
(C3) From 'A holds of every B' infer 'B holds of some A'.

A perfection by way of conversion works in the following way. Suppose as premisses that:

(1) A holds of no B,

and:

(2) A holds of every C.

Then from (1), by (C1), infer:

(3) B holds of no A.

And now, by the second syllogism in the first figure (*Celarent*), we may infer from (3) and (2) to:

(4) B holds of no C.

---

[5] Later versions of syllogistic produce *four* figures; and there is a large – and largely futile – literature on the origin and value of the fourth figure. See 47,12 note.

[6] For the 'names' of the syllogistic forms see below, pp. 212-15.

[7] Strictly speaking we should write:

(C1*) From a proposition of the form 'A holds of no B' infer the corresponding proposition of the form 'B holds of no A'.

But here and hereafter we shall follow the harmlessly inaccurate custom of citing propositional forms as though they were propositions and syllogistic forms as though they were syllogisms.

Thus we have shown that (4) follows from (1) and (2). A syllogism with premisses of the forms (1) and (2) and with a conclusion of the form (4) is in the second figure – it is a syllogism of the form *Cesare*.[8]

The method of reduction to the impossible works as follows. Suppose as premisses:

(1) A does not hold of some B.
(2) C holds of every B.

Hypothesize in addition that:

(3) A holds of every C.

Then, by *Barbara*, we may infer from (3) and (2) to:

(4) A holds of every B.

But (4) is 'impossible'; or rather, (4) is inconsistent with premiss (1). Hence if both (1) and (2) are true, (3) cannot be true. Hence if both (1) and (2) are true, it follows that the contradictory of (3) is true, i.e. that:

(5) A does not hold of some C.

Thus we have shown that (5) follows from (1) and (2). A syllogism with premisses of the forms (1) and (2) and with a conclusion of the form (5) is in the third figure – it is a syllogism of the form *Bocardo*.[9]

The third method, the method of exposition, is more controversial.[10] Alexander's interpretation, which has been generally rejected on inadequate grounds, is roughly this.[11] Suppose as premisses that:

(1) A holds of every B.
(2) C holds of every B.

Now 'expose' or set out some particular B, say b. Then from (1) we may infer:

(3) A holds of b,

and by (2) we may infer:

(4) C holds of b.

But from (3) and (4) it follows that A holds of something of which C also holds. Hence that:

(5) A holds of some C.

Thus we have shown that (5) follows from (1) and (2). A syllogism with premisses of the forms (1) and (2) and with a conclusion of the form (5) is in the third figure – it is a syllogism of the form *Darapti*.[12]

---

[8] Some may prefer a more formal presentation of the argument, thus:

1 (1)	A holds of no B	prem
2 (2)	A holds of every C	prem
1 (3)	B holds of no A	1, (C1)
1, 2 (4)	B holds of no C	3, 2 *Celarent*

[9] More tormally:

1 (1)	A does not hold of some B	prem
2 (2)	C holds of every B	prem
3 (3)	A holds of every C	hyp
2, 3 (4)	A holds of every B	3, 2 *Barbara*
1, 2 (5)	A does not hold of some C	1, 2, 3, 4 reductio

[10] See 32,33 note.

[11] In fact Alexander thinks that Aristotle uses two distinct types of exposition: see 100,17 note.

[12] The formal version requires the interpolation of of few steps:

1(1)	A holds of every B	prem
2(2)	C holds of every B	prem
1(2*)	B holds something	1
2+(2+)	B holds of b	exp
1, 2+(3)	A holds of b	1, 2+

Of the forty-eight possible premiss pairings, *An. Pr.* 1.4-6 proves fourteen syllogistic. Moreover, Aristotle also proves that none of the remaining thirty-four pairings yields a conclusion of the form 'A holds of C'. (The method by which he proves pairings to be non-syllogistic has been described in the Introduction.[13]) In 1.7, Aristotle signals two further developments. He indicates a way of reducing all syllogisms to the first two syllogisms of the first figure (i.e. to *Barbara* and *Celarent*); and he observes that there are certain other syllogistic forms in addition to the fourteen which have been set out in 1.4-6. For the former development it should be enough to con Alexander's close commentary; for the latter we may refer to the long note to 70,21 and to the descriptions in the second part of this Appendix.

II

Against each syllogistic form in the following list we have set its standard mediaeval name. (Like most writers on syllogistic, we have found it convenient to refer to the syllogistic forms by their traditional names.) The names, which were collected into halting hexameters, are significant.[14] The first three vowels in each name indicate the quantity and quality of the premisses and conclusion of the syllogism. (A marks a universal affirmative, E a universal negative, I a particular affirmative, O a particular negative.) The initial consonant indicates to which first figure syllogism a derived syllogism may be reduced: a syllogism beginning with 'B' reduces to *Barbara*, with 'C' to *Celarent*, with 'D' to *Darii*, with 'F' to *Ferio*. 'S' indicates that the syllogism can be reduced if the premiss marked by the preceding vowel is converted by an application of rule (C1) or (C2); 'P' indicates a conversion by rule (C3). A 'C' – except an initial 'C' – indicates the need for reduction to the impossible. The other letters in the names have no significance.[15]

We give first the standard fourteen syllogisms, in their three figures and in the order in which Aristotle gives them.[16]

First figure

Barbara
A holds of every B
B holds of every C

———————————

A holds of every C

Darii
A holds of every B
B holds of some C

———————————

A holds of some C

1, 2+ (4)	C holds of b	2, 2+
1, 2+ (5)	A holds of some C	3, 4
1, 2 (5*)	A holds of 'some C	2*, 2+, 5 EE

(Why does (2*) follow from (1)? Because (within Aristotle's logic) if A holds of every B, then A holds of some B; hence something is B.)

[13] Above, pp. 12-13.

[14] See e.g. Bochenski (1956), pp. 244-50; Thom, p. 54.

[15] Except 'M', which indicates that the premisses must have their order changed – but this is not a logical operation.

[16] Note that the later Peripatetics changed the Aristotelian order of the syllogisms in the third figure: see 97,12 note.

Celarent
A holds of no B
B holds of every C
___
A holds of no C

Ferio
A holds of no B
B holds of some C
___
A does not hold of some C

Second figure

Cesare
M holds of no N
M holds of every O
___
N holds of no O

Festino
M holds of no N
M holds of some O
___
N does not hold of some O

Camestres
M holds of every N
M holds of no O
___
N holds of no O

Baroco
M holds of every N
M does not hold of some O
___
N does not hold of some O

Third figure

Darapti
P holds of every S
R holds of every S
___
P holds of some R

Datisi
P holds of every S
R holds of some S
___
P holds of some R

Felapton
P holds of no S
R holds of every S
___
P does not hold of some R

Bocardo
P does not hold of some S
R holds of every S
___
P does not hold of some R

Disamis
P holds of some S
R holds of every S
___
P holds of some R

Ferison
P holds of no S
R holds of some S
___
P does not hold of some R

Next, we list the additional syllogisms divided into the three groups which we distinguish in the note to 70,21. The roman numeral in brackets after the name of each syllogism indicates which figure it belongs to.

Group A

Baralipton [I]
A holds of every B
B holds of every C
___
C holds of some A

Cesares [II]
M holds of no N
M holds of every O
___
O holds of no N

Dabitis [I]
A holds of every B
B holds of some C
_____
C holds of some A

Cesares [II]
M holds of no N
M holds of every O
_____
O holds of no N

Disami [III]
P holds of some S
R holds of every S
_____
R holds of some P

Camestre [II]
M holds of every N
M holds of no O
_____
O holds of no N

Daraptis [III]
P holds of every S
R holds of every S
_____
R holds of some P

Datisis [III]
P holds of every S
R holds of some S
_____
R holds of some P

Group B

Fapesmo [I]
A holds of every B
B holds of no C
_____
C does not hold of some A

Firesmo [II]
M holds of some N
M holds of no O
_____
O does not hold of some N

Frisemo [III]
P holds of some S
R holds of no S
_____
R does not hold of some P

Frisesomorum [I]
A holds of some B
B holds of no C
_____
C does not hold of some A

Fapemo [III]
P holds of every S
R holds of no S
_____
R does not hold of some P

Group C

Barbari [I]
A holds of every B
B holds of every C
_____
A holds of some C

Celantos [I]
A holds of no B
B holds of every C
_____
C does not hold of some A

Celaront [I]
A holds of no B
B holds of every C
_____
A does not hold of some C

Cesaro [II]
M holds of no N
M holds of every O
_____
N does not hold of some O

Camestrop [II]
M holds of every N
M holds of no O

N does not hold of some O

Cesaros [II]
M holds of no N
M holds of every O

O does not hold of some N

Faresmo [II]
M holds of every N
M holds of no O

O does not hold of some N

Appendix 3
Textual Notes

This appendix collects together the various textual suggestions which are scattered in the footnotes to the translation.

2,5	Delete τὸ μόριον.
3,6	Delete ὄν.
3,12	Read ἐν αὐτῇ for ἐν αὐτοῖς.
3,25	Read περιττόν, with the MSS. (Wallies prints τερπνόν, after the Aldine edition.
4,18	Read πρὸς τοῦτο for πρὸς τούτῳ.
7,30	Remove the comma after προτάσεις and add a comma after τὸ εἶναι (with Wallies, *in Top.*, p. 711).
7,31	Read που αὐτόν (Aldine) for τινα αὐτῶν.
8,3	Read ἀεί (conjectured by Wallies) for δεῖν.
9,6	Read προθείς for προσθείς.
9,17	Read περί (Aldine) for πᾶν.
9,22	Perhaps read διὰ [or μετὰ] ἀποδείξεως for περὶ ἀποδείξεως?
11,8	Read ἀντιφάσεως for ἀποφάνσεως (see 11,10-11).
11,22	Retain τί before κατά, with the MSS (Wallies deletes).
13,27	Read καὶ τὶ μή, with the MSS. (Wallies prints ἢ μή, after the Aldine edition and our MSS of Aristotle.)
14,15	Omit καί before ἐνδόξου, with LM (see Aristotle, *Top.* 100b23–5.)
15,18-19	Add τό before μετὰ τοῦ ἐστίν.
15,23	Read προστιθεμένου for συντιθεμένου.
16,14	Retain λέγοιτο, with the MSS. (Wallies emends to λέγοι τό.)
17,4	Add ἢ ἐν τῇ ἐρωτήσει after ἐντολῇ (see p.16 n.83).
18,3	Read τἄλλα for ταῦτα.
18,16	Read ἡμέρα, with B and the Aldine edition (and Wallies, *in Top.*, p.711) for φῶς.
19,16	Read τῷ ἑτέρῳ for τῷ ἑπομένῳ.
19,22	Delete τῆς συλλογιστικῆς συμπλοκῆς.
20,13	Transpose οὐ γάρ ... ζῷον εἶ (20,16–18) to follow παρέχεται.

20,21–2	Place ἢ μᾶλλον . . . γίνεται between parentheses.
22,4	Delete θεώρημα.
22,11–12	Delete τῶν ἀντικειμένων.
23,2	Read εἶπεν for εἶπον (see Aristotle, *Soph.El.* 168b22–6).
25,17	Omit εἰπεῖν περὶ τοῦ κατὰ μηδενός, after the Aldine edition.
29,24	Read τέως for πως.
31,13–14	Read ἐναργῶν συλλογιστικῶς for ἐναργῶς [ἐναργῶν, M] συλλογιστικῶν.
31,18	Read πλεῖστα, with LM and the Aldine, for πλείστῳ.
33,8	Omit τούτῳ (with L). (M offers τό, the Aldine τοῦτο.)
35,6	Read αὐτῇ, with B and the Aldine (if Wallies reports correctly). Wallies prints αὐτῇ; L and M have ἑαυτῇ.
36,6	Read καταφάσεως, with LM and the Aldine, for ἀντιφάσεως (B, followed by Wallies).
37,9	Read οὐδενὶ ἐνδέχεται, with L and B² (ἐνδέχεσθαι, M), for οὐδενὶ ἀνάγκη.
37,13	Read μηδενὶ ἐνδέχεται for μηδενὶ ἀνάγκη.
37,16	Read ταύτῃ for ταύτης.
39,19	Perhaps read δυνατοῦ for ἐνδεχομένου?
41,28	Read ἀποφατικῇ (Aldine) for καταφατικῇ.
42,8–9	Read σχῆμα for σχημάτων.
43,24	Read ὁ δέ . . . πίστιν: ὁ δέ. . . πιστόν, MSS; ὃ δή . . . πιστόν, Wallies.
44,4	Read καὶ πῶς for πως.
47,9–10	Delete τὶς ἄρα οὐσία ἔμψυχός ἐστιν.
54,16	Read λαβεῖν after ἐστί, with M and the Aldine edition (Wallies omits).
55,11	Read συλλογιστικῶν for συλλογισμῶν τῶν.
56,24	Omit καὶ τὸ ζῷον κατ' οὐδενὸς λίθου: the phrase, printed by Wallies, is found in the Aldine edition but not in the MSS.
62,2	Read καί for ἤ.
64,17	Read ἐκκειμένην: ἀντικειμένην, MSS; εἰρημένην, Wallies after the Aldine edition.
66,20	Delete τῷ before μηδενί.
67,7	Delete μή before ὑπάρχοι (see 66,2–3).
68,26	Read αὐτά for αὐτήν.
70,6	Read τέλεον for τέλειοι, with Wallies (in his *corrigenda*, p.426).
72,11	Read λέξεως, with LM and the Aldine, for τάξεως.
73,8	Read τῷ οὗ for τῷ δι' ὄν.
73,14–15	The text is corrupt, but no convincing cure suggests itself. *Exempli gratia* add ἐκεῖνο δέ before ἐγγυτέρω and delete ὁ ἵππος ἤπερ ἄνθρωπος.

74,11	Read ὥστε for οὕτως.
78,28	Read ὁ δέ (conjectured by Wallies, in the Index Verborum to *in Top.*) for ὅδε.
80,15	Read ἄρα for γάρ.
81,22	Read ἓν γένος: ἐν γένεσι, MSS; ἐν γενέσει, Aldine; ἐν γένει, Wallies.
81,26	Follow LM and the Aldine edition: after παραδείγμασιν B has ἀλλ᾽ ὥσπερ, with τε written above περ; Wallies prints ἄλλως τε.
85,2	Retain ἐχόντων which Wallies emends to ἐχουσῶν.
85,27	Add ἅ after κατὰ τὰ μόρια αὐτοῦ (Wallies prints κατὰ ἃ μόρια αὐτοῦ).
86,12	Perhaps read ἀνομοίων for ἀνομοιοσχημόνων (see 85,17).
86,30–87,1	Delete τὸ ἀσυλλόγιστον.
90,19	Add τοῦ μὲν μηδενί before ἄνθρωπος.
90,25–6	Read τὸ Α τινὶ τῷ Γ (with M and the Aldine) for τὸ πρῶτον τινὶ τῷ τρίτῳ.
91,1–3	Remove Wallies' parentheses.
91,3	Perhaps read ἀπαγωγή for συναγωγή?
91,6	Omit γάρ, added by Wallies.
92,10	Retain μηδέ (μηδενός, Wallies).
95,17–18	Read τὰ ἄλλα σχήματα, τό τε δεύτερον λέγω καὶ τὸ τρίτον for τῶν ἄλλων σχημάτων, τοῦ τε δευτέρου λέγω καὶ τοῦ τρίτου.
100,10	Delete τὸ ἐκκείμενον, which Wallies emends to τῷ ἐκκειμένῳ.
100,15	Delete διττὸν τὸ μέσον ἐστὶ <καί>.
104,1	Read τι for τοῦτο (τι τοιοῦτο, Aldine).
112,14	Read προκειμένου for κειμένου.
112,20–1	Remove the commas after γίνεται and ἔδειξεν; add a comma after τρίτῳ.
113,12	Read ὁμολογουμένως συλλογιστικῶν for ὁμολογουμένων.
114,27	Read δύο τούς, with the Aldine edition: δύο τούτους, MSS; δύο τούτου τούς, Wallies.
116,33	Perhaps read εἶπον for εἶπεν (see 103,16–19)?

Texts and Abbreviations

The list has a double purpose: it expands the various abbreviations which appear in the notes to the Introduction and the Translation; and it indicates which editions of the ancient texts we have taken as standard.

Albinus
  Didasc.   *Didascalicus* [ed. Hermann, in vol. VI of the Teubner Plato]

Alexander
  in An. Pr.   *Commentary on Aristotle's Prior Analytics* [ed. Wallies, *CAG* II 1]
  Conv.[1]   *On Conversion* [ed. Badawi (1971)]
  DA   *On the Soul* [ed. Bruns, *CAG* suppt II 1]
  Fat.   *On Fate* [ed. Bruns, *CAG* suppt II 2]
  in Metaph.   *Commentary on Aristotle's Metaphysics* [ed. Hayduck, *CAG* I]
  Quaest.   *Questions* [ed. Bruns, *CAG* suppt II 2]
  in Top.   *Commentary on Aristotle's Topics* [ed. Wallies, *CAG* II 2]

[Alexander][2]
  in Metaph.   *Commentary on Aristotle's Metaphysics* [ed. Hayduck, *CAG* I]
  in SE   *Commentary on Aristotle's Sophistical Refutations* [ed. Wallies, *CAG* II 3]

Ammonius
  in An. Pr.   *Commentary on Aristotle's Prior Analytics* [ed. Wallies, *CAG* IV 6]
  in Int.   *Commentary on Aristotle's On Interpretation* [ed. Busse, *CAG* IV 5]
  in Porph. Isag.   *Commentary on Porphyry's Introduction to Philosophy* [ed. Busse, *CAG* IV 3]

[Ammonius]
  in An. Pr.[3]   *Commentary on Aristotle's Prior Analytics* [ed. Wallies, *CAG* IV 6]

---

[1] We have used an English translation generously made for us by Mr. Robert Hoyland of Pembroke College, Oxford.

[2] Square brackets around an author's name mark inauthenticity: the pseudo-Alexandrian commentary on *SE* is rightly ascribed to Michael of Ephesus.

[3] References using upper case roman numerals pick out texts printed in the Introduction to Wallies' edition.

anonymous
  in Int. An. Pr.   *Commentary on Aristotle's On Interpretation and Prior Analytics* [ed. Mynas (Paris, 1844)]

  in Theaet.   *Commentary on Plato's Theaetetus* [edd. Diels-Schubart]

  Logica   *Logic and the Quadrivium* [ed. Heidberg (Copenhagen, 1929)]

Apollonius Dyscolus
  Conj.   *On Conjunctions* [ed. Schneider, *Grammatici Graeci* II 1]

  Synt.   *Syntax* [ed. Schneider, *Grammatici Graeci* II 2]

Apuleius
  Dog. Plat.   *On Plato and his Doctrines* [ed. Beaujeu, Budé]
  Int.   *On Interpretation* [ed. Thomas, Teubner]

Aristotle
  An. Pr.   *Prior Analytics* [ed. Ross, OCT]
  An. Post.   *Posterior Analytics* [ed. Ross, OCT]
  Cael.   *On the Heavens* [ed. Allan, OCT]
  Cat.   *Categories* [ed. Minio-Paluello, OCT]
  DA   *On the Soul* [ed. Ross, OCT]
  EE   *Eudemian Ethics* [edd. Walzer-Mingay, OCT]
  EN   *Nicomachean Ethics* [ed. Bywater, OCT]
  GC   *On Generation and Corruption* [ed. Joachim (Oxford, 1922)]
  HA   *History of Animals* [ed. Dittmeyer, Teubner]
  Int.   *On Interpretation* [ed. Minio-Paluello, OCT]
  Metaph.   *Metaphysics* [ed. Ross (Oxford 1924)]
  Meteor.   *Meteorology* [ed. Fobes (Cambridge Mass., 1918)]
  PA   *Parts of Animals* [ed. Peck, Loeb]
  Phys.   *Physics* [ed. Ross, OCT]
  Pol.   *Politics* [ed. Dreizehnter (Munich, 1970)]
  Rhet.   *Rhetoric* [ed. Kassel (Berlin, 1976)]
  SE   *Sophistical Refutations* [ed. Ross, OCT]
  Top.   *Topics* [ed. Brunschwig, Budé; Ross, OCT]

[Aristotle]
  Probl.   *Problems* [ed. Bekker (Berlin, 1831)]

Aristoxenus   *Harmonics* [ed. da Rios (Rome, 1954)]

Boethius
  in Cic. Top.   *Commentary on Cicero's Topics* [edd. Orelli-Baiter, in vol. V of *Ciceronis Opera* (Zurich, 1833)]

  in Int.   *Commentary on Aristotle's On Interpretation* [ed. Meiser, Teubner]

  Int. Syll. Cat.   *Introduction to Categorical Syllogisms* [ed. Migne, Patrologia Latina 64]

  Syll. Cat.   *Categorical Syllogisms* [ed. Migne, Patrologia Latina 64]

CAG   *Commentaria in Aristotelem Graeca*

Cassius Dio   *Histories* [ed. Boissevain (Berlin, 1895-1901)]

Cicero
  Nat. Deorum   *On the Nature of the Gods* [ed. Ax, Teubner]
CMG   *Corpus Medicorum Graecorum*

David
  in Porph. Isag. — *Commentary on Porphyry's Introduction to Philosophy* [ed. Busse, *CAG* XVIII 2].
Dexippus
  in Cat. — *Commentary on Aristotle's Categories* [ed. Busse, *CAG* IV 2]
Diodorus Siculus — *History* [ed. Dindorf, Teubner]
Diogenes Laertius — *Lives of the Philosophers* [ed. Long, OCT]
Elias
  in. An. Pr. — *Commentary on Aristotle's Prior Analytics* [ed. Westerink (1961)]
  in Cat. — *Commentary on Aristotle's Categories* [ed. Busse, *CAG* XVIII 1]
  Proleg. — *Prolegomena* [ed. Busse, *CAG* XVIII 1]
Epictetus
  Diss. — *Discourses* [ed. Schenkl, Teubner]
Euclid — *Elements* [ed. Heidberg/Stamatis, Teubner]
Eudemus
  F *n* Wehrli — fragment *n* in Wehrli
Eusebius
  PE — *Preparation for the Gospel* [ed. Mras/des Places, *Die griechischen Christlichen Schriftsteller* VIII 1-2]
Eustathius
  in Od. — *Commentary on Homer's Odyssey* [ed. Stallbaum (Leipzig, 1825/6)]
Eustratius
  in An. Post. — *Commentary on Aristotle's Posterior Analytics* [ed. Hayduck, *CAG* XXI 1]
FDS — *Fragmente zur stoischen Dialektik* [see Bibliography: Hülser]
Galen
  Anat. Admin. — *Anatomical Procedures* [ed. Kühn (Leipzig, 1821-33)]
  in Hipp. Aph. — *Commentary on Hippocrates' Aphorisms* [ed. Kühn (Leipzig, 1821-33)]
  in Hipp. Fract. — *Commentary on Hippocrates' On Fractures* [ed. Kühn (Leipzig, 1821-33)]
  in Hipp. Off. — *Commentary on Hippocrates' On the Surgery* [ed. Kühn (Leipzig, 1821-33)]
  Inst. Log. — *Introduction to Logic* [ed. Kalbfleisch, Teubner]
  Lib. Prop. — *On My Own Books* [ed. von Müller, Teubner][4]
  Meth. Med. — *On Therapeutic Method* [ed. Kühn (Leipzig, 1821-33)]
  Opt. Sect. — *On the Best Sect* [ed. Kühn (Leipzig, 1821-33)]
  PHP — *On the Doctrines of Hippocrates and Plato* [ed. de Lacey, *CMG*][5]
  Sem. — *On Semen* [ed. Kühn (Leipzig, 1821-33)]
  Simp. Med. Temp. — *On the Mixture and Powers of Simple Drugs* [ed. Kühn (Leipzig, 1821-33)]
Gellius — *Attic Nights* [ed. Marshall, OCT]
Herodotus — *Histories* [ed. Hude, OCT]

[4] References are given by Kühn numbering.
[5] References are given by Kühn numbering.

Iamblichus
   Comm. Math. Sc.   *On the Common Science of Mathematics* [ed. Festa, Teubner]
Martianus Capella   *The Marriage of Philosophy and Mercury* [ed. Dick, Teubner]
Ocellus Lucanus   *On the Nature of the Universe* [ed. Harder (Berlin, 1926)]
OCT   Oxford Classical Texts
Olympiodorus
   in Gorg.   *Commentary on Plato's Gorgias* [ed. Westerink, Teubner]
   in Meteor.   *Commentary on Aristotle's Meteorology* [ed. Stuve, *CAG* XII 2]
Pappus   *Collection* [ed. Hultsche (Berlin, 1976-8)]
Papyri
   PFayum   *Fayum Towns and their Papyri* [edd. Grenfell-Hunt-Hogarth (London, 1900)]
   PGen   *Les Papyrus de Genève* [ed. Nicole (Geneva, 1896-1900)]
   PHeid   [see Bibliography: Carlini, 1978]
   PMon   [see Bibliography: Carlini, 1986]
   POxy   *The Oxyrhynchus Papyri* [edd. Grenfell-Hunt, et al. (London, 1898-)]

Philodemus
   Rhet.   *Rhetoric* [ed. Longo Auricchio (Naples, 1977)]
Philoponus
   in An. Pr.   *Commentary on Aristotle's Prior Analytics* [ed. Wallies, *CAG* XIII 2]
   in An. Post.   *Commentary on Aristotle's Posterior Analytics* [ed. Wallies, *CAG* XIII 3]
   in Cat.   *Commentary on Aristotle's Categories* [ed. Busse, *CAG* XIII 1]
   in DA   *Commentary on Aristotle's On the Soul* [ed. Hayduck, *CAG* XV]
Plato[6]
   Rep.   *Republic* [ed. Bury, OCT]
Plutarch
   Ser. Num.   *On God's Slowness to Punish* [edd. Pohlenz-Sieveking, Teubner]
   Stoic. Rep.   *On Stoic Self-contradictions* [ed. Cherniss, Loeb]
Porphyry
   Vit. Plot.   *Life of Plotinus* [edd. Henry-Schwyzer, in vol. I of the OCT Plotinus]
Posidonius
   F n EK   fragment n in Edelstein-Kidd
Proclus
   in Eucl.   *Commentary on the First Book of Euclid's Elements* [ed. Friedlein, Teubner]
   in Rep.   *Commentary on Plato's Republic* [ed. Kroll, Teubner]

---

[6] For all Plato's works we have used Bury's OCT.

in Tim.	*Commentary on Plato's Timaeus* [ed. Diehl, Teubner]
Ptolemy	
Synt.	*Almagest* [ed. Heiberg, Teubner]
scholia to Aristotle	[ed. Brandis, in vol IV of *Aristotelis Opera*, ed. Bekker (Berlin, 1836)]
Seneca	
Ep.	*Letters* [ed. Reynolds, OCT]
Sextus	
M	*Against the Mathematicians* [ed. Mutschmann/Mau, Teubner]
PH	*Outlines of Pyrrhonism* [ed. Mutschmann/Mau, Teubner]
Simplicius	
in Cat.	*Commentary on Aristotle's Categories* [ed. Kalbfleisch, *CAG* VIII]
in DA	*Commentary on Aristotle's On the Soul* [ed. Hayduck, *CAG* XI]
in Phys.	*Commentary on Aristotle's Physics* [ed. Diels, *CAG* IX-X]
SVF	*Stoicorum Veterum Fragmenta* [see Bibliography: von Arnim]
Syrianus	
in Metaph.	*Commentary on Aristotle's Metaphysics* [ed. Kroll, *CAG* VI 1]
Themistius	
Max.	*Reply to Maximus* [ed. Badawi (1971); French trans. in Badawi (1987)]
Theophrastus	
F *n* Graeser	fragment *n* in Graeser

Bibliography

The bibliography lists all the books and articles referred to in the Introduction and in the notes to the translation. A full bibliography on Alexander, up to 1986, can be found in Sharples (1987); new items may be tracked down in the regular bibliographical sections of the journal *Elenchos*.

Paolo Accattino: 'Alessandro di Afrodisia e Aristotele di Mitilene', *Elenchos* 1, 1985, 67-74

J. L. Ackrill: review of Patzig, *Mind* 71, 1962, 107-117

Allan Bäck: 'Philoponus on the Fallacy of Accident', *Ancient Philosophy* 7, 1987, 131-146

Abdurrahman Badawi: *Commentaires sur Aristote perdus en grec* (Beirut, 1971)

—— *La transmission de la philosophie grecque au monde arabe* (Paris, 1987²)

Jonathan Barnes: 'Aristotle's Theory of Demonstration', *Phronesis* 14, 1969, 123-152 [reprinted in J. Barnes, M. Schofield and R. Sorabji (edd.), *Articles on Aristotle* I (London, 1975)]

—— *Aristotle's Posterior Analytics* (Oxford, 1975)

—— review of Hintikka (1973), *Journal of Hellenic Studies* 1977, 97, 183-186

—— [1980a]: 'Proof Destroyed', in M. Schofield, M. F. Burnyeat and J. Barnes (edd.), *Doubt and Dogmatism* (Oxford, 1980)

—— [1980b]: 'Aristotle and the Methods of Ethics', *Revue Internationale de Philosophie* 133, 1980, 490-511

—— 'Proof and the Syllogism', in E. Berti (ed.), *Aristotle on Science: the Posterior Analytics* (Padua, 1981)

—— 'Terms and Sentences', *Proceedings of the British Academy* 69, 1983, 279-326

—— [1985a]: 'Theophrastus and Hypothetical Syllogistic', in J. Wiesner (ed.), *Aristoteles: Werk und Wirkung* I (Berlin, 1985)

—— [1985b] 'Uma terceira espécie de silogismo: Galeno e a lógica das relações', *Análise* 2, 1985, 35-61

—— 'Peripatetic Negations', *Oxford Studies in Ancient Philosophy* 4, 1986, 201-214

—— 'Bits and Pieces', in J. Barnes and M. Mignucci (edd.), *Matter and Metaphysics* (Naples, 1988)

—— [1990a]: 'Logical Form and Logical Matter', in A. Alberti (ed.), *Logica, Mente e Persona* (Florence, 1990)

—— [1990b]: 'Galen and the Utility of Logic', in J. Kollesch (ed.), *Proceedings of the Fourth International Galen Congress* (Berlin, 1990)

—— [1990c]: *The Toils of Scepticism* (Cambridge, 1990)

—— [1991]: 'Ammonius and Adverbs', in H. Blumenthal and H. M. Robinson (edd.). *Aristotle and his Successors*, Oxford Studies in Ancient Philosophy, supplementary volume 1991

Albrecht Becker: *Die aristotelische Theorie der Möglichkeitsschlüße* (Berlin, 1933)

Oskar Becker: 'Über die vier Themata der stoischen Logik', in his *Zwei Untersuchungen zur Antiken Logik* (Wiesbaden, 1957)

Linos G. Benakis: 'Commentaries and Commentators on the Logical Works of Aristotle in Byzantium', in R. Claussen and R. Daube-Schackat (edd.), *Gedankenzeichen: Festschrift für Klaus Oehler zum 60. Geburtstag* (Tübingen, 1988)

I. M. Bochenski: *La Logique de Théophraste* (Fribourg, 1947)

—— *Ancient Formal Logic* (Amsterdam, 1951)

—— *Formale Logik*, Orbis Academicus III 2 (Freiburg/Munich, 1956)

F. Bömer: 'Der Commentarius', *Hermes* 81, 1953, 210-250

Jacques Brunschwig: 'Observations sur les manuscrits parisiens des *Topiques*', in G. E. L. Owen (ed.), *Aristotle on Dialectic* (Oxford, 1968)

—— 'La proposition particulière et les preuves de non-concluance chez Aristote', *Cahiers pour l'Analyse* 10, 1969, 3-26 [reprinted in A. Menne and N. Offenberger (edd.), *Zur modernen Deutung der aristotelischen Logik* I (Hildesheim, 1982)]

—— 'L'objet et la structure des *Seconds Analytiques* d'après Aristote', in E. Berti (ed.), *Aristotle on Science: the Posterior Analytics* (Padua, 1981)

—— ' "Indéterminé" et "Indéfini" dans la logique de Théophraste', *Revue philosophique de la France et de l'Etranger* 172, 1982, 359-370

Walter Burkert: *Lore and Science in Ancient Pythagoreanism* (Cambridge Mass., 1972)

—— 'Xenarchos statt Poseidonios: zu Pap. Gen. inv. 203', *Zeitschrift für Papyrologie und Epigraphik* 67, 1987, 51-55

Myles Burnyeat: 'The Origins of Non-deductive Inference', in J. Barnes, M. F. Burnyeat and M. Schofield (edd.), *Science and Speculation* (Cambridge, 1982)

Antonio Carlini: 'Su alcuni papiri "platonici" ', *Proceedings of the XIVth International Congress of Papyrologists* (London, 1975)

—— (ed.): *Papiri letterari greci* (Pisa, 1978)

—— (ed.): *Papiri letterari greci della Bayerische Staatsbibliothek di Monaco di Baviera* (Stuttgart, 1986)

John Corcoran: 'Aristotle's Natural Deduction System', in J. Corcoran (ed.), *Ancient Logic and its Modern Interpretations* (Dordrecht, 1974)

F. Edward Cranz: 'Alexander Aphrodisiensis', in P. O. Kristeller (ed.), *Catalogus Translationum et Commentariorum* I (Washington D.C., 1960)

Marina del Fabbro: 'Il commentario nella tradizione papiracea', *Studia Papyrologica* 18, 1979, 69-132

H. Diels and W. Schubart (edd.): *Anonymer Kommentar zu Platons Theaetet*, Berliner Klassikertexte 2 (Berlin, 1905)

John Dillon: *Iamblichi Chalcidiensis in Platonis dialogos commentariorum fragmenta*, Philosophia Antiqua 23 (Leiden, 1973)

Pierluigi Donini: *Le scuole, l'anima, l'impero* (Turin, 1982)

William E. Dooley: *Alexander of Aphrodisias: on Aristotle. Metaphysics 1* (London, 1989)

Heinrich Dörrie: *Der Platonismus in der Antike* I (Stuttgart, 1987)

Sten Ebbesen [1981a]: *Commentators and Commentaries on Aristotle's Sophistici Elenchi*, Corpus Latinum Commentariorum in Aristotelem Graecorum VII (Leiden, 1981)
—— [1981b]: 'Analyzing Syllogisms, or Anonymous Aurelianensis III – the (presumably) earliest extant Latin commentary on the Prior Analytics, and its Greek model', *Cahiers de l'Institut du Moyen-Age Grec et Latin* 37, 1981, 1-20
—— 'Ancient scholastic logic as the source of mediaeval scholastic logic', in N. Kretzmann, A. J. P. Kenny and J. Pinborg (edd.), *The Cambridge History of Later Mediaeval Philosophy* (Cambridge, 1982)
—— 'Philoponus, "Alexander", and the origins of mediaeval logic', in Sorabji (1990b)
Theo Ebert: 'Zur Formulierung prädikativer Aussagen in den logischen Schriften des Aristoteles', *Phronesis* 22, 1977, 123-145
—— 'Warum fehlt bei Aristoteles die 4. Figur?', *Archiv für Geschichte der Philosophie* 62, 1980, 13-31
L. Edelstein and I. G. Kidd: *Posidonius: I The Fragments*, Cambridge Classical Texts and Commentaries 13 (Cambridge, 1972)
Kevin Flannery: 'A Rationale for Aristotle's Notion of Perfect Syllogisms', *Notre Dame Journal of Formal Logic* 28, 1987, 455-471
P. M. Fraser: *Ptolemaic Alexandria* (Oxford, 1972)
Michael Frede [1974a]: *Die stoische Logik* (Göttingen, 1974)
—— [1974b]: 'Stoic vs. Aristotelian Syllogistic', *Archiv für Geschichte der Philosophie* 56, 1974, 1-32 [reprinted in his *Essays in Ancient Philosophy* (Oxford, 1987)]
J. Geffcken: 'Zur Entstehung und zum Wesen des griechischen wissenschaftlichen Kommentars', *Hermes* 67, 1932, 397-412
Gabriele Giannantoni: *Socraticorum Reliquiae* (Naples, 1983)
John Glucker: *Antiochus and the Late Academy*, Hypomnemata 56 (Göttingen, 1978)
—— review of Tarrant (1985), *Journal of Hellenic Studies* 109, 1989, 272-273
H. B. Gottschalk: 'Aristotelian Philosophy in the Roman World from the time of Cicero to the end of the second century AD', in W. Haase (ed.), *Aufstieg und Niedergang der Römischen Welt* II 36.2 (Berlin, 1987)
—— 'The earliest Aristotelian Commentators', in Sorabji (1990b)
Richard Goulet: *Dictionnaire des Philosophes Antiques* I (Paris, 1989)
Andreas Graeser: *Die logischen Fragmente des Theophrast* (Berlin, 1973)
William M. A. Grimaldi: *Aristotle*, Rhetoric I: *a commentary* (New York, 1980)
A. Gudeman: 'Scholien', *Pauly-Wissowas Realencyclopaedie* IIA (Stuttgart, 1923), 625-704
Ilsetraut Hadot: 'Les introductions aux commentaires exégétiques chez les auteurs néoplatoniciens et les auteurs chrétiens', in M. Tardieu (ed.), *Les règles de l'interprétation* (Paris, 1987)
Pierre Hadot: 'Les divisions des parties de la philosophie dans l'antiquité', *Museum Helveticum* 36, 1979, 201-223
B. J. Hijmans: 'Apuleius, Philosophus Platonicus', in W. Haase (ed.), *Aufstieg und Niedergang der Römischen Welt* II 36.1 (Berlin, 1987)
Jaakko Hintikka: *Time and Necessity* (Oxford, 1973)
—— 'Aristotelian Induction', *Revue Internationale de la Philosophie* 133/134, 1980, 422-439
—— and U. Remes: *The Method of Analysis* (Dordrecht, 1974)

Karlheinz Hülser: *Die Fragmente zur Dialektik der Stoiker* (Stuttgart, 1987-88)
Katerina Ierodiakonou: *Analysis in Stoic Logic* (diss. London, 1990)
Werner Jaeger: review of Merki, in his *Scripta Minora* II (Rome, 1960)
E. Kapp: 'Syllogistic', in J. Barnes, M. Schofield and R. Sorabji (edd.), *Articles on Aristotle* I (London, 1975)
I. G. Kidd: *Posidonius:* II *The Commentary*, Cambridge Classical Texts and Commentaries 14 (Cambridge, 1988)
John S. Kieffer: *Galen's Institutio Logica* (Baltimore, 1964)
William and Martha Kneale: *The Development of Logic* (Oxford, 1984⁸)
Erich Lamberz: 'Proklos und die Form des philosophischen Kommentars', in J. Pépin and H. D. Saffrey (edd.), *Proclus, lecteur et interprète des anciens* (Paris, 1987)
Jonathan Lear: *Aristotle and Logical Theory* (Cambridge, 1980)
Tae-Soo Lee: *Die griechische Tradition der aristotelischen Syllogistik in der Spätantike*, Hypomnemata 79 (Göttingen, 1984)
A. C. Lloyd: *Form and Universal in Aristotle* (Liverpool, 1981)
—— *The Anatomy of Neoplatonism* (Oxford, 1990)
A. A. Long: 'Reply to Jonathan Barnes: "Epicurean Signs" ', *Oxford Studies in Ancient Philosophy*, supplementary volume 1988
Jan Łukasiewicz: *Aristotle's Syllogistic* (Oxford, 1957²)
John Lynch: *Aristotle's School* (Berkeley, 1972)
Henry Maconi: 'Late Greek Syllogistic', *Phronesis* 30, 1985, 92-98
Heinrich Maier: *Die Syllogistik des Aristoteles* (Tübingen, 1899/1900)
Italo Mariotti: *Aristone d'Alessandria* (Bologna, 1966)
Miklós Maróth: *Ibn Sina und die Peripatetische 'Aussagenlogik'* (Budapest, 1989)
Benson Mates: *Stoic Logic* (Berkeley, 1961²)
H. P. F. Mercken: 'The Greek Commentators on Aristotle's *Ethics*', in Sorabji (1990b)
H. Merki: *Homoiôsis Theôi* (Fribourg, 1952)
Mario Mignucci: *Aristotele: gli Analitici Primi* (Naples, 1969)
—— '*Hôs epi to polu* et nécessaire dans la conception aristotélicienne de la science', in E. Berti (ed.), *Aristotle on Science: the Posterior Analytics* (Padua, 1981)
—— 'La teoria della quantificazione del predicato nell'antichità classica', *Anuario Filosofico* 16, 1983, 11-42
Paul Moraux: *Der Aristotelismus bei den Griechen*, Peripatoi 5 and 6 (Berlin, 1973/1984)
—— *Le Commentaire d'Alexandre d'Aphrodisie aux 'Seconds Analytiques' d'Aristote*, Peripatoi 13 (Berlin, 1979)
—— [1986a]: 'Diogène Laërce et le *Peripatos*', *Elenchos* 7, 1986, 245-294
—— [1986b]: 'Les débuts de la philologie aristotélicienne', in G. Cambiano (ed.), *Storiografia e dossografia nella filosofia antica* (Turin, 1986)
Ian Mueller: 'Stoic and Peripatetic Logic', *Archiv für Geschichte der Philosophie* 51, 1969, 173-187
—— 'Greek Mathematics and Greek Logic', in J. Corcoran (ed.), *Ancient Logic and its Modern Interpretations* (Dordrecht, 1974)
Iwan von Mueller: *Über Galens Werk vom wissenschaftlichen Beweis*, Abhandlungen der königlichen Bayerischen Akademie der Wissenschaften 20 (Munich, 1897)

Vivian Nutton: 'Galen in the Eyes of his Contemporaries', *Bulletin of the History of Medicine* 58, 1984, 315-324
——— 'Galen's Philosophical Testament: "On My Own Opinions"', in J. Wiesner (ed.) *Aristoteles: Werk und Wirkung* II (Berlin, 1987)
J. H. Oliver: *Marcus Aurelius – Aspects of Civic and Cultural Policy in the East*, Hesperia supplement 13 (Princeton, 1970)
Dominic O'Meara: *Pythagoras Revived* (Oxford, 1989)
Günther Patzig: *Aristotle's Theory of the Syllogism* (Dordrecht, 1968)
R. Pfeiffer: *A History of Classical Scholarship* (Oxford, 1968)
Shlomo Pines: 'Omne quod movetur necesse est ab aliquo moveri: A refutation of Galen by Alexander of Aphrodisias and the Theory of Motion', *Isis* 52, 1960, 21-54 [reprinted in his *Studies in Arabic Versions of Greek Texts and in Mediaeval Science* (Jerusalem, 1986)]
Karl Praechter [1909a]: review of *CAG*, *Byzantinische Zeitschrift* 18, 1909, 516-538 [reprinted in his *Kleine Schriften* (Hildesheim, 1973); English translation in Sorabji (1990b)]
——— [1909b]: review of Diels-Schubart, *Göttinger Gelehrter Anzeiger* 171, 1909, 530-547 [reprinted in his *Kleine Schriften* (Hildesheim, 1973)]
Carl Prantl: *Geschichte der Logik im Abendlande* (Leipzig, 1855)
E. Puglia: 'La filologia degli Epicurei', *Cronache Ercolanesi* 12, 1982, 19-34
Nicholas Rescher: *Galen and the Syllogism* (Pittsburgh, 1966)
Joyce Reynolds: *Aphrodisias and Rome*, Journal of Roman Studies monograph 1 (London, 1982)
Marcel Richard: '*Apo Phônês*', *Byzantion* 20, 1950, 191-222
Lynn E. Rose: *Aristotle's Syllogistic* (Springfield, 1968)
W. D. Ross: *Aristotle's Prior and Posterior Analytics* (Oxford, 1949)
D. M. Schenkeveld: 'Stoic and Peripatetic Kinds of Speech Act and the Distinction of Grammatical Moods', *Mnemosyne* 37, 1984, 291-353
D. N. Sedley: 'Philosophical Allegiance in the Greco-Roman World', in M. Griffin and J. Barnes (edd.), *Philosophia Togata* (Oxford, 1989)
R. W. Sharples: 'Alexander of Aphrodisias: Problems about Possibility I', *Bulletin of the Institute of Classical Studies* 29, 1982, 91-108
——— 'Alexander of Aphrodisias: Problems about Possibility II', *Bulletin of the Institute of Classical Studies* 30, 1983, 99-110
——— 'Alexander of Aphrodisias: Scholasticism and Innovation', in W. Haase (ed.), *Aufstieg und Niedergang der Römischen Welt* II 36.2 (Berlin, 1987)
——— 'The School of Alexander?', in Sorabji (1990b)
Ineke Sluiter: *Ancient Grammar in Context* (Amsterdam, 1990)
Timothy Smiley: 'What is a Syllogism?', *Journal of Philosophical Logic* 2, 1973, 136-154
Robin Smith: 'What is Aristotelian Ecthesis?', *History and Philosophy of Logic* 3, 1982, 113-127
——— *Aristotle: Prior Analytics* (Indianapolis, 1989)
Richard Sorabji [1990a]: 'The ancient commentators on Aristotle', in Sorabji (1990b)
——— (ed.) [1990b]: *Aristotle Transformed* (London, 1990)
Jürgen Sprute: *Die Enthymemtheorie der aristotelischen Rhetorik* (Göttingen, 1982)
Gisela Striker: 'Aristoteles über Syllogismen "aufgrund einer Hypothese"', *Hermes* 107, 1979, 33-50
G. Strohmaier: 'Al-Iskander al-Afrudisi', in G. van Donzel (ed.), *Encyclopaedia of Islam* IV (Leiden, 1978²)

Eleonore Stump: *Dialectic and its Place in the Development of Mediaeval Logic* (Ithaca, 1989)

M. W. Sullivan: *Apuleian Logic* (Amsterdam, 1967)

Leonardo Tarán: 'Amicus Plato sed magis amica veritas', *Antike und Abendland* 30, 1984, 93-124

Harold Tarrant: 'The Date of anon. *In Theaetetum'*, *Classical Quarterly* 33, 1983, 161-187

—— *Scepticism or Platonism?* (Cambridge, 1985)

Pierre Thillet: *Alexandre d'Aphrodise: Traité du Destin* (Paris, 1984)

Paul Thom: *The Syllogism* (Munich, 1981)

E. Thouverez: 'La IVme figure du syllogisme', *Archiv für Geschichte der Philosophie* 15, 1902, 49-110

Robert B. Todd: 'Lexicographical Notes on Alexander of Aphrodisias' Philosophical Terminology', *Glotta* 52, 1974, 207-215

—— *Alexander of Aphrodisias on Stoic Physics*, Philosophia Antiqua 28 (Leiden, 1976)

E. G. Turner: *Greek Papyri* (Oxford, 1968)

Martin M. Tweedale: 'Alexander of Aphrodisias' Views on Universals', *Phronesis* 29, 1984, 279-303

Mario Untersteiner: *Problemi della filologia filosofica* (Milan, 1980)

Hermann Usener: review of *CAG*, in his *Kleine Schriften* III (Stuttgart, 1913)

G. Volait: *Die Stellung des Alexander von Aphrodisias zur aristotelischen Schlußlehre* (Bonn, 1907)

Hans von Arnim: *Stoicorum Veterum Fragmenta* (Leipzig, 1903-1905)

Heinrich von Staden: *Herophilus: the art of medicine in early Alexandria* (Cambridge, 1989)

Maximilian Wallies: 'Zur Textgeschichte der Ersten Analytik', *Rheinisches Museum* 72, 1917/1918, 626-632

Fritz Wehrli: *Eudemos von Rhodos*, Die Schule des Aristoteles 8 (Basel, 1955)

L. G. Westerink: 'Elias on the *Prior Analytics'*, *Mnemosyne* 14, 1961, 126-139 [reprinted in his *Texts and Studies in Neoplatonism and Byzantine Literature* (Amsterdam, 1980)]

—— *The Greek Commentaries on Plato's Phaedo* (Amsterdam, 1976)

—— 'The Alexandrian commentators and the introductions to their commentaries', in Sorabji (1990b)

Wolfgang Wieland: 'Die aristotelische Theorie der Konversion von Modalaussagen', *Phronesis* 25, 1980, 109-116

Mark F. Williams: *Studies in the Manuscript Tradition of Aristotle's Analytics*, Beiträge zur klassischen Philologie 161 (Königstein, 1984)

Eduard Zeller: *Die Philosophie der Griechen* III i (Leipzig, 1923⁵)

F. W. Zimmermann: *Al-Farabi's Commentary and Short Treatise on Aristotle's* de Interpretatione, Classical and Mediaeval Logic Texts 3 (London, 1981)

Indexes

English-Greek Glossary

The Glossary lists all and only those English words which occur in the Greek- English index.

absurd: *atopos*
accidentally: *kata sumbebêkos*
account: *logos*
accusative: *aitiatikos*
actual: *huparkhousa*
add (v.): *prostithenai*
addition: *prosthesis, prosthêkê*
adjunct: *prosrêsis*
affirm (v.): *kataphaskein*
affirmation: *kataphasis*
affirmative: *kataphatikos*
agree (v.): *homologein*
agreement: *homologêma*
aim: *skopos*
alter together with (v.): *summetaballein*
analyse (v.): *analuein*
analysis: *analusis*
analytic: *analutikos*
annex (v.): *prostithenai*
apply to (v.): *harmozein, epharmozein*
appropriate: *oikeios*
argument: *logos*
art: *tekhnê*
aspect: *skhesis*
assert (v.): *apophainein*
assertion: *apophansis*
assertoric: *apophantikos*
assume (v.): *lambanein [lêpsis]*
assumption: *lêmma*
authoritative: *kurios*
axiom: *axiôma*

beginning: *arkhê*
betoken (v.): *dêloun*

cancel (v.): *anairein [anairetikos]*
case: *ptôsis*
change (v.): *metapiptein [summeta-
    piptein, summetaskhêmatizein]*

clear: *dêlos*
clear, make (v.): *dêloun [dêlôtikos]*
co-assume (v.): *proslambanein
    [aproslêptos]*
co-assumption: *proslêpsis*
coincide with (v.): *sumpiptein*
combination: *suzugia*
combine (v.): *suzeugnunai*
common: *koinos*
common usage: *sunêtheia*
common use, in: *sunêthês*
complementarily: *enallax, parallax*
compound (v.): *suntithenai*
compounded, be (v.): *sunkeisthai*
compounding: *sunthesis*
concede (v.): *sunkhôrein*
conclude (v.): *perainein, sumperainein*
conclusion: *sumperasma*
conditional: *sunêmmenon*
conflict: *makhê*
conflict (v.): *makhesthai*
congruous: *katallêlos*
conjectural: *stokhastikos*
conjunction: *sumplokê*
connect (v.): *suntattein*
connection: *suntaxis*
construct (v.): *sunistanai*
construction: *sustasis*
contingent, be (v.): *endekhesthai*
continue (v.): *epipherein*
continuous: *sunekhês*
contradiction: *antiphasis*
contradictory: *antikeimenon, anti-
    phatikos*
contradictory pair: *antiphasis*
contrary: *enantios*
contribute (v.): *suntelein*
converse: *antistrophê*
conversion: *antistrophê*

230

convert from (v.): *antistrephein* + *pros*
convert with (v.): *antistrephein* + dative
co-ordinate (v.): *antidiairein*
co-predicate (v.): *proskatêgorein*
counterpredicate (v.): *antikatêgorein*

deduce (v.): *sunagein*
deduction: *sunagôgê*
deductive: *sunaktikos*
define (v.): *horizein*
definition: *horismos*
definitional: *horistikos*
demand: *aitêsis*
demand (v.): *apaitein*
demonstrate (v.): *apodeiknunai*
demonstration: *apodeixis*
demonstrative: *apodeiktikos*
deny (v.): *apophanai, apophaskein*
destroy (v.): *anairein*
determination: *diorismos*
determine (v.): *diorizein*
diagram: *katagraphê*
dialectical: *dialektikos*
difference: *diaphora*
differentia: *diaphora*
directly: *autothen*
discovery: *heuresis*
disjoin (v.): *apozeugnunai, diazeugnunai*
disjoint: *diairetikos*
disjunctive: *diazeuktikos*
disposition: *hexis*
disprove (v.): *diaballein*
dispute (v.): *amphisbêtein*
dissimilar in form: *anomoioskhêmôn*
distinguish (v.): *diairein, khôrizein*
divide (v.): *diairein*
doctrine: *doxa*
duplicated: *diphoroumenos*

encompass (v.): *perilambanein* [*perilêp-sis, sumperilambanein*]
end: *telos*
equal: *isos*
equivalent: *isos*
equivalent, be (v.): *ison dunasthai, isodunamein*
establish (v.): *kataskeuazein*
example: *paradeigma*
exceed (v.): *huperballein, huperek-piptein, huperekhein, huperpiptein*
excel (v.): *pleonektein*
existence: *huparxis*
explanation: *aitia*
explanatory: *aitios*
exposition: *ekthesis* [*ekthetikos*]
expression: *lexis*

external: *exôthen*
extreme: *akron*

fall (v.): *piptein*
fall in (v.): *peripiptein*
false: *pseudês*
figure: *skhêma*
find (v.): *heuriskein*
follow from (v.): *akolouthein, hepesthai*
form: *eidos* [*eidopoiein*]

general: *koinos*
genus: *genos*
give (an account of) (v.): *apodidonai* [*apodosis*]
greater length, at: *epi pleon*

help: *boêtheia*
hold (of) (v.): *huparkhein* [*sunuparkhein, asunuparktos*]
homonymous: *homônumos*
homonymy: *homônumia*
hypothesis: *hupothesis*
hypothesize (v.): *hupotithenai*
hypothesized, be (v.): *hupokeisthai*
hypothetical: *hupothetikos*

immediately: *eutheôs, euthus*
imperfect: *atelês*
implication: *akolouthia*
impossible: *adunatos*
include (v.): *periekhein*
incongruous: *akatallêlos*
indemonstrable: *anapodeiktos*
indeterminate: *adioristos*
indicate (v.): *endeiknunai*
indifferent: *adiaphoros*
individual: *atomos*
indivisible: *adiairetos, atomos*
induction: *epagôgê*
infer (v.): *epipherein*
inferior: *kheirôn*
inseparable: *akhôristos*
instrument: *organon*
intelligible: *noêtos*
introduce (v.): *paralambanein* [*sum-paralambanein*]
investigate (v.): *zêtein*

justification: *pistis*
justified: *pistos*
justify (v.): *pisteuein, pistousthai*

keep (v.): *têrein*
knowledge: *gnôsis, epistêmê*
known: *gnôrimos*

separated: *khôristos*
separative: *khôristikos*
set down (v.): *paratithenai* [*parathesis*]
set out (v.): *ektithenai*
set out, be (v.): *ekkeisthai*
share (v.): *koinônein* [*koinônia*]
shared: *koinos*
show (v.): *deiknunai* [*deiktikos*]
sign: *sêmeion*
signify (v.): *sêmainein* [*sêmantikos*]
similar in form: *homoioskhêmôn*
single-assumption: *monolêmmatos*
sophist: *sophistês*
sophistical: *sophistikos*
sound: *hugiês*
species: *eidos*
starting-point: *arkhê*
statement: *axiôma*
strict: *kurios*
study: *pragmateia*
study (v.): *pragmateuesthai*
subaltern: *hupallêlos*
subcontrary: *hupenantios*
subject for, be (v.): *hupokeisthai*
subject for, make (v.): *hupotithenai*
subordinate (v.): *hupotattein*
subpart: *morion*
subsistence: *hupostasis*
substance: *ousia*
subsume (v.): *hupagein*
subsyllogistical: *huposullogistikos*

superior: *beltiôn*
suppose (v.): *hupotithenai*
supposed, be (v.): *keisthai, hupokeisthai*
supposition: *keimenon*
syllogism: *sullogismos*
syllogistic: *sullogistikos*
syllogize (v.): *sullogizein*

take (v.): *lambanein*
term: *horos*
theorem: *theôrêma*
theoretical: *theôrêtikos*
theorise (v.): *theôrein*
theory: *theôria*
transform (v.): *metalambanein*
transformation: *metalêpsis*
'tropic': *tropikon*
true: *alêthês* [*sunalêtheuein*]

unclear: *adêlos*
universal: *katholikos, katholou*
unmethodical: *amethodos*
unreliable: *adokimos*
utterance: *logos*

verb: *rhêma*

wider extension, of: *epi pleon*
whole: *holoklêros*
whole, in as in a: *en holôi*
word: *onoma, phônê*

Greek-English Index

Wallies' edition of *in An. Pr.* contains an adequate *index verborum*, and we have not thought it necessary to duplicate his work: this Index limits itself, with a few exceptions, to Alexander's logical terminology (but it understands the word 'logical' in a generous sense). We have not listed every occurrence of every logical term in our portion of *in An. Pr.* Where a word occurs more than about twenty-five times, we have given the first six or seven occurrences and then indicated (by a figure printed in bold type and between square brackets) approximately how many examples of the word a complete list would contain. (The listings exclude occurrences in lemmata or citations from Aristotle's text.) The Ibycus system, which we used in making this Index, is widely available; and any reader who wishes to scan all the occurrences in our text of, say, the word '*sullogismos*' will find it far easier to consult Ibycus than to contemplate a sequence of 290 numerical references.

For each Greek word we have given the English translation or translations which we have normally used. (Note that the translations are normal and not invariable.) In a few cases we have indicated that a word is normally paraphrased rather than translated: we set between angle brackets the word or words normally used in the paraphrase.

adêlos, unclear, 5,29.31; 18,24
adiairetos, indivisible, 81,21.22
adiaphoros, non-different, indifferent, 18,17; 72,18
adioristos, indeterminate, 11,19; 13,30; 27,18; 30,29; 49,14.15; 51,25 [70]
adokimos, unreliable, 52,24.24; 56,25; 62,5; 64,21; 65,1; 85,22; 104,19.20
adunatos, impossible, 22,11; 24,6.12.16; 31,10.11; 33,11 [125]
aisthêsis, perception, 4,4; 5,7; 33,1; 99,32; 100,1
aisthêtikos, perceptual, 32,33; 33,14; 113,1
aisthêtos, perceptible, 4,3.6.9; 32,33; 33,2.3; 53,23; 100,4.5.7.12.17.22.23; 101,5; 104,4
aitêsis, demand, 14,2; 43,21
aitia, reason, explanation, 5,8; 17,24; 21,13.13.15.16 [30]
aitiatikos, accusative, 9,7.8
aitios, explanatory, 8,16; 10,29; 14,13; 21,17.21; 23,2; 24,2.16; 42,23; 47,22; 55,18; 67,17; 68,16; 75,18; 83,14; 87,20; 94,6.22; 95,4; 96,9; 101,19; 104,32; 106,30; 107,16
akatallêlos, incongruous, 15,24
akhôristos, inseparable, 4,13; 26,19.20

akolouthein, to follow, 17,31; 20,32; 21,7; 35,16; 55,10.10; 87,13; 112,12.30
akolouthia, implication, 7,1; 11,20; 17,30
akron, extreme, 33,27; 46,19.21; 47,3.4.11.15 [50]
alêthês, true, 5,13; 6,9.10; 8,24.25.26.27.29 [130]
amethodos, unmethodical, 21,30; 22,18.24; 24,1.9; 68,23.32
amphisbêtein, to dispute, 43,8.26; 44,14.15
anagein, to reduce, 7,18.25; 24,5; 58,21; 77,4; 98,26; 100,31 [65]
anagôgê, reduction, 7,12.26.31; 97,29; 113,16; 115,14.17.36; 118,20.25.28
anairein, to destroy, to reject, to cancel, 22,27.27.28.28; 24,16; 31,13.14; 50,31; 55,31; 56,2.5.30; 57,2; 64,3.9; 87,25; 88,25; 90,10.26.28; 91,9; 105,6; 107,21; 112,29
anairesis, rejection, 30,24; 36,5; 77,24; 84,26
anairetikos, <cancel>, 55,26; 90,8.12; 91,25.32
analuein, to analyse, 7,15.20.22.22.23.25

234

analusis, analysis, 6,28;
7,12.13.14.19.26.27; 58,19; 97,29.30
analutikos, analytic, 4,30;
6,15.30.32.33; 7,11.27; 8,1.2; 9,6;
11,9; 12,3.23; 14,13.19; 25,12; 42,24;
110,20
anankaios, necessary, 4,11.18; 8,33;
9,25; 12,24; 17,27.28 [115]
anankê, necessity, 2,1; 7,3; 17,26.31.32;
20,32; 21,2 [50]
anaphora, reference, 2,10.12.14.17.35;
3,16.24; 8,5
anapodeiktos, indemonstrable, 6,25;
24,4.11; 49,5; 54,12; 55,3; 60,21.25;
69,28; 70,3; 77,5.16; 79,7; 83,13;
102.30; 110,7; 111,12.18; 113,7
anomoioskhêmôn, dissimilar in form,
70,8; 71,29; 76,21.23; 82,9.18; 86,12;
96,5; 104,13; 106,3; 108,4; 109,9.17
antidiairein, to co-ordinate, 1,16.18;
2,12; 11,2
antikatêgorein, to counter-predicate,
72,23
antikeisthai, to be opposed to [*antikeimenon*, opposite, contradictory],
12,32.33; 15,13; 19,11.12.16.18 [95]
antiphasis, contradictory pair, contradiction, 11,10.11; 12,28; 13,5; 14,5;
18,28.29.29; 19,3; 31,17; 36,5.6.12;
45,31; 56,1.5; 57,1; 80,1; 89,33.34;
90,15
antiphatikos, contradictory, 30,1; 31,23;
46,1; 99,14
antistrephein, to convert [+ *pros*, convert from; + dative, convert with],
6,35; 28,9; 29,2.8.9.10.13 [160]
antistrophê, conversion, converse,
24,3.5.14; 27,23.26; 28,5.6 [140]
antithesis, opposition, 29,10.16;
45,15.18.24; 46,8.9
apagein, to reduce, 6,4
apagôgê, reduction, 24,6; 31,10.11.15;
34,5.17; 76,11 [55]
apaitein, to demand, 4,24; 9,7
apodeiknunai, to demonstrate,
12,25.32.34; 13,16; 49,9
apodeiktikos, demonstrative, 1,4;
9,19.21.21.22.23; 12,8.22.27;
13,14.22; 14,11.19; 18,24; 20,26;
28,2.27; 49,6.7.9
apodeixis, demonstration, 2,25;
4,21.24.25.33; 6,10.12 [35]
apodidonai, to give (an account of), to
present, 10,14; 11,21;
12,3.9.11.14.18; 13,13.18; 16,22;
23,18; 25,13.17.28; 41,5; 42,19; 44,13;

53,2.5; 54,6; 69,24
apodosis, <*apodidonai*>, 9,8; 10,7;
14,28
apophainein, to assert, 5,22
apophanai, to deny, 91,22
apophansis, assertion,
10,13.16.17.27.27; 11,7.8.28
apophantikos, assertoric, 10,19.30;
11,12; 14,2; 27,8
apophasis, negation, 10,6.25.30;
11,5.13.15.23.23.27.27; 13.22.26;
14,3; 15,11.13.27.28.32.34; 16,2.4;
22,16.16; 37,7; 41,14; 72,22
apophaskein, to deny, 73,13.18;
74,1.2.10.11.15.18.19.21.22
apophatikos, negative, 10,18; 11,26.31;
13,24; 14,9; 15,10.30 [405]
apozeugnunai, to disjoin, 31,7.8.8.9;
34,14.14
aproslêptos, <co-assume>, 20,18
arkhê, principle, beginning, starting-
point, 4,12; 7,14.14.15.17; 8,12.14
[30]
asullogistos, non-syllogistic, 6,22;
20,14.19.23; 42,13; 47,18; 52,19 [120]
asunuparktos, not holding at the same
time, 90,2
atelês, imperfect, 6,25.25; 7,24; 10,1;
23,19.21.23.24 [30]
atomos, indivisible, individual,
65,24.25.28; 73,23.28; 100,14
atopos, absurd, 16,15; 20,27; 34,20
autothen, directly, 6,24; 13,9; 54,18;
116,36; 117,12.17.23; 118,19
axiôma, axiom, statement, 1,19;
44,18.21

beltiôn, superior, 3,6.7; 51,11.13.18;
71,17
boêtheia, help, 24,10; 77,8.20.28; 78,22

deiknunai, to prove, to show, 2,2;
4,27.32.33; 5,27; 12,9.16 [345]
deiktikos, <prove, show>, 34,13; 43,25;
54,2; 75,18; 79,20; 104,23; 109,17;
111,18; 112,16
deixis, proof, 4,22.26; 7,17; 18,21; 23,28;
28,14.16; 31,6 [80]
dêlos, clear, 3,20; 5,2; 13,5; 15,12; 16,23;
18,31; 28,19 [35]
dêlôtikos, <*dêloun*>, 11,24; 13,30;
15,9.11; 16,24; 18,8; 20,31; 21,4.13;
26,16; 42,9.17; 59,32; 62,12; 71,6;
76,13; 93,3
dêloun, to make clear, to mean, to
betoken, 11,5; 12,16; 13,26.29; 14,23;

---

[1] See also 63,13.

---

[2] Excluding the few occurrences in which *meizôn* means 'greater'.

[3] Excluding occurrences which form part of the phrases *en merei, epi merous* and *kata meros*.

---

[4] Excluding the numerous non-technical occurrences.

Index of Passages

Numbers in **bold** type refer to the works cited; numbers in ordinary type refer to the pages of this book.

ALBINUS

Didasc. **153**, 47 n.40; **158H**, 108 n.36; **158-64H**, 7 n.51; **156-7H**, 49 n.50; **157H**, 50 n.53; **158-9H**, 31 n.137; **158-60H**, 73 n.129; **158H**, 49 n.49, 56 n.25; **161H**, 45 n.22; **179-80H**, 47 n.40

ALEXANDER

in An. Pr. **121,15-123,9**, 174 n.36; **121,15-123,24**, 88 n.24; **123,28-124,7**, 82 n.167; **124,8-30**, 113 n.58; **125,3-6**, 7 n.52; **125,30**, 3 n.23; **126,1-8**, 87 n.20; **125,26-8**, 116 n.71; **126,29-127,2**, 113 n.58; **127,16**, 3 n.23; **129,9**, 133 n.140; **136,1-2**, 109 n.41; **140,14-141,6**, 93 n.45; **144,4-6**, 53 n.3; **151,14-16**, 53 n.3; **155,20-25**, 93 n.45; **156,27-157,2**, 93 n.45; **158,24-161,2**, 99 n.66; **164,17-165,15**, 98 n.60; **164,23-165,6**, 43 n.11; **164,30**, 66 n.87; **165,8-15**, 98 n.61; **165,10**, 98 n.62; **168,31-169,10**, 98 n.60; **173,32-174,19**, 113 n.58; **188,16**, 3 n.23; **191,17**, 3 n.23; **193,21**, 3 n.23; **199,7-10**, 99 n.66; **201,21-24**, 93 n.45; **203,3-5**, 133 n.140; **203,15-35**, 132 n.137; **207,35**, 3 n.23; **210,30-2**, 53 n.3; **213,11-27**, 9 n.60; **213,26**, 3 n.23; **214,12-18**, 9 n.60; **218,20-4**, 99 n.66; **219,35-221,5**, 100 nn.68, 69; **219,35-221,13**, 98 n.63; **221,6**, 133 n.140; **221,16-227,9**, 100 n.67; **236,8-11**, 9 n.60; **238,22-38**, 9 n.60, 10 n.65; **238,37**, 3 n.23; **240,32-241,9**, 9 n.60; **249,15-250,2**, 10 n.65; **249,25-32**, 9 n.60; **249,38**, 3 n.23; **250,2**, 3 n.23; **256,12-14**, 23 n.107; **256,32-258,25**, 108 n.36; **257,1-4**, 70 n.112; **257,6-12**, 64 n.71; **257,8-13**, 64 n.72; **258,24**, 23 n.107; **259,8-260,6**, 77 n.148; **260,23-261,2**, 73 n.127; **261,25-6**, 23 n.107; **262,5-9**, 67 n.93; **262,29-31**, 69 n.103; **262,32-5**, 65 n.79; **263,11-12**, 69 n.103; **263,26-36**, 67 n.93; **266,8-267,27**, 133 n.143; **266,8-270,8**, 101 n.1; **268,7-8**, 73 n.127; **270,6-8**, 9 n.60; **270,10-28**, 82 n.168; **271,16-272,10**, 108, n.37; **271,2-6**, 145 n.26; **275,32-7**, 49 n.50; **282,14-15**, 17 n.85; **283,3**, 17 n.85; **284,17**, 3 n.23; **284,20**, 17 n.85; **284,29**, 17 n.85; **297,4-23**, 122 n.94; **297,22-3**, 105 n.25; **300,3**, 98 n.61; **301,9-19**, 139 n.7; **317,31-318,10**, 77 n.148; **326,31-2**, 118 n.83; **328,6**, 3 n.23; **328,10-30**, 13 n.77; **329,30-330,5**, 82 n.168; **331,12-24**, 49 n.49; **340,11-12**, 48 n.42; **343,21-344,6**, 71 n.118; **344,9-13**, 65 n.78; **344,9-346,6**, 72 n.125; **344,27-31**, 65 n.78; **345,18-20**, 134 n.135; **346,10-14**, 74 n.133; **348,29-32**, 64 n.67; **349,5-7**, 107 n.34; **350,11-16**, 71 n.118; **350,30-352,26**, 130 n.125; **372,26-373,9**, 50 n.60; **372,29-30**, 154 n.65; **373,16-30**, 154 n.65; **379,20-1**, 65 n.78; **379,14-380,27**, 116 n.71; **381,8-12**, 139 n.7; **381,28-386,2**, 50 n.62; **386,5-30**, 67 n.93, 77 n.148, 102 n.5; **388,18-399,9**, 136 n.157; **390,3-4**, 65 n.79; **390,9**, 3 n.23; **392,19-26**, 31 n.139; **406,32-5**, 62 n.55, 105 n.26; **411,35-7**, 82 n.168; **414,9-10**, 116 n.71; **415,10-12**, 116 n.71

Conv. **83** n.1; **56**, 48 n.43; **56-7**, 108 n.36; **57-9**, 49 n.49; **59**, 51 n.68; **60**, 4 n.25, 83 n.4, 136 n.157; **60-1**, 83 n.5; **61**, 85 n.12, 116 n.71; **63**, 84 n.10, 89 n.27, 90 n.34; **64-5**, 87 n.19; **65**, 86 n.14, 90 n.33; **65-6**, 91 n.38; **66-8**, 85 n.12; **69**, 84 n.11; **69-74**, 84 n.11; **76-7**, 92 n.41

DA **2,4-9**, 9 n.62; **90,2-9**, 67 n.90; **90,10-91,6**, 47 n.40

Fat. **164,1-3**, 1 n.1; **164,14-15**, 1

in Metaph. **1,10-2,3**, 46 n.29; **2,3-21**, 47 n.34; **2,24-5,13**, 46 n.31; **17,5-18,14**, 47 n.34;

APOLLONIUS DYSCOLUS
   Synt. **265,9-10**, 50 n.56; **326,11-327,12**, 50 n.56
APULEIUS
   Dog. Plat. **126,3-6**, 47 n.40
   Int. 7 n.50; **176,1-3**, 41 n.4; **176,13-14**, 62 n.59; **177,3-10**, 56 n.25; **177,15-17**, 86
       n.13; **178,1-18**, 61 n.49; **179,16-181,17**, 106 n.29; **181,6**, 19 n.93; **181,19-183,6**,
       83 n.1; **183,15-21**, 110 n.47; **183,22-6**, 104 n.20; **184,19-23**, 65 n.75; **184,23-31**,
       66 nn.87, 88; **185,10-20**, 103 n.7, 104 nn.12, 13; **185,23-186,10**, 111 n.54; **186,5**,
       12 n.75; **186,5-10**, 112 n.57; **188,4-11**, 48 n.45; **189,19-27**, 168 n.18; **189,23-5**,
       136 n.157; **190,15-191,5**, 145 n.30; **190,25-191,5**, 170 n.21; **192,30-193,5**, 31
       n.137; **193,7-13**, 136 n.157; **193,9-16**, 113 n.62; **193,16-20**, 136 n.157; **194,23**, 12
       n.75
ARISTOTLE*
   An. Pr. **24a10-11**, 71 n.113; **24a10-15**, 51 n.66; **24a12-13**, 76 n.143; **24a17**, 60 n.41,
       81 n.162; **24a30-b1**, 60 n.43; **24b10-12**, 60 n.45; **24b18-22**, 75 n.142, 104 n.17,
       154 n.67; **24b20**, 134 n.147; **24b22-6**, 144 n.25; **24b23-4**, 135 n.149; **24b26-8**,
       116 n.72; **25a14-17**, 147 n.40; **25a20-22**, 88 n.22; **25a29-34**, 92 n.41; **25a38-9**,
       93 n.43; **25b14-15**, 95 n.55; **25b19-25**, 99 n.64; **25b22**, 61 n.54; **25b27**, 102 n.4;
       25b29, 49 n.48; **25b30**, 48 n.41; **25b32-5**, 107 n.34; **26a2-9**, 124 n.113, 131
       n.131, 175 n.40, 185 n.4; **26a9-12**, 12 n.76; **26a13-14**, 121 n.92; **26a15**, 17 n.85;
       26a17-29, 127 n.116; **26a20-21**, 127 n.111; **26a25-8**, 174 n.39; **26a28-30**, 113
       n.62; **26a29-30**, 86 n.13; **26a30-31**, 123 n.95; **26a36-9**, 185 n.4; **26b10-16**, 159
       n.86; **26b11-13**, 132 n.139; **26b14-20**, 159 n.85; **26b21-5**, 129 n.121, 164 n.100;
       26b33, 135 n.152; **27a5-9**, 145 n.32; **27a5-14**, 121 n.93, 169 n.19, 189 n.19;
       27a9-14, 146 n.34; **27a18-20**, 159 n.84; **27a20**, 156 n.76; **27a20-23**, 158 n.82;
       27a23, 164 n.103; **27a23-5**, 151 n.58; **27a26-b2**, 163 n.98; **27a32-6**, 157 n.81,
       189 n.20; **27a36-b1**, 190 n.21; **27a36-b3**, 170 n.20, 173 n.30; **27b3-36**, 163 n.99;
       27b4-6, 154 n.70; **27b6-8**, 151 n.55, 185 n.4; **27b20-3**, 132 n.137; **27b27-9**, 132
       n.137; **28a16**, 145 n.26; **28a17-23**, 191 n.24; **28a18-22**, 194 n.34; **28a18-23**, 188
       n.12; **28a22-26**, 89 n.26; **28a22-26**, 89 n.28; **28a26-9**, 194 n.34; **28a26-30**, 178
       n.48, 191 n.24; **28a30-33**, 180 n.52, 185 n.4; **28a33-6**, 182 n.58; **28a36-8**, 185
       n.4; **28a37-b4**, 176 n.41; **28b7-11**, 193 n.32; **28b11-14**, 192 n.27; **28b15-20**, 194
       nn.35, 38; **28b31-5**, 182 n.57, 192 n.27; **28b15**, 181 n.55; **28b15-20**, 155 n.71;
       28b22-4, 155 n.72; **28b24-31**, 132 n.137; **29a19-27**, 135 n.156, 136 n.157;
       29a27-9, 86 n.13, 113 n.62; **29b24**, 196 nn.43, 44; **29b29-32**, 79 n.157; **30a5-14**,
       174 n.36; **30b35-40**, 93 n.45; **32a18-b2**, 79 n.157; **32a29-b1**, 99 n.66; **32a31-b3**,
       99 n.64; **32b18-22**, 98 n.60; **34a16-19**, 64 n.72; **34b7-18**, 79 n.157; **36b35-37a31**,
       98 n.63, 100 n.67; **38a29-31**, 12 n.75; **38b18-20**, 12 n.75; **39b3-6**, 12 n.75;
       40b30-7, 64 n.72; **40b36**, 67 n.93; **41a2-20**, 108 n.36; **41a23-32**, 77 n.148;
       41a39, 67 n.93; **41b6-22**, 133 n.143; **41b6-31**, 101 n.1; **41b33**, 145 n.26;
       41b36-42a40, 64 n.71; **41b36-42b26**, 108 n.37; **44a13**, 118 n.83; **43b3**, 118 n.83;
       43b17-22, 122 n.94; **43b32-6**, 98 n.60; **43b43-44a2**, 88 n.21; **46b40-47b14**, 50
       n.59; **47a16-20**, 74 n.136; **47a22-3**, 65 n.75; **47a22-31**, 74 n.133; **47b15-50a4**, 50
       n.60; **49b37-50a1**, 103 n.7; **50a5-15**, 50 n.62; **50a16-28**, 64 n.69; **50a16-b4**, 102
       n.5; **51a2, 3, 18, 22**, 50 n.58; **51b3-52b34**, 99 n.64; **53a3-14**, 135 n.154, 136
       n.157, 186 n.7; **53b16-23**, 64 n.72; **59b8-10**, 27 n.119; **59b8-11**, 106 n.30;
       61a18-33, 77 n.148; **62a9-10**, 125 n.106; **63b23-30**, 106 n.30; **64a15-17**, 103 n.7;
       64b11-13, 103 n.7; **64b28-65a37**, 70 n.112; **65a38-b40**, 74 n.137; **68b8-14**, 102
       n.6, 103 n.7; **68b13-37**, 104 n.14; **68b35-7**, 104 n.16; **68b38-69a19**, 104 n.14;
       69a13-16, 103 n.7; **69a16-19**, 103 n.7; **70a2-b38**, 72 n.119
   An. Post. **71b20-72a24**, 58 n.34; **71b21-2**, 60 n.44; **71b22**, 72 n.120; **72a8-9**, 56 n.21;
       72a13-14, 56 n.22; **73a7-11**, 64 n.72; **73a29**, 79 n.157; **73b26-7**, 57 n.30;
       73b26-7, 78 n.153; **75b25-6**, 79 n.157; **77a22-3**, 150 n.51; **77b30**, 122 n.94;
       79a17-32, 110 n.52; **79a29-32**, 109 n.40; **79b23-5**, 125 n.104; **85a13-86b39**, 110
       n.48; **87a1-30**, 181 n.54; **87a36**, 150 n.48; **87b19-27**, 98 n.60; **96a8-19**, 98 n.60;
       97b37-9, 75 n.139; **99b15-17**, 53 n.6

* See also: SCHOLIA.)

PHILODEMUS
  Rhet. v 34-vi 19, 98 n.61
PHILOPONUS
  in An. Pr. 7 n.54; **2,14**, 64 n.74; **2,22-4,14**, 49 n.49; **4,26-9**, 46 n.27; **5,15-6,6**, 48 n.42;
    6,19-9,20, 41 n.1; **7,31**, 43 n.9; **9,28-32**, 53 n.6; **9,28-10,25**, 53 n.4; **10,3-25**, 53
    n.1; **11,25-36**, 55 n.12, 104 n.20; **12,5-12**, 78 n.152; **12,23-20,3**, 56 n.18; **21,20-3**,
    4 n.28; **22,4-15**, 104 n.20; **22,23-23,17**, 58 n.32; **25,30-30,20**, 61 n.52; **26,5**, 7
    n.54; **33,6-10**, 64 n.67; **33,10-23**, 64 n.72, 65 n.75; **33,23-6**, 66 n.88; **34,7-10**, 12
    n.75; **34,10-14**, 104 n.13; **34,12-30**, 103 n.7; **34,21-6**, 104 n.12; **36,5-13**, 72
    n.125; **36,19-37**, 75 n.141; **37,16-38,29**, 77 n.148; **39,15-24**, 78 n.151; **39,32-
    42,34**, 83 n.1; **42,20**, 84 n.8; **42,22**, 106 n.28; **43,18-44,1**, 80 n.160; **46,25-47,11**,
    116 n.71; **47,14-15**, 89 n.30; **48,11-18**, 86 n.14; **48,18-49,5**, 84 n.11; **49,6-31**, 87
    n.19; **52,4-56,5**, 92 n.40; **52,27-9**, 92 n.41; **53,15-56,5**, 99 n.64; **56,15-57,13**, 93
    n.44; **57,24-58,27**, 94 n.50; **61,16-62,4**, 98 n.60; **63,12**, 19 n.93; **63,19-64,7**, 100
    n.70; **64,11-15**, 64 n.74; **65,4-66,26**, 108 n.38; **65,20-23**, 139 n.7; **67,18-30**, 109
    n.42; **67,18-68,8**, 140 n.11; **67,27-30**, 143 n.19; **68,8-69,29**, 113 n.61; **69,30-
    71,17**, 111 n.54; **71,12-17**, 113 n.58; **74,30-75,15**, 12 n.75; **77,22-9**, 123 n.95;
    79,4-5, 86 n.13; **79,4-9**, 113 n.62; **79,10**, 136 n.157; **79,10-20**, 136 n.157;
    82,1-84,11, 29 n.127; **82,21-7**, 128 n.120; **82,34-83,4**, 128 n.120; **87,10-19**, 140
    n.11; **87,30-88,2**, 145 n.26; **88,26-33**, 145 n.30; **90,20**, 86 n.16; **92,9-12**, 151 n.55;
    94,3-7, 145 n.30; **98,4-12**, 29 n.127; **98,6**, 19 n.93; **105,28-106,2**, 170 n.21;
    109,20-1, 128 n.120; **112,21-113,20**, 136 n.157; **123,12-17**, 113 n.58; **126,21**, 4
    n.28; **129,16-19**, 113 n.58; **162,16-28**, 50 n.53; **188,20-1**, 87 n.20; **198,19-20**, 87
    n.20; **201,18-19**, 87 n.20; **243,4-8**, 69 n.103; **243,8-10**, 67 n.93; **255,27-9**, 145
    n.26; **277,26-32**, 122 n.94; **277,29-31**, 105 n.25; **302,17-19**, 118 n.83; **307,6-8**, 49
    n.50; **321,7-322,18**, 72 n.125; **321,12-14**, 134 n.145; **388,18-399,9**, 136 n.157;
    451,15-453,33, 70 n.112; **456,24-457,7**, 74 n.137
  in An. Post. **111,31-112,6**, 4 n.28; **155,24-5**, 105 n.25; **301,26-8**, 150 n.48; **334,25-
    335,3**, 50 n.57; **416,13-31**, 75 n.139
  in Cat. **11,20**, 104 n.20
  in DA **21,20-3**, 4 n.28
PLATO
  Cratylus **431B**, 61 n.49
  Laws **730C**, 47 n.33
  Phaedrus **249C**, 47 n.39
  Philebus **33D2**, 75 n.140; **55E-56C**, 98 n.61
  Rep. **408C**, 73 n.129; **511BC**, 49 n.52; **526C-527C**, 45 n.22; **528D-530C**, 45 n.21;
    566B, 103 n.9; **613A**, 47 n.40
  Sophist **262D**, 61 n.49
  Theaetetus **155AB**, 105 n.22; **176B**, 47 n.40; **191C8-9**, 75 n.140; **206D**, 61 n.49
PLUTARCH
  Ser. Num. **550D**, 47 n.40
  Stoic. Rep. **1034E**, 51 n.68
PORPHYRY
  Vit. Plot. **14**, 2 n.13, 6 n.41
PROCLUS
  in Eucl. **21,15-22,16**, 45 n.22; **38,4-10**, 45 n.21; **43,18-21**, 49 n.52; **211,18-212,4**, 50
    n.53
  in Rep. **II 96**, 6 n.41
  in Tim. **I 75,30-76,10**, 5 n.36
PTOLEMY
  Synt. **6,21-7,4**, 45 n.21
SCHOLIA TO ARISTOTLE
    139a36-140a10, 53 n.1; **140a35-41**, 49 n.50; **145a30-7**, 125 n.106; **146a9-18**, 61
    n.48; **146a19-27**, 62 n.56; **146a24-7**, 63 n.61; **147b47-148a2**, 65 n.75; **151a46-
    b4**, 108 n.38; **155b8-19**, 170 n.21; **156b43-157b9**, 6 n.45, 75 n.141; **157a13-24**,
    86 n.14; **188a4-12**, 136 n.157; **294b23-9**, 66 n.87

Index of Persons

Names in quotation marks occur only in examples.

Index of Subjects

actual, 30, 71, 79, 79 n.157, 195, 209
affirmative, 27, 55-7, 187
agreement, 104-5
analysis, 22, 49-50, 121, 170-1, 171 n.24
Aristotle criticized, 7, 9, 9 n.60, 11, 84
    n.11, 87, 87 n.19, 92-3, 92 n.41, 99
    n.66, 128 n.120, 129, 134, 170, 170
    n.21
assertion, 55
assumption, 104-5
astronomy, 45, 45 n.21
axioms, 23 n.109, 105

Baralipton, 136 n.157, 213
Barbara, 77 n.148, 117, 136 n.157, 189,
    210, 212
Barbari, 136 n.157, 214
Baroco, 77 n.148, 152-3, 158, 190, 213
begging the question, 70 n.112
Bocardo, 155, 177-8, 211, 213

Camestre, 168 n.17, 214
Camestres 136 n.157, 147-8, 168 n.18,
    169, 189, 213
Camestrop, 136 n.157, 215
canonical premisses, 73
categories, 45, 45 n.24, 142
Celantes, 136 n.157, 213
Celantos, 136 n.157, 214
Celarent, 117-8, 136 n.157, 189, 212
Celaront, 136 n.157, 214
Cesare, 136 n.157, 147, 168 n.18, 169,
    189, 210-1, 213
Cesares, 168 n.18, 214
Cesaro, 136 n.157, 214
Cesaros, 215
co-assumption, 24, 67 n.93, 70, 72-3
combination, 23, 105, 107-8, 114-15
    non-syllogistic, 12-13, 21, 114-15,
    118-20, 124-30, 133-4, 150-1,
    155-64, 175-6, 178-80, 181-3
commentaries, 4-7
    on Aristotle, 6-7
    canons of, 8, 8 n.57, 9 n.62
    on Plato, 5-6
conclusion, 66-71, 105, 112

conditional propositions, 65 n.79, 70
    n.111
conjectural arts, 98, 98 n.61
contingency, 29-30, 71, 79-80, 79 n.157,
    84, 95-100
    kinds of, 93, 95, 96-8
contradictories, 26-7, 56, 56 n.22, 106,
    119, 160-1
contraries, 27, 106, 125, 157, 160
conversion, 3, 31, 65 n.77, 106-7, 164-5,
    181, 181 n.54, 195, 210-11
    and generation of figures, 109, 109
    n.44, 138-9, 168, 170
    modal, 82, 84, 91-100
    of particular affirmatives, 87, 89, 90-1,
    121-2
    and particular negatives, 85 n.12, 91
    and reduction, 76, 81, 83, 135, 144,
    145-6, 169, 170, 185, 186, 188, 189,
    192
    types of, 83-4
    of universal negatives, 84 n.11, 86-90,
    140
    used in reduction, 147-8, 152, 172, 174,
    176, 177, 180
co-predication, 61, 80, 99
copula, 61-3, 105 n.26

Dabitis, 136 n.157, 214
Darapti, 88 n.21, 89, 136 n.157, 168 n.18,
    171-4, 188, 191, 211, 213
Daraptis, 136 n.157, 168 n.18, 214
Darii, 123-4, 127, 136 n.157, 149, 168
    n.18, 190-1, 213
Datisi, 136 n.157, 176-7, 192-3, 213
Datisis, 214
definition, 63-4, 63 n.64, 74
demonstration, 20, 24, 45, 46, 67, 71, 81,
    82, 110, 148
    and the *Analytics*, 48-9, 51, 53-4, 53
    n.1, 71, 102
    and syllogism, 48, 102
demonstrative propositions, 57, 57-60
diagrams, 139, 139 n.7, 140 n.9, 146, 171
    n.26

dialectical arguments, 24, 51, 67, 81, 82, 110

dialectical propositions, 57, 57-60

dictum de omni et nullo, 87, 87 n.20, 116-17, 117 n.35, 124, 135

differentia, 63-4

Disami, 214

Disamis, 136 n.157, 176, 192-3, 213

disjoint arguments, 67-9, 67 n.92

disjunction, 131 n.128

disproof, 12-13, 85, 91, 159, 160

dissimilar in form, 27, 156 n.77, 184-5

double negation, 66 n.81

duplicated arguments, 66-7, 66 n.88, 69-70

enthymeme, 103 n.7

eristic arguments, 67

etymologies, 44 n.17, 64 n.74

every, of, 54, 77-8

existence, 23 n.106, 62

explanation, 72, 72 n.122

exposition, 26, 88, 88 n.24, 130 n.126, 159, 169, 173, 174 n.36, 175, 177, 178, 189, 211

Fapemo, 136 n.157, 214

Fapesmo, 136 n.157, 214

Faresmo, 215

Felapton, 174-5, 178, 191, 213

Ferio, 124, 127, 149, 161 n.93, 191, 213

Ferison, 180-1, 192-3, 213

Festino, 152, 157, 189, 213

figures, 32, 48, 91, 101, 107-8, 209-10
  first, 108-16, 212-13
  fourth, 108, 108 n.36, 210 n.5
  ranking of, 108-10
  second, 110, 138-9, 154, 213
  third, 110, 154, 166-8, 213

Firesmo, 136 n.157, 214

form, 30, 45, 48, 50, 114, 119

for the most part, 97-8, 98 n.60

Frisemo, 136 n.157, 214

Frisesomorum, 136 n.157, 214

generation of figures, 108-10, 109 n.41, 138-9, 166, 168, 170-1, 171 n.24, 186

genus, 45, 49, 55-6, 56 n.18, 63-4, 67, 140-2, 140 n.13

geometry, 44-6, 49-50, 50 n.53, 59, 73, 86-7

gods, 44, 47, 47 n.40

hypotheses, 25, 59, 179

hypothetical propositions, 23, 56, 56 n.25, 64

hypothetical syllogisms, 3, 6 n.45, 102, 102 n.5

imperfect syllogisms, 21, 50, 75-6, 135, 146, 149, 183, 210

indemonstrables, 21, 76, 117, 189

indeterminacy, 28-9, 29 n.127
  = absence of quantifier, 85-6, 86 n.13, 111, 113-14, 113n.62, 124, 125, 126, 164, 167-8, 187, 209 n.3
  of particulars, 130-1, 131 n.128, 132-3, 157, 158, 159, 162, 163, 164, 180, 182

induction, 66, 71, 103-4, 103 n.7, 104 n.12

is, 62, 105

justification, 19, 102-4, 103 n.7, 109, 110

knowledge, 46

lemmata, 8, 8 n.58, 15, 17, 17 n.85

letters, 16, 116 n.71, 146, 172

logic, 41-3, 67
  Stoic [see Index of Persons, s.v. Stoics]
  utility of, 41, 43, 43 n.11, 46 n.27, 66, 70, 82, 97-8, 104
  value of, 46-8

logoi, kinds of, 64, 64 n.66

major term, 32, 109, 109 n.43, 140-4, 167 n.11, 176

major premiss, 109, 167, 167 n.11

matter, 30, 45, 48, 50, 58, 59, 81-2, 81 n.165, 85, 114, 116, 119

meaning, 154

medicine, 98, 98 n.62

metaphor, 74

middle term, 32, 105, 107-8, 115, 138, 146, 166, 171, 209

minor term, 32, 109, 109 n.43, 140-4, 166, 167 n.11

minor premiss, 109, 167, 167 n.11

mixed modes, 9 n.60, 82 n.167

modal propositions, 79-80, 79 n.157, 80 n.158

modal syllogisms, 9 n.60, 29 n.128, 82

modes, 29-30, 80-1, 81-2, 116, 195, 209

nature, 97-8

necessity, 29, 79-80, 79 n.157, 80 n.160, 81 n.165
  of the consequence, 71
  kinds of, 93
)(syllogism, 21, 65, 66, 134, 162

negative, 27, 55, 57, 59, 143-4, 187

non-differently concluding arguments, 66, 66 n.87